Peter Ross

The Scot in America

Peter Ross

The Scot in America

ISBN/EAN: 9783743331792

Manufactured in Europe, USA, Canada, Australia, Japa

Cover: Foto ©ninafisch / pixelio.de

Manufactured and distributed by brebook publishing software (www.brebook.com)

Peter Ross

The Scot in America

CONTENTS.

CHAP.	I.	INTRODUCTORY	1
CHAP.	II.	PIONEERS	53
CHAP.	III.	EARLY COLONIAL GOVERNORS	75
CHAP.	IV.	REVOLUTIONARY HEROES	103
CHAP.	V.	MINISTERS OF THE GOSPEL	141
CHAP.	VI.	ARTISTS AND ARCHITECTS	174
CHAP.	VII.	SCIENTISTS AND INVENTORS	194
CHAP.	VIII.	MERCHANTS AND MUNICIPAL BENEFACTORS	221
CHAP.	IX.	EDUCATORS	282
CHAP.	X.	STATESMEN AND POLITICIANS	301
CHAP.	XI.	AMONG THE WOMEN	319
CHAP.	XII.	PUBLIC ENTERTAINERS	334
CHAP.	XIII.	MEN OF LETTERS	347
CHAP.	XIV.	AMONG THE POETS	376
CHAP.	XV.	SCOTTISH-AMERICAN SOCIETIES	411

PREFACE.

THE materials for the present volume have been gathered from many and varied sources, and their collection has provided for the author a pleasant relaxation from other studies during several years. A wide acquaintance among Scots resident in this country and in Canada has not only directed him to original sources of information, but has, in various ways and for many reasons, shown him the desirability of the compilation of such a work.

Even as now presented, the theme cannot be said to be exhausted. What is printed has been mainly selected from a mass of material, for it was found that the subject was too extensive to be fully covered in a single volume, while every day brings to the front some fresh incidents in this history-making age which deserve a place in such a record. Still, enough has been written, it is thought, to bring out into clear relief the main purpose the author had in entering upon its compilation, the demonstration of the fact that in the building up of this great Republic in all that has contributed to its true greatness and perfect civil and religious liberty, Scotsmen have, at least, done their share.

It is a pity that a work like this was not attempted a century ago, for much of the early history of the Scot in America has now been lost or has become so mingled with the general trend of events that it has become undistinguishable from the mass. Most of the early Scotch colonists crossed the sea in search of fortune, but a large number found a domicile in America under circumstances which, though sad, reflected honor upon themselves. Devotion to principle is a wonderful factor in the greatness of any country, and such prisoners as those landed in

Boston from the John and Sara in 1652 (as related at Page 48) must have done much to supplement and strengthen the stern uprightness inculcated upon New England by the Pilgrim Fathers. These expatriated Scots fought for a principle at Dunbar, and the principle that makes men take up their arms in its defense on the field of battle is one that is not likely to be abandoned merely on account of worldly reverses or a backward tide in the fortunes of war. So, too, in the time of the Covenant, we find many traces of men and women who, after suffering imprisonment at home for their religious sentiments, were shipped to America as the easiest way to further punish and silence them. Thus the student of Scottish history comes across many items like the following, which is quoted from the statistical account of the Parish of Glassford, Lanarkshire, written in 1835 by the Rev. Gavin Lang, whose son, bearing the same name, afterward became a minister in Montreal and one of the best-known clergymen in Canada. It is an extract from the records of the Kirk Session of Glassford. "*Item*— In 1685 Michael Marshall and John Kay were both taken prisoners for their nonconformity, and banished and sent over sea to New Jersey in America. The said Michael stayed several years in America. After the late happy revolution, [1688,] designing to come home, he was taken prisoner at sea and was carried to France, where he was kept a year and a half in prison and endured great hardships before he was delivered."

It may be supposed from the above that the Covenanter, Kay, remained in New Jersey, or, at all events, in America, and it seems a pity that, if he left any descendants, their pedigree should not be known, as next to descent from a Mayflower Pilgrim, no more honorable start for an American genealogical tree than the name of this Presbyterian martyr could be imagined. It is, in fact, an interesting study to follow the fortunes of Scotch families in America, and while sometimes they drop out of sight among what John Knox pleasantly called the "rascall multitude," the majority remains in the van in whatever sphere of life they have attained.

The descendants of Principal Witherspoon of Princeton can be traced in honorable positions in the ministry and the professions to the present day. Andrew Wodrow, the eldest son of Robert Wodrow, the famous Scotch Church historian, emigrated to Virginia in 1768, and when the Revolutionary War broke out he entered the ranks of the Colonists and did his part in consolidating the Colonies into a nation, rising in the service to the grade of Lieutenant Colonel of Cavalry. Many of the descendants of the old historian are yet to be found in America, mainly in Virginia, principal among whom may be mentioned the President of South Carolina College, the Rev. Dr. J. Woodrow, the additional vowel having been introduced in the name to preserve its sound, a custom which is widely prevalent, and which has helped more than aught else to obliterate many traces of the doings of the early American Scots. This fashion of altering the spelling of names is unfortunately much more common than is generally supposed. Thus Douglas becomes "Douglass"; Watt, "Watts"; Urquhart, "Urkart"; Patrick, "Partrick"; Napier, "Napper"; Mackintosh "Mackentash"; Gibson "Gipson"; Semple "Sarmple," and so on.

A case in point is that of the Gilmor family of Baltimore, whose original patronymic in Scotland was Gilmour. As the history of this family in America is an interesting one, not only for showing how each successive generation has kept in the front ranks of professional and business society, but for illustrating how the Scot by intermarriage soon becomes a member of the most aristocratic local families, the following notice, from "Harper's Magazine" for June, 1882, may not inappropriately be introduced here, especially as, further on, it will be found that the early New York Scots, the Livingstones, Barclays, Watts, and others equally strengthened their social position in the community by marrying into the old Dutch families —the salt of the New Amsterdam community:

"Four generations of the Gilmor family have been prominent in the business and social circles of Baltimore. Robert Gilmor, the founder of the family in this country, was born at Paisley on the 10th of November, 1748, and christened the same day by the Rev. Dr. John Witherspoon, afterward of Princeton College. John Gilmor, the father of Robert, was a wealthy manufacturer. At the early age of seventeen his son displayed so great an aptitude for business that his father took him into partnership. Within a year, however, from this time, Robert, who had previously made several successful business trips to London, now determined to further extend his commercial enterprises, and with an assortment of goods suitable for the American market, he embarked in 1767 for this country, and landed at Oxford, Maryland, toward the end of September. This little place was then much resorted to by the British vessels to obtain the products of the country. The young man realized $1,500 from his venture, and being pleased with the country, determined to settle there. While on a visit to Dorchester County he made the acquaintance of his future wife, Miss Louisa Airey, daughter of the Rev. Thomas Airey, with whose brother he formed a partnership before he had been in the country one year. On the 25th of September, 1771, he married, and after being engaged in business on the Eastern Shore of Maryland for over ten years, he removed to Baltimore, believing it offered a wider field for his business. Mr. Gilmor soon developed a character of great prudence and industry, and showed a decided talent for making money.

"Among Mr. Gilmor's business correspondents at this date were Messrs. Thomas Willing and Robert Morris of Philadelphia, both of whom were members of the Continental Congress, and the latter one of the Signers of the Declaration of Independence. They traded under the firm of Willing & Morris. These gentlemen, together with Mr. William Bingham, Mr. Willing's son-in-law, anticipating a treaty of peace after the surrender of Cornwallis, were desirous of forming an establishment at Amsterdam for the purpose of exporting more largely the staple products of Maryland and Virginia, and deeming Mr. Gilmor a suitable person to represent the concern in Holland, they offered him a copartnership, which was accepted. In accordance with this arrangement, Mr. Gilmor sailed with his family on the 27th of November, 1782, and arrived safely on the 12th of January, 1783, at his destination, where they met Captain Joshua Barney, on his way to America with the preliminary treaty of peace between Great Britain, France, and the United States. At Paris Mr. Gilmor met John Adams, one of the negotiators of the treaty of peace, who gave him a letter addressed to Messrs. Wilhelm & Jan Willink, the bankers of the United States in Holland, and one of the richest houses in Europe. This was the beginning of a commercial connection between the Gilmors and the Willinks which continued from father to son for upward of fifty years, during which transactions took place to the amount of many millions of dollars.

"The house in Amsterdam, under the management of Mr. Gilmor, soon commanded an extensive business, extending all over Europe, and to the West Indies and the United States. Eventually the firm thus constituted was broken up by the death of Mr. Samuel Inglis, one of the Philadelphia partners. Mr. Bingham, who was at that time living in London, wrote to Mr. Gilmor to come there, with a view of arranging a partnership with him. He did so, and the result was the establishment of the firm of Robert Gilmor & Co. of Baltimore, in which Mr. Bingham was the other member. By his successful enterprises to all parts of the world, Mr. Gilmor, in the course of fifteen years, became one of the merchant princes of Baltimore.

"In 1799 the business connection with Mr. Bingham was dissolved, and Mr. Gilmor associated his two sons, Robert and William, with him, under the firm name of Robert Gilmor & Sons. The correspondents of the old firm were continued to the new, and many years of commercial prosperity followed. Robert Gilmor, Jr., did most of the traveling for the firm, and was thus enabled to combine pleasure with profit. He continued to take the deepest interest in the prosperity of Baltimore to the last, and died in 1849, universally lamented.

"His younger brother, William, was married at an

early age to Mrs. Marianne Drysdale, a young widow of nineteen. She was a daughter of Isaac Smith of Northampton County, Virginia. Mr. and Mrs. Gilmor had twelve children. Their eldest son, Robert, was graduated at Harvard in 1828, and afterward went to Europe as attaché to the legation with Mr. Rives, our Minister to France. After remaining abroad, visiting places of interest, and meeting with a great deal of attention, he returned in the Autumn of 1829. It was his good fortune during this trip to spend several days at Abbotsford with Sir Walter Scott, and often referred to it with pleasure. Mr. Gilmor's country seat was Glen-Ellen, in Baltimore County. He married Ellen Ward, daughter of Judge Ward, of Baltimore, whose memory is cherished as one of the most admired ladies that ever graced Baltimore society. The Hon. Robert Gilmor, who has been for more than twelve years one of the Judges of the Supreme bench of Baltimore, is a son of this lady. He possesses the love of art which is hereditary in his family, and owns a number of fine paintings and engravings formerly possessed by his relative. Mr. William Gilmor, who married Miss Key, a descendant of Francis S. Key, and Col. Harry Gilmor, who won distinction as a dashing cavalry officer in the Confederate service during the late war, are brothers of Judge Gilmor."

We might find similar accounts of the Scotch families in the local histories of all the States, but the subject is really limitless, and it presents itself to us in all sorts of biographical reading, both in the old land and the new. For instance, we read that Thomas Carlyle's favorite sister still resides in Canada, which has been her home for many years, and a brother of Dr. Livingstone long carried on business at Listowell, in Ontario. A brother of Mungo Park, an earlier African traveler, left three daughters, all of whom crossed the Atlantic, but every trace of them has been lost. In the course of this work many instances are given of the descendants of famous Scots taking up their residence in the Western Hemisphere, and in several cases the fortunes of entire families have been followed from their transatlantic beginning to the present day. There is no more delightful or interesting feature in connection with the Scot in America than this branch of the subject.

In many portions of this work the author might be criticised for having permitted the *perfervidum ingenium Scotorum* to carry him apparently to extreme lengths in speaking in terms of praise of his native land. If in this respect the bounds of decorum have been exceeded, it has arisen from no want of appreciation of or devotion to the magnificent Republic of which he is proud to be a citizen, and in which for many years he has found a happy home. But there is nothing out of place in a heart beating as strongly at the sight of the Stars and Stripes as at a blink of the blue banner of old St. Andrew. The two countries represented by these emblems have so much in common that love for the one necessarily implies love for the other. But if some ultra American critic should condemn the writer on this score, he submits that he has gone no further in his admiration than Americans themselves. In a letter to the writer a Roman Catholic prelate, well known for his literary ability and for his devotion to America, his native land, says:

" While Scotsmen and their descendants all over the world do not make as clamorous and sometimes offensive show of their love for the Old Country as does the Celt of Ireland, their devotion to the beauty, honor, success, and grandeur of the dear old land is, in my opinion, far deeper and far more justified. It is wonderful, especially in view of the scarcity of population, of the comparative poverty of the soil, and from the unfavorable situation of Scotland as regards the rest of Europe, what a noble worldwide history she has, and how many great men she has produced. While Scotland was ultimately benefited by the Union, in the sense of material prosperity, the smaller and poorer country exerted far more influence on the politics, literature, and commerce of the wealthier one. It is no idle boast that Scotsmen reduced Canada, conquered India, suppressed the Sepoy mutiny, and have furnished the United States with an immense number of the most intelligent and loyal citizens."

Equally laudatory was the following tribute by another American citizen, Consul Jenkinson of Glasgow, when he said: "The great body of the American people not only entertain a feeling of friendship for the people of Scotland, but also a sense of obligation, for much of what they are they owe to the teaching and example of Scotland. If they believed in liberty and independence, it was mainly due to what the Scots had taught them. If they tried to elevate mankind morally and socially by a thorough system of popular education, they but follow the example of Scotland. If they refused to put on and wear the shackles which bound the consciences of men and prevented a full and free religious worship, they but accepted the results of the long and severe contest waged by the people of Scotland. They had not only drawn upon the teaching and the example of the Scotch, but they had to some extent appropriated their wisdom and their genius in putting these into practice. At all times since the history of their people began they had had among them many distinguished statesmen who were Scotsmen."

After such tributes—and they might be multiplied by the hundred—from men not to the manner born, the author may be forgiven any apparent excess of enthusiasm to which he has been beguiled in the course of inditing the following pages. At the same time, no effort has been made to cover up the backsliding of any particular individual, and now and again the author has felt it necessary to expose the shortcomings of some compatriot who, to put it in the least offensive way, did not come up to the national standard. There are not many such, although it must be confessed the author has not exerted himself very exhaustively in trying to discover them. Still, even with the most diligent search, the number of black sheep in the Scottish flock would be found comparatively few. The national record in America is, on the whole, a grand one. An instance is not on record of a Scotsman being tried by Lynch law, or, with a single exception, of one being tarred and feathered. But that solitary, disagreeable event happened so long ago that it is difficult to understand the true inwardness of the case, and for all we really do know the victim might have been a martyr instead of an evildoer. He seems to have been rather a dubious character, however, judging by the following account of him written by the late Benson J. Lossing, the American historian.

"John Malcolm was a Scotsman who settled in North Carolina after the famous rebellion of 1745. He was aide to Gov. Tryon in 1771, when he went against the Regulators. He afterward became a Custom House officer at Falmouth, (now Portland,) in Maine, and early in 1774 he was in a similar position in Boston. He was an insolent man. One day he struck a tradesman for an alleged insult, and a warrant was issued for his arrest. The constable pretended he could not find him. A mob gathered about his house, when he thrust a sword through a broken window and wounded one of them. They broke in, found him in a chamber, lowered him by a rope from a window to a cart, took off his clothes, tarred and feathered him, and dragged him through several of the streets with a rope around his neck to Liberty Tree. From there he was taken to a gallows on Boston Neck, beaten, and threatened with death. In the course of an hour he was conveyed to the extreme north end of the town, and then, after being bruised, and benumbed with cold for four hours, they took him back to his house. What became of him afterward is not on record. He was despised by both parties, and became equally malevolent toward Whigs and Tories."

Considerable space might have been devoted to the humor of the Scot in America, but it was felt that such a theme might more properly be left as the subject of a monograph by some other investigator. Such a compilation would not only be interesting in itself, but would show that the race had lost none of its native pawkiness by being transplanted, nay, would demonstrate rather that it was broadened, that it was less dry, that it did not require so much "thawing out" under the influence of a few years' alternate baking and freezing beneath an American sky. Still, in these stories the Scot would be there with all his noted characteristics. Here is an illustration in a story concerning dour Scotch obstinacy, which was once told to a group in a New York hotel by a middle-aged man of alert appearance and rapid, nervous movements: " My father," he began " came over about seventy-five years ago and settled in Michigan, which, in that part, at any rate, was a semi-wilderness. As the country grew more settled my father, from the mere fact of his having been a pioneer, became very prominent in civic affairs in the community. He was very conscientious, but extremely impatient of contradiction, never understanding why a person could disagree with him, when he was so plainly correct in his position.

" Well, one night, contrary to his usual custom, he did not come home to supper. Eight o'clock came and the whole family was in bed and still he had not arrived. It was after 1 o'clock in the morning that his heavy step was heard on the stairs. My mother, who had been anxious, met him with a light in her hand.

" ' Where have you been?" she asked, looking at him seriously.

" ' Been on a jury,' he growled.

" ' Why did you stay so late?'

" ' Stay so late? There were eleven obstinate devils on that jury and it took me all night to convince them.' "

But such vain frivolities must not occupy us further, and, besides, as this preface is already too long, we must acknowledge several obligations, and so bring it to a close.

In a volume like this many sources have been culled to contribute in some way to its completeness, to furnish information of more or less importance. It has been difficult to determine in every case the printed authority for much of the work, but where it has been possible the authority has been pointed out. In a more general way the author has been indebted to many of the publications of Gen. James Grant Wilson, son of the sweet Scottish poet of Poughkeepsie. To the volume on "Scottish Poets in America," by John D. Ross, LL. D., is due much of the information concerning living bards contained in

Chapter XIV. Much useful information has also been received from Mr. Robert Whittet of Richmond, Va.; Mr. John Johnston, Milwaukee, and several others. Some of the data contained in the chapter on Scottish societies has been condensed from an earlier work by the author, "St. Andrew: the Disciple, the Missionary, and the Patron Saint," now nearly out of print.

It may be noticed that the references to the Scot in Canada have not been by any means as full as they might be. In fact, the writer has wandered across the St. Lawrence only at intervals. To do otherwise would have simply flooded these pages with sketches of a great majority of the very men who have made Canada a nation, and, besides, the work has already been done in a thoroughly appropriate and lovable manner by W. J. Rattray of Toronto. It may be mentioned, too, for reasons that will be apparent and easily understood by any one who has had any acquaintance with bookmaking in the United States during the past thirty years, that only in a comparatively few instances, and then merely to emphasize some paricular point, have references been made to living personages.

The writer now commends the volume to his countrymen and to all lovers of Scotland, with the fervent hope that it may be the means of increasing, even in a little degree, the reverence which has in the past been freely rendered to the dear old land in the Great Republic of the West.

THE SCOT IN AMERICA.

CHAPTER I.

INTRODUCTORY.

THE Scots in America, with truth, claim to be equally loyal to the land they left and to the land of their adoption. Were it at all necessary to prove how perfectly just is this claim an abundance of evidence could readily be presented. But the claim is generally allowed even by the most rabid believers in " Know Nothingism." From time to time movements have sprung up in America directed against a particular race or nationality, but no such attack has ever been made directly or indirectly upon those hailing from Scotland. They have generally been acknowledged as good exemplary citizens, people who had, as a people, no axe to grind, and who in all matters pertaining to America acted as citizens, and from the standpoint of citizenship unswayed by any claims of nationality. No politician, so far as is known, ever figured on " the Scotch vote," nor did any Scotch aspirant for political office ever count on the " solid support " of his countrymen. In all matters pertaining to the country the citizen of Scottish birth completely sinks his own original nationality and takes his place simply and individually with the other citizens in whatever matter is at issue.

The Scots at home somehow do not understand this. They do not see how it is possible for a Scotsman to remain loyal in heart to his own land and yet fight against its government, as in the time of the Revolutionary War, nor even how a feeling of regard for the old nationality can remain in the breast of one who willingly takes an oath which absolves him from all fealty to the land of his birth.

But the Americans fully understand and appreciate it all, and, as a result, no new citizens are more cordially welcomed to the great republic than those who hail from the Land o' Cakes. All over the country the Scot is looked up to with respect. He is regarded as an embodiment of common sense, a natural lover of civil and religious liberty, a firm believer in free institutions, in the rights of man, in fair play, and exemplary in his loyalty to whatever cause he may have adopted. They laugh at his reputed want of wit, at his little idiosyncrasies, at his dourness, at his dogged determination, at his want of artificiality, and several other peculiarities, but admire intensely the effectiveness of his work, the habit he has of "getting there" in whatever he sets out to do, the quiet way in which he so often climbs to the top, whether in banking or professional or military circles, the public-spiritedness he shows in all walks of life and his truly democratic spirit.

The fact is, from the beginning of their history the Scots have been model colonizers and have had the happy faculty of making themselves perfectly at home in all climes and in all circumstances. If we like to believe the earliest traditions, the Scots were originally a tribe of Greece. The tribe went to Egypt and their leader, as might be expected, became commander in chief of the forces in that country and married Scota, the daughter of the Pharaoh who flourished at that time, as was eminently fitting and characteristic. This Scotch warrior and his followers, or some of them, had sense enough not to be caught in the Red Sea when it swallowed up so many Egyptians, and when that catastrophe occurred they left Egypt. Poverty stricken and desolate, the original Scottish chiefs had no further use for the country, and so sought for other fields of usefulness. Making their way to Portugal they settled there, and naturally enough their leading chief, Galethus by name, became King. One of his descendants went to Ireland with a host of followers and became monarch of that unhappy country. They journeyed afterward to Scotland, but where they will go next the believers in this legend do not inform us, although some people assert that the migratory movement has already set in, with America as its objective point. There are other legends of the early wandering habits of the primitive Scots, some of which make them travel from Iceland, from Central Europe, and from Asia, without ever touching at Ireland at all. In fact, by the believers in these last theories the Irish idea is regarded as a national slander. Then if we credit the legend that Gaelic was the language spoken by Adam and Eve while they resided in the Garden of Eden and that Welsh was what they conversed in after their ignominious expulsion from that earthly paradise, we get an idea not only of the high antiquity but of the lost estate of the early Scots.

However we may regard these legends, they all point in an indefinite way to one fact—and some fact can always be evolved out of the wildest and most incoherent mass of legends—that the pioneers of the Scottish people of to-day were wanderers. This characteristic is borne out by their later and better authenticated history. We find them early noted in the military services of the continent of Europe, fighting with courage and fidelity, true soldiers of fortune, under whatever flag they happened to be enrolled, sometimes indeed, as in the case of the famous Scots Guard of France, trusted with interests deemed too sacred for the subjects of the realm they served to protect. We find them, also, occupying leading positions at the various seats of learning, and the history of such institutions as the Scots Colleges at Paris and Rome yet testify to the high regard in which the intellectual qualities of the nation were held even at a time when the general standard of education in Scotland itself was by no means high. There was hardly a position of importance in Europe in which the influence of the Scottish race was not at one time or other more or less directly felt, and what has been called the "ubiquitousness of the Scotch" has given rise to many curious yet amusing stories, which, however, all have more or less truth for their foundation. It is often asserted that when the north pole shall be discovered a Scotchman will be found astride of it, and we have read stories of Chinese mandarins, Turkish pashas, and South Sea Island chiefs who turned out on occasion to be natives of Scotland and proud of their nationality.

A story which illustrates this is given in Peter Buchan's "Historic and Authentic Account of the Ancient and Noble Family of Keith." It refers to an incident in the life of the greatest of the Earls Marischal—Frederick the Great's most honored Field Marshal. It was copied by Buchan from Dr. James Anderson's "Bee," a forgotten weekly publication issued for three years, between 1790 and 1793. "The Russians and the Turks, in their war, having diverted themselves long enough in murdering one another, for the sake of variety they thought proper to treat of a peace. The commissioners for this purpose were Marshal General Keith (born at Inverugie) and the Turkish Grand Vizier. These two personages met, with the interpreters of the Russ and Turkish betwixt them. When all was concluded they arose to separate; the Marshal made his bow with his hat in his hand, and the Vizier his salaam with turban on his head. But when these ceremonies of taking leave were over, the Vizier turned suddenly, and, coming up to Keith, took him freely by the hand and, in the broadest Scotch dialect, spoken by the lowest and most illiterate of our countrymen, declared warmly that 'it made him very happy, now that he was sae far frae hame, to meet a countryman in his exalted station.' Keith stared with all his eyes, but at last the explanation came and the Grand Vizier told him: 'My father was bellman of

Kirkcaldy, in Fife, and I remember to have seen you, sir, and your brother occasionally passing.'"

The Scot abroad, however, does not always occupy high places. Sometimes he misses the tide which leads to fortune, but even then his national philosophical spirit does not leave him, and he makes the best of his circumstances, whatever they may be. An instance of this, and beyond question a true one, is given in the Rev. Dr. William Wright's very interesting work on "The Brontës in Ireland." He says: "On the coast of Syria I once arranged with a ragged rascally looking Arab for a row in his boat. My companion was a Scotch Hebrew Professor. It was a balmy afternoon and we enjoyed and protracted our outing. We talked a little to our Arab in Arabic and much about him of a not very complimentary character in our own tongue. I happened to drop some sympathetic words regarding the poor wretch, and suddenly his tongue became loosened in broad Scotch and he told us his story. It was very simple. Twenty years before, the English ship on which he served as a lad had been wrecked at Alexandretta, on the northern coast of Syria. He swam ashore, lived among the people of the coast till he became one of themselves, and at the time we met him he was the husband of an Arab woman and the father of a dusky progeny. He was content with his squalid existence and never again wished to see his native heather."

The correctness of the last sentence is open to very grave doubt; in fact, it could only have been written by one who did not understand the Scottish character. Doubtless it is true that the Arab boatman did not want to revisit his native land in that character, and with its attendant poverty. But could he have managed to gather a few shekels together, the hope which every Scotsman abroad has in his heart of hearts of returning once more to his native land, even for a brief glimpse, would have been ever present, and ever increasing in intensity, as time passed on.

In spite, however, of their successes abroad, the Scots at home, especially in these later days, do not seem to value the services which their wandering countrymen have rendered to the glory of the old land, and have in fact made its name be honored and respected all over the world. Possibly this arises from a popular misconception of one of Sir Walter Scott's most carefully delineated creations—Sir Dugald Dalgetty. He has been held up to ridicule as a timeserver, a cut-throat, a man without principle, and an embodiment of self. But there was nothing in his character as portrayed by Sir Walter's matchless pen to indicate that he was anything but the honorable cavalier he invariably described himself as being. His sword was his fortune, and he sold it to the highest bidder, but he never broke an agreement or betrayed a trust. He served the flag under which he was enrolled with the best of his ability, and his crowning hope was to gather enough money to enable him to spend his later years where his life began. His only fault was his poverty, and his life was devoted to the removal of that fault. After all, poverty at home has really been the cause which has always inspired the Scot to roam away from his native land. Said a well-known Scotch banker in New York once to the writer: "—— is poor, but then we were all poor when we came here. If we had not been poor there is not a Scotsman in the banking business in New York who would ever have dreamed of leaving Scotland. Why should we?"

To the Scot in America, the New World is a practical reality and Scotland a reminiscence, a sentiment. He throws himself with ardor into all things American, gives to it his best endeavors, takes up all the duties of citizenship, and does everything that lies in his power to promote the general wealth of the country by building up its commerce, by developing its resources, and by adding to its higher aspirations by widening and popularizing its educational, artistic, and literary aspirations and opportunities. He becomes an integral part by active citizenship in a commonwealth where the mere knowledge of his nationality secures him at the outset a warm welcome, and is a factor in the individual or general favor which enables him to mount ever higher without cliciting jealousy or ill-feeling or ill-nature on the part of the native element.

But he never forgets Scotland even though it becomes simply a sentiment, although even when the chance comes he does not forsake the interests and friendships which have grown around him and return to his own land, spend his gear, and enjoy a blink of affluent sunset before the darkness of the long night comes on. All over Scotland we find traces of the practical love which the Scot in America entertains for the " Land o' Cakes."

In the parish records of Kirkcudbright is an entry of the sum of £31 being left in 1803 by James R. Smyth of New York, the interest of which was to be devoted to the purchase of Bibles for the poor, and Robert Lenox of the famous New York family of that name was munificent in his gifts to the poor in the Stewartry. Miss Harriet Douglas, afterward Mrs. Congar of New York, gave during her lifetime £100 to the service of the poor in Castle Douglas and Gelston. Mr. John S. Kennedy gave a beautiful piece of statuary to adorn the West End Park of Glasgow, in which city he first learned the elements of business. Mr. Thomas Hope, merchant, New York, bequeathed a considerable sum for the erection and endowment of a hospital in his native place, Langholm, Dumfrieshire, and that charitable foundation, after considerable legal bickering, is now in successful operation. John McNider, once a noted merchant in Quebec, left at his decease £40 to the poor of his native town of Kilmarnock, and another Quebec merchant, John Muir, left £50 to be distributed among the needy in the beautiful Lanarkshire parish of Dalserf, where he started out on the journey of life. Such evidences of kindly remembrance of the old land might be multiplied almost indefinitely, and instances are constantly being added, from the munificent donations of Andrew Carnegie, to the smaller sums sent by less affluent but not less kindly wanderers " furth " of Scotland.

A noted Scottish-American benefactor of his native parish was Robert Shedden of Beith, who was born there in 1741 and was the representative of an ancient

Ayrshire family. He went to Norfolk, Va., in 1759 and entered into business there as a merchant. He married a Virginia lady and evidently intended to settle permanently in the country. When the Revolution broke out he remained loyal to Britain and was compelled to take refuge with his family on a British vessel, and soon afterward his property in Virginia was confiscated. After a short stay in Bermuda he went to New York, and there remained so long as the city was in the hands of the British. Then he went to England, where he resumed business as a merchant. His death took place in London in 1826. The lands of Gatend, Beith, were purchased by him and transferred to trustees, so that the rent, to the annual value of £50, might be distributed in annuities not exceeding £10 and not less than £5 among residents of the parish. In connection with the same branch of the Sheddens a celebrated case was tried in the Scotch courts in 1861, in which a romantic story with incidents on both sides of the Atlantic was unfolded. Its occasion was the attempt of an American family of the name to be declared legitimate and so acquire considerable property in Ayrshire. But the attempt was not sustained by the Scotch courts, nor by those in London before which the case was carried on appeal.

In writing of the Scot in America we find the subject so vast that it is difficult to present an adequate view of the theme within the compass of a volume of ordinary size. The materials are so extensive and the subjects are to be found in so many and such varied walks of life that what is here written can only be indicative, or suggestive, of the important services the nationality has performed in the mighty work of building up the North American continent. We find the Scot wherever we turn in banking circles, colleges, legislative halls, pulpits, the fighting and the civil services, in editors' sanctums, merchants' offices, and in the mechanics' workshops and factories. About the only sphere in which they have not shone is that of the prize ring, although a gang of six New York Bowery toughs once found to their cost that the Scots were born fighters, when a simple looking wayfarer from Stranraer whom they essayed to rob had them all sprawling on the sidewalk in front of him before they exactly realized what had happened. It is very seldom, too, that we hear of a Scot becoming what is known as a practical politician, a political "boss," with all that the designation implies. The nearest approach to it in the knowledge of the writer was the late Police Justice Hugh Gardner of New York, who was for several years regarded as the real leader of the Republican party in that city. Judge Gardner was born at Paisley in 1818, and long carried on business as a dyer in New York in partnership with the late Matthew McDougall, a native of Kilbarchan, who for many years held the office of United States Consul at Dundee. Gardner drifted into politics soon after his arrival here, and was at one time a Police Commissioner, but, although mixed up in all the "deals" and tricks and schemes which then, as now, disgraced local politics in his adopted city, "Hugh," as he was familiarly called, passed through them all unscathed in his personal character, and died, as he had lived, with the reputation of an honest politician. He was a warm-hearted man and an enthusiast about Scotland. He delighted, in a quiet way, in doing a good turn to his countrymen, by exerting his influence in getting them appointed to official or other employment over which he had any control; but woe to the misguided wretch who openly boasted that the ties of a common motherland gave him any undue claims for assistance. Such a man in Gardner's eyes was a "fule." The only instance on record when he publicly did a good turn to a Scotsman, as such, was in connection with the first case he tried after his elevation to the bench. The prisoner had been arrested for being "drunk and disorderly," and in a Scotch accent promptly acknowledged his guilt. "Where are ye frae?" asked the Judge. "Frae Paisla," replied the prisoner. "Ye're dischairged, but dinna mak a fule o' yersel again," was the Judge's decision. The next prisoner, a hod-carrier, "with the map of Ireland depicted all over his face," as the Judge said when telling the story afterward, "tried the Paisley game, but I gied him a lang enough sentence to make up for the ither fellow, an' sae justice was satisfied." Hugh Gardner was brusque in his manner, but he was liberal, generous, and sympathetic, and showed these qualities in many ways, but always in each instance with the admonition to "say naething aboot it."

In treating of the influence of the race, the question of what is being done by people of Scottish descent should be borne in mind, although it is difficult at times to trace out the line of descent in a country where few people claim an ancestral tree, and where 99 per cent. of the population boast of having Scotch blood in their veins. It is not proposed here to deal with the achievements of others than natives of Scotland except in a few instances which are adduced mainly for the sake of showing that the influence of a Scottish progenitor goes on through many generations. An instance of this, one that most readily occurs at the moment, is that of the American family founded by John Graham.

Mr. Graham was a native of Edinburgh, where he was born in 1694, and claimed descent, whether rightly or wrongly there are no means of determining, from one of the Marquises of Montrose. He was educated for the medical profession at Glasgow, practiced for a short time in Londonderry, and with some emigrants from the North of Ireland crossed the Atlantic in 1718 and took up his residence at Exeter, New Hampshire. While there he studied for the ministry, and in time became a minister at Stafford, Conn. From that charge he resigned for the frankly expressed reason that its emoluments were insufficient for his support, and in 1733 he became pastor of a church at Woodbury, Conn., where he remained for about forty years, or till his death in 1774. Mr. Graham was a powerful and popular preacher and was the author of several works, all of which, being controversial in their nature, are now very properly forgotten. His son, Andrew, was intense in his American patriotism. He was one of the most outspoken advocates for separation from the motherland when the events began which led to the Revolution of 1776, and in the war which accompanied it he took an active part. At the battle of White Plains he was captured by the British, but was released after the surrender of Cornwallis. Later he represented Woodbury for many years in the Connecticut Legislature. One of the sons of this patriot—Andrew—became recognized, before his death in 1841, as the most noted criminal lawyer in New York, and yet another son, John Hodges Graham, entered the navy as a midshipman in 1812 and two years later had command of Commodore McDonough's flagship in the famous engagement on Lake Champlain. In 1849 he became a Captain in the American navy, and died, full of years and honors, in 1878. Another grandson of the Scottish preacher, John Lorimer Graham, long a lawyer of eminence in New York, was Postmaster of that city between 1840 and 1844, and his services as such were recognized as being of great value to the community.

Then, too, we find Scotsmen doing good work for the country and for humanity in ways that can hardly be classified for the purposes or scope of this work. A case in point is that of William Steel, once one of the most noted and practical of that band of Abolitionists and social reformers who did so much to mitigate the horrors of slavery, to make it unpopular, and finally were the means of bringing about the removal of that most baneful of institutions from the American social system. Steel was born at Biggar, Lanarkshire, in 1809, and settled in or near Winchester, Va., with his parents, in 1817. Afterward he moved to Ohio. There he was soon noted for his hatred of slavery, and he became one of the most successful workers on the once mysterious "underground railroad" by which so many slaves were carried to places where their liberty was secure, where the words in the Declaration of Independence that "all men are created equal" meant more than a figure of speech or were held to apply to any particular class or race. Steel used to boast that no slave was ever retaken after getting into his hands, and the boast was amply borne out by facts. He had many curious experiences, many hairbreadth escapes while carrying on this humane work, but he passed through them all unscathed. As for many years he was regarded as the leader of the abolitionists in Ohio, he was a marked man and, had circumstances permitted, the slave owners, in Virginia especially, would have made of him a terrible example. Indeed, they at one time offered a reward of $5,000 for his head, but he only laughed at all such evidences of ill-will and even offered to carry his head on his own shoulders into the enemy's territory if the money was placed in responsible hands so that he was sure it would be paid after they had completed their intentions and satisfied their hate. Notwithstanding his engrossing labors in connection with the anti-slavery crusade, Steel acquired a moderate fortune in business, but it was swept away in the financial panic of 1844. He lived to see the principles for which he had worked so hard become completely successful, although at a terrible cost, and the last few years of his life were pleasantly spent with his sons, at Portland, Oregon. There he died in 1881.

Mention might be made here also of another noted abolitionist worker, Judge James Brownlee of Ohio. He was born in a hamlet near Glasgow in 1801, and used to boast that many of his ancestors had fought "For Christ's Crown and Covenant." He settled in the United States in 1827, and three years later his parents and the rest of the family followed him. They bought a beautiful tract of land in Mahoning County, Ohio, and prospered greatly. In his "Historical Collections of Ohio" Henry Howe writes: "For his first thirty years in this country Judge Brownlee was engaged chiefly in the buying and selling of cattle, purchasing yearly thousands and thousands of cows and beeves for the great markets of the West and East. He was always active in politics, an enthusiastic and ardent Whig; but while acting with the Whigs he astonished the Abolitionists by attending an indignation meeting held at Canfield against the passage of the Fugitive Slave law, when he drew up a resolution so audacious that the committee feared to adopt it, it seeming treasonable. He offered it personally, and it was carried in a whirl of enthusiasm. It was ' Resolved, That, come life, come death, come fine or imprisonment, we will neither aid nor abet the capture of a fugitive slave; but, on the contrary, will harbor and feed, clothe and assist, and give him a practical godspeed toward liberty.' * * * Judge Brownlee held many positions of public and private trust. For years he held his life in jeopardy, having repeatedly heard the bullets whistling around his head when obliged to visit certain localites still remembered for their opposition to the [civil] war and the operations of the revenue system. He died January 20, 1879, at Poland, Ohio. He was a stanch Presbyterian, and his friends were numbered among the rich and the poor, who found in him that faith and charity which make the whole world kin." A daughter of this typical Scot—Mrs. Kate B. Sherwood—has contributed several volumes of high-class verse, including many stirring lyrics, to the literature of her own country, the country of her father's adoption.

In quite another although possibly less important department of usefulness old John Allan, the once noted antiquary and book collector, might be recalled. He was born at Kilbirnie, Ayrshire, in 1777. His father was a " small farmer " there and, like most people of his class, had a hard task in constantly wrestling with the soil to produce enough to make ends meet, and so the family became scattered in early life, after their schooling was completed. John crossed the Atlantic in 1794 and, settling in New York, got a position as clerk. Afterward he became a collector of accounts and real estate agent, but he never acquired what would even then be called moderate wealth. Therefore it is extraordinary how he managed to gather such a wonderful variety of curiosities, antiquities and literary treasures of all sorts. His house at 17 Vandewater street was a veritable museum. It was crowded from cellar to attic with books, pictures and knick-knacks of all ages and countries. Allan had a particular *penchant* for collecting snuff-boxes —a hobby which was once a favorite one among Scotch antiquaries—and his possessions in this field were more numerous than had ever before been gathered together in America. He had also a craze for illustrating books—a craze which is by no means to be commended, or which would ever be entertained by one who loved literature for its own sake—and his "illustrated" copies of such works as the life of Washington and the poems of Robert Burns were extraordinary not merely for their bulk, but for the wealth and variety, and sometimes the rarity and uniqueness of the material which had been used in them. The destructiveness of this form of literary amusement, if such it can be called, is fully set forth in a delightful passage on "Grangerites" in John Hill Burton's "Bookhunter," for the hobby is not, as has sometimes been said, an American invention, but had its rise in England, or was at least in vogue there long before it crossed the sea. Allan took no special interest in Scotland, mixed rarely, if ever, among his countrymen in the city in which he had his home, but devoted his time and his means to increasing his collections. After his death they were dispersed at public auction, and realized nearly $38,000.

In studying the history of the Scot in America we come upon many curious facts in the early history of the continent. For instance, the first paper mill ever erected in Canada was due to the business enterprise of James Crooks, a native of Kilmarnock, where he was born in 1778. He was a good soldier as well as business man, and served with distinction in the royal army in the battle of Queenstown Heights and in other engagements of the War of 1812. Afterward he won eminence as a representative of the people in the legislative chambers of Canada, and died full of years and honors at West Flamborough, Ontario, in 1860. During the course of these pages several other instances will be recorded of the first steps in important industries being undertaken by Scotsmen.

Then knowledge of the race in America comes to us in indirect ways. In the poems of our national bard are several in honor of Miss Jeannie Jaffrey, whose "two lovely een o' bonnie blue" apparently played havoc with the heart of the poet. Miss Jaffrey was the daughter of the Rev. Andrew Jaffrey, minister of Lochmaben. She married a gentleman named Renwick, and, after residing several years in Liverpool, removed with her husband to the United States. Scott Douglas, in his library edition of Burns's poems, says: "Her husband's name was [William] Renwick, and her position in the chief city of the United States was one of distinguished respectability. Washington Irving was proud of her friendship and society, and some years after her death, in October, 1850, her memoirs were published along with a collected volume of her writings." Her son James (born in Liverpool) became in 1820 Professor of Natural Philosophy and Chemistry in Columbia College, New York, and was one of the Commissioners who laid out the early boundary line of the Province of New Brunswick and a frequent and welcome writer, mainly on scientific subjects. He died in 1863. One of his sons, Henry B. Renwick, who died in 1895, was a noted engineer and expert in patent cases and was the first Inspector of Steam Vessels for the Port of New York. He was engaged by the United States Government in many important engineering works, notably the construction of the Sandy Hook and Egg Harbor breakwaters. He was also one of the Government surveyors in the matter of fixing the boundary line between Maine and New Brunswick. Another son, James, who also died in 1895, was the architect of Grace Church, the Roman Catholic Cathedral on Fifth Avenue, and other important buildings in New York, the Smithsonian Institution and the Corcoran Gallery, Washington, and of Vassar College. The whole of the Renwick family, however, were of more than ordinary ability, as might be expected from the descendants of a "heroine of Burns," and who was one of the sprightliest and most charming of Scottish-American ladies.

If it was thought necessary to introduce sensational matters in a volume of this kind, very considerable space might be given to the exploits of Allan Pinkerton, the ablest detective who ever assisted justice in America.

Sketches of this man's career, however, are plentiful enough, and his successes and experiences have been told in a series of volumes bearing his name, but evidently written by some literary gentleman who seems to have been a believer in the art of embellishing truth with fiction, so much so that it is impossible to know what to regard as truth and what to place to the credit of embellishment. Pinkerton was born at Glasgow in 1819, his father being a policeman. He certainly became the best-known detective in America, acquired a national reputation, in fact, and was a terror to evildoers of all classes. He died at Chicago in 1884.

One Scotsman whose influence is still felt in this country, although not on account of any practical work he did while in it, was John Loudon Macadam. He was born in the parish of Carsphairn, Kirkcudbrightshire, according to the article in the Statistical Account of Scotland on the parish of Carsphairn by the Rev. David Welsh. Some authorities state, however, that his birthplace was Ayr, and the date September 21, 1756, and as this claim is also put forward in the volume of the same statistical account relating to that country, an example is afforded of how even an authority can differ on a matter on which no such confusion should exist. That the family belonged to Carsphairn there is no doubt, however, and there was a tradition in it that their original name was MacGregor, that the MacAdams were descended from that once formidable Highland clan, and that the patronymic was assumed when the original name was proscribed by law. Macadam was educated at Maybole, and when a young man was sent, on the death of his father, to an uncle, who was a merchant in New York. He became himself a successful merchant, but as he retained his loyalty at the time of the Revolution, he lost the greater part, if not the whole, of his property. For a time he acted as agent for the sale of prizes at the Port of New York, but in 1783 was compelled to leave the country. He secured an appointment in England and it was while residing at Bristol and holding the office of a local road trustee that he showed his genius for

INTRODUCTORY.   17

roadmaking and put into effect the system which still bears his name and which is everywhere recognized as the best ever conceived. Its principle is simply to have the roadbed made level and to cover it with about three inches of rock broken into fragments of two cubic inches each. The fame of the roads built under his superintendence and according to his ideas quickly spread all over England, and soon he and his sons had more business on hand as road surveyors and builders than they could easily handle. Mr. Macadam's last years were pleasantly spent in Scotland, where he was recognized as a public benefactor and as a generous-handed friend to the poor. He refused the honor of knighthood, which, however, was bestowed on one of his sons, and in 1836 passed away to his reward, at Moffat, at the ripe age of eighty-one. It is possible that it was the wretched condition of the roads in America, and the fact that the means to improve them were on hand on every side, that first turned his thoughts to the subject of the improvement of public highways. America was slow to appreciate the need and utility of anything beyond a clearing being required for a highway, but now that a demand for "good roads" has sprung up all over the continent, the cry for "macadamized" streets, boulevards and thoroughfares of all sorts shows that the lifework of this ingenious Scot has become an important factor in the current thought and endeavor of the land where he once had his home and where he doubtless intended to round out the entire measure of his existence.

This chapter having dealt in a promiscuous and offhand sort of way with a few representative Scots in varied walks of life, it may not be out of keeping with its tenor to introduce here notices of one hero who owes his prominence mainly to the caricature of a novelist and of two others who might have claimed to belong to the race, although they are not generally regarded from a Scotch standpoint. In Smollett's novel of "Humphrey Clinker" a peculiar type of Scotsman is introduced — Lieutenant Lismahago. According to the story, this warrior, while serving in America, was captured by the

French and escaped, only to be recaptured by a tribe of Indians. The treatment Lismahago and his companion in misery received at the hands of their savage captors need not be retailed here, but its harrowing details ended with the marriage of the Lieutenant to Squinkinacoosta, the princess of the tribe. "The Lieutenant," according to the novel, " had lived very happily with his accomplished squaw for two years, during which she bore him a son, who is now the representative of his mother's tribe; but at length, to his unspeakable grief, she had died of a fever occasioned by eating too much raw beef which they had killed on a hunting excursion. By this time Mr. Lismahago was elected Sachem, acknowledged first warrior of the Badger tribe, and dignified with the name or epithet of Occacanastaogarora, which signifies 'nimble as a weasel.'" It is said that the original of this Caledonian-Indian Chief was Richard Stobo, a native of Glasgow, where his father was a wealthy merchant. He was born in 1724 and about 1743 went to Virginia, where he engaged in business but without, apparently, meeting with much success. He held a good social position, however, and probably he sacrificed his business prospects to further his military ambition. In 1754 he was appointed Captain in a regiment that was raised to meet the French and of which George Washington was in command. It was Stobo, who designed the works which formed the stronghold which Washington grimly called "Fort Necessity," and when it was surrendered Stobo was one of the two hostages given to the French. While in durance at Fort Duquesne, Stobo kept his eyes open, and managed to send to his own side of the lines a letter containing a plan of the fort and suggestions for its capture. One part of his letter " breathes a loyal and generous spirit of self-devotion," as Washington Irving says in his life of the first American President. "Consider the good," Stobo wrote, " of the expedition without regard to us. When we engaged to serve the country it was expected we were to do it with our lives. For my part I would die a hundred deaths to have the pleasure of possessing this fort for one day. They are so vain of their success at the Meadows it is worse than death to hear them. Haste to strike."

One of Stobo's letters fell into the hands of his captors, and as a result he and his fellow captive were sent to Quebec. From that fortress he escaped, was captured, and condemned to death as a spy. He again escaped, was recaptured after three days, escaped once more by means of a birch canoe, and in thirty-eight days, after encountering all sorts of adventures, reached the British forces before Louisbourg. During his enforced absence he had been promoted Major in his Virginia regiment, and so much were his services appreciated and his sufferings pitied that the Legislature of that colony voted him a grant of £1,300. Going to England in 1760 Stobo was commissioned Captain in the Fifteenth Infantry and served in the West Indies. Returning to England in 1770 he settled down as a man of leisure, cultivated literature and the friendship of literary men, among others of Tobias Smollett, and published a little book descriptive of his adventures in America, a work which is now very rare. How much of Smollett's descriptions of penury and adventure of which Lismahago is the theme be exactly true, we cannot of course determine, but it is certainly not a very flattering picture for one friend to draw of another, to say nothing of the existence in the heart of the novelist of a sentiment of national pride which might have induced a softening of the sketch. Lockhart, in his brilliant life of Burns, excuses or accounts for this peculiar state of things as a sort of deference to the prevailing dislike of Scotsmen entertained in London at the era when Smollett wrote. " A still more striking sign of the times," Lockhart says, " is to be found in the style adopted by both of these novelists, (Dr. Moore and Smollett), especially the great masters of the art, in their representations of the manners and characters of their own countrymen. In 'Humphrey Clinker,' the last and best of Smollett's tales, there are some traits of a better kind, but, taking his works as a whole, the impression it conveys is certainly a painful, a disgusting one. * * * When such high-spirited Scottish gentlemen, possessed of learning and talents, and, one of them at least, of splendid genius, felt or fancied the necessity of making such submissions to the prejudices of the dominant nation, and did so without exciting a murmur among their own countrymen, we may form some notion of the boldness of Burns's experiment, and in contrasting the state of things then with what is before us now it will cost no effort to appreciate the nature and consequences of the victory in which our poet led the way, by achievements never in their kind to be surpassed."

But however the personality of the doughty Lieutenant may be obnoxious to us, and however much it may belie the fair name or distort the true story of the career of Richard Stobo, many originals for such stories may be found in the early history of the Indian tribes of North America; that is, their early history so far as their associations with Europeans go. One of the more noted chiefs of the Creek nation—one of the most powerful on the continent—in the eighteenth century was Alexander McGillivray. His father was Lachlan McGillivray, a native of Mull and said to have belonged to the house of McGillivray of Dunmaglas—a branch of the Clan Chattan—probably on account of the same degree of relationship that makes all Stewarts " sib " to the King. Alexander's mother was a Creek princess whose father had been a French officer of Spanish descent, so that Alexander had Scotch, Indian, Spanish and French blood in his veins, and as his uncle, his father's brother, was a Presbyterian minister at Charleston and a member of the St. Andrew's Society there, he could boast, at least, that he was respectably connected. McGillivray was a genius, a born diplomat, a natural leader, and in time became acknowledged as the supreme head of his tribe. He was by turns a speculator, merchant, politician, diplomatist, and always a warrior. He was well educated, his early years having been passed under the care of his uncle the clergyman, and it was expected that he would, on reaching manhood, cling to his father's people. But he preferred his maternal relatives and returned to the haunts and adopted the ways of the Indians so completely that he became not only their most trusted leader, but the virtual autocrat of the Creek nation and its allies.

McGillivray once visited New York, in 1790, in his capacity of leader of the Creeks, and the incidents attending that visit are thus told in Booth's history of that city, "Colonel Marinus Willett * * * invited McGillivray to go with him to New York to talk with the Great Father. To this proposal McGillivray consented, and set out in the beginning of the Summer, accompanied by twenty-eight chiefs and warriors of the nation. Their arrival excited considerable interest in the city. On landing they were met by the Tammany Society, arrayed in Indian costume, which escorted them to their lodgings on the banks of the North River, at the tavern known henceforth as 'The Indian Queen.' Here they remained for more than six weeks, negotiating the terms of a treaty with General Knox, and, the matter being at length satisfactorily arranged, the treaty was ratified in true Indian style in Wall Street on the 13th of August. At 12 o'clock the Creek deputation was met by the President and his suite in the Hall of the House of Representatives, where the treaty was read and interpreted, after which Washington addressed the warriors in a short but emphatic speech, detailing and explaining the justice of its provisions; to each of which, as it was interpreted to them, McGillivray and his warriors gave the Indian grunt of approval. The treaty was then signed by both parties, after which Washington presented McGillivray with a string of wampum as a memorial of the peace, and with a paper of tobacco as a substitute for the ancient calumet, grown obsolete and unattainable by the innovations of modern times. McGillivray made a brief speech in reply, the 'shake of peace' was interchanged between Washington and each of the chiefs, and the ceremony was concluded by a song of peace, in which the Creek warriors joined with enthusiasm. The warriors indeed had good reason to be satisfied with this treaty, which ceded to them all the disputed territory and distributed presents and money liberally among the nation. * * * The visit of the Indians closed the official career of New York as the capital city of the United States."

According to all accounts, McGillivray was a brave man, had wonderful powers of endurance, and possessed all the noted Indian traits of stolidity and deception in abundance. His enemies never knew very well what to make of him, but all courted his friendship as long as possible, and he was probably the only man who ever lived who at one and the same time was a British Colonel, a Spanish General, and a General in the forces of the United States. With all his brilliant qualities, however, he had few admirers, and one of his adversaries, Gen. Robertson, summed up his character in these unmistakable words: " The Spaniards are devils, but the biggest devil among them is the half Spaniard, half Frenchman, half Scotsman, and altogether Creek scoundrel, McGillivray." This redoubted warrior died in Florida in 1793.

Quite a similar case in many ways was that of William McIntosh, another Creek chief, who was born in Georgia in 1775. His father was a Highland officer and his mother a Creek princess. He cast in his lot with his mother's tribe and became its chief. During the war of 1812 he fought against the British and held the dignity of Major in the United States Army. He was one of the first Indians to perceive that the white man had taken possession of the country for good, and the policy of his life seems to have been to conciliate the whiteskins and to live with them on the best terms attainable. This policy, undoubtedly the most far-sighted and prudent that could have been adopted, led to his death, for he was assassinated in his native State in 1825 by some Indians who were opposed to an agreement he had entered into

INTRODUCTORY.

which involved the selling of some of the lands held by the Creeks to the United States Government.

Many weird tales are yet told along the eastern coast of the wild doings of Capt. Kidd, many romances have been evolved out of his career, romances which have terrified the nursery and aroused the sympathetic ardor of lovers of fiction in the parlor. Thousands of dollars, too, have been spent in the search after Capt. Kidd's treasures, and hardly a Summer passes without bringing us a story or two of expeditions being organized. William Kidd was born at Greenock about 1650, and was, it is said, the son of a clergyman. Of his early training and career nothing is known. The first authentic glimpse we get of him is from the records of the New York Colonial Assembly for 1691, when on one occasion he was thanked for services rendered the commerce of the colony, and on another when £150 was voted him for similar services. What these were is not exactly clear, but it has been surmised, and the surmise is plausible, that he acted as a sort of protector to the coast commerce from pirates and unlawful depredators. In 1696, Capt. Kidd was placed by Gov. Bellamont in command of a vessel, with the view of sweeping the coast of pirates, and he did his work so well that after his first cruise he was awarded a fresh grant of money, this time of £250. Then he started on another cruise, and leaving the coast, started out as a pirate on his own account. He sailed to the Indian Ocean, made Madagascar his headquarters, and committed such depredations, scuttling, stealing, and robbing ships, that his name became famous and feared throughout the maritime world. After a time he returned to America, and, it is said, had any number of hiding places along the seaboard. His headquarters were, however, mainly on Long Island, and for safe keeping he is reported to have buried his treasures in different localities, but where has been the puzzle to succeeding generations of those acquainted by reading or tradition with his career. The stories in connection with this section of Capt. Kidd's life story are of the most vague and unintelligible order, but the following from the pen of Mr. D. W. Stone of the New York "Commercial Advertiser" is as moderately written and as reliable as anything that has appeared:

"It is beyond doubt true that Long Island contained several of his hiding places. 'Kidd's Rock' is well known at Manhasset, up on Long Island, to this day. Here Kidd is supposed to have buried some of his treasures, and many have been the attempts of the credulous in that section to find the hidden gold. There is also no doubt that he was wont to hide himself and his vessel among those curious rocks in Sachem's Head Harbor, called the 'Thimble Islands.' In addition to the 'Pirates' Cavern,' in this vicinity, there is upon one of these rocks, sheltered from the view of the Sound, a beautiful artificial excavation in an oval form, holding, perhaps, the measure of a barrel still called 'Kidd's Punch Bowl.' It was here, according to the traditions of the neighborhood, that he used to carouse with his crew. It is also a fact beyond controversy that he was accustomed to anchor his vessel in Gardner's Bay. Upon an occasion in the night he landed upon Gardner's Island and requested Mrs. Gardner to provide a supper for himself and his attendants. Knowing his desperate character, she dared not refuse, and, fearing his displeasure, she took great pains, especially in roasting a pig. The pirate chief was so pleased with her cooking that on going away he presented her with a cradle blanket of gold cloth. It was of velvet inwrought with gold and very rich. A piece of it yet remains in the possession of the Gardner family, and a still smaller piece is in my possession, it having been given to my father, the late Col. William L. Stone, by one of the descendants of that family. On another occasion, when he landed upon the island, he buried a small casket of gold containing articles of silver and precious stones in the presence of Mr. Gardner, but under the most solemn injunctions of secrecy.

"Repairing, soon after this occurrence, to Boston, where Lord Bellamont chanced to be at the time, he was summoned before His Lordship and ordered to give a report of his proceedings since he had sailed on his second voyage. Refusing, however, to comply with this demand, he was arrested on the 3d of July, 1699, on the charge of piracy. He appears to have disclosed the fact of having buried treasure on Gardner's Island, for it was demanded by the Earl of Bellamont and surrendered by Mr. Gardner. I have seen the original receipts for the amount, with the different items of the deposits. They were by no means large, and afford no evidence of such mighty ' sweepings of the sea ' as have been told of by tradition. Of gold, in coins, gold dust and bars, there were 750 ounces; of silver, 506 ounces, and of precious stones, 16 ounces."

But there are hundreds of places along the Hudson and the New England and New Jersey coasts where search has been made for more treasure, and at Asbury Park may still be seen steel divining rods which were once used by experts who located one or more of the pirate's chests where Ocean Grove and Bradley Beach are now located.

Kidd was sent to Britain in 1701, tried for piracy on the high seas, and also for murder, and, with six of his crew, was hanged in chains at Execution Dock, London, in the same year. The news of his fate recalled attention to his exploits, the notoriety of his name increased, and rumor magnified his daring, his crimes, his depredations and everything connected with him a thousandfold, and even formed themes for a score or so of ballads. So far as we know, he was the only Scottish-American who ever was celebrated by the rhymes of the sheet vocalist and wandering minstrels of the curb and kitchen.

Of course, nothing can be said in defense of piracy, and even though Kidd was guiltless of the crime of murder or of any of the acts of cruelty and barbarism attributed to him, his course as an adventurer on the high seas would still leave his memory badly tarnished. Robbery is plain, vulgar robbery, whether committed on land or sea. It is a pity, however, that more of the history of this redoubtable pirate was not known, for we are convinced that his character would appear in a more amiable light under the microscope of truth than it seems in the misty haze of tradition. Indeed, we fancy it would then be seen that the services for which the New York Legislature granted him gifts of money were really little short of acts of piracy in whose proceeds they shared and which they negatively authorized. "Connivance at piracy," writes Mr. Ellis H. Roberts, in his interesting volumes on the history of the State of New York, " was a charge not infrequent against prominent persons in the Colonies at this time (around 1700). Privateering was encouraged by the Government, and reputable persons became partners in vessels sent out under daring sailors to secure prizes. The sailors did not always observe nice distinctions when such captures were possible, and privateering not infrequently fell more and more into audacious piracy. * * * He (Capt. Kidd) cannot have deemed himself a criminal in any great degree, if at all, for, after selling his ship, he appeared openly in Boston, where the Earl of Bellamont recognized him and put him under arrest." The trouble with Kidd was that the stories of his having hidden treasure withdrew from him the support of his confederates among the authorities. As modern Americans would say, he lost his " pull," and so his power. In considering the case of Capt. Kidd we should remember that among his partners in his privateering expeditions were such men as King William, the Earl of Bellamont, and Robert Livingston, and while this does not justify Kidd's conduct in any way, it makes him simply a spoke in a wheel of corruption evolved by others and sanctioned and protected in high places, instead of the hub of a wheel which he had cut out and fashioned for himself.

We cannot close this chapter with such a dubious character as a representative of the nationality, and therefore, as a sort of redeeming offset, turn to the long list of heroes for an example or two, and this we do with the more readiness, as the chapter which will deal with heroes will treat mainly of those who fought on the popular side during the War of the Revolution.

In the early history of the United States and Canada, Highlanders, as we have seen and will frequently be reminded in the course of this volume, were welcomed as settlers, and in many places, as in Nova Scotia, Cape Breton, Glengarry, North Carolina, and around Caledonia, N. Y., as well as in other localities, the direct descendants of these pioneer immigrants from Albyn may yet be found. In many places they yet speak the language of their ancestors; in others they are still distinguished by their manners, their ways, their industry, thrift, and godliness. Several bands of Highlanders came over here in military service, and their prowess, endurance, skill, and intrepidity are freely acknowledged in the ordinary histories. Such was notably the case in Canada with Fraser's Highlanders, and in the other colonies, as well as in America, with the Black Watch. But there were other Highland soldiers whose deeds were equally worthy of record with those generally mentioned; but they are simply spoken of as Highlanders without any more definite designation.

Such was the case with as gallant a band as ever maintained the name of the Scottish soldier in foreign lands—Montgomerie's Highlanders. Famous as they were in their day, they are now practically forgotten; but there are few commands which earned a better record as soldiers and as men. They were formally enrolled as the Seventy-seventh Regiment, and were only in existence some six years when they were disbanded. Thus in glancing over their career we can start out with them on their campaign and remain with them until their flags were finally furled without undertaking a very considerable task. Their history is a brief one; but, brief as it is, there is no lack of incident in the story. It is full of interest from beginning to end for Highlanders everywhere, and particularly for all who love to read about the early doings of the Scot in America.

In 1756, after considerable wirepulling, Major Archibald Montgomerie got permission to raise a regiment of Highlanders for service in North America. So successful was he that he soon was at the head of a body of about 1,400 officers and men, and in January, 1757, he received his commission as Colonel. Col. Montgomerie was a military man of great promise and was very popular among all classes. He was a son of the ninth Earl of Eglinton, and ultimately succeeded to that title himself. His father, of course, was a nobleman, but he was one of those aristocrats who believed the country was made expressly for their benefit. He was a shrewd business man, it is said, made three fortunate marriages, turned everything into cash, and even sold his vote to England for £200, at the time the Treaty of Union was being considered. Col. Montgomerie's mother, the Countess Susannah, was one of the most beautiful women of her time, and was noted for her wit and her love of literature. It was to her that Allan Ramsay dedicated his "Gentle Shepherd." Col. Montgomerie appears to have inherited the qualities which made his mother so popular and so generally beloved, without any of the sordid spirit which was his father's main characteristic.

The regiment embarked at Greenock in 1758. Its officers, with two exceptions, all bore good old Highland names—as Grant, Campbell, Mackenzie, Macdonald, and the like. The two exceptions were the Colonel and his young kinsman, Capt. Hugh Montgomerie, who in turn succeeded to the earldom. The regiment landed at Halifax and was at once sent *en route* to Fort Duquesne (Pittsburgh) as part of a force which was to capture that stronghold from the French or their Indian allies. It was a terrible journey at that time, but the Highlanders stood its fatigues and dangers nobly, although there is no doubt they were glad when they reached Philadelphia and enjoyed a brief season of rest in its new and comparatively comfortable barracks before starting out again for their destination.

The Philadelphia barracks extended between Second and Third Streets, from St. Tamany to Green Street, and the buildings were arranged in the form of a hollow square. The officers' section faced on Third Street, and consisted of a large three-story brick house, while the soldiers' quarters were two stories high, and of wood, with a veranda running on a level with the second floor. In the centre of the square was a drillyard, or parade ground. Many Highland regiments were quartered there from first to last, and at times, when its accommodations were overtaxed, the officers took rooms in the house of a Scotch widow, Mrs. Cordon, who kept a high-class boarding establishment for many years on Front Street. It is said that at one time her house was filled with the officers of the Forty-second Highlanders. The barracks, which seem to have been first occupied by Montgomerie's regiment, have been built over long ago.

The expedition against Fort Duquesne was an imposing one, as such things went in those days. Gen. Forbes was in chief command, and one of the officers was George Washington, who rendered good service by his knowledge of the country. The first stopping place for more than a night was Raystown, ninety miles from the fort. From there a smaller expedition was sent on to Loyal Hannen, fifty miles from Duquesne, and in this expedition were Montgomerie's Highlanders. From Hannen a still smaller expedition set out commanded by James Grant of Ballindalloch, Major in the Highland regiment. He had with him some 400 of his own comrades and 500 Colonial troops. Having no knowledge of Indian warfare, Major Grant advanced upon the fort in grand style, with drums beating and pipes playing. The soldiers in the fort made a gallant resistance, and being helped by a large band of Indians, poured a terrible fire into the ranks of the invaders, while they themselves were protected by the foliage of the surrounding forest. It was an awful massacre. The Highlanders were unaccustomed to fight an unseen enemy, and when it was found useless to continue the contest any longer, 230 of them were lying on the field, dead or wounded. Only 150 made their way back to Loyal Hannen. Several were taken prisoners by the Indians, who at once set about killing them with all the atrocities for which those redskins were famous. After seeing a dozen of his comrades butchered with the most horible cruelty, one of the Highlanders, Allan Macpherson, revolved a little scheme in his mind. When his turn came he told his captors that he knew the secret of an herb, which, when applied to the skin, would make it resist the strongest blow from sword, knife, or tomahawk. An herb of this sort was the very thing the Indians wanted, and they agreed to let him go to the woods, under escort, to gather the herb, the conditions being that he should rub the stuff on his own neck and so prove its efficiency. Macpherson gathered some roots, boiled them, and then, anointing his neck with the liquid, declared himself ready, and invited the strongest man to try to break his skin. A most powerful Indian stepped forward and with one terrific blow cut Macpherson's head off, and sent it flying through the air for several yards. The Indians then understood that the Highlander had outwitted them, and escaped the lingering death to which he had been doomed. It is said that they were so pleased with his ingenuity that they desisted from inflicting further cruelties upon the remaining prisoners.

Disastrous as was the fate of this adventure, the defenders of Fort Duquesne, however, saw that they had a determined force to deal with, and so when the main body of the invading expedition came up they evacuated their stronghold, leaving behind them their cannon, stores, and provisions. Gen. Forbes, on taking possession, changed the name of the place to Pittsburgh. There the Highlanders enjoyed another respite from field service.

In May, 1759, they were part of Gen. Amherst's forces at Ticonderoga, and along Lake Champlain and Lake George, and then returned to Pennsylvania and marched in fighting order as far as the border of Virginia. Their numbers during these campaigns were not strengthened by recruits from Scotland or elsewhere; but they certainly

made up in determination, courage, and endurance for
their want of numbers. They were now veteran campaigners, and as careful of ambuscades as before they
were careless. They understood Indian fighters and
methods as well as any battalion of frontier scouts. As
usual, too, with Highland regiments, even to this day,
the more dangerous and difficult the task the more certain was it to be allotted to them by whoever was commander in chief.

Such a task was the expedition to Martinique, in which
Montgomerie's Highlanders and the Forty-second
(Black Watch) next took the most important part. When
that trouble was over, both these regiments went to New
York, and Montgomerie's men remained there, while the
Forty-second was sent to Albany. Two companies of
Montgomerie's regiment, which had previously been detached from the main body, had formed part of a force
which was sent to St. John's, Newfoundland, to capture
that town from the French. When this was accomplished
the two companies—or what was left of them—rejoined
the rest of the regiment in New York, where the Winter
of 1762 was passed. Next Spring peace was declared between Great Britain and France, and the former became
mistress of the French colonies in America. Then Montgomerie's Highlanders were disbanded, and, while some
of the veterans returned to their "ain countrie," not a
few took advantage of the offer of grants of land and
settled in America.

Such in brief is the story of an old Highland regiment,
whose doings are well worthy of being recalled. They
who fought in it were an honor to the country which
sent them forth, and their deeds at Pittsburgh, as well
as at Ticonderoga and elsewhere, entitle them to a prominent place in the long list of Scotland's military heroes.

It would be an interesting study to follow the fortunes
of the gallant Black Watch in North America, or to
relate the stirring story of such regiments as the old
Seventy-first, but such records would occupy a volume
in telling, and even a recapitulation of them would swell

this work beyond due proportions. This is all the more unnecessary as the records of such commands are easily accessible.

As an example of the men who fought in these commands, we select the name of John Small, who was born at Strathardale, Perthshire, in 1720, and died at Guernsey, with the rank of Major General, in 1796. Early in life he entered the army, and his career throughout was an eventful one. He first saw service with the Scotch Brigade in the Dutch Army, and then received an ensigncy in the Black Watch, being promoted to Lieutenant soon after joining that corps. He was under Abercombie in the attack on Ticonderoga in 1758, was in Montreal two years later, and then went to the West Indies, where he won his Captaincy. In 1775, after holding a commission for a short time in the Twenty-first Regiment, he was commissioned Major in the Second Battalion of the regiment known as the Royal Highland Emigrants, raised in Nova Scotia to aid the Crown, and was present at the battle of Bunker Hill. In Trumbull's painting of that skirmish, Major Small's figure occupies a prominent place. This regiment, mention of which is again made in the closing chapter of this volume, was named the Eighty-fourth, and Small was continued in command of the Second Battalion, and with it served mainly in the State of New York under Sir Henry Clinton. The regiment was disbanded in 1783, after the conclusion of hostilities, and many of the officers and soldiers in Small's battalion retired to Nova Scotia, where they received grants of land—5,000 acres to a field officer, 3,000 to a Captain, 500 to a subaltern, 200 to a Sergeant, and 100 to a private. Before leaving America Small was gazetted a Lieutenant Colonel and was Military Governor of the Island of Guernsey at the time of his death.

So much for an officer. In an old issue of the London magazine, "The Humanitarian," we read an account of one of those who served in the ranks in the same campaign, under Sir Henry Clinton, with Major Small. As the story is interesting, we quote it in full:

INTRODUCTORY.

"An old Highland soldier—Sergt. Donald Macleod, of the Forty-second Highlanders—was in 1791 an out-pensioner of Chelsea Hospital, in the one hundred and third year of his age. This veteran was a native of Skye, born at Ulinish on the 20th of June, 1688, as appears from the parish register of Bracadale. He enlisted in the Royal Scots, and his first campaign was under Marlborough in 1704-13, where he served with his regiment in the battles of Blenheim, Ramillies, &c.; he was in the Hanoverian Army in 1715, and greatly distinguished himself against his own countrymen at Sheriffmuir; he then saw foreign service again at the battle of Fontenoy; after this we find that he was in America under Gen. Wolfe. At the battle of Quebec Sergt. Macleod had his shin bone shattered by grape shot, and received a musket ball in his arm; but when Gen. Wolfe was seriously wounded the old soldier offered his plaid, in which his beloved commander was borne to the rear by four Grenadiers. Owing to his wounds Macleod was invalided, and returned to England in November, 1759, in the frigate that bore the body of Gen. Wolfe. On arriving in England he was admitted an out-pensioner of Chelsea Hospital on the 4th of December, 1759. His wounds soon healed, and he went on a recruiting expedition to the Highlands, where he married his third wife. Although now seventy-two years of age, he again took to the wars on the outbreak of hostilities, and served as a volunteer under Col. Campbell on the Continent, and in the course of different engagements during the campaign of 1760-61 he was wounded several times. Even these hard knocks were not sufficient to end the old man's military career, as we find him again in America under Sir Henry Clinton."

Passing over the kittle times of the Revolution and the War of 1812, we find many instances of the continuity of the heroic side of the story of Scotland's sons in America. Take the career of Col. John Munroe as one which is an example of a thousand others, too soon, alas, forgotten. Munroe was born in Ross-shire in 1796 and settled in America with his parents when a boy. In 1814 he graduated at West Point and was appointed to the United States Army as a Third Lieutenant. Promotion in Uncle Sam's Army, except at fortunately rare intervals, is rather slow, and it was not till 1825 that Munroe received his commission as Captain. In 1838, for brilliant services against the Florida Indians, he was brevetted Major, and in 1846 was appointed Major in the Second Artillery. That same year he was Gen. Zachary Taylor's Chief of Artillery, and was brevetted Lieutenant Colonel for gallantry at Monterey, and Colonel for his services at Buena Vista. For over a year (1849-50) he was military and civil Governor of New Mexico, and made an admirable Executive. After retiring from the army he took up his residence in New Brunswick and died there in 1861.

This warrior's death brings us down to the opening of the great civil war—a conflict in which, on both sides, Scotsmen exhibited the native valor of their country. We cannot even estimate the number of Scotsmen who took part in that political convulsion—possibly 50,000 would be under the mark—as the volunteer records at Washington do not define nationality. But it is acknowledged on all sides that Scotsmen did their full duty according to their consciences, whether they wore blue or gray.

One of the earliest commands to answer the call of President Lincoln was the Highland Guard of Chicago, which was originally formed in 1855. It commenced its term of active service in 1861, under Capt. J. T. Raffen, and made a brilliant record. Its first commander was John McArthur, who was born at Erskine in 1826, and was originally a boilermaker. In the civil war he bore himself with great gallantry and rose step by step until he was brevetted Major General at the battle of Nashville for conspicuous bravery. After the war he returned to Chicago and entered into business, which was interrupted by his four-year term of service as Postmaster of Chicago, an office he administered with great tact and executive ability.

Another Scotsman who rose to the rank of General in the civil war was Gen. James Lorraine Geddes, who died at Ames, Iowa, in 1887. There were many, very many, Scotch field officers in the war, so many that it seems somewhat invidious to single out any one, but Gen. Geddes had such a varied career and, on the whole, was so typically representative of the Scot abroad that we cannot refrain from relating its most salient points. It is very few nationalities that can point to a son who begins life as a private soldier and ends as the President of a college. Geddes was born at Edinburgh in 1829, and in 1837 was taken by his father to Canada. As soon as he was old enough, after he had received his schooling, he went to sea. But he soon got tired of that life, and, while in Calcutta, enlisted in the Royal Artillery. He fought under Sir Charles Napier and Sir Colin Campbell in the Crimea, and received the regulation silver medal and clasp. When he was discharged he made his way back to Canada, where after a time, he was elected Colonel in a local cavalry organization. In 1857 he left the Dominion and settled at Vinton, Iowa, where he got employment as a teacher. When the civil war broke out he enlisted (Aug. 8, 1861,) as a private in the Eighth Iowa Volunteers, and went to the front. His promotion, as might be expected from his past experience, was rapid, and by 1865 he had passed upward through all the intermediary grades and was brevetted a Brigadier General. He was wounded at Shiloh, and was once taken prisoner, but soon exchanged, and he served under Grant at Vicksburg and under Sherman at Jackson, Miss. While acting as Provost Marshal at Memphis, he saved that city from being taken by the Confederate forces under Gen. Forrest, and during the Mobile campaign his capture of Spanish Fort was regarded as the most brilliant feat of that chapter in the history of the great interstate struggle. When the war was over Gen. Geddes returned to Vinton, and for some time had charge of the blind asylum there, but his later years were identified with the Iowa College, at Ames, in which, besides directing in an executive capacity, he was Treasurer and Professor of Military Tactics. He was a poet as well as a soldier and teacher, and wrote several popular war songs, among which "The Soldiers' Battle Prayer" and "The Stars and Stripes" are still remembered and have won a place among the national songs of America.

This record of men of war may fittingly terminate with a reference to the Seventy-ninth Highlanders of New York, which made a record worthy of auld Scotia in the civil war. The nucleus of this command was a company called the Highland Guard, which, with uniforms patterned after those of the Black Watch, used to delight the eyes of the Scotch residents of New York in the fifties. The regiment was practically organized in 1861 and promptly offered its services to the national Government. It was accepted, and it fought through the entire struggle, "fighting more battles and marching more miles than any other New York regiment," as the State record sums up its story. Its first Colonel, Cameron, was killed at the first battle of Bull Run, and it was afterward commanded by several noted officers. On the conclusion of peace the regiment returned to New York, was mustered out of service and at once enrolled as a State regiment of militia. It was finally mustered out in 1875, when under the command of Col. Joseph Laing, a native of Edinburgh, and a good soldier. The deeds of this gallant regiment have been fully told in a portly volume, and thus a knowledge of the details of its campaigns is fairly on record and can be read by all Scots who desire additional topics for illustration of Scottish heroism on American soil.

Probably the central figure of the Seventy-ninth Highlanders—the fighting Seventy-ninth—during the war was Col. David Morrison, who died in New York in February, 1896. His career is an illustration of that of hundreds of good men who took up arms in response to the call from Washington at the outbreak of the civil war. David Morrison was born at Glasgow in 1823, and learned the trade of a brassfounder. After a short term in the British Army, Morrison settled in New York and soon started in business. When the war broke out he went with the Seventy-ninth to the front as one of its Captains, and steadily rose until he was made Colonel, and commanded the regiment. He proved a brilliant leader and his personal bravery was beyond question. His men loved him, trusted him, and executed whatever order he gave unquestioningly, and he was the personal friend of every man who marched under the Seventy-ninth's banners. He, with the regiment, and while acting as commander of a brigade, took part in many battles and skirmishes, and the story of their campaigns is one of the most wonderful in the history of the conflict. When the struggle was over, Col. Morrison returned to New York with the brevet rank of Brigadier General, and again resumed his business, prospering day after day—as he deserved. Except to attend a meeting of the Seventy-ninth veterans, or a St. Andrew's Society dinner, he devoted his spare time to his home and family, and was rarely seen at public gatherings. But he gave away liberally in charity, and many a war veteran was helped over an emergency by his thoughtful generosity. "A brave soldier, a good man, and a Christian gentleman" was what one of his comrades said in speaking of his merits when the news of his death became public, and a whole volume of anecdote could not more fittingly or truthfully describe the man.

We give one anecdote, as it occurred long after the tie between Gen. Morrison and the Seventy-ninth had become merely one of sentiment, and shows that his heart continued warm to his old comrades until the end, for the incident occurred only a few years before his death. "A year or two ago," says our informant, writing in 1896, "the members of old St. Andrew's Division in the course of their temperance work, learned of the case of an old member of the Seventy-ninth Regiment who was steadily 'going down into the depths' from a love for liquor. The man held a fair social position, had a lux-

uriously furnished home, a good business, and but for
' the drink ' would have had a happy life all round. The
St. Andrew's men who were interested in the case pleaded with the man, but to no avail. Then it was suggested
that Gen. Morrison should be told of the matter and his
aid invoked. The trouble was laid before him and he at
once willingly volunteered to accompany the division
folk on a night that was designated. When the night
arrived, however, it was feared that the General would
not turn up. It was one of those Winter evenings when
it was raining one minute, freezing the next, and with an
interval of sleet between. The streets were slippery, the
rain was drenching, and those who knew how fond Gen.
Morrison was of his home did not believe it possible that
he would venture out. But, exact to the moment agreed
upon, he turned up at the home of the then head of the
division, Mr. Thomas Cochrane, plumber, a native of
Glasgow, and when wonder was expressed at his presence under the circumstances he said he felt that a duty
had been assigned to him and it would take queer
weather to make him fail. It was not long before we
were in the home of the man we were trying to aid, and
without any preliminary fencing, the General quietly
opened fire. He did not say much, but what he did say
was so sincere, so evidently from the heart, that in a very
short time the man was in tears and promised not only
to abstain, but to join the division. We do not wish to
repeat what was said, for the proceedings were private,
but we never heard a shorter or better temperance lecture than the General gave. It was practical, kindly, and
touching. After the promise was given we spent a very
happy night, and when we were escorting the General to
the cars he expressed the pleasure he would feel if he
thought he had been of service, and said St. Andrew's
Division had a right to call on him or any one else to
help in its work. Perhaps had New-York contained more
Scotsmen of his stamp the division might have been
alive to-day. The strange thing was that none of us ever
questioned whether Gen. Morrison was himself a teeto-

taller or not. We had implicit faith that he would help us to do what was right and that such a faith existed is as green a wreath as can be placed on the grave where now, alas! rest his honored remains."

It is interesting to know how widely scattered become the members of a command like the Seventy-ninth after fighting together for nearly four years in defense of the Union. The veterans' organization of the old soldiers of the regiment numbers 168 members at present. The number is decreasing yearly, but that, in the nature of things, is to be expected. The following notes of the present whereabouts and standing of several of the best known of the veterans is taken from the " New York Scottish-American," the information being called forth in connection with the death of Gen. Morrison. "Col. Joseph Laing was Captain of G Company when the regiment first went to the front. He was wounded on several occasions—once severely—and his comrades are unanimous in bearing testimony to the pluck and soldierly qualities he showed on the field. His place of business, at the corner of Fulton and Water Streets, this city, where he is an engraver and print-seller, has long been a house of call, both for old members of the regiment and soldiers belonging to other corps. Col. A. D. Baird is a prosperous citizen of Brooklyn. A few years ago he was the Republican candidate for Mayor, and at present he is a Commissioner for the new East River bridge. Along with his son, he carries on extensive stone works in the Eastern District. He is, now that Gen. Morrison has gone, the association's best friend. Capt. Robert Armour, again, is at the head of an important bureau in the Quartermaster's Department of the War Office at Washington. Mr. Crammond Kennedy, the Chaplain of the regiment, who was once known as the "boy preacher," now practices law with success at the national capital. Major Hugh Young, who is a resident of this city, has acquired a competency from a patent of his invention which is used in all stone yards. Dr. David McKay has a good practice as a physician in Dallas, Texas, and Dr. Charles F. Locke is the owner of silver mines in Colorado, and a member of the State Senate. Lieut. D. G. Falconer, who lost a leg in the war, is a prominent lawyer in Lexington, Ky. Mr. Thomas Moore, who was President of the association when it visited Louisville, is a manufacturer of horse collars in Pearl Street, this city. He is prominent in the Masonic fraternity, and has been honored with some high offices in the brotherhood, being at present Trustee of its hall and asylum. William Webster, who was a private in the regiment, went after the war to the Old Country, and became a Captain in the Coldstream Guards, a position which he only recently resigned. Mr. John Spence, who was also a private, has a large and profitable plumbing business in the upper part of this city. Sergt. James McLean is a manufacturer of ice-boxes and butchers' fixtures, his works being in Eleventh Avenue. Private John H. Grant was for more than twenty-five years a police Sergeant, and is now Acting Captain at One Hundred and Twenty-fifth Street. Sergt. Major Joseph Stewart, having faithfully served the city for more than twenty years in the Police Department, is now a retired Sergeant, and a respected and trusted employe of the Nassau Trust Company of Brooklyn. A good number of the other members also reside in this city and neighborhood, among them Adjt. Gilmour, is connected with the business of his father-in-law, the late Gen. Morrison; Capt. John Glendinning is employed by the Board of Works, Capts. Thomas Barclay, F. W. Judge, and Robert Gair live in Brooklyn; Capt. William Clark is employed in the Post Office here, Lieut. John S. Dingwall resides up town, and Mr. J. S. Martin, popularly known as 'Crackers,' keeps his comrades in a state of merriment at all their social gatherings. Mr. Malcolm Sinclair, who was well known here, is now at Cumberland, Md. The rest of the veterans are scattered far and wide over the country. There are a good number in Staten Island, several in Chicago, some in the Soldiers' Homes at Hampton, Va., Kearny, N. J., or elsewhere.

Some are living happily with their friends the enemy down in Dixie, while Middletown, Conn., Syracuse, N. Y., Auburn, Neb., Denver, Col., Davenport, Iowa, Pittsburgh, Penn., Sterling, Kan., and various other places are among the addresses found on the roster. Wherever they are they are all animated by one feeling—that of pride in the record of their old regiment.

The names mentioned in this rambling introductory chapter will give an idea of the ramifications and ways through which the history of the Scottish race in America is to be traced. The men we have already spoken of are mainly random instances, but all, even the Scoto-Indian chiefs, did something toward making the country what it is to-day. As we proceed we will find much more direct and important examples of the influence of the nationality and of the good work that influence accomplished. It is a knowledge that Scotsmen have done their share in building up the great Republic that makes them proud of its progress and inspires them to add to its glories and advantages in every way. Scotsmen, as a nationality, are everywhere spoken of as good and loyal citizens, while Americans who can trace a family residence of a century in the country are proud if they can count among their ancestors some one who hailed from the land of Burns, and it is a knowledge of all this, in turn, that makes the American Scot of to-day proud of his country's record and his citizenship and impels him to be as devoted to the new land as it was possible for him to have been to the old had he remained in it. In America, the old traditions, the old blue flag with its white cross, the old Doric, are not forgotten, but are nourished, and preserved, and honored, and spoken by Scotsmen on every side with the kindliest sentiments on the part of those to whom they are alien. Americans know and acknowledge that the traditions and flag and homely speech have long been conserved to the development of that civil and religious liberty on which the great confederation of sovereign republican States has been founded. In the United States, Sir Walter Scott has more readers and quite as enthusiastic admirers as in Scotland, and if Americans were asked which of the world's poets came nearest to their hearts, the answer would undoubtedly be—Robert Burns.

CHAPTER II.

PIONEERS.

AS might be expected of a race which began, so far as we know to the contrary, in Greece, sojourned in Egypt, Portugal, and other places, and at present has its headquarters in the northern portion of the island of Great Britain, the Scots early began to turn their attention to America. Indeed, it has been gravely argued that America was really discovered long before Columbus was heard of by a band of Scotch mariners who were driven by stress of weather on the coast of Newfoundland, and a full account of the discovery now reposes in the " transactions " of some learned society. It is alleged that the mariners' boat was too much battered by the waves to be of any more practical service out at sea, and as the Scots got a hearty welcome from the natives they concluded there was no use of struggling with wind and weather any longer and they settled down, were adopted by the aborigines, and married among them. The Captain, as was natural, married a princess. Most all Europeans of whom we have record who married into Indian families got princesses for their brides, and from that we infer that princesses were more plentiful than were young women of ordinary degree. Had the Captain only written home an account of the adventures of himself and his crew, what priceless documents the epistles would have been to-day! His name would have been revered as the discoverer of America, while we would have been erecting statues in his honor and celebrating his anniversary! But he missed his opportunity, and, as Scotsmen, Scotsmen abroad especially, very seldom do that, we are rather inclined to doubt the whole story.

Mr. J. M. Le Moine, in his interesting paper on "The Scot in New France," suggests that among Cartier's crew, when that discoverer made his first acquaintance with Canada, were several Scots seamen. "Herué, Henry," he says, "seems to us an easy transmutation of Henry Herué, or Hervey." Again, in reference to another, he remarks that "Michel Herué sounds mightily in our ears like Michael Harvey, one of the Murray Bay Harveys of Major Nairn." With reference to the facility with which names may be changed or adapted to circumstances, Mr. Le Moine gives an illustration which came under his own observation. "We once knew, at Cap Rouge, near Quebec, a worthy Greenock pilot whose name was Tom Everell. In the next generation a singular change took place in his patronymic; it stood transformed thus: Everell Tom. Everell Tom in the course of time became the respected sire of a numerous progeny of sons and daughters—Jean Baptiste Tom, Norbert Tom, Henriette Tom, and a variety of other Toms."

In the same interesting monograph, Mr. Le Moine brings to our notice a veritable Scotch pioneer in the following words: "Who has not heard of the King's St. Lawrence pilot, Abraham Martin dit l'Ecossais— Abraham Martin alias the Scot. Can there be any room for uncertainty about the nationality of this old salt— styled in the Jesuits' 'Journal' 'Maitre Abraham,' and who has bequeathed his name to our world-renowned battlefield (the Plains of Abraham). * * * The exhaustless research of our antiquarians has unearthed curious particulars about this Scotch seafaring man—the number, sex, and age of his children; his speculations in real estate; his fishing ventures in the Lower St. Lawrence. Sometimes we light on tid-bits of historical lore anent Master Abraham not very creditable to his morality. Once he gets into chancery; as there is no account of his being brought to trial, let us hope the charge was unfounded—a case of blackmail originated by some 'loose and disorderly' character of that period or by a spiteful policeman. On September 8, 1664, the King's pilot closed his career at the ripe age of seventy-five."

There is, however, something mythical and unsatisfactory in all we know of this industrious and enterprising personage, and we turn with satisfaction to consider a greater man in every respect, although by a curious freak of fortune his name has not been immortalized by any world-renowned landmark like the Plains of Abraham. This was the Earl of Stirling, in many ways one of the most extraordinary men of his time, a man who was restless in his activity, who won fame in many walks of life, who was one of the most extensive landowners of which the world has any knowledge, yet who died poor—a bankrupt. William Alexander was born at Menstrie, Stirlingshire, in 1580. Through the influence of the Argyll family he obtained a position at Court, and became tutor to Prince Henry, eldest son of James VI. He soon won the good graces of the sovereign by his learning, his shrewdness, and his poetical abilities, and when the crowns of Scotland and England were united Alexander followed the King to London. That Alexander enjoyed much popular favor and high reputation during his lifetime as a poet is undoubted, although few except students of literature venture to read his productions now. They are heavy, discursive, and, with the exception of a few of his sonnets and his "Paraenesis to Prince Henry," rather monotonous. But the evidence that he was a slave to the mannerisms and affectations of the age cannot blind us to the fact that he was really possessed of a rich share of poetic ability. With his poetical writings or his merits as a poet, however, we have nothing to do in this place, nor do we need to discuss the question as to whether or not he wrote King James's "Psalms," or even the nature of his statesmanship as exemplified in his official relations with his native country. We have to deal with him simply as a colonizer.

one of the first to colonize America. His career at Court may be summed up by mentioning that he was knighted in 1609, created Lord Alexander of Tullibody and Viscount Stirling in 1630, Earl of Stirling and Viscount Canada in 1633 and Earl of Dovan in 1639. A year later he died.

Lord Stirling found that the English were striving to establish colonies on the American seaboard, and thought, like the patriot which he undoubtedly was, that his own countrymen should have a share in the rich lands across the sea. Early in 1621 he sent a petition to King James for a grant of territory in America on which he hoped to induce Scotsmen to settle. "A great number of Scotch families," he told his sovereign, "had lately emigrated to Poland, Sweden, and Russia," and he pointed out that "it would be equally beneficial to the interests of the kingdom, and to the individuals themselves, if they were permitted to settle this valuable and fertile portion of His Majesty's dominions."

The petition was granted by the King—probably that was satisfactorily arranged before it had been committed to paper—and indorsed by the Privy Council. When these formalities had been gone through, Lord Stirling entered on formal possession of what is now mainly included in Nova Scotia, New Brunswick, Prince Edward Island, a goodly portion of the State of Maine and of the Province of Quebec. This territory was to be known as New Scotland—Nova Scotia the charter dignifiedly called it—and over it the new owner and those acting for him were supreme even to the establishment of churches and of courts of law. For some reason, not now exactly known, Lord Stirling at once handed over a part of his new dominion to Sir Robert Gordon of Lochinvar. That part is known as Cape Breton, but it was then given the more national name of New Galloway.

Sir William Alexander, to give Lord Stirling the name by which he is probably best remembered, sent out his first expedition to colonize New Scotland in March, 1622. These pioneers, with the exception of an adventurous clergyman, were of the humblest class of agricultural laborers, and only a single artisan—a blacksmith—was among them. The voyage was a rough one, and after sighting the coast of Cape Breton the emigrants were glad to shape their course back to Newfoundland, where they spent the Winter. Next Spring Sir William, who had been advised of the failure of the first expediton, sent out another ship with colonists and provisions. The early reports of the land on which the new colony was to settle were communicated to him by some of his people soon after they managed to get landed—which they did in the guise of an exploring party. These reports were submitted by him to the world, with all the attractiveness of a modern advertising expert, in his work entitled "An Encouragement to Colonies." The explorers described the country they visited (mainly the coast of Cape Breton) as presenting "very delecate meadowes, having roses white and red growing thereon, with a kind of wild Lilly, which hath a daintie smell." The ground " was without wood, and very good, fat earth, having several sort of berries growing thereon, as gooseberries, strawberries, hindberries, raspberries, and a kind of wine berrie; as also some sorts of grain as pease, some eares of wheat, barly, and rie growing there wilde. * * * They likewise found in every river abundance of lobsters, cockles, and all other shel-fishes, and also, not only in the rivers, but all the coasts alongst, numbers of several sorts of wilde-fowle, as wild-goose, black Ducke, woodcock, crane, heron, pidgeon, and many other sorts of Foule which they knew not. They did kill as they sayled alongst the coast, great store of cod, with severall other sorts of great fishes. The countrie is full of woods, not very thick, and the most part Oake; the rest Firre, Spruce, Birch and some Sicamores and Ashes and many other sorts of Wood which they had not sene before." All this information so cunningly and attractively set forth by Sir William in his book of encouragement—which, by the way, had a map of the territory in which Scottish names are given to every point and section and river—failed to attract settlers, and the projector found himself some £6,000 out of pocket by his patriotism. To reimburse him, and at the same time to add a little to the royal treasury, the Order of Baronets of Nova Scotia was founded, on the pattern of the Order of Ulster. Even this move was not substantially successful, although the terms were reasonable and the lands accompanying the honor were "three myles long vpon the coast and ten mile vp into the countrie."

We need not follow the details of Sir William's colonizing scheme any further. They belong really to the history of Canada. Each failure seemed to be compensated for by a fresh grant of territory, and if we may believe a map issued long after by one of the many claimants for his hereditary titles and "land rights" the Alexander family held "by right of charters," the sort of documents which the Duke of Argyll believes to be the most sacred on earth, not only about the whole of Canada, but the States of Maine, New Hampshire, Vermont, New York, Massachusetts, Rhode Island, Connecticut, Pennsylvania, Ohio, Maryland, and an undefined territory two or three times as large as all that has been named put together.

Sir William never saw his possessions on this side of the Atlantic, but his eldest son, known as Lord Alexander, did, and "efter his returne from his sea voyage, gave to the puir of Stirling fifty-aught pundes money"—the first of a long series of gifts to Scotland from Scots who have enjoyed a blink of fortune's sun on the western side of the Atlantic.

Among the first actual settlers from Scotland of whom we have record in what is now the United States, were the passengers on the ship "John and Sara," which arrived in Boston Harbor in 1652. That there were Scotsmen settled and doing business—perhaps making sillar and meditating speeches about St. Andrew—before that time there is no doubt. Of the fact, indeed, there is plenty of evidence, but these arrivals came in a body and under such sad circumstances that the early Scottish-American history of the time, especially in New England, crystallizes about them. They were prisoners of war, captured by Cromwell's forces after the battle of Dunbar, and sentenced to be transported to the American plantations and sold as slaves. This was done. Some appear to have been traded off in New England for a term of years; others were sent to the West Indies. The entire "cargo" was soon disposed of in one way or another, and for various terms of servitude, and there were other consignments of unfortunates about the same period and for many years after sent to the New World. The John and Sara prisoners, however, stand out in bold and creditable relief from the rest, as it was due to their plight that the Scots' Charitable Society of Boston was established in 1657. The same class of prisoners, staunch, stern Presbyterians, were the founders of colonies on the Elizabeth River, Virginia, and in Maryland, and it was invariably the case that one of the first structures in each settlement was a church, although the tabernacle was only built of logs.

The Scottish population received many of its earlier recruits from soldiers belonging to the Highland regiments who completed their terms of service while in this country or were disbanded after the close of the war for possession with the French. Large colonies of these settled in the Carolinas and Virginia, and through them many immigrants were induced to join them from the home country. Canada enjoyed its full share of these settlers, and after the Revolution it had a monopoly of them, while they in turn monopolized a good deal themselves. Indeed, it is said that up to the year 1810 there was not a merchant in the French City of Quebec who did not hail from the "Land o' Cakes."

"After the termination of the Seven Years' War," writes Bancroft in his great History of the United States, "very few of the Highland regiments returned home, soldiers and officers choosing rather to accept grants of land in America for settlement. Many, also, of the inhabitants of Northwestern Scotland, especially of the clans of Macdonald and Macleod, listened to overtures from those who had obtained concessions of vast domains and migrated to Middle Carolina, tearing themselves, with bitterest grief, from kindred whose sorrow at parting knew no consolation. Most who went first reported favorably of the clear, sunny clime where every man might have land of his own; and from the isles of Raasay and Skye whole neighborhoods formed parties for removal, sweetening their exile by carrying with them their costume and opinions, their Celtic language and songs." Marlborough, Bladensburg, Maryland, the Cape Fear, Wilmington, North Carolina, York and Rappahannock Rivers, Virginia, Delaware, Albemarle Sound were among the places at which, or near to which, Scotch colonies settled whose history is really an interesting part of that of the early Commonwealths.

In the State of New York there were many such colonies and one in particular deserves notice for the publicity it received at the time, and the scandal it created among the local politicians. In 1738 Captain Laughlin Campbell, an Argyllshire man, sold off his Scotch estate and expended the proceeds in conveying across the Atlantic eighty-three families from his own countryside. He had obtained a grant of 47,450 acres in what is now Washington County, on the borders of Lake George, and proposed to settle down there as a feudal baron, with his retainers around him. Many of the emigrants were indebted to him for the entire cost of their passage; all were his debtors to a greater or less extent, and the people, numbering some 500, were to recoup him by their labor after settling in America. His means were practically exhausted after bringing that host across the sea, and his indignation and sorrow may be imagined when, after landing, some of them refused to settle on his lands. They would pay what they owed him as soon as they earned any surplus, but they intended to earn that surplus in their own way and asserted that they had no idea, when they left Scotland, of simply exchanging a system of vassalage from Scotch landlords to one in America. It was a terrible, an unexpected muddle. The Colonial Assembly interfered. The Governor, George Clarke, asked that some provision be made for those who were penniless, which seems to have been the whole lot, and a motion was made to donate £7 to each family to start them in their new career. The contracts Campbell had made with the Colonial authorities and with his people were perfectly legal, and after considerable bickering and argument all around, his party or most of them reached Washington County and settled down on the tract which had been awarded to their leader. There they experienced the hardships which are the usual accompaniments of pioneer life. But the majority appear to have overcome these hardships and to have succeeded fairly well in bettering their condition. "By this immigration," writes Mr. Ellis H. Roberts in his "History of New York," "the province secured a much-needed addition to its population, and these Highlanders must have sent messages home not altogether unfavorable, for they were the pioneers of a multitude whose coming in successive years was to add strength and thrift and intelligence beyond the ratio of their numbers to the communities in which they set up their homes." However the others may have fared, Captain Campbell was ruined by the scheme, and we cannot say that we feel even a sentiment of regret over his misfortune, for his policy was dictated by selfishness from first to last. The tract on which these Highlanders settled was named by them Argyle, and when it was incorporated in 1764 with Duncan Reid, Neil Shaw, Alexander McNachten, and Neil Gillespie as trustees, they had begun to have high notions as to its future. They drew up a plan on paper—thus showing that they had become thoroughly Americanized—of the town, and its principal avenue was there seen to be a broad thoroughfare called The Street and extending in a fairly straight line for seven miles. They divided their property into city lots and farm lots, and, apparently, hoped to get rich quickly; but their hopes did not materialize, and Argyle, North

Argyle, and South Argyle, populated by Livingstones, Campbells, Gillies, McRaes, and others of such patronymics still retain to this day much of their original and delightful rural simplicity.

Quite a Scotch colony settled at one time, too, in what is now Putnam County, N. Y. The town of Patterson was mostly settled by Scotch and New England Presbyterians before 1750. The town got its name from Matthew Patterson, a Scotch mason who settled in New York several years before the Revolution. As a Captain of volunteers he served under General Abercrombie in the northern campaign against the French troops. At the Revolution he took the side of the Colonial Whigs, and was much respected for his honesty and superior intelligence. He was nine times elected a member of the New York Legislature, and was nine years a County Judge. He purchased 160 acres of land, which had belonged to the Beverley Robinson forfeited estate, and on this he erected a mansion which was long the most prominent in Patterson.

The names of the Scottish families which settled in the place were McLean, Grant, Fraser, and Fleming; and there was a Capt. Kidd—no relation, however, of the pirate of the same name we have already spoken about. Several fugitives from the massacre of Wyoming, made classic by the genius of Campbell, found refuge and homes in Dutchess County; and among the number was a Scotch family of the name of Stark.

We would like to refer to other colonies, notably that of Glengarry in Ontario, but that, and such settlements as those at Pictou, Antigonish, and others all over the Lower Provinces would require a volume to themselves. As this work is indicative rather than exhaustive we have said enough for the present to show the existence of such colonies, while several others will be mentioned in connection with various matters during the course of our present study. We will therefore devote the remainder of this chapter mainly to recalling the experiences and adventures of a few individuals who may be regarded as representative of the grand army of pioneers.

In the last decade of the eighteenth century no man was better known throughout Western New York for his success and energy as a promoter and pioneer than Charles Williamson. He was born at Edinburgh in 1757 and was the scion of a respectable Dumfries-shire family. In early life he held a commission in the British Army, and it was in the course of his military duty that he first crossed the ocean to visit America. He landed at Boston, however, as a prisoner of war, the vessel on which he was a passenger having been captured by a French privateer. While on parole in Boston he fell in love with the young daughter of the family with whom he boarded —or she fell in love with him—and when he obtained his release the two were married under what some people might think romantic circumstances. The pair left the country in 1781, and for several years resided at Balgray, Scotland. In 1790 he returned to this country as the principal agent of what was known as the Pulteney estate, from the name of Sir William Pulteney, the leading spirit of a British syndicate which had purchased a tract of 1,200,000 acres of land in Western New-York for colonization purposes from Robert Morris, the representative of the United States Government. This property included mainly what is now Steuben County, and, although Sir William Pulteney was nominally the head of the syndicate and another Englishman, John Hornby, was a leading shareholder, its moving spirit was Patrick Colquhoun. This notable Scot was born in Dumbarton in 1745 and was a cadet of the family of Luss. When a youth he was sent to Virginia, and there he engaged in business and was very successful during the few years of his sojourn. In 1766 he left the country and settled in Glasgow, where he soon became one of the most noted local figures. He was three times elected its Lord Provost, organized the city's Chamber of Commerce and obtained a royal charter for it, and was generally regarded as the most influential of its citizens. In 1789 he removed to London, became one of the Police Magistrates of the British metropolis, and distinguished himself by his untiring energy in that capacity, by his plans for the protection of the property in the city and on the Thames, as well as by his writings on police, indigence, and other practical social questions. He died in 1820, and like so many other kindly Scots at all times, bequeathed a part of his accumulated savings to help the poor of his native parish, that of Dumbarton. Colquhoun retained during his long career a deep interest in America and was one of the most enthusiastic believers in its future greatness and importance. His residence in Virginia and the share he took in developing the Pulteney syndicate are sufficient to account for and illustrate this, but there were probably other ways now forgotten in which his actions commended him to the good will of many in America. How otherwise can we account for the presence of a marble memorial tablet, bearing a long, biographical and highly flattering inscription, in one of the churches at Canandaigua? It was erected there soon after Colquhoun's death, in 1820, and was removed, for some unknown reason, and by ignoble hands, about 1880.

It was undoubtedly through Colquhoun that Williamson received the appointment to take charge of the lands of the Pulteney syndicate. He arrived at Norfolk, Va., in 1791 and spent the Winter of that year mainly in Pennsylvania. But while resting he was conceiving schemes for the future management of the property intrusted to him, and on a flying visit which he paid to the land in midwinter he located the site of a future town which was to bear his name—and still bears it, although its intended greatness has not yet materialized. He also became a citizen and received a deed of the lands of the syndicate, as the law did not permit aliens to own real estate in New York. Next Spring, 1792, he entered on his duties in earnest and soon had "things hummin'," as the Yankees say. The property was quickly surveyed and improvements begun. He opened roads, built bridges, laid out farms, erected schoolhouses and hotels, and, more important than all, had the tract widely talked about and induced intending settlers to visit the territory and buy or lease its lands. His greatest energy was devoted, however, to the town of Bath, named after Lady Bath, the only daughter of Sir William Pulteney, which he founded in 1793. It was to be a metropolitan city, and he hustled to make it great. It had a newspaper, a theatre, a racecourse, and, for a time, was the centre of a great amount of business, of real estate speculation, and of schemes of all sorts. Naturally all that attracted crowds to the place, and its population increased; but the throng was mainly composed of speculators, gamblers, and adventurers of various sorts—hardly the sort of people to give a settlement any permanence. But while the boom lasted, Bath enjoyed the luxury of indulging in hopes of a glorious future, and every month seemed to add to Capt. Williamson's importance, while the members of the syndicate in London, when they looked at the neat maps of the estate and the extensive plan of the City of Bath, had visions of unexampled wealth lying in their coffers. Williamson was elected to the State Legislature, was appointed a Judge, had Steuben County created, and was its representative in the Assembly, and became Colonel of the local militia. He had a large establishment, kept open house, and entertained lavishly. Among his other guests were the Duke de la Rochefoucault and his suite, and that nobleman afterward wrote an interesting account of his sojourn in the collection of small houses which formed the Williamson home, and which had been built from time to time, just as increased accommodation was required. Afterward Williamson erected for himself a stately mansion, which was long the most imposing private residence in the county. Williamson's schemes and plans would certainly have had wonderful results had he been allowed to carry them on in his own way. But his doings were on an extravagant and costly scale, and as no dividends were being remitted to London, the syndicate became restive. All retired, selling their interests to Pulteney, and that capitalist in

1800 revoked Williamson's appointment. The latter remained in Steuben for a few years, attending to his own affairs and seeing the work he had inaugurated and so hopefully developed gradually falling into a state of decay. Domestic troubles helped to make his position additionally embarrassing and his prospects more gloomy, and in 1806 he went back to Scotland. Two years later he got an appointment from the British Government in connection with the Island of Jamaica, and while on the journey there died of yellow fever at New Orleans, in September, 1808.

Bath soon fell into decay and never regained its prominence, nor did much success attend the town of Williamson, or that of Cameron, which latter was founded not far away and about the same time by Dugald Cameron, who accompanied Williamson from Scotland to help him in the work of the agency. But if the Scotch people did not found towns very successfully, they gave to the county a race of settlers who, to the present day, are proud of their ancestry and have developed the agricultural resources of Steuben to their fullest extent.

It must not be inferred from the failure of Williamson's schemes that either his judgment or methods were at fault. The trouble lay simply in the impatience of the people at headquarters, who expected an immediate profit upon their capital. Nor are Scotsmen to be regarded as failures in respect to town founding in America. Half of the towns in Canada, the centres which are the marts of the country, were founded by Scotsmen, and, indeed, to the present day are controlled by people whose boast is that they are either native-born Scotch or of Scotch descent. The City of Chicago was really founded by John Kinzie, an Indian trader and agent, the son of a Scotsman, John McKenzie, although the name got twisted round a little to suit the people who could not catch hold of the grand old Scotch name, just as a well-known New York clergyman whose name was Menzies when he landed, and pronounced it like a true Scot "Meengies," found himself so often addressed as Mingins that he was forced to adopt that very peculiar modification of an old Celtic name. Kinzie was born at Quebec in 1763, and died in the city he had founded in 1828, probably without much idea of its ultimate greatness. Another example of a prosperous American town founded by a Scot is Paterson, N. J., which owed its origin to the public spirit of Alexander Hamilton, Washington's Secretary of the Treasury, and until the present day its Scottish residents have been regarded as among its most representative citizens.

An instance of a pioneer in humble life, although a pioneer very much against his will, is that of Peter Williamson, a sort of universal genius, who acquired more than local fame by being the first to introduce the penny post into Edinburgh and more than fleeting reputation by having his portrait done by Kay, the Edinburgh engraver and miniature painter, and included in the published collection of that noted caricaturist's works. From that wonderful storehouse of quaint information we learn that Williamson, who was a native of the Parish of Aboyne, was kidnapped in Aberdeen when only eight years of age. The ship a month later started on a voyage to America, when Williamson and some other young unfortunates were permitted to go on deck and assigned to various duties. The ship was wrecked off Cape May, but no lives were lost, and the crew camped in the woods for three weeks, when the kidnapped lads were taken to Philadelphia and sold for £16 a head. Williamson's master appears to have been a rather kindhearted sort of fellow, and he made his bondsman as comfortable as possible. He died, however, when Williamson was seventeen years of age, leaving him £120 in cash, a horse, and other valuables. For seven years more Williamson worked wherever he could find employment, being his own master, and managed to save a little money. Then he determined to settle down for life, and, marrying the daughter of a planter, received with her a gift of a farm of some 200 acres on the Pennsylvania frontier. His troubles then began.

It was not long after he had gotten fairly settled down that one evening, his wife being absent, making a call, he heard the terrible Indian war whoop, and soon his house was surrounded and he was forced to surrender to the savages. After they had destroyed his buildings and stock they carried him off with them on their march of destruction. They committed many fiendish cruelties as they proceeded, burning and destroying all they could not take away, murdering without scruple, and carrying into captivity a few unfortunates who took their fancy, principally as fit subjects for torture. Williamson's treatment was something terrible even to read about, and he appears to have been the most gently handled of the lot. They tied him so tightly to trees that the blood oozed from his finger nails; they applied burning faggots to various parts of his body, threw tomahawks at him, beat him unmercifully, forced him to carry the heaviest possible loads, starved him, and, to put it mildly, made him emphatically decide that life really was not worth living. After several months of this sort of pioneering, Williamson managed to make his escape, and at the close of a series of startling adventures reached his father-in-law's house, only to find that his wife had died shortly after his capture. For three years Williamson served with the military forces of the Commonwealth of Pennsylvania, repaying the Indians with interest for what he had suffered, and rose to the rank of Lieutenant in the army by his bravery and success as an Indian fighter. This pleasant occupation was stopped at length by his capture by the French. On being released he was taken to Plymouth, England, and, being there found unfit for further service, was graciously discharged from His Majesty's service with six shillings in his pocket. His after career in his native land was full of startling incidents, but they do not concern us here. He died at Edinburgh, in poor circumstances, in 1799.

Some people might deny that Williamson was exactly a pioneer, as he did not betake himself to open up new fields, or of his own volition went into sections of the country which, prior to his time, had not been under the observation or the sway of white men. But he was there, nevertheless, and his experiences and observations were of value in the struggle for possession then going on. If we turn, however, to the careers of such men as Donald Mackenzie or Robert Stuart, we will meet with pioneers whose claim to the title not even the most fastidious in the choice of words and terms will affect to deny. A great deal of the adventures of these two men and of several other Scotch pioneers, is to be found in Washington Irving's delightful work, "Astoria," which possibly presents a more graphic and truthful description of old American frontier life than any other volume. Donald Mackenzie was born in Scotland in 1783, spent his early manhood in the service of the Northwest Company, and became one of the partners in Astor's American Fur Company, mainly because promotion in the other concern was slow, and under new conditions and auspices he saw a chance of bettering his prospects. Like most of the other Scots who joined Mr. Astor as partners in the new company, he apprehended that he might be called upon to take part in opposition to his own countrymen, but the fact that the British Minister to the United States, to whom the whole matter had been privately submitted by two of the Scotch partners, saw no reason why men owning allegiance to the British flag should not take part in an American expedition to trade in a territory which was at that time no-man's land, quieted his scruples, as it did that of the others. Irving tells us that prior to joining the Astor Company, Mackenzie " had been ten years in the interior in the service of the Northwest Company and valued himself on his knowledge of 'woodcraft' and the strategy of Indian trade and Indian warfare. He had a frame seasoned to toils and hardships, a spirit not to be intimidated, and was reputed to be a remarkable shot, which of itself was sufficient to give him renown on the frontier." His adventures are fully related in the pages of "Astoria," and, indeed, if the doings of Stuart, Mackenzie, Mackay, and other Scots were taken out of that book, its subject matter would occupy only a few pages. Mackenzie seems to have been intended by nature for a pioneer. His soul revelled in the trackless woods; he knew no sense of fatigue or fear, was perfectly happy with each day's work, had no care for the future, took a delight in getting the best of the Indians in any transaction, warlike or peaceful; was always ready for any expedition, no matter how hopeless it seemed, and had that degree of chivalrous daring which was most likely to inspire admiration in the hearts of friends and foes alike. An instance is given so graphically in Irving's narrative that we cannot forbear quoting it here, although that volume is happily still widely read. A rifle belonging to one of Mackenzie's associates was held as a trophy in an Indian village after its owner had fallen into the hands of the redskins. Being near that same village with a small party, Mackenzie determined to make an attempt to recover the rifle, and along with two of his men, who volunteered to accompany him, started on his dangerous mission. "The trio," wrote Irving, "soon reached the opposite side of the river. On landing, they freshly primed their rifles and pistols. A path, winding for about a hundred yards among rocks and crags, led to the village. No notice seemed to be taken of their approach. Not a solitary being—man, woman, or child—greeted them. The very dogs, those noisy pests of an Indian town, kept silence. On entering the village, a boy made his appearance and pointed to a house of larger dimensions than the rest. They had to stoop to enter it. As soon as they had passed the threshold, the narrow passage behind them was filled up by a sudden rush of Indians, who had before kept out of sight. Mackenzie and his companions found themselves in a rude chamber of about twenty-five feet in length and twenty in width. A bright fire was blazing at one end, near which sat the chief, about sixty years old. A large number of Indians, wrapped in buffalo robes, were squatted in rows, three deep, forming a semi-circle round three sides of the

room. A single glance sufficed to show them the grim
and dangerous assembly into which they had intruded,
and that all retreat was cut off by the mass which blocked
up the entrance. The chief pointed to the vacant side of
the room, opposite the door, and motioned for them to
take their seats. They complied. A dead pause ensued.
The grim warriors around sat like statues, each muffled
in his robe, with his fierce eyes bent on the intruders.
The latter felt they were in a perilous predicament.
'Keep your eyes on the chief while I am addressing
him,' said Mackenzie to his companions. 'Should he
give any sign to his band, shoot him and make for the
door.' Mackenzie advanced and offered the pipe of peace
to the chief, but it was refused. He then made a regular
speech, explaining the object of their visit and proposing
to give in exchange for the rifle two blankets, an axe,
some beads, and tobacco. When he had done the chief
arose, began to address him in a low tone, but soon became
loud and violent, and ended by working himself
up into a furious passion. He upbraided the white men
for their sordid conduct in passing and repassing
through their neighborhood without giving them a blanket
or any other article of goods merely because they
had no furs to barter in exchange, and he alluded with
menaces of vengeance to the death of the Indian killed
by the whites in the skirmish at the falls. Matters were
now verging to a crisis. It was evident the surrounding
savages were only waiting a signal from the chief to rush
on their prey. Mackenzie and his companions had gradually
risen to their feet during the speech, and had
brought their rifles to a horizontal position, the barrels
resting in their left hands; the muzzle of Mackenzie's
piece was within three feet of the speaker's heart. They
cocked their rifles; the click of the locks for a moment
suffused the dark cheek of the savage, and there was a
pause. They coolly but promptly advanced to the door;
the Indians fell back in awe and suffered them to pass.
The sun was just setting as they emerged from the
dangerous den. They took the precaution to keep along

the tops of the rocks as much as possible on their way back to the canoe and reached the camp in safety, congratulating themselves on their escape and feeling no desire to make a second visit to the grim warriors of Wish-ram."

After a life of such adventure it is wonderful to record that Mackenzie spent a short season of repose before he died at Maysville, N. Y., in 1851.

Stuart was a man much superior, intellectually, to Mackenzie, although he had all his qualities of hardihood, daring, and an equal experience of frontier life. He was born at Callander in 1785, a scion of one of the recognized septs of the Stuarts, and the grandson of Alexander Stuart, Rob Roy's most bitter enemy. He crossed the Atlantic in 1806. Irving describes him as "an easy soul and of a social disposition. He had seen life in Canada and on the coast of Labrador; had been a fur trader in the former and a fisherman on the latter, and in the course of his experiences had made various expeditions with voyageurs. He was accustomed, therefore, to the familiarity which prevails between that class and their superiors, and the gossipings which take place among them when seated round a fire at their encampments. Stuart was never so happy as when he could seat himself on the deck with a number of these men around him in camping style, smoke together, passing the pipe from mouth to mouth, after the manner of the Indians; sing old Canadian boat songs, and tell stories about their hardships and adventures, in the course of which he rivalled Sinbad in his long tales of the sea, about his fishing exploits off Labrador." This personage occupies a very prominent position throughout the volume on Astoria, and, indeed, he was one of Mr. Astor's most trusted partners in that expedition. Particular care is devoted to relate his memorable journey across the continent—he was the third to attempt such a task—which lasted from June, 1812, until the middle of the following year. For the details of this journey the inquirer cannot do better than study the pages of Irving's book, and there he will find much additional information about Scottish and other pioneers connected with early Oregon.

In 1819, Stuart left Oregon and settled at Mackinaw, Mich., where he continued to act as a fur trader and was appointed by the Federal Government Commissioner for the Indian tribes of the Northwest. In 1834 he settled in Detroit, and among other important offices, served as Treasurer of Michigan. His honesty was of the most scrupulous order, and when he died, at Chicago, in 1848, his loss was regretted by the Indian tribes over whom he had exercised authority, for they recognized in him a true friend, one whose word was his bond, and a man who was ever ready to further their welfare. Such a man deserves to be held in kindly remembrance. He was faithful to every trust imposed upon him. Whatever duty was intrusted to him was well done. His whole life had all the elements of romance, but its entire series of events were always controlled by some useful, practical purpose and of direct benefit to the country of which he became a citizen. His devotion to the land of his adoption was reproduced in the career of his son, David, who was born at Brooklyn in 1816. Educated as a lawyer, he became very popular in public life and served in Congress, as one of the Representatives of Michigan, from December, 1853, to March, 1855. Then he removed to Chicago to become attorney for the Illinois Central Railroad. In 1861, when the war broke out, he went to the front as Colonel of the Fifty-fifth Illinois Infantry, and commanded a brigade under Sherman. After being wounded at Shiloh, he was laid aside from military service for a while, but soon returned to active duty, and, being appointed a Brigadier General of Volunteers, performed brilliant service at Corinth and other places. At that time, however, political feeling ran high, and, being a Democrat, Congress failed to confirm his appointment, so he retired from the army and resumed the practice of law at Detroit. He died there in 1868.

The Scotch pioneers may be divided into three classes

—those whose efforts were directed to wholesale colonizing, those who braved the dangers and discomforts of the new land as individual settlers, and those who were simply explorers. In the first of these classes, a most noted figure is that of Thomas, fifth Earl of Selkirk—the brother of that Lord Daer whose only title to remembrance, or immortality, as some would say, lies in the fact that he invited Robert Burns to dinner, and that the latter wrote a poem about it. Lord Selkirk was born in 1771, and in 1799 succeeded to his ancestral title and estates. Like nearly all the rest of his family, he was possessed of much public spirit. He visited America in 1802-3, and was so struck by the benefits which were likely to accrue to his countrymen through organized immigration that throughout his career he never ceased to advocate all measures tending to promote the settlement in Canada of Scotch colonies. His appearance while traveling in America is thus described in a letter written by Mrs. Thomas Morris: "I recollect a short visit from Prince Ruspoli, Grand Master of the Knights of Malta, and in a few days from Lord Selkirk on his journey to visit a settlement he was forming in Canada—far to the north. He struck me as a reserved, diffident young man, almost austere in his dress, with heavy, dusty shoes tied with leather thongs; but then, to support his aristocratic pretenses, he had a dandy servant, who laid out his toilet like a lady's." His first experience as a colonizer, in Prince Edward Island, was very encouraging. In the history of that island by the late Duncan Campbell, we read: "The Earl of Selkirk brought out to his property about 800 souls. They were located on land north and south of Point Prim, which had been previously occupied by French settlers, but a large portion of which was now again covered with wood and thus rendered difficult of cultivation. Many of His Lordship's tenants became successful settlers." He also settled a colony in Kent, Ontario, which proved very prosperous.

But the settlement by which Lord Selkirk is best remembered in the annals of Canada is that of the Red

River colony, in what is now the Province of Manitoba. While residing in Montreal he heard many stories of the wonderful fertility of the Northwest, and saw in that section an unlimited field for settlement. He bought largely of the stock of the Hudson Bay Company, and through the influence he thus acquired, he was enabled to induce that corporation to sell him a vast tract of land in the Red River Valley in 1811. The lands were fertile and eminently suited for an agricultural community. Nature had done everything possible to aid man to reap a rich harvest from the soil, and even the severity of the Winters had their advantages. The settlers, mainly from Kildonan, Sutherlandshire, arrived in the Fall of 1812, and were given holdings around Fort Garry—the site of which is now included in the thriving City of Winnipeg. It was a wild time. The rivalries of the different fur-trading companies often culminated in a fight in the settlement, and the Indians harassed the colonists' lives and destroyed their crops. The first Winter's experience disheartened many, and a memorable march was made by the faint-hearted ones back to civilization. Those who remained encountered many misfortunes and disasters, and we read that in a battle in June, 1819—the battle of Seven Oaks—twenty of the colonists lost their lives. Then they had to abandon their holdings and were reduced to terrible straits. The Earl returned to America in 1817 and, learning of the troubles in the Red River Valley, started there with a small but sufficient force to re-establish his authority. This was successful, life and property were rendered safe, and the last vestige of the Indian claims on the lands was removed by a solemn treaty with the chiefs of the Salteaux and Cree tribes. Lord Selkirk died at Paris in 1821, and in 1836 the Hudson Bay Company repurchased the lands from his heirs for £84,000. From 1817, however, Manitoba gradually advanced in population and importance, not by any "boom," but slowly and surely, and to-day it is one of the most progressive of the provinces in the Canadian federation. In its entire history Scotsmen crop out in every page and predominate in all the commercial, financial, manufacturing, mining, educational, legislative, and other interests over those of all other nationalities.

The Mackenzie River, one of the great waterways of Northwestern Canada—a navigable stream for over 800 miles from the Great Slave Lake to the Arctic Ocean—takes its name along with the name of the bay at its mouth from its discoverer, Sir Alexander Mackenzie. This indefatigable traveler was a native of Inverness, where he was born in 1755. He was a merchant in Canada, and after he became connected with the Northwest Fur Company, was able to indulge in his desire for exploration. He traveled through the entire Northwest, penetrating over the Rockies to the Pacific, and told the story of his adventures and discoveries, notably that of the Mackenzie River, in 1789, in a modest sort of way in a work he published in 1801. In the following year he was knighted. Another Canadian merchant who became an explorer was Duncan McTavish, a native of Strathherrick, Inverness-shire. For twenty-four years he traveled through the Northwest in furtherance of the interests of the Northwest Company. He managed to win the entire confidence of the Indians, among whom his business transactions chiefly lay. While engaged in this service he anticipated one of the purposes of the Canadian Pacific Railway by conceiving the idea that the natural course of trade between the Orient and Europe was through Canada, and it was while making explorations with a view to mapping out a route for this trade that he was drowned, with six companions, near Cape Disappointment, on the Northern Pacific Ocean, in 1815. The name of McTavish has been a prominent one in the history of the far Western Provinces of Canada. John George McTavish, one of the partners of the Northwest Company, was the conqueror at Astoria when that port had to be abandoned, and dictated the terms of surrender, although he did it on a liberal and honorable basis. Another of the same sept, William McTavish, who left Scotland in 1833 and entered the Hudson Bay Company as a clerk, became its chief factor in 1852. Afterward, as Governor of Assiniboia and of Rupert's Land, he did much good work by the introduction of law and order into those then wild territories. He died in Liverpool, while on a European trip in search of health, in 1872.

Among the thousands of Scotsmen whose labors and enterprise made the Hudson Bay Company as important as it was to the early discovery and development of Canada, and its dividends so satisfactory to the pockets of its stockholders, none held a higher place or did more good work than George Simpson. He was a native of Lochbroom, Ross-shire, and commenced his business career as a clerk in a merchant's office in London. He there attracted the attention of Lord Selkirk, and through that nobleman's interest got an appointment in the service of the Hudson Bay Company. Early in 1820 Simpson sailed for Canada, and almost as soon as he reached Montreal started off to his post of duty in the then unknown lands around Lake Athabasca. His first Winter there was one of great privation, but he liked the work and saw in it an opportunity for a prosperous future. At that time the rivalry between the Hudson Bay Company and the Northwest Company was at its height, but Simpson acted with such energy that when, in 1821, the rivals pooled their issues, he was appointed Governor of one of the departments. Indeed, it is asserted on good grounds that it was at his suggestion and through his diplomacy that the coalition of the rival companies was effected. Subsequently he was appointed Governor of Rupert's Land and General Superintendent of the Hudson Bay Company's affairs. It was while holding these responsible positions that he promoted those schemes of discovery by which his name is most generally recalled. Under his direction most of the Arctic coast was surveyed, and his liberality, his apparently intuitive estimate of the capabilities of the men he employed, or was associated with, or called to his assistance, and his good judgment in planning the various expeditions he fitted out were rewarded with knighthood in 1841. In that year he made a tour round the world, an account of which he afterward published in two handsome volumes. Sir George's closing years were spent at Lachine, near Montreal, and he took a leading part in financial affairs in that city. His hospitality was unbounded, and only a few days before his death, in 1860, he entertained the Prince of Wales in a manner befitting the heir to the British throne.

This representative Scot had a brother, Alexander Simpson, who was a trusted official of the Hudson Bay Company, was for a long time afterward British Consul at Hawaii, and enriched the literature of travel by the compilation of several volumes descriptive of places he had seen. The intellectual genius of the family, however, was Thomas Simpson, a cousin of the two already mentioned. He was born at Dingwall in 1808, and had a brilliant career at Aberdeen University, where he won, among other honors, the Huttonian Prize. On completing his studies, he went to Canada and entered the service of the Hudson Company. His immediate work seems to have been more scientific than commercial, however, and in 1836 he was placed in command of an expedition which succeeded in tracing the coast line from the mouth of the Mackenzie River to Point Barrow, and from the mouth of Coppermine River to the Gulf of Boothia. This expedition occupied over three years, and it was while returning from it, in 1840, that he was murdered by some Indians near Turtle River. He claimed in some of his memoranda and letters to have discovered a clear water passage between the Atlantic and the Pacific, and his claim was well founded, although the passage has been of no service to commerce. The dream of most of these Scotch explorers was to find a way for opening up a direct trade with India and China, either through Canada or by water. At that time railroads were still in the stages of early experiment, and a practical waterway would have settled the question, while a route across the continent would have been more difficult, and as tedious and costly as the long voyage around the Cape, which it was hoped to avoid. Nowadays the Suez Canal and the transcontinental railroad systems have brought the East very much nearer to the commercial centres of Europe and taken all the practical interest out of the once burning question of a Northwest passage.

Another name connected with the New Canada is that of Sir James Douglas, who passed away at Victoria, British Columbia, in 1877. He was born in Demerara, British Guiana, of Scotch parents. His father died when James was a lad, and he went with an elder brother to Canada. There he entered the service of the Northwest Company and was soon recognized as one of its most adventurous and indomitable agents. When that company consolidated with its great rival he was advanced to the dignity of chief factor. In that capacity he visited even the most distant and outlying posts of the company and became as well acquainted with the "primeval forests and everlasting hills" as the Indians themselves. His adventures were many and dangerous. Once, for instance, he was kept a close prisoner for six weeks by some Indians, and was so long prevented from reporting his whereabouts that he was supposed to have been killed by the red men, or to have died in the bush. In 1833 he became chief agent of the region west of the Rocky Mountains, and in 1851 was made Governor of the infant colony of Vancouver. In 1859, when Vancouver was made a Crown colony, he was appointed its Chief Executive by the Government, and made a Companion of the Bath. In 1863 he received the honor of knighthood, and a year later retired to private life to enjoy a few years of well-earned rest before answering to the last great call—the call that summons all men.

We have said that one of Sir George Simpson's qualifications as a successful administrator lay in his ability to judge of the capacity of the men over whom he had control. An instance of this is given in the career of one of his most trusted associates, that of Robert Campbell, who died at Winnipeg in 1890, at the ripe old age of eighty-six. Few adventurers attain such wealth of years, but it is noticeable of the Scotch pioneers in the Canadian Northwest that they were a long-lived race, in spite of the hardships and privations and dangers through which they passed. Campbell was born in Perthshire and worked on his father's farm until his twenty-second year, when he entered the Hudson Bay Company's service. One of his first duties was to take part in an expedition to Kentucky to purchase a lot of sheep and convey them into the company's territory. The journey from Kentucky to Canada with the animals was a long and tedious one, and most of them died on the way. It was the result of his experiences on this trip that induced Campbell, long afterward, to import to Manitoba West Highland cattle, a breed which is better adapted for standing the climate than any other. In 1834 he became attached to the agency at Fort Simpson, and showed his mettle by volunteering to establish a post on Dease's Lake, a position of great danger, as the Indians there were in the service of Russian traders and bitterly opposed to the incursions of the British adventurers. He held his position there in spite of jealousies and dangers, and made it fairly remunerative.

Enough has been said to show the pioneer services of the Scottish race, and we leave that branch of our subject here, although it might be extended almost indefinitely. Such names as those we have dwelt upon, and hundreds of others that might be mentioned, are really part and parcel of the history of the Northwestern provinces, and when that history comes to be fittingly written, the names of these Scotch pioneers, traders, and merchants will certainly, if the history be an honest one, receive due and deserved prominence. Nor is the race extinct even yet. The pioneers are no longer fur traders, but Government surveyors, and year after year the immense territory to the north of the settled strip along the great lakes is being made known to the world by a number of hardy scientists, and such names among them as

Gordon, Ogilvie, Ross, Robertson, and McLatchie are sufficiently indicative that Scotland is still to the front in bringing a knowledge of the resources of Canada to the civilized world. It was one of these pioneers, Andrew R. Gordon, a native of Aberdeen, who first demonstrated the advisability of a railroad connection between Winnipeg and Hudson's Bay, and when his plans are carried out, as they are certain sooner or later to be, Manitoba will be in direct, cheap, and comparatively easy communication with Europe for at least six months in each year, while Winnipeg will rival Glasgow as a commercial centre.

Nor is the spirit of colonizing yet dead. It is still helping to people Manitoba and other new Canadian provinces, and every now and again we hear of fresh colonies arriving from the old land and settling down on the far West in this country as well as in Canada, and even in some of the Southern States. Sometimes such colonies turn out disastrously, as did one or two that settled a few years ago in North Carolina, mainly because they were badly managed and because the ground selected was unfitted for cultivation. In short, the colonies failed because the colonists were the victims of land sharks, and had not taken the precaution of fully acquainting themselves with all the facts in the case. But such failures are exceptions, and these colonies are generally successful, even when they cast their lot in some of the older settled portions of the continent. In 1873 a colony was settled in Victoria County, New Brunswick, certainly not a part of Canada which is very extensively "boomed" for its fertility or its future. A recent visitor to the settlement writes: "The colony was organized by a Capt. Brown, belonging to Kincardineshire, who brought the people over in the Castilia, a steamer of which he was commander. A large proportion of these colonists were from the Mearns, some from Aberdeen, Montrose, Forfar, Kirriemuir, and Glasgow. One man, I found, was from Inverarity, and his wife from Dundee. This lady told me she had been born and brought up in

Dundee, but had never been down the length of the [Broughty] Ferry. Those who have been most successful and are the most contented are those who have been at farm service in the Old Country. Here, they say, they enjoy a degree of independence, comfort, and style of living which they never could have attained at home."

Thus, among the pioneers of the American Continent, in all classes, dignified and humble, we find the Scot holding a position which is everywhere honorable to his nationality and helpful to the continent itself. His efforts have ever been on the side of law and order, have ever been on conservative lines, and have been accomplished with a disregard of personal danger worthy of the representative of a nation whose struggle for civil and religious freedom has made personal heroism to be accepted by the world as one of the most noted characteristics of the race.

CHAPTER III.

COLONIAL GOVERNORS.

ONE of the most interesting figures in the military service of King William III. and of Queen Anne was Lord George Hamilton Douglas, son of Duchess Anne of Hamilton and her husband, William, Earl of Selkirk, who was created Duke of Hamilton at her request. Lord George was born in 1666 and was bred a soldier. In 1690 he was made a Colonel and two years later was in command of the Royal Scots Regiment. His skill and bravery in the field, in Ireland and Flanders, commended him to King William, who awarded him the rank of Brigadier General, and in 1696 conferred on him the old Scotch title of Earl of Orkney. To complete his happiness, the King gave the wife of the new peer a grant of most of the private estates in Ireland of King James II. Queen Anne was profuse in her favors to the Earl of Orkney, who served with distinction in her wars, under Marlborough, and helped very materially to win such victories as Blenheim, Ramillies, and Oudenarde. She commissioned him a Lieutenant General, made him a Privy Councillor, a Knight of the Thistle, and he was one of the peers of Scotland who were returned to Parliament after the Union. King George I. continued the series of royal favors which marked the career of this favorite of fortune. He appointed him a "Gentleman Extraordinary" of the Bedchamber, an honorary office which gave the Earl a position at Court; Governor of Edinburgh Castle, Lord Lieutenant of Lanarkshire, a Field Marshal, and he died at London in 1737, in possession of all his faculties and honors.

Another of the honorary offices held by this much favored individual was that of Governor of Virginia. The Earl of Orkney never saw America and knew nothing of Virginia except its name, and probably cared little about it except for the emoluments his office as its Governor brought him. Such titular honors were very numerous in the history of the royal families of Europe, and America since its discovery has furnished a goodly share of them. If Lord Orkney did Virginia no good, he certainly did it no harm, and that, at all events, is more than can be said of many of those who tried their hands at serious statesmanship by muddling and marring its affairs. His possession of the office gives him a sort of left-handed claim to recognition in a work like this, although he more properly belongs to the story of the Scot in Europe, in which, indeed, his achievements and honors make him a striking figure. Hardly as much can be said of a later Governor of Virginia, whose connection with the province was also merely titular, and who never saw it, although he served with the army in America. That was John Campbell, fourth Earl of Loudoun, whose rather inglorious military career in America, as commander in chief of the forces, lasted a little over a year, and was terminated by his sudden recall. He was appointed Governor in 1756, but his time in America was devoted entirely to his military duties. His transatlantic failure did not apparently affect his standing at home, and he continued the recipient of many honors until his death, in 1782.

William Drummond, who was Governor of "Albemarle County Colony," was as active and aggressive in American affairs as the two personages just named were not. Drummond, who was a native of Perthshire, justly ranks as one of the earliest of American patriots. He took a prominent part in Nathaniel Bacon's insurrection in 1676, an insurrection that was brought about by the insolence and pig-headedness of Sir William Berkeley, then Governor of Virginia, to which Albemarle County (North Carolina) was subject. Drummond, who is described by Bancroft as a " former Governor of North Carolina," did good work in that uprising in supporting the rights of the people, and, though he has been blamed for the part he took in the burning of Jamestown, it might be pleaded that that act was, in the opinion of himself and his comrades, a grim necessity of war. When the insurrection was crushed by circumstances which could not be foreseen, and Drummond was led a prisoner to the presence of Berkeley, that cowardly braggadocio said, exultingly: " You are very welcome. I am more glad to see you than any man in Virginia. You shall be hanged in half an hour." Glorifying in the part he had taken in the movement for individual liberty, Drummond met his fate like the brave man that he was, his only concern being about the future of his wife and children. So many lives were sacrificed in furtherance of the Governor's desire for revenge that even Charles II., who really valued no life but his own, exclaimed when the news was brought to him: " The old fool has taken away more lives in that naked country than I for the murder of my father!" Drummond's wife and little ones were thrust from their home and reduced to actual want, their necessities being relieved only by the charitable kindness of the neighboring planters.

The most notable of the Scottish Colonial rulers of Virginia in many ways was Alexander Spottiswood, who served as Lieutenant Governor from 1710 to 1722. He was a scion of a noted family—the Spottiswoods of Spottiswood in Berwickshire, the descent of which could be traced back to the time of Alexander III. One of his ancestors fell at Flodden, and another at the time of the Reformation adopted the new tenets, became one of the leaders of the Kirk, was Superintendent (a title that did not exactly mean Bishop, but rather something like foreman minister,) of Lothian, and was very prominent in national and church affairs until a few years before his death, in 1581. The Superintendent's son became Archbishop of St. Andrews. The Archbishop's second son,

Sir Robert Spottiswood, President of the Court of Sessions and Secretary of State for Scotland, was beheaded for his devotion to the cause of the royal family of Stuart. One of the sons of this unfortunate statesman left Scotland to seek his fortune, and became physician to the garrison at Tangiers. Governor Spottiswood was the only son of this wanderer. Spottiswood entered the army in early life, and served in Flanders under Marlborough, with the utmost credit. He was severely wounded at Blenheim. Among his friends in the army was the Earl of Orkney, with whose name we opened this chapter, and when that nobleman was appointed Governor of Virginia he secured the selection of Spottiswood as Lieutenant. He proved a wise ruler in his executive relations, and probably was the most popular of all the representatives of the crown who ever administered the affairs of the province. His first act, that of promulgating the habeas corpus law, was in itself an opening wedge to a term of popularity, and he availed himself of it to the utmost. He conciliated the red men and tried to improve their condition. He promoted education, and was enthusiastic over the fortunes of the recently established William and Mary College. He gave considerable thought to agricultural improvement, and was especially anxious and helpful in improving the cultivation of tobacco, at that time Virginia's great export and principal source of wealth. He also introduced the manufacture of iron into the province, and sought by the aid of exploring parties to give to the world a correct conception of its resources and extent. Under him Virginia enjoyed a period of great prosperity, and its importance in every way was greatly augmented. Had all the Colonial Governors been men of his stamp and brains there would have been no Revolution, for the need would never have arisen.

Perhaps the secret of Governor Spottiswood's success lay in the fact that he seems to have made up his mind to settle permanently in the country. He was not a carpet-bagger in the modern sense, or a gentleman adventurer, as that term was employed in the reign of good Queen Anne. He aimed to promote the best interests of the country, to preserve the peace within its bounds by conciliating all classes, by encouraging trade, and by protecting to the extent of his ability life, property, and personal liberty. He was a true patriot, and a true American citizen, and as his home was with the people he ruled, he had no temptation to grow rich at their expense, that he might go elsewhere and have no further interest in the colony beyond the agreeable fancies of pleasant reminiscences.

In many respects a Lieutenant Governor of a very different stamp was Robert Dinwiddie, who ruled over the destinies of Virginia from 1752 to 1758. He was born near Glasgow in 1690, his father being a merchant in that city, and his mother the daughter of one of its magistrates. Dinwiddie has often been spoken of as the discoverer of George Washington, as he was the first to call the "Father of His Country" into the public service, but if he ever entertained any regard for Washington it did not last very long. The time during which Dinwiddie stood at the helm in Virginia was one that required the exhibition of the most statesmanlike qualities, and these Dinwiddie does not seem to have possessed. His mind was not of the comprehensive order; he could not look beyond the exigencies of the hour; he was fretful and spiteful, and more fond of exhibiting the powers than the graces of his office. Washington Irving sums up his character in these stinging words, which seem to be a logical arraignment of his shortcomings if we may judge by the known facts in his career: "He set sail for England in 1758, very little regretted, excepting by his immediate hangers-on, and leaving a character overshadowed by the imputation of avarice and extortion in the exaction of illegal fees and of downright delinquency in regard to large sums transmitted to him by Government to be paid over to the province in indemnification of its extra expenses, for the disposition of which he failed to render an account. He was evidently a sordid, narrow-minded, and somewhat arrogant man; bustling rather than active; prone to meddle with matters of which he was profoundly ignorant, and absurdly unwilling to have his ignorance enlightened." It seems a pity for the sake of Dinwiddie's good name that he had not remained in Glasgow and become a merchant, possibly a deacon, like his father and a bailie like his maternal grandfather.

One of the titled Governors of Virginia who was much more than a mere nonentity was John, fourth Earl of Dunmore. His family was an offshoot of the ducal one of Athol. He was destined for a military career, but was poor and unable to add much to his wealth by the chance of war, while his wife, though a daughter of the ancient house of Galloway, did not bring him any very tangible accession to his worldly goods. When, therefore, he received the appointment, in 1770, of Governor of New York, he gladly accepted it, because he saw in the appointment a chance of increasing his personal resources. In short, he crossed over to America simply to make as much money as he could out of it, and without much concern as to whether or not the country was to be benefited by his services. It was, however, a period demanding the utmost tact and diplomacy, qualities Lord Dunmore either did not possess, or did not deem it worth his while, when he had the chance, to exhibit; and in these facts lie the causes for his ignoble American career, and the poltroonery, the crime, the silliness by which it was most distinguished. The Revolutionary movement at the time of Lord Dunmore's arrival in America was approaching a crisis. Discontent was in the air, uneasiness was prevalent everywhere. But the Virginians were then loyal to the crown, and a wise Governor should have strengthened that loyalty by every means in his power, instead of acting in a manner, as Lord Dunmore did, to deepen the discontent, to fan the flames of sedition and to drive the people into open revolt. Had his Lordship really been a statesman he had the opportunity while in America of doing yeoman service for his sovereign, but his actions while in the country failed to exhibit any signs of his possession of that quality. He was for self first, last, and all the time, and when Virginia was too hot to hold him—he ran away.

While in New York Lord Dunmore was very popular, for his term of service did not last long enough to bring any of his ignoble qualities to the front, but he seems to have attended strictly to his "ain" business and acquired some 50,000 acres of land in the State. He was transferred to the much more valuable post of Virginia in less than a year, and was heartily welcomed on his arrival in his new sphere of usefulness. His first act bound him closely to the hearts of the Virginians, for he indorsed cordially their remonstrances to the Home Government against the continuation of the slave trade. This popularity continued for two or three years, during which time he waxed rich in land and fees and concealed his personal schemes with the utmost craft. In 1774, when he was joined by his Countess, the Assembly presented her with an address of welcome, and got up a grand ball in her honor. When her daughter was born she named it Virginia in honor of a province which had so warmly welcomed her. A year later the poor woman was glad to take refuge on a British vessel, as she considered her life in danger at the hands of these same Virginians. Lord Dunmore's troubles came on him all in a heap. He had had a little war with the red men, and had conducted it so successfully and had brought about such a favorable peace that the Legislature gave him a sort of vote of confidence, in which his management of affairs was spoken of as "truly noble, wise, and spirited." His agents, however, were out trying to annex lands, and win fees, as far West as Cincinnati, and some even operated on the soil of Pennsylvania, inviting trouble and complaint from that quarter. Then, when the troubles with the home country were elsewhere approaching a crisis, he precipitated the outbreak in Virginia by seizing the powder stored in Williamsburg, by his arrogant manner, by his threatening to arm the negroes and the Indians against the white residents, and by several other unwise sayings and doings. It is not to be wondered at that Lady Dunmore was soon joined on the vessel in which she had taken refuge by her husband, himself a fugitive, and that Virginia quickly threw off her allegiance and ranged herself on the side of the Revolutionists. The rest of Dunmore's American story is equally contemptible. His wanton destruction of Norfolk cannot be defended on grounds either of military necessity or the demands of statesmanship, and when he finally returned to Britain, it was with anything but the record of a hero. But his prestige does not appear to have suffered, although it might truly be said that his foolishness and personal greed had lost Britain a province. He continued to be elected to Parliament by his brother peers of Scotland, and in 1787 he was sent to the Bahamas as Captain General and Governor, and there resided, an inoffensive figurehead, for several years before he returned home again to adorn society until his death, in 1806.

It is refreshing to turn from such a personage to recall the nobler career of George Johnstone, who was nominated in 1763 Governor of Florida, when that colony was ceded by Spain to Great Britain. Johnstone, who belonged to the family of Johnstone of Westerhall, was a Captain in the Royal Navy, a hero in every sense of the word, and a capable man of affairs, as was abundantly proved by his course in Florida, and his career in Parliament. In 1778 he was one of the Commissioners sent out by the British Government to try and restore peace in America, and was noted as being outspoken in his sympathy with the American people, and in his condemnation of the wrongs which had driven them into revolt. But events had by that time progressed so far that peace could only be procured through independence or annihilation, and so the commission accomplished no practical result, but Johnstone, by a curious turn in his thoughts and sympathies, then changed his ideas of the American people and thenceforth was among their bitterest detractors. Gov. Johnstone's term of office is additionally interesting in that it was the means of bringing James Macpherson, the translator of Ossian, to the country, although only for a short time. In Mr. Bailey Saunders's interesting monograph on that literary hero, we read: " In October (1763) one George Johnstone was gazetted Governor of the Western Provinces and ordered to Pensacola. Like most of the other American Governors, Johnstone was a Scotchman. Macpherson was offered an appointment as his secretary, and, in addition, the posts of President of the Council and Surveyor General. It was a strange shift in the breeze of his fortune, and of the reasons which led him to yield to it we have no knowledge. He may have resented the treatment which he was receiving from men of letters in London, or he may have found himself in pecuniary or other difficulties. Certain it is, that in the early part of the following year, he set his sails for America. He was absent about two years, but only a portion of that time was spent at Pensacola, for he soon quarrelled with his chief and departed on a visit to some of the other provinces. After a tour in the West Indies he returned in 1766. As Surveyor General, he had received a salary of £200 a year. In a day when pensions formed a larger part of the machinery of the State than at present, Macpherson was allowed to retain it for life on the condition, so far as can be gathered, that he should devote himself henceforth to political writing." America seems, however, to have made little impression on the hero of the Ossianic controversy, if we may estimate the extent of that impression by his silence.

A notable and lovable, and, in every way commendable, career was that of Gabriel Johnston, who was Governor of North Carolina from 1734 till his death, in Chowan County, in that State, in 1752. Little is known of his early career in Scotland except that he was born there in 1699 and that he studied medicine at St. Andrews University, but he had a predilection for the study of languages and never practiced. Instead, he became Professor of Oriental Languages at St. Andrews, and taught for several years. Then he removed to London and became a literary hack, his most notable employment being under Lord Bolingbroke on the latter's periodical, "The Craftsman." Johnston crossed the Atlantic in 1730, intending to settle in America, and three years later, through the influence of the Earl of Wilmington, he was appointed Lieutenant Governor of North Carolina, and showed his gratitude, among other ways, by naming the town of Wilmington after his benefactor. Johnston's life here was one of peacefulness. His administration was in every way wise and beneficent, and, although even in his time there were murmurs against the Home Government, he kept his charge well in hand and thoroughly loyal to the Crown. One of his first acts as Governor was to urge upon the Colonial Assembly the need of making provision for a thorough school system, and in educational matters he took a deep personal interest to the end. It was during his administration, too, that the great influx of Scotch Highlanders took place into North Carolina. Thousands of these people settled in the Counties of Bladen, Cumberland, Robeson, Moore, Richmond, and Hamet, among others, and their descendants predominate in these sections till the present day. At Gov. Gabriel's suggestion, his brother, John Johnston, crossed to America from Dundee in 1736, and settled in North Carolina. Among the rest of this man's family was a child who had been born in Dundee three years before. This was Samuel Johnston, afterward a noted figure in the history of the State. At the Governor's suggestion, Samuel studied for the bar, and in a short time after he had passed was in possession of a large practice. When he grew to manhood he knew no other country except that in which he had been raised, and was one of the earliest to earn the title of patriot. When the troubles with the mother country began to take practical shape, Samuel Johnston was one of the trusted leaders of the Americans in the State. In 1775 he was elected Chairman of the Provincial Council, and as such, by force of circumstances, which need not be enlarged upon here, virtually Governor of the State. Bancroft says of him at this juncture: "On the waters of Albemarle Sound * * * the movement [for freedom, or at least a removal of oppression] was assisted by the writings of young James Iredell, from England, by the letters and counsels of young Joseph Hewes, and by the calm wisdom of Samuel Johnston, a native of Dundee, in Scotland, a man revered for his integrity, thoroughly opposed to disorder and revolution, if revolution could be avoided without yielding to oppression." When the die was finally cast and absolute separation from the mother country was demanded, Johnston did not flinch, but cast in his lot with those who demanded independence. He was a member of the Continental Congress in 1781 and 1782, was elected Governor of his State in 1788, served four years in the Senate of the United States, and from 1800 to 1803 was a Justice of the Supreme Court of the United States. He closed his long, useful, and patriotic career at Edenton, North Carolina, in 1816, and his memory is yet one of the greenest in that beautiful State.

Besides furnishing in these later days a popular Governor General to the Dominion of Canada, in the person of the Marquis of Lorne, the house of Argyll has given at least two Governors to territories south of the St. Lawrence. One of these was Lord William Campbell, youngest son of the fourth Duke of Argyll. He served in the Royal Navy and held the rank of Captain when, in 1766, he was appointed Governor of Nova Scotia. He arrived at Halifax on Nov. 27 of that year, and at once assumed control of affairs. He proved a satisfactory, if not a brilliant administrator and enjoyed the confidence of the people. He faithfully carried their representations to the Home Government and preserved the relations of the colony to the mother country unimpaired. He was watchful over the morals of the people, too, and in one of his orders he peremptorily forbade public horse racing at Halifax on account of its tending to "gambling, idleness, and immorality." In 1763 he married Sarah Izard, belonging to

a wealthy South Carolina family, and sister of that Ralph
Izard who became distinguished as an American patriot,
as a warm friend and unwavering supporter of Washington, and as the first representative of South Carolina in
the United States Senate. It was his union with this lady
that led, in one way or another, to his receiving the
appointment, in 1775, of Governor of South Carolina, and thither he removed in that year. Before he left
Nova Scotia he was presented with an address of thanks
from the Legislature, extolling his career as Governor
and regretting that circumstances should sever their
pleasant relations. Lord William was probably not very
long at his new sphere of duty ere he joined in that regret. The Commonwealth was really in a state of rebellion when Lord William arrived, and the address
which the Provincial Council addressed to him on that
occasion must have sounded strange in his ears. " No lust
of independence," it said, " has the least influence upon
our councils; no subjects more sincerely desire to testify
their loyalty and affection. We deplore the measures
which, if persisted in, must rend the British Empire.
Trusting the event to Providence, we prefer death to
slavery." What was wanted in such a crisis was a policy
of conciliation, an exhibition of statesmanship. Lord
William tried an opposite policy and appears to have been
utterly destitute of the necessary qualities to guide a
statesman in a storm. His supercilious contempt for the
claims and opinions of the Carolinians helped only to
embitter them still more. He held out no hope of relief
or remedy in connection with the wrongs which had
driven them to take the stand they did. In place of trying
to adjust these wrongs, to soften the people's thoughts,
to induce them to reason with him, he contented himself
with indulging in threats. " I warn you," he foolishly
said to the Legislature, " of the danger you are in; the
violent measures adopted cannot fail of drawing down
inevitable ruin on this flourishing colony." His value as
a statesman in a crisis may be judged from the fact that
he was unable to grasp the meaning of the American

troubles or the extent of the feeling in the hearts of the people. " Three regiments, a proper detachment of artillery, with a couple of good frigates, some small craft, and a bombketch would do the whole business here and go a great way to reduce Georgia and North Carolina to a sense of their duty. Charleston is the fountain head from whence all violence flows; stop that, and the rebellion in this part of the continent will soon be at an end." It was not long after writing this rigmarole that Lord William had to take refuge on a small British warship, " The Tamer," and to leave the affairs of his province to be managed by its people. After a vain attempt to overawe the Colonists by a show of resistance from the water, he passed from American view, to reappear again about a year later in an unsuccessful naval attack on Charleston Harbor, and in that engagement he was mortally wounded. Like most of his race, he was a brave man, but he really had little administrative ability. In the loyal quietness of Nova Scotia he did well enough, but when he became a prominent figure in " the time that tried men's souls," he was a distressing failure. At the moment he assumed its government, South Carolina, says Bancroft, " needed more than ever a man of prudence at the head of the administration, and its new Governor owed his place only to his birth."

New Jersey in the Colonial days was a favorite settling place for Scotch refugees, and, naturally, for Scotch Governors. Many of the Presbyterian exiles sought the liberty of conscience which was denied them at home in its then wild but fruitful territories, and among the early " proprietors " we find the names of many Scotch noblemen and official dignitaries, and it was after one of them, an Earl of Perth, that the once great rival of New York, Perth Amboy, was named. The Quakers, too, began to see in it a place where their doctrines could be lived up to without molestation, and one of the most famous of their number, Robert Barclay of Ury, was appointed Governor of East Jersey in 1682. Barclay, author of the still classic " Apology for the Quakers," never visited his territory; but, nevertheless, his influence in it was great, and while Quaker influence predominated—a period of about twenty years—the colony enjoyed wonderful prosperity. Barclay appointed as his deputy Gavin Laurie, a native of Edinburgh, a man of peace, who devoted himself to developing the resources of his charge, and the comfort and well-being of its people. He was a good ruler, and as much may be said of Alexander Skene, another Quaker Governor, a native of Aberdeen.

Lord Neil Campbell, son of the ninth Earl of Argyll, visited New Jersey as its Governor in 1687, having previously bought, or secured in some way, the lands of Sir George Mackenzie—the "Bluidy Mackenzie" of the Covenanters. Lord Neil, however, stayed little longer than to see some of the land over which he was thus nominally ruler, and does not appear to have meddled with its affairs in any way. His deputy, Andrew Hamilton, made up in practical work for his lordship's qualities of nonentity. Hamilton was born at Edinburgh about 1627, and for a time was a merchant in that city. He was sent to New Jersey as agent for the Scotch "proprietors," and on Lord Neil Campbell's departure became acting Governor. He was an aggressive sort of personage, and his official career was rather a stormy one, but he did good service to the young country. He was the first to organize a postal service in the Colonies, having obtained a patent for a postal scheme from the Crown in 1694. Gov. Andrew Hamilton died at Burlington, New Jersey, in 1703. His son John, who died at Perth Amboy in 1746, was also for a time acting Governor of New Jersey, and his grandson, James, was the first native-born Governor of Pennsylvania.

Another Governor of Pennsylvania of Scotch descent was Thomas McKean, who entered public life as a Deputy Attorney General in 1756, and retired in 1808, having in the intervening years held almost every office in the gift of the people, in State Legislature, in Congress, in the field as a soldier, on the bench as Chief Justice of Pennsylvania for twenty years, and as Governor of the State for nine years. He enjoyed a rare record for a career of usefulness, in the course of which he exhibited the highest qualities of an orator, a jurist, and an executive. He was proud of his descent from Scotch forbears, and showed his pride publicly in 1792, when he joined the ranks of the Philadelphia St. Andrew's Society.

The most notable of the Scotch Governors of Pennsylvania, however, was Sir William Keith, who was born at Peterhead in 1680, and was the son of Sir William Keith. He was Governor from 1717 till 1726, but left behind him a record for vanity, intrigue and misgovernment, all of which, however, occupies so large a space in the early history of Pennsylvania as not to need recital here. Keith was a man of the world. He lived for self and his life was a failure, for he died in London in 1749, while a prisoner for debt, in the Old Bailey.

New York had its full quota of Scottish Governors. The first of them in point of time, and in many ways the most distinguished, was Major Gen. Robert Hunter, grandson of Patrick Hunter, of Hunterston, Ayrshire, the head of an ancient family. Robert Hunter was born at Hunterston and commenced life as a soldier. In 1707 he was commissioned Governor of Virginia and started out to take possession of his political prize, but on the voyage the ship in which he was a passenger was captured by a French vessel, and the budding Governor was carried to Paris, a prisoner of war. He never saw Virginia, and his appointment to the high office of its chief Executive has been doubted, but his commission is still extant and carefully preserved among the curiosities of the Historical Society of Virginia

Gen. Hunter's real American experience commenced in June, 1710, when he entered upon his duties as Governor of New York. He accepted the appointment with the primal view of adding to his fortune, but he had a conscience that prevented him from seeking to increase his wealth by means which were in direct variance to the welfare of the community among whom his lot was cast. After being about a year in his office he saw that the development of the colony could only be hastened by adding to its population by means of immigration, and, having conceived a scheme about the manufacture of naval stores by which he might enrich himself, he proceeded to develop the resources of the country and increase his own wealth by the introduction of some 3,000 German laborers from the Palatinate. These people were settled on the banks of the Hudson River, mainly on lands belonging to the Livingstons, and were to produce tar and turpentine. Their passage money was to be repaid out of their earnings, and on the same terms they were to be supplied at first with the necessaries of life. As might be expected, the scheme was a failure. The immigrants were virtually contract slaves and were soon so dissatisfied with their lot that they refused to work, and, when he washed his hands of the affair and left the immigrants to shift for themselves, the Governor was crippled financially very seriously. His greatest claim to remembrance is his establishing of a complete Court of Chancery in the colony, and, although he doubtless saw in such a court a rich harvest of fees and opportunities for patronage, the good accomplished by a tribunal of that description, especially in a developing colony, where new and intricate questions were daily demanding decisions—decisions which were for all time to rank as precedents—should not be ignored. In many ways Gov. Hunter was a model ruler. In questions of religion he was extremely tolerant, and he believed in every man being permitted to worship as he thought best. He indulged in no wildcat schemes and encouraged no extravagant outlay of public money. He understood the art of managing men and was on equally good terms with all the parties in the colony. Very popular he was not, and never could be, for he represented a sovereign power in the person of the King, while all round him in New York was developing the theory that the source of all power, even the power to name Governors and Judges, should be the people concerned. Still he preserved intact the supremacy of his royal master and maintained peace or harmony in the colony, although he foresaw very clearly that a struggle between the two was certain sooner or later. "The Colonies are infants at their mother's breast," he wrote to Lord Bolingbroke, then British Secretary of State for Foreign Affairs, "but such as will wean themselves when they become of age."

When Gov. Hunter retired from the Colony, in 1719, the Assembly gave him an address in which they lauded his administration of affairs and expressed the opinion that he had "governed well and wisely, like a prudent magistrate; like an affectionate parent." This praise seems to have been thoroughly well deserved, and even American writers acknowledge that his official record was not only an able, but a clean one. He was possessed of more than ordinary talent, was a warm friend of such men as Addison, St. John, Steele, Shaftesbury, and especially of Dean Swift, who appears to have entertained for him as undoubted sentiments of respect and friendship as he entertained for any man. "Hunter," wrote John Forster, in his unfinished life of the great Dean of St. Patrick's, "was among the most scholarly and entertaining of his (Swift's) correspondents; some of Swift's own best letters were written to this friend, and the judgment he had formed of him may be taken from the fact that when all the world was giving to himself the authorship of Shaftesbury's anonymously printed 'Letter on Enthusiasm,' Swift believed Hunter to have written it."

Gov. Hunter married the widow of an old companion in arms in the Marlborough campaigns, Lord John Hay, son of the second Marquis of Tweeddale, and Colonel of the Scots Greys. She was the daughter and heiress of Sir Thomas Orby, a Lincolnshire Baronet, and brought him considerable wealth. He, however, continued in official harness to the last and died at Jamaica in 1734, while holding the post of Governor of that island, one of the plums of the then colonial service.

Gov. Hunter's successor in New York was also a Scotsman—William Burnet. This amiable man was the son of the famous Bishop Burnet, and grandson of Robert Burnet of Crimond, one of the Scotch Lords of Session. William Burnet was educated at Cambridge and admitted to the practice of the law. He appears to have been fairly successful, but lost all his means in the South Sea bubble, and, finding himself ruined, looked around so that he might use his great family influence to secure for him a colonial appointment. His success was quick, and in September, 1720, he found himself in New York as its Governor. His administration was as able and as honest as that of his predecessor, and he made himself immensely popular by his prohibition of trade between the Indians of New York and the merchants in Canada, and he even built a fort at his personal expense to help in protecting the trade of the colony over which he ruled. The Home Government, however, refused to indorse Burnet's course in this instance, but that only added to his personal popularity. He lost it all, however, by the policy he adopted toward the Court of Chancery. Briefly stated, he wanted to make that body independent of public sentiment and above public interference, while Colonial sentiment was that all Judges and all courts should be subject to the control of the people, either directly or through their elected representatives. Things reached such a pass that the Assembly threatened to declare all acts and decrees of the Court of Chancery as null and void, and reduced all its fees as a preliminary step in that direction. The crisis between the Governor and the people was ended, greatly to the former's relief, in 1728, when he was transferred to the Governorship of Massachusetts. He had not much time to make a name for himself there, for he died at Boston in 1729.

Another Scotsman, John Montgomerie, was sworn in as Burnet's successor in the New York Governorship on April 15, 1728. He was a scion of the noble house of Eglinton, being the son of Francis Montgomerie of Giffen, who was a son of Alexander, sixth Earl of Eglinton. John Montgomerie was an officer in the Guards and was a member of Parliament from 1710 to 1722. He occupied a high position in society and married a daughter of the Earl of Hyndford; but his habits were erratic, his tastes extravagant, and he became inextricably involved in debt. His ancestral estate had to be sold and he was glad to accept a minor post at the Court of George I.— the 'wee, wee, German lairdie." It was in the hope of benefiting his fortunes that he secured the appointment as the royal representative in New York, but his usefulness was gone. His service as Governor was not marked by any matter of importance. He seemed to be in weak health from the day he landed, and he died July 31, 1731.

If, however, Gov. Montgomerie occupies but a small share in the historical annals of the colony, Gov. Colden, the last of the Scottish Governors, or British Governors, whose executive rights were recognized by the people, had a very important position in public affairs for the fifteen years preceding the Revolution. Cadwallader Colden was born at Dunse in 1688. His father, the Rev. Alexander Colden, was minister of Dunse, and Cadwallader was educated at Edinburgh University, with the view of entering the ministry. His own inclination, however, led him to study medicine, and he appears to have practiced that profession in London. In 1710 he crossed the sea to Philadelphia. His stay there was comparatively short, for we find him again in London in 1715, when he moved in the highest intellectual and literary circles. In 1716 he returned to Scotland and married a Kelso girl, the daughter of a minister, and soon after left his native land again for America. After practicing medicine for a time in Philadelphia, he visited New York and won the friendship of Gov. Hunter, who invited him to settle in the territory under his jurisdiction. This he agreed to, mainly because Hunter backed up his professions of friendship by the more tangible offer of the position of Surveyor General of the Colony. Two years later Colden had so fortified his position with the ruling powers that he obtained a grant of 2,000 acres of land in Orange County and there built a country home for himself and founded a village, to which he gave the name of Coldenham, which it still retains. His influence was increased after he was appointed, in 1722, a member of His Majesty's Provincial Council, when Gov. Burnet had commenced his rule, and he became that personage's most trusted counsellor. After Burnet went to Boston, Colden retired to Coldenham, and there interested himself in those literary and scientific pursuits which gave him a prominent position in contemporary learned circles. He had a wide correspondence with scientists on both sides of the Atlantic, and to a suggestion in one of his letters was due the formation of the American Philosophical Society of Philadelphia. As a member of Council, however, Colden still continued to be active in the politics of the province, and, as usual, came in for a full share of popular and official criticism and abuse. In 1760, as senior member of Council, he was called upon to administer the Government on the sudden death of Gov. De Lancey. Thereafter, with a few interruptions, he served as Lieutenant Governor until June 25, 1775, when the progress of the Revolution laid him on the shelf by wiping out the royal office. Had Colden thrown in his lot with the Revolutionists, he might have attained a high place in the affections of the leaders of the successful side, but he remained steadfast in his loyalty and to the official oaths he had taken to be faithful to the Home Government, and while his sympathies were always with the people and his views were decidedly against unwarranted State interference and against taxation without representation, he was too old to renounce his allegiance, too near the end of his pilgrimage to change his flag. Besides, he was of the opinion that all the evils which led to the Revolution could be amended by united and firm representation to the sovereign and his immediate advisers, and that, therefore, open rebellion was needless. So when the crash finally came, and his proclamations, promises, explanations, diplomacy, and entreaties proved unavailing, the old Governor retired to a farm near Flushing, L. I., and died of a broken heart a few months later, in September, 1776, when in the eighty-eighth year of his age. After the bitterness of the contemporary struggle had passed away, the public services and brilliant talents of this most accomplished of all New York's royal Governors was more apparent than at the time when he was an actor in the drama of history, and his loyal devotion to the duties of his high office became fully acknowledged on all sides. "Posterity," wrote Dr. O'Callaghan in his "Documentary History of the State of New York," in summing up the life work of Colden, "will not fail to accord justice to the character and memory of a man to whom this country is most deeply indebted for much of its science and for many of its most important institutions, and of whom the State of New York may well be proud." And H. G. Verplanck said: "For the great variety and extent of his learning, his unwearied research, his talents, and the public sphere in which he lived, Cadwallader Colden may justly be placed in a high rank among the most distinguished men of his time." The grandson of Governor Colden was Mayor of New York from 1818 to 1821, and in that office had an enviable record.

For a brief period, in 1780, James Robertson was the nominal Governor of New York. He was born in Scotland in 1710, and was a soldier by profession. His record in America, while he held office under his commission as Governor, is not, it must be confessed, a creditable one, and we may dismiss him with the statement that his office as Governor was merely a titular one, and he never assumed legislative functions. He was a soldier pure and simple, and, had the Revolutionists been defeated, might have swayed executive power. But the crisis was virtually passed when he came upon the scene, and we need not follow his doings further than to say that he returned to Britain in safety from the conflict and died in England in 1788.

After the Revolution, the history of the United States presents us with several instances of Scotsmen holding the office of Governor in one of the confederated Commonwealths. Among the earliest of these was Edward Telfair, who was for several years (1786, 1790-3) Governor of Georgia. He was born in the Stewartry of

Kirkcudbright, in 1735, and educated at the Kirkcudbright Grammar School. He left Scotland in 1758, to become agent in America for a commercial house, and, after residing in Virginia and North Carolina, removed, in 1766, to Savannah, Ga., where he engaged in business. When the Revolutionary troubles commenced, he heartily espoused the American side, and became known locally as an ardent advocate of liberty. He was elected in 1778 a delegate to the Continental Congress, and served in that capacity also from 1780 to 1783. In the latter year he was appointed a Commissioner to treat with the Cherokees, then, as before, and long after, a troublesome problem in Georgia. Telfair was regarded as the foremost citizen of his adopted State, and his death, at Savannah, in 1807, was deeply mourned, not only in that Commonwealth, but by all throughout the country who had taken any part in the struggle which gave the Stars and Stripes a place among the flags of the nations. His son, Thomas, who graduated at Princeton in 1805, gave promise of a brilliant career. He was a member of the House of Representatives from 1813 to 1817, and but for his untimely death, in 1818, would doubtless have attained higher honors in his State and in the nation.

A good example of the later Governors is found in W. E. Smith, who in 1877 and in 1879 was elected to the Executive Chair of Wisconsin by large popular votes. Mr. Smith was taken to America when a boy, and his earlier years were spent in the States of New York and Michigan. Finally, he settled at Fox Lake, Wis., where he engaged in business and acquired considerable means. In 1851 he served his first term as a member of the State Legislature, and was Speaker of that body in 1871. On retiring from public life, Governor Smith devoted himself to religious and philanthropic enterprises. He was a member of the Baptist Church, and took a keen interest in its progress, and in all movements for the relief of misery or for improving the moral tone of the community in which he was recognized as a leader. Governor

Beveridge of Illinois, Governor Moonlight of Kansas, and Governor Ross of New Mexico, are among the other Governors the Scottish race has furnished to American Commonwealths.

Turning to the history of Canada, we find that one of its earliest rulers was Samuel Veitch, who was Governor of Nova Scotia, and had in many respects the career of a typical Scot abroad. He was born at Edinburgh in 1668, and was the son of a noted Presbyterian minister. After studying at the University of Edinburgh, he passed over to Holland and entered the College of Utrecht. Although a clerical career had been proposed for him, his inclinations were for the army, and he attached himself to the Court of William of Orange, and accompanied that Prince to England in 1688. Veitch afterward served with much distinction with the army in Flanders, rose to the rank of Colonel, and returned to England after the peace of Ryswick, in 1697. He next attempted to become a money-maker, and took a deep interest in the Darien scheme, one of the causes of much ill-feeling against the administration of King William in Scotland. He was one of the Councillors of the Darien Colony of Caledonia. He proceeded to Darien in 1698, and when the colony was wiped out by the Spaniards he made his way to the North, and settled at Albany, where he engaged in trading with the Indians, and seems to have been fairly successful, for in 1700 he married Margaret, daughter of Robert Livingston. For several years his most notable employment was connected with schemes to forcibly wrest Canada from the hands of the French. In 1710, in the course of hostilities, he was appointed Governor of Nova Scotia, and held the office for three years. His duties, however, were military rather than civil, and it seems a pity, for the sake of his personal comfort and fortunes, that he ever saw the province. In 1713 he was removed from his office, was soon after reappointed to it, and again was removed without ceremony. Then he went to Boston and petitioned the crown for a place or a pension, but without meeting with any success; nor were his petitions to the Department of State any more fortunate. He went to England to push his claims in person, but failed to receive either recognition or recompense for his services and losses, and he died in London in 1732, a sadly disappointed and broken man. He possessed great ability, was active and conscientious in all the duties which fell to him, but he was of a stern and unyielding disposition, strong in his prejudices and utterly unfitted by a want of suavity in his manner for making himself popular either with the people or the Court.

James Murray, fifth son of the fourth Lord Elibank, who from 1763 to 1767 was Governor General of Canada, occupies a prominent place in the military and political history of the Dominion. Beginning life as a soldier, he early saw service on the Continent of Europe. He took part in Wolfe's expedition to Quebec. He commanded a brigade at the battle on the Plains of Abraham, and after Quebec had fallen and Wolfe had " died victorious " the command of the city and its forces devolved upon him. He at once put the place in order to meet any attack which might be made upon it. All through the Winter of 1759-60 he continued his preparations, and early in Spring found his charge invested by a French force of 12,000 men, under De Levis, one of the most brilliant of French Generals, while his own available force was barely 3,000. He offered De Levis battle, and in the "second engagement of Quebec," as it has been called, although he lost his guns and did not break the investing lines, he only suffered a loss of 300 men, while the enemy owned up to 1,800. This sally, brilliant as it was, severely crippled his resources, and he had a hard, ceaseless, and ever-perplexing struggle to keep the enemy out of Quebec. In spite of the great odds against him, he maintained his position with brilliant success. But the struggle was a terrible one until the strain was relieved when the news came that aid had landed in Canada from Great Britain, and the French forces retreated from before the city. Had Quebec fallen into the hands of the French that Winter the British would have lost Canada, for the time at least. When all danger was past, Murray went to Montreal and there joined Lord Amherst, and with the capitulation soon after of that city the French struggle for the retention of Canada ceased, and it became " one of the fairest gems in the British crown," as some one has truthfully described it.

As Governor General, to which post he was almost immediately appointed, General Murray made a brilliant record. Mr. Henry J. Morgan, in his " Sketches of Celebrated Canadians," says: " During his administration the form of government and the laws to be observed in the new colony were promulgated; the many evils that arose therefrom caused much dissatisfaction among the French people, and Governor Murray did all in his power to alleviate the discontented feeling, but with only partial success. Nevertheless, he won the good will and esteem of the whole French race in Canada, and lost that of a part of his countrymen because he would not conform to their prejudices against the poor natives and those of French origin." On leaving Canada, he served in the army with his accustomed brilliancy in other parts of the world, and refused on one occasion a bribe of one million pounds sterling to surrender Minorca. He died in 1794 and was buried in Westminster Abbey, where rest the remains of so many brilliant Scotsmen whose abilities made them famous in all walks of life.

Another military Governor of Canada who won a brilliant record for his administrative qualities was General Peter Hunter, a brother of the celebrated founder of the Hunterian Museum at Glasgow. He was descended from the same family as Governor Hunter of New York, and was born at Long Calderwood, Lanarkshire, in 1746. Choosing the military profession, he soon rose steadily and acquitted himself with credit in many hard fought campaigns. When appointed Governor of Upper Canada and Commander in Chief of the Forces, in 1799, he had attained the rank of Lieutenant General, and his appointment is an evidence of the confidence felt in his military and administrative qualities by the British authorities, for the time was one of the most critical in the history of Canada, and the services of a diplomat were needed as much as those of a soldier. Governor Hunter's course in Canada fully justified the confidence of the appointing power. He ruled wisely and well, instituted many improvements in all branches of the Government, and was equally watchful over the contemporary prosperity and the opportunities for future development of the country. But, while constantly reforming the details of government and formulating laws and orders which were designed to benefit the country then and thereafter, and which seem to have been understood and appreciated by the people, Governor Hunter kept a close watch on the defenses and the military resources of his province, and it was while on a tour of inspection of the outposts of Canada that he died, at Quebec, in 1805. His career was in every way an honorable one to himself and his country, and the words on the memorial erected in the English Cathedral at Quebec by his brother, Dr. John Hunter, the famous anatomist, are as truthful as they are fitting: " His life was spent in the service of his King and country. Of the various stations, both civil and military, which he filled, he discharged the duties with spotless integrity, unwearied zeal, and successful abilities."

A volume might be written about the incidents in the career of Sir James H. Craig, the last of the family of Craig of Dalnair, near Edinburgh, who became Governor of Canada in 1807. He was born in 1750 at Gibraltar, where his father held an appointment as Judge. Entering the army in 1763, he received his military training in Gibraltar. He was present at the battle of Bunker Hill, and thereafter took part in most of the American campaigns. In 1794, with the rank of Major General, he went to the Cape of Good Hope, was instrumental in bringing that settlement under British rule, and was appointed its Governor. Thereafter he served for several years with distinction in India, and, as Lieutenant General, had command of the troops in the Mediterranean in

1805. Illness compelled him to retire from active service, but a short interval of rest seemed to recuperate him so much that he accepted the Governorship of Canada. His life there was not an enviable one. His constitution was broken and he suffered terribly from dropsy and a complication of diseases. The country was unsettled, the French and British did not get along harmoniously together, and Craig made a few serious errors—errors which brought upon him much savage abuse. But he meant well, his honesty and patriotism were unimpeachable, and he strove earnestly to benefit the country over which he ruled. Probably had he been in perfect health, had sedition been less ripe, had party spirit less blinded the people to his purpose, he might have succeeded better than he did. They called him an oppressor, and in connection with that charge, directly made, he issued the following pathetic statement: " For what should I oppress you? Is it from ambition? What can you give me? Is it for power? Alas, my good friends, with life ebbing not slowly to its period under the pressure of diseases acquired in the service of my country, I look only to pass what it may please God to suffer to remain of it in the comfort of retirement among my friends. I remain among you only in obedience to the commands of my King. What power can I wish for? Is it then for wealth I would oppress you? Inquire of those who know me whether I regard wealth. I never did when I could enjoy it; it is now of no use to me. To the value of your country laid at my feet I would prefer the consciousness of having, in a single instance, contributed to your happiness and prosperity." Such a man could not remain long misunderstood, and though in some quarters the wrangling and criticism prevailed while he continued at the head of affairs, (and indeed long after,) the true sentiments of the people forced themselves to the front when it was announced that he was about to relinquish his post and leave the country. Addresses of regret were sent to him from all quarters, and on the way to the vessel that was to carry him across the Atlantic a throng took the horses from his carriage and pulled it to the wharf. In the "History of Canada," by Robert Christie, is the following mention of Governor Craig, which, so far as it goes, seems a truthful tribute to some of the excellencies of his character: "Although hasty in temper, he was, like most men who are so, far from implacable, and as we have seen, easily reconciled to those who may have incurred his displeasure. Hospitable and princely in his style of living, he was also munificent in his donations to public institutions, and to charitable purposes a generous patron; and, lastly, we shall mention, though not the least of his virtues, a friend to the poor and destitute, none of whom applying at his door ever went away unrelieved."

In one respect, Governor Craig was far ahead of his contemporaries. That was in connection with the land question. He had no faith in the policy which handed over thousands of the most fruitful acres in Canada to adventurers who applied for them, to favorites who believed themselves entitled to such gifts, or to land speculators who grasped what they could, and then made fortunes by selling their gifts of territory. In 1808, as we learn from one report, 179,786 acres were "granted" in Upper Canada; in 1809, 105,624; in 1810, 104,537; and in 1811, 115,586; while in Lower Canada the liberality of the Government was equally marked. Governor Craig protested on every opportunity against this purposeless prodigality, and gave the home authorities at least one very good object lesson illustrative of its result. A new barracks and a military hospital were needed in 1811 for Quebec, but no site was available for their construction. The Government had by that time actually granted away every vacant piece of ground within the walls, and the Governor could only recommend the purchase of a site. In doing so, however, he did not refrain from pointing out the folly of the whole principle of miscellaneous and indiscriminate awarding of the public lands. To actual settlers he did not begrudge an acre, but to no others would he have given a single foot. Governor Craig died in England, in 1812, a year after he left Canada.

Sir James Kempt, a native of Edinburgh, was another noted soldier-Governor of Canada. He fought under Sir Ralph Abercrombie in Egypt, under Sir James H. Craig in the Mediterranean, under Wellington in the Peninsula and at Waterloo, and received many royal honors from his own and the allied sovereigns. In 1820 he succeeded Lord Dalhousie as Governor of Nova Scotia, and eight years later followed the same nobleman in the Governorship of Canada. His administration was an admirable one, and has been commended on all sides. He found the country on the verge of rebellion, and he quelled, gently and without force, all traces of discontent, so that when he retired he left it enjoying the blessings of assured peace and carried with him affectionate addresses from all sorts of public bodies. His death took place at London in 1855.

A very different type of Canadian Governor may be studied in the comparatively quiet, but none the less useful careers of such men as Miles Macdonnel—a native of Inverness, who was born there in 1767, was Lord Selkirk's right-hand man in the Red River Valley Settlement, became Governor of Assiniboia, and died at Port Fortune, on the Ottawa River, in 1828—and of the bulk, in fact, of the Lieutenant Governors of the different Provinces and territories, before and after Confederation. Such names, too, as Lord Dalhousie, Lord Elgin, and Lord Lorne, are indissolubly associated with Canadian history, and that sturdy Scotch soldier, Sir Colin Campbell, a native of Kilninver, tried his hand at the mysteries of civil administration as Governor of Nova Scotia before becoming Governor of Ceylon.

Taken as a whole, the Scotch Governors, royal or otherwise, on this side of the Atlantic, were fairly creditable to, and representative of, the Scot abroad. One or two of the royal appointees were more mercenary in their disposition than anything else—sort of executive Andrew Fairservices; but only one—Robertson—can be classed as a rascal. The faults which most of them committed were due, in a great measure, to the system under which they were appointed, or to the measures they were to bring about and the policy they were to enforce, all of which were completely at variance with the conditions under which the continent was progressing. This is illustrated in a very significant manner, even in the brief summary contained in this chapter. It will be observed that those Chief Magistrates who came to the United States—to the American Colonies rather—to stay, to make their homes in the new land, to become part and parcel of its citizenship, to throw in their entire future with it, made good executive officers, and have left records which are equally creditable to America and Scotland. Such men as Spottiswood, Johnston, Hamilton, and Colden, for example, still command the admiration of American historical writers, and now that the bitterness of the Revolution has long been buried—let us hope forever—the fact that they were at one and the same time loyal to the people over whom they ruled and to the sovereign they served is freely admitted. Those who came after the Revolution were invariably noted for their honesty, their superiority to mere party spirit, and for their moderation, their wisdom and their sturdy adherence to the principles of the Constitution and of law and order. Carpet-bag rulers have never been much in favor in America at any part of its history, not even in the South after the war, in the reconstruction period, and they are now unknown in the States, and, with the exception of the direct representative of the sovereign, in the Dominion of Canada.

CHAPTER IV.

REVOLUTIONARY HEROES.

THERE was much in the Revolutionary movement which resulted in the formation and independence of the United States to attract Scotsmen to the cause. In Scotland the people were by no means intense in their loyalty to the Orange King or the Hanoverian dynasty, and in the Highlands especially, the fact that " a stranger filled the Stuarts' throne " rankled in the hearts of every one. Even in the Lowlands, where the majority of the people were not in favor of the restoration of the " Auld Stuarts," movements looking to greater freedom under the prevailing Government were rife. Such movements were termed seditious and were repressed with all the severity and cruelty possible. Many of those concerned in these movements were glad to fly to America, and we can easily imagine that their views anent human freedom and the right of all citizens to a voice in the affairs of State did not change after they had crossed the sea. The close of the seventeenth century and the whole of the eighteenth was a period of unrest in Scotland as well as in Continental Europe, and would probably have found vent in the end in rebellion there, if not in revolution, as in France and America, had not Robert Burns crystallized the sentiments of the people into many of his matchless lyrics and inspired them with hope for the future in such reassuring prophetic-like words as those of " A man's a man for a' that."

The Scotch soldiers who were settled on grants of land in the States, as a reward for their military services, were steadfast in their loyalty to Britain at the outbreak of hostilities. They still regarded themselves as soldiers of

King George, and considered, in view of their land holdings, that they were under obligation to continue to fight his battles when occasion demanded, without any consideration as to the merits of the question which was to be settled by a resort to arms. The well-known loyalty of these men and their military reputation drew upon them —and, to a certain extent, upon their countrymen—the ill-will of many, and caused some of the patriots to describe the Scots as being generally anti-revolutionary in their ideas, although, had they chosen to look around a little, exactly the opposite truth might become apparent to them. It was on this erroneous idea that John Trumbull of Connecticut wrote the doggerel lines of "McFingal." Describing that fictitious hero, Trumbull says:

> "His high descent our heralds trace,
> To Ossian's famed Fingalian race;
> For tho' their name some part may lack
> Old Fingal spelt it with a Mac;
> Which great McPherson, with submission
> We hope will add, the next edition.
> His fathers flourished in the Highlands
> Of Scotia's fog-benighted islands."

In commenting on this passage, the late Benson J. Lossing, the latest and best editor of the poem, wrote:
"The Scotch were noted for their loyalty, in this country, and were generally found among the Tories, especially in the Carolinas. This fact and the odium that rested upon the Jacobites in the Mother Country made the Americans, during the Revolution, look with suspicion upon all Scotsmen. Jefferson manifested this feeling when he drew up the Declaration of Independence. In the original draft he alluded to 'Scotch and foreign mercenaries. This was omitted on motion of Dr. Witherspoon, who was a Scotsman by birth. In most minds the word Jacobite was synonymous with Popery. Trumbull showed his dislike of the Scotch by his choice of a hero in this poem. Frenau, another eminent poet of the

Revolution, also evinced the same hatred. In one of his poems, in which he gives Burgoyne many hard rubs, he consigns the Tories, with Burgoyne at their head, to an ice-bound, fog-covered island off the north coast of Scotland, thus:

> ' There, Loyals, there, with loyal hearts retire;
> There pitch your tents and kindle there your fire,
> There desert nature will her strings display,
> And fiercest hunger on your vitals prey.' "

The bulk of the Scots who crossed the Atlantic, other than those in the military service, from 1700 till the outbreak of the Revolution, and long after, were discontented with the prevailing condition of things at home. Some wonder, knowing the intense loyalty of the Scots of the present day, that settlers of that country should have taken such an active part in the pre-Revolutionary movements in America, and been so ready to throw off their allegiance; but no one who has studied the history of the people, particularly in the period named, will be in the least surprised. The exiles of Dunbar and of Cromwell's régime may have had some sentimental regard for the King they fought for, but the news of his doings after the " blessed restoration " crushed it out. The prisoners of the Covenanting frays had little reverence for the royal authority and their descendants had none. After religious liberty had been won, the movement for civil liberty commenced in earnest and men were sent to prison for holding sentiments as well as for standing out in actual opposition to " the powers that be." Even such sentiments as " The nation is essentially the source of all sovereignty " and " Equal representation, just taxation, and liberty of conscience " were deemed treasonable enough to cause the arrest of their utterers, and such policy sent hundreds of good men and true across the sea. These wanderers found in America an opportunity for securing that religious liberty and that freedom and perfect equality before the law they could not obtain at home. When the Revolutionary troubles began they or their descendants entertained no loyalty for King George or his dynasty; they knew that Scotland had suffered deeply, not only at the hands of the last two Kings of the old royal house, but at those of King William " of blessed memory." Besides, from the time that John Knox had established in the Kirk the most perfect form of republican government of which the world has yet had knowledge, a growing sentiment, although in most instances an unconscious sentiment, in favor of a republican form of government for State as well as for Kirk existed in the country. These are some of the reasons which made Scotsmen in America, or rather the majority of them, be as devoted to the principles at stake in the American Revolution as were any of the native patriots.

Thus, in the highest circle of American patriotism, among the Signers of the Declaration of Independence we find the Scottish race well represented. Quite a number were of Scotch descent, such as George Ross, who was the son of a Scottish minister, and Thomas McKean, afterward Governor of Pennsylvania. Two were natives of Scotland. One of these was James Wilson, a representative of Pennsylvania, who was born near St. Andrews, Fifeshire, in 1742. He was educated at the university in that ancient city and also at the Universities of Glasgow and Edinburgh. After settling in America he was employed for a time as a teacher in Philadelphia, and won a high reputation for his knowledge of the classics. Then he turned his attention to the study of the law and in due time was admitted to the bar and practiced, among other places, in Annapolis, Md., and in Reading, Pa., afterward making his home again in Philadelphia. He was a prominent advocate of the rights of the Colonies, and in the Congress of 1775, of which he was a member, he strongly advocated independence as the only possible means of escape from the evils which had brought the various Commonwealths into such a state of turmoil and dissatisfaction. In 1779 he was appointed Advocate General for the French Government in the United States, but resigned the office in 1781. He continued, however, to give professional advice to the French Government until 1783, when he received from Paris a gift of 10,000 livres in recognition of his services. He served in Congress in 1783 and 1786, and in 1789 became, by appointment of George Washington, one of the Justices of the Supreme Court of the United States. A capable lawyer, an upright and honorable citizen, wise in his counsels, and moderate, yet determined, in all his public utterances, we can easily understand that Judge Wilson held a high position in the Revolutionary councils, and how, after the turmoil of the struggle was over, he should be elevated to a seat on the highest tribunal of the country and so assist in placing the legal system of the new nation on a sure foundation. He died, while on a circuit journey, at Edenton, N. C., in 1798.

One of the most notable figures among the group of Signers, and said by some to have indeed been the real author of the Declaration, was the Rev. Dr. John Witherspoon, President of Princeton College. This great and good man was born at Yester, Haddingtonshire, in 1722. He could trace his descent from John Knox in the female line and on the other side from John Knox's heroic son-in-law, the Rev. Mr. Welsh. His father was the minister of the parish of Yester, and Witherspoon was educated for the pulpit in the University of Edinburgh. His first charge was the parish of Beith, Ayrshire, and there the excellence of his pulpit discourses, the high standard of his published writings and his natural qualities as a leader soon won for him a high rank among the Scottish clergy. In the General Assembly he became a power on the side of the Evangelical party—the party that was trying to rouse the Church from the lethargy into which it had been thrown by the rhetoric, the phrases, the artificiality of the " Moderates." Probably his work on " Ecclesiastical Characteristics," published in 1753, and directed against the Moderate party in the Scottish Church, was the most pithy and pungent bit of genuine sarcasm which Scottish theological writing had up to that time produced, and it proved the literary sensation of the hour. In 1757 he accepted a call from Paisley, and, although he had afterward calls from Dublin, Dundee, Rotterdam and other places, he remained in "Seestu" until 1768, when he accepted a demand for his services as presiding officer over Princeton College, a demand which when made on a previous occasion he had refused.

Dr. Witherspoon was a noted man before crossing to America; he had attained by his preaching and his literary capacity the highest rank among his contemporaries. In America he soon became equally popular and influential. Princeton College quickly became, under his direction, the foremost in the country, and it would have soon been regarded as among the noted seats of learning in the world had not the troubles of the Revolution paralyzed its usefulness, as they did that of all the higher educational institutions in the country. The college was finally compelled to close its doors, for around Princeton the tide of war for a time beat rudely. While the duties of his assigned office thus fell away from him, however, Dr. Witherspoon assumed others, which have given him a commanding place in the history of the Revolution. "He assisted," writes Lossing, "in framing a republican Constitution for New Jersey, and in June (1776) he was elected to a seat in the Continental Congress, where he hotly advocated independence and signed his name on the Declaration thereof. He was a faithful member of Congress until 1782 and took a conspicuous part in military and financial matters." In 1783 the time seemed ripe for renewing the activity of Princeton, and Dr. Witherspoon turned his attention from secular affairs to engage solely in that work, and he combined teaching and preaching until his death, in 1794. The saddest feature of his closing years was a visit he paid to his native land, primarily in search of financial assistance to carry on the work of his college. He was deeply pained to find his efforts in this direction a failure, but the saddest blow came from the personal treatment he received, mainly at the hands of his brother clergy. He was denounced as a traitor on every side and shunned by many who knew him well and were his friends and allies before he threw in his lot with the new republic. That sort of treatment was, however, to be expected, and it seems that even Witherspoon dreaded it when he left America on his journey to his native land. The clergy of Scotland at that time (1785) were by no means the believers in popular liberty their predecessors were, and it needed the discipline of the Disruption to bring them, as a class, once more to appreciate the power and influence of the people when rightly enlisted and directed.

Dr. Witherspoon was by no means the only Scottish clergyman who was active on the side of the Revolution. There were in reality very many such, and, indeed, it might be said that the Presbyterians and the great majority of those then classed as "nonconformists" were outspoken in favor of independence. A noted example was that of the Rev. John Roxburgh, who was born at Berwick in 1714 and settled in America in 1740. He studied for the ministry at Princeton, graduating from there in 1761, and soon after was ordained as pastor of a church in Warren County, New Jersey. In 1769 he assumed a pastorate at the Forks of Delaware and held that charge at the time of his death. He was early distinguished by his emphatic views in favor of separation, and soon after the conflict broke out he joined in the formation of a military company from his own vicinity. He became chaplain of a battalion of militia and served during most of the New Jersey campaign. At the battle of Trenton, in 1777, he was taken prisoner by a gang of Hessians and brutally murdered.

As ardent an American patriot, although less militant in his disposition, was the Rev. Henry Patillo, who was taken to America from Scotland, where he was born, in 1736, when only nine years of age. Beginning life as a clerk in a store, he studied for the ministry, was ordained in 1758, and settled in North Carolina. His ministerial labors were confined thereafter to that State, and among the negroes, especially, his work was very effective. He ranked as an excellent classical scholar, and his published volume of sermons prove him to have been a preacher of more than ordinary power. From the first, as might have been expected, he was in favor of the complete independence of the Colonies, and spoke on that once dangerous topic on every possible occasion. He was a member of the Provincial Council in 1775 and had the satisfaction of seeing the country fairly started in its national career long before he died, in 1801.

Another Scottish clergyman deserves to be recalled here, because he was outspoken in his advocacy of the principles at stake in the Revolution while still residing in Scotland and preaching there. This was the Rev. Charles Nisbet, who was born at Long Yester, Haddingtonshire, where his father was a schoolmaster, in 1728. He was educated at Edinburgh University and became pastor of a church at Montrose. It was while there that his utterances in favor of the American Revolution were delivered, and his justification of Washington and his associates was regarded with disfavor by the leading people of the district and caused him to be considered as, politically, a suspicious character. In 1783, when John Dickinson of Delaware founded at Carlisle, Pa., as a Presbyterian college, the institution which still bears his name, an offer of the Presidency was tendered to Nisbet, and he gladly accepted. He was even anxious to leave Scotland and take up his abode in a country where his sentiments concerning human liberty would be regarded as orthodox, or where at least he would have opportunity of expressing and ventilating those sentiments without giving offense. In the Statistical Account of Haddington, written in 1835, by the Rev. John Thomson, we read the following summary of Nisbet's American experiences: "Although a man of distinguished attainments, he seems to have enjoyed little comfort and less worldly prosperity in 'the land of liberty.' Although the names 'college' and 'President' sounded well, yet he found that his situation was neither more profitable nor more respectable than that which his worthy father held before him. On one occasion he wrote to his friends that 'America was certainly a land of promise, for it was all promise and no performance.'" This dolesome report was probably sent to Scotland soon after Nisbet's settlement at Carlisle, for he had at the beginning some disagreement with the trustees of the college, and he resigned his position within a few months after assuming it. The matter was, however, arranged to his satisfaction, for he was re-elected to the Presidency and continued his connection with the institution until his death, in 1804. Besides acting as President, Nisbet lectured on philosophy, systematic theology, logic, and belles-lettres. His collected writings were published in 1806, and show him to have been a man of wide reading and great ability, and a just estimate of his career, and of its value in the cause of American education, may be found in the excellent memoir which was published in 1840, by Dr. Samuel Nullis. Long after his death President Nisbet's library, a large and extensive collection, including many very rare works, was presented by his grandsons to the library of Princeton College, so that to the present day some of the usefulness of his lifetime may be said to continue in active operation.

Seeing that the clergy were so active in the Revolution, it is an easy matter to turn from them to those who in the tented field bore the brunt of the struggle and willingly encountered the horrors of war to secure the independence of the land in which they were born or which they had adopted as their own.

One of the most renowned of these heroes was Hugh Mercer, who was born at Aberdeen in 1721. He graduated in medicine at Aberdeen University and served as a surgeon or assistant surgeon in the army of Bonnie Prince Charlie, closing his Scottish military career on the field of Culloden. As soon after that as possible he crossed the Atlantic, and in 1747 we find him practicing as a physician near what is now the pleasant town of Mercersburg, in Pennsylvania. He was, however, fonder of military matters than of his own profession, and he took an active part in the campaign of General Braddock, that ended so disastrously for that warrior's reputation. In the defeat on the Monongahela, Mercer was severely wounded, and either wandered from the main force of the retreating troops or was left behind by them intentionally as being so near death that there was no use of being cumbered with him. The business of human butchery does not inspire men with kindly feelings toward each other any more than the butchery of sheep invests the breast of the butcher with pity for his bleating victims. Mercer found himself alone in the unknown forest, but with the energy so characteristic of his countrymen in many like cases, he determined to attempt, at least, to gain the nearest settlement, Fort Cumberland, about a hundred miles distant. The journey occupied several weeks, and each day had its story of remarkable adventure and constant peril. On one occasion he escaped from the clutches of a band of Indians by climbing into the trunk of a hollow tree and remaining there till they disappeared. For his bravery and suffering in this campaign he received a medal from the city of Philadelphia. Afterward he was placed in command, for a time, of Fort Duquesne.

Mercer removed, when that campaign was over, to Fredericksburg, Va., to resume the practice of his profession. By that time, however, the Revolutionary tide had fairly set in, and Mercer's abilities as a soldier were too well known to Washington and the other leaders in Virginia to allow him to remain in a peaceful walk of life when sterner work had to be done. Besides, Mercer's own entire sympathies were with the movement and he was pronounced in his views for independence as soon as the first glimmer of its light was seen. One who had already fought against King George in Scotland was not very likely to be enthusiastic in his support in America, even although circumstances led him to fight under a General (Braddock) who was one of the commanders in the victorious army at Culloden. He agitated with all his might for the maintenance of the rights of the Colonies, and in 1775 organized the afterward famous Minute Men of Virginia. He also put the militia of the State in readiness for campaigning. In 1776 Congress commissioned him a Brigadier General, on the advice of Washington, and he at once took a high place in the forces of the young republic. His military career was cut short, however, in the campaign in New Jersey. After leading the forces in a night march on Princeton, he was mortally wounded in the battle at that place on January 3, 1777, and expired a few days later. The loss of this brave man was deeply regretted by General Washington and the nation, and Congress resolved not only to erect a monument to his memory at Fredericksburg, but to educate his infant son. The body of the hero was interred in Laurel Hill Cemetery, Philadelphia, and the funeral is said to have been attended by 30,000 persons. Among the associations represented in the throng was the Philadelphia St. Andrew's Society, of which he had been a member, and which still possesses, as its most precious relic, his sword. The American writers of the Revolution vie with each other in their tributes to his honesty of purpose, his valor, and his abilities as a leader, and the words of General Wilkinson may be regarded as stating the general sentiment when he wrote: " In Mercer we lost, at Princeton, a chief who for education, talents, disposition, integrity and patriotism was second to no man but the Commander-in-Chief, Washington, and was qualified to fill the highest trusts in the country."

A much more varied, and, on the whole, a much sadder American career was that of Arthur St. Clair. This brave and at one time greatly maligned man was born at Thurso in 1734, and learned the " sodgerin' trade " in the British Army. He entered the British service as an ensign and served under Amherst at Louisbourg and under Wolfe at Quebec. In 1762 he resigned his commission, but continued his residence in America. On the outbreak of the Revolutionary War he threw in his lot with the Colonists, and was commissioned Colonel. His services and bravery were so conspicuous that in 1777 he was raised to the rank of Major General, and placed in command of the important post of Ticonderoga. That post was regarded by many of the most experienced officers as untenable, and even St. Clair was compelled to abandon it to General Burgoyne on July 5, 1777. Although some fault might be found with the details of St. Clair's defense, there was no way of evading the inevitable result, for at best the most he could have done was to delay the further movements of the enemy. The surrender of the place, however, was learned with much disfavor by the American troops, and to appease their dissatisfaction St. Clair was deprived of his active position in the forces and tried by court-martial. That tribunal completely exonerated him, and he remained with the army as a volunteer, gradually winning back by his services in that capacity his former popularity and influential position. He served in Congress from 1785 to 1787, and presided over its deliberations in the latter year. From 1788 to 1802 he was Governor of the Northwest. His last military service was in command of an expedition against the Miami Indians, in 1791, when he suffered a humiliating defeat and lost over 700 men. This disaster again turned the tide of popularity against him, and the loud censures then pronounced were more distinguished by their bitterness than by their logic. A defeated soldier, defeated under any circumstances, is never an object of much respect or regard, and although St. Clair was honorably acquitted of all blame by a committee of Congress, he never again recovered his former reputation. When, in 1802, Ohio was admitted into the sisterhood of States, St. Clair relinquished, or had to relinquish, his Governorship, and retired into obscurity and private life. He was old, poor, and dispirited, and even suffered, it is said, the terrors of poverty—the most relentless foe of old age. At length, Congress voted him a pension of sixty dollars a month, and with that his few wants were abundantly supplied and the evening gloom was not tortured by the spectre of actual want. The veteran died in 1818 at Greensburg, and over his grave a handsome monument was erected several years later by his brethren of the Masonic fraternity.

A type of military commander evolved out of the warlike exigencies of the time without previous military training, many more recent examples of which were furnished by the civil war, was Alexander McDougall, who was born in Argyllshire, in the year 1731, and settled in America with his father in 1755. He was a seaman at times, but appears to have learned, somehow, the printing trade. When the dissatisfaction with the home government had nearly reached its height, McDougall became noted in New York as one of the leading members of the Sons of Liberty, an organization called into existence by the opposition to the Stamp Act, in 1765. The feeling of loyalty which the rescinding of that act aroused did not, for various reasons, last very long. One would almost think, by reading the history of the time, that the Home Government really wanted to drive the Colonists into open rebellion, and in 1769 McDougall was arrested and thrown into prison as being the author, or chief compiler, of an address to the people, which was decreed by the authorities to be "an infamous and seditious libel." His career as a popular hero dated from the moment of his incarceration. In Booth's "History of the City of New York" we read: "A daily ovation was rendered him by his friends, who regarded him as a martyr to the cause of liberty. The ladies flocked in crowds to the cell of the imprisoned patriot, and so numerous were his visitors that, in order to gain leisure for the defense of his cause, he was obliged to publish a card fixing his hours for public receptions. He remained in jail to the April term of the court, when the Grand Jury found a bill against him, to which he pleaded not guilty. A few days afterward he was released on bail." When war was declared, McDougall went to "the front" as Colonel of the regiment from New York City. His military merit was such that he was speedily raised to the rank of Major General, and he was particularly conspicuous in the battles of White Plains and Germantown. Between 1778 and 1780 he had command of the forts along the Hudson River, one of the most important posts in the American Army, and fulfilled his trust to the entire satisfaction of his colleagues. In 1781 he was elected to Congress, was for a time Minister of Marine, and was sent to the United States Senate in 1783. He died some three years later, while still filling that position, to the great regret of General Washington and all who were associated with him in military or political life.

Another instance of evolution from civil life to high military command is afforded by the career of Lachlan McIntosh, who from being a merchant's clerk and a land surveyor developed into a Brigadier General. His father, John Mohr McIntosh, was head of a small sept of the MacIntosh clan, and in 1736 settled in Georgia, with 100 of his followers, on a place to which they gave the name of Inverness, but which is now known as Darien. Lachlan was born at Badenoch, Inverness-shire, in 1727, accompanied his father to Georgia, and grew up an enthusiastic American patriot. When the war broke out he volunteered his services, and was commissioned Colonel, becoming a General in 1776. As a result of a duel, in which he mortally wounded Button Gwinnett, one of the Signers of the Declaration of Independence, considerable ill-feeling was aroused against him in Georgia, although he was not the challenger in the duel, and was acquitted after standing his trial on a charge of murder. The trouble, however, was so serious that McIntosh was given for a time a command in the West, with headquarters at Pittsburgh. In 1779 he was second in command at the siege of Savannah, and took part in the defense of Charleston. When that town was surrendered, in 1780, McIntosh was made a prisoner, and with that terminated his military career. He retired to Virginia until the close of the war, and then settled in Savannah. His closing years were marked by poverty, and he was undoubtedly glad when his period of waiting came to an end, and he entered into rest, in 1806.

In many ways one of the most prominent figures in the Revolutionary struggle was the hero who was known to his contemporaries as the Earl of Stirling. He was generally addressed by his title; but he was a devoted adherent of the republic, and the son of a man who was in every respect as ardent an American patriot as he became. With the justice of his claim to be Earl of Stirling, we have nothing here to do. He preferred the claim in due form to the British House of Lords in 1759 and backed it up with various proofs, notably a genealogical tree showing his descent from John, the uncle of the first Earl. The House of Lords took nearly three years to digest the material placed before it, and then decreed against the validity of the claim. He refused to acquiesce in this decision, and continued to assume the title until the end of his career. The American family commenced with James Alexander, who, for his share in the rebellion of 1715, had to leave Scotland. He settled in New York and was appointed its Surveyor General, and Governor Burnet made him a member of his council. He was held in high esteem, and, along with Benjamin Franklin and others, was one of the founders of the Philosophical Society of America. By his marriage with the Scotch widow of an American trader, he had four daughters (one of whom married General John Reid, founder of the Chair of Music in Edinburgh University and composer of the famous song " In the Garb of Old Gaul ") and one son, the claimant of the Stirling peerage and its acknowledged holder in America. He died in 1756.

Major William Alexander, or the Earl of Stirling, as he preferred to be called, and as, for that reason if for no other, we will call him, was born in New York in 1726. After a short experience in commercial affairs, he became private secretary and aide-de-camp to General Shirley, then commanding the Colonial forces, and when that officer was recalled, Lord Stirling accompanied him to England. His time there was mainly devoted to the prosecution of his peerage claims, with the unfavorable result already mentioned. On his return to America, he was appointed Surveyor General of New York and a member of the Council in New Jersey. He threw himself with the utmost ardor into the movement for independence, although thereby he knew that he dissipated any chance he might have for a legal acknowledgment of his claims to the peerage, and started in the war as Colonel of a regiment. His promotion was rapid and his military career brilliant. In January, 1776, he captured a British transport in the Bay of New York with a small force, and in March of that year he was placed in command of New York and dexterously fortified the city and harbor. He was taken prisoner near Brooklyn, on Long Island, but exchanged, and took part in the battles of Brandywine, Germantown, and Monmouth. In 1781, with the rank of Major General, he was placed in command of the Northern Army, with headquarters at Albany, and he died in that city in 1783. "It is a singular fact," says Lossing, "that during the War of Independence, Lord Stirling had command at different times of every brigade in the American Army, except those of South Carolina and Georgia." By his marriage with Sarah, eldest daughter of Philip Livingston, Lord Stirling had two daughters, but no son, and so the claims of his branch of the Alexander family to the peerage died with him. In the brilliant galaxy of Revolutionary heroes, he holds an honored place, but his memory is perhaps now held in greener remembrance for the services he performed for Columbia College, of which he was for a long time one of the Governors.

These soldiers we have just named are all recognized as leaders in the Revolutionary cause, and their deeds and lives have become part and parcel of American history. There were hundreds of others less prominent, however, but by no means less brave, less loyal to the cause, less self-sacrificing, or, in a sense, less needful. That struggle was one in which all who took part in it had to do their utmost and to fulfill the duties allotted to them with scrupulous fidelity, and when every man's work was really necessary to success. Among these now less known heroes mention may be made of Colonel John Murray, one of the bravest of men, who represented Pennsylvania in the struggle. He was born in Perthshire in 1731 and settled near the town of Dauphin, Pa., with his father, in 1766. He commenced his active career as a military patriot in March, 1776, when he was appointed to the command of a company in a regiment of rifles. A year later he had won the rank of Major, and in 1778 was Colonel of the Second Pennsylvania Regiment. He continued in active service until the termination of hostilities, in 1783, having been present at the battles of Long Island, White Plains, Trenton, Princeton, Germantown, and Brandywine, besides skirmishes innumerable. When the struggle was over he retired to Dauphin County, was appointed a Justice of the Peace in 1791 and so continued in the duties of active citizenship until his death, in 1798. A brother of this hero, James Murray, who came from Scotland with the rest of the family, served through the war, mostly as Captain in the Pennsylvania troops.

Another Scottish-American who figured very conspicuously in Pennsylvania's quota of patriots was William Leiper, who was one of the founders of the famous Philadelphia City Troop, and served with it during the greater part of the war. He was born at Strathaven in 1745, settled in Maryland in 1763, but removed to Philadelphia two years later, and thereafter made it his home. He engaged in the business of storing and exporting tobacco and the manufacture of tobacco and snuff, and amassed a large fortune. For years he was looked upon as one of the most public-spirited of the citizens of Philadelphia, and every scheme for the advancement of the city or for the promotion of its interests found in him a liberal and thoughtful patron. The first tramway in America was laid under Leiper's direction, in 1809, and as President of the Philadelphia Common Council he proved a model official by the interest he took in every matter pertaining to the welfare of the city. He served also as a Presidential Elector, and was one of the first, if not the first, to nominate Andrew Jackson, his beau ideal among America's public men, for the Presidency. Mr. Leiper's later years were spent in dignified retirement, and as he survived till 1825, he had the satisfaction of seeing his adopted country prosperous and progressive after almost half a century of independence.

William Fleming, who was born in Lanarkshire in 1740, may serve as a type of the Southern soldier. He emigrated when twenty years of age and settled on a large tract of land at Botecourt, Augusta County, Va. His property steadily increased in value until, in the prime of life, Fleming could regard himself as a fairly rich man. In the district in which he had settled he was very popular. He had received a good education, was well read, and was a man of fine appearance, and these qualities, joined with his fondness for athletic sports, together with a commonly credited report that he was really of aristocratic parentage, his generous hospitality, and his interest in public affairs, won him hosts of friends. When the outbreak with the mother country was imminent, Fleming raised a regiment which he afterward commanded at the battle of Point Pleasant. His military career ended with that engagement, however, for in it he received a wound, from the effects of which he never fully recovered. Colonel Fleming is said by some authorities to have served for a short time as Governor of Virginia during the troubles.

Of all the soldiers in the Revolution, none had, on the whole, a more extraordinary career than James Swan, who was born in Fifeshire in 1754 and settled in Boston when a young man. He was for a time a mercantile clerk, but soon became more noted for his advocacy of the movement for independence than for his business abilities, although, as long subsequent events showed, his business qualities were of a high order. He formed one of the celebrated "Boston Tea Party" and acted as an aide de camp to Gen. Warren at Bunker Hill. In that famous skirmish he was severely wounded. Afterward as a Captain in Crafts's regiment of artillery Swan saw much active service, and he was in the expedition that compelled the British forces to leave Boston Harbor. As Secretary to the Massachusetts Board of War, as member of the State Legislature, and as Adjutant General of the State, he rendered a series of magnificent services to the Commonwealth. But while thus winning honors as a patriot his private fortunes were not flourishing, and, despairing of meeting with much financial success in the then unsettled state of the country, Swan retired from public life and went to France. There in a few years he accumulated a fortune, and when he returned to the United States, in 1795, he was noted equally for his wealth, his charity, and his munificence. In 1798 he returned to Europe and engaged in large commercial ventures, all of which were wonderfully successful. In 1815 his career was cut short by his being arrested and lodged in prison on charges preferred by a German with whom he had had dealings. He remained in durance until 1830, living meantime in a style of the greatest luxury and enjoying the additional prodigality of a score of lawsuits. A year later he died in Paris. Swan was a man of brilliant genius, of that there is no doubt, and he possessed many of the qualities of a statesman, as well as those of a soldier and a merchant. His pamphlets on the fisheries of Massachusetts show that he was alive to the importance of an industry then wholly unappreciated, while his work against the slave trade, published at Boston in 1773, demonstrated his belief that all men, black and white, are born free and equal, long before that sentiment became recognized, even as a figure of speech, in the Declaration of Independence.

It is singular to find that several Scots took part in the battle of Bunker Hill, and, having just mentioned one who fought on the American side, it may not be out of place to recall another Scot, and also another native of Fifeshire, who was in the opposing ranks—in the ranks of King George. This was John Pitcairn, son of the Rev. David Pitcairn, minister of Dysart, and a representative of the old Fifeshire house of Pitcairn of Pitcairn. John Pitcairn, when twenty-five years of age, became a Captain in the Royal Marines, and was commissioned a Major in 1771. He was for a considerable time stationed at Boston, and had the reputation of being the only British officer who showed any consideration for the people in their frequent petty troubles with the soldiery. On April 19, 1775, he was in command of the British squad in the famous skirmish at Lexington, generally regarded as the opening contest in the Revolutionary War. Bancroft says: " Pitcairn rode in front, and, when within five or six rods of the Minute Men, cried out: ' Disperse, ye villains! Ye rebels, disperse! Lay down your arms! Why don't you lay down your arms and disperse?' The main part of the countrymen stood motionless in the ranks, witnesses against aggression; too few to resist, too brave to fly. At this Pitcairn discharged a pistol and with a loud voice cried ' Fire!' The order was followed first by a few guns which did no execution, and then by a close and deadly discharge of musketry." This very circumstantial story has, however, been denied in most of its details by other historians, and Pitcairn himself always averred that it was the Minute Men who fired the first shot. Seven of the latter were killed, among them being Robert Munroe, a Scotsman, who as an ensign in one of the Highland regiments had helped to win Louisbourg for his country from the French in 1758. In the retreat from Concord on the afternoon of the Lexington affray Pitcairn had to abandon his horse and pistols, and very nearly lost his life. At Bunker Hill he was conspicuous for his bravery. In the last assault made on the hill he was the first to climb to the redoubt, which he did, crying: " Now for the glory of the marines! " but fell mortally wounded by a shot fired by a negro—the last shot, it is said, fired in the fight. Major Pitcairn was carried to the City of Boston, and died within a few hours. He had married early in life Elizabeth, daughter of Robert Dalrymple of Annefield, Dumfries-shire, and left her a widow with eleven children. She secured a pension of £200 a year from the British Government, and her eldest son, David, became one of the most noted physicians in London, dying in that city in 1809, the recognized head of his profession.

We have probably said enough about the military heroes of the Revolution—adduced sufficient instances to prove the importance of the Scotch element in it. We may, therefore, turn to another field—that of statesmanship—which was as essential to the success of the movement as the military prowess of the warriors. Had the advice of the Scotch settlers, or of the majority of the Scotch representatives of the Home Government, been taken, there would never have been any revolution at all—at least at the time and under the circumstances it did. Alexander Kennedy, for example, who was Collector of Customs at the Port of New York, and in 1750 a member of the Provincial Council, was continually, in his letters to headquarters, in his reports, and in his published writings, urging the importance of the American Colonies to the mother country and advocating measures and giving suggestions which, if carried out, would undoubtedly have strengthened their loyalty and added to their wealth and prosperity. But no attention was paid to such warning voices. Kennedy, who became Receiver General of the Province of New York—proof sufficient that he was a man possessing some influence with the home powers—was descended from the third Earl of Cassilis. He married a Miss Massam of New York, and when he died, in 1763, left a son, Archibald. This son became a Captain in the Royal Navy, and in 1792, on the death of the tenth Earl of Cassilis without issue, succeeded to the Earldom. He had married Anne, sister of John Watts, at one time President of the St. Andrew's Society of New York, and their descendants still hold the old title and the newer one of Marquis of Ailsa. Anne Watts lies buried in the Chapel of Holyrood under a plain flat stone. One of the younger sons of this marriage married the sister of Alexander Macomb, who, in 1828, became Commander in Chief of the United States Army.

The most brilliant statesman of the Revolution was Alexander Hamilton, who was born in the island of Nevis, British West Indies, his father being a native of Scotland and his mother a Frenchwoman. He learned business routine in a mercantile house at St. Croix, and when sixteen years of age came to this country with his widowed mother. He then entered King's College and studied law. His public life may be said to have begun when, at the age of seventeen years, he commenced making speeches in favor of freedom, and in 1775 he helped the Sons of Liberty to carry off the cannon from Fort George, (now the Battery,) New York. To trace this man's career would be to write the history of the country during its continuance. He served in the war, in Congress, and was Secretary of the Treasury in Washington's first Cabinet. No one enjoyed to a greater extent the confidence of the "Father of his Country," and when, in 1798, Washington assumed command of the provisional army it was with the distinct understanding that Hamilton should be his chief associate. His later years were spent in New York in the prosecution of his private law business, but he took the keenest interest in politics and national affairs. It was this interest and a knowledge of the influence he deservedly exerted that led to a dispute with the notorious Aaron Burr and to the latter sending him a challenge to a duel. According to the fashion of the time, Hamilton had to accept, and the parties met near Weehawken on July 11, 1804, almost on the spot where Hamilton's son had been killed in a similar encounter a few years before. Hamilton fired in the air. Burr shot straight at his opponent, who fell, mortally wounded, and died the next day. There was a terrible outburst of public indignation when the news of the duel spread abroad, and Burr was denounced as a murderer, and for the remainder of his long life was not only ostracised by society, but was everywhere shunned, and he sank into obscurity. Hamilton was interred with all possible honors in Trinity Churchyard. He was throughout his life proud of his Scotch descent; joined the New York St. Andrew's Society in 1784, and that organization marked the spot where he fell by a neat memorial stone. That monument has long ago disappeared—removed by relic hunters for the most part—and although the erection of another stone on the site has often been discussed by New York Scotsmen in recent years nothing practical has resulted. It is even doubtful if the exact site could now be determined, so great have been the changes in the vicinity.

The family of Watts was a conspicuous one in the Revolution, and, like many others, was divided by that outbreak into loyalists and Americans. According to Gen. De Peyster, the present able and cultured representative of the family, its American progenitor was John Watt of Rosehill, near Edinburgh, who settled in America toward the close of the seventeenth century. His son, John, became a noted figure in local affairs, and, had the Revolution been suppressed, would have been Lieutenant Governor of the Colony of New York. He represented the city in the Assembly for many years and was a member of Council. As one of the wealthiest landed proprietors in the colony, he was munificent in his private charity and in his public benefactions. He was one of the founders and Trustees of the New York Society Library, and in 1760 was the first President of the New York City Hospital. In the early Revolutionary struggle he was noted for his strong loyalist proclivities, and when hostilities began he went to England and there remained till his death, in 1789. By his marriage with the daughter of Stephen De Lancey he had a large family. "Robert, the eldest son," writes Gen. De Peyster, "married Mary, eldest daughter of William Alexander, titular Earl of Stirling; Ann, their eldest daughter, married the Hon. Archibald Kennedy and became Countess of Cassilis; Susan married Philip Kearney and was mother of Major Gen. Stephen Watts Kearney, the conqueror of New Mexico and California; Mary married Sir John Johnston, Bart., and, like her father, suffered the pains of exile and confiscation of property; Stephen, the famous Major Watts of Oriskany, and John, the public benefactor." We give this really correct genealogical record as an examplification of the way in which most of the old Scotch families have spread through what are now regarded as leading American houses, very few of which at the present day cannot point to some Scotch name in their family tree.

John Watts, the son of this expatriated colonist, was bred to the study of the law, and was the last of the Royal Recorders of New York, serving in that capacity from 1774 to 1777. As he threw in his lot with the winning side in the war, a large proportion of the confiscated estate of his father was returned to him and his brothers. He became Speaker of the New York Assembly—from 1791 to 1794—served in Congress for two years, and in 1806 became first Judge of Westchester County, N. Y. He performed many good services to his country and deserved all the honors he enjoyed, but his memory is best preserved by his noble act in founding and endowing with a legacy that came to him under distressful circumstances the Leake and Watts Orphan House, in New York, a charity which to the present day continues its beneficent work. Like his father, he showed his partiality to his ancestral country by joining the ranks of the St. Andrew's Society, and in many other ways he demonstrated his warm heart for the old land. A fine statue of this patriot-jurist, representing him in his robes as Recorder, has been erected in Trinity Churchyard, New York, by his descendant, Gen. J. Watts de Peyster. A more suitable site for such a memorial could not be found, excepting, perhaps, the corner of Twenty-sixth Street and Second Avenue, on the grounds upon which Bellevue Hospital is now located—grounds which formerly belonged to his family.

A much less known statesman than any of those we have yet mentioned, yet a man whose services were of the utmost consequence to the young republic, was John Ross, a native of Tain, who, in his day—a day before the Revolutionary sentiment developed into war—was one of the wealthiest citizens of Philadelphia. Ross had learned the principles of business in Perth, to which his family had removed when he was very young. He settled in Philadelphia in 1763, and soon was noted for his enthusiastic advocacy of the principles which were tending to political independence; and for separation as the natural and only possible outcome of the entire sea of troubles brought about by the incapacity or carelessness or arrogance, or all three combined, of the Home Government, he was decidedly outspoken. In 1776 he was appointed by Congress to attend to the purchase of stores—clothing, arms, ammunition, wagons, camp utensils, &c.—for the army, and his whole business energy and tact were devoted to his duties in that connection. He was too honest a man to fill such a position—one of the few honest army contractors on record—and his own means were liberally placed at the disposal of his office. He proved his patriotism by his bawbees, and cheerfully invested his whole fortune in supplementing the grants given by Congress for the purposes of his department. In this way he not only exhausted his own resources, but found himself confronted by debts amounting to over £20,000. This sum he had to make good, for Congress was unable to pay it, and dallied over the matter, as is customary for deliberative bodies on too many occasions when real business has to be transacted. Mr. Ross was a man of great intelligence, and enjoyed the friendship of such men as Washington, Benjamin Franklin, and Robert Morris. After the war he resumed business in Philadelphia, and died in that city in 1800, in the seventy-first year of his age.

Another Scot who did much in his own sphere to bring about the Revolution was William Murdoch, who was born at Glasgow in 1720. He came to America with his father, the Rev. George Murdoch, when that gentleman was appointed Rector of Prince George County, Maryland, by Lord Baltimore. William was a member of the lower house of the General Assembly of Maryland from 1745 till 1770, and was determined in his opposition to all tax edicts not imposed by or sanctioned by the people. He became recognized as one of the leaders of the House, and it was mainly through him that it was placed so clearly on record on the popular side. In the resistance to the Stamp act he was particularly conspicuous, and there is no doubt he would have taken the field to support his principles had he not died in 1775, just as the crisis had been reached.

Hitherto we have been dealing with honorable men—

men who, however much people might differ with them as to their views or actions, were still entitled to be respected on account of the honesty of their motives and the uprightness of their conduct, if for no other reasons. It may be well, therefore, for the sake of variety to recall one who was a timeserver and traitor, the only one deserving of these epithets which the writer of this book has met with (with the exception, probably, of Gen. Andrew Williamson, who for his dubious conduct at Charleston and elsewhere was called "the Benedict Arnold of the South,") in his study of the part Scotsmen took in the founding of America. This was John Allan, a native of Edinburgh. He was taken to Nova Scotia by his father when only three years of age, so that on behalf of puir auld Scotland we may take what comfort we can in the reflection that the good influences of Auld Reekie did not have much to do with the molding of his character—a fortunate thing for the reputation of Auld Reekie. John prospered in the colony. He studied law, became Clerk to the Supreme Court, and from 1770 to 1776 was a member of the House of Assembly. He sided with the Americans in the Revolutionary War, although Nova Scotia was intense in its loyalty, and he used his position to aid the Revolutionists against the Home and Colonial Governments. He secretly sent them information, tried to sway over the Indians to their side, and in many other ways attempted to weaken the influences which held Nova Scotia aloof from the Revolution, and all the while that he was bound by his oath and his office and salary to protect British and Colonial interests. His perfidy was at last discovered, and he found it expedient to fly across into Maine. His wife was imprisoned by the authorities in the hope of learning from her as much as possible of the extent of his machinations, while his angry neighbors burned his house to the ground. He seems, however, unlike most traitors, to have been very well repaid for his losses and troubles by those to whom he had rendered his foul services. In 1792 Massachusetts gave him a gift of 22,000 acres of land, (on part of which the town of Whiting now stands,) and in 1801 Congress granted him 2,000 acres in Ohio. It seems impossible to say a word in favor of this man's course. Had he openly avowed his attachment to the principles of the Revolution and, like the heroes of that struggle, candidly thrown off his allegiance to Britain, no stigma could have attached itself to his memory, but to act the part of a traitor is inexcusable. This man, in a minor degree, simply played the part which Benedict Arnold played, and deserves to be held in proportionate contempt.

Many well-known American families date their rise into prominence from the part their progenitors on this side took in the pre-Revolutionary movement, as well as in the struggle itself, and several of them can trace their descent clearly from well-known and ancient Scottish houses. The Rutherfurds, for instance, are descended from Sir John Rutherfurd of Edgerston, whose eldest son fought in America in 1758, and was killed in the attack on Ticonderoga that year, and through him from a Bishop of Caithness, from whom Sir Walter Scott claimed descent. The late Gen. Winfield Scott, who was in command of the American Army at the outbreak of the civil war, a position which he attained after a long series of distinguished services, and from which he retired on account of the infirmities of age, was the grandson of a Scot who fought for Prince Charlie at Culloden and was glad to make his escape to Virginia. His son, the General's father, was a determined advocate of separation when the crisis came, and the General himself lived in retirement until May, 1866—long enough to learn that the Nation had emerged from the greatest civil war on record, with the Stars and Stripes still the flag of the country from the lakes to the Gulf. Another noted and earlier warrior of the same name was Gen. John Morin Scott, who was born in America in 1730 and was fourth in descent from Sir John Scott of Ancrum, one of the first baronets of Nova Scotia, descended in his turn from the Scotts of Balwearie—the head of the house. Gen. J. Morin Scott was a graduate of Yale University, and, possessing a ready and vigorous pen, used it with marked purpose in assailing the measures by which the British Government finally drove the Colonies into armed opposition. He was long a member—and a very influential one—of the Provincial Council of New York, and in 1776, having been appointed a Brigadier General, he fought with distinction at the battle of Long Island and elsewhere. In 1777 he was Secretary of State for New York; for a time he was at the head of a Committee of Safety when the exigencies of the struggle left the Government of New York in a chaotic condition, and he closed a memorable and in every way honorable career by serving in Congress for three years. He retired from active work in 1783, died a year later, and was buried in Trinity Churchyard—the historic God's-acre of New York.

But by far the most noted of the Scottish American families of the Revolutionary period and after, from a national, State and municipal point of view, was that of the Livingstons. A family which numbers among its members one of the greatest of the old Patroons, a Chancellor of the State of New York, a Signer of the Declaration of Independence, a Justice of the United States Supreme Court, a Secretary of State of the United States, a Governor of New Jersey, besides soldiers, poets, and statesmen of all degrees, is surely entitled to be regarded as pre-eminent. A volume or two would be required to relate its story, and in this place there is no opportunity for doing more than briefly indicating what the family has done to mold and develop the great republic of to-day. It is commonly said that the American patriots had no fathers, meaning by that, of course, that their fathers were of the commonplace order and were not worth mentioning except as links in a genealogical chain, of no more importance than the links in the chain supporting a gorgeous badge of office are to the gorgeous badge itself. But the Scotch ancestor from whom the American Livingstons sprung had a life history as interesting as any individual who ever founded a family, and in many ways more important than most others. For that reason we refer to it here, for, although John Livingstone of Ancrum was not a Scottish-American and never saw

America, it was not his fault. He made the attempt and the elements were against him. It is difficult to learn much about the progenitors of the American Revolutionary heroes, to know what manner of men they were, how far their careers were likely to influence their children, and the principles which animated them while they were engaged in the battle of life. But the character of the immediate ancestor of the American Livingstons is known by all who care to read his writings or study the records of his career and of his opinions, which he himself and others have handed down to us. In him we find all the features which made the family in America so prominent in public life. He was a typical Scotsman. He was steadfast, brave, outspoken, yet cautious. He stood resolutely for the truth, sacrificed everything rather than give up his convictions, and would have preferred passing through life in the character of a humble but devoted minister of the Gospel rather than that of the public defender of a principle which, in the long run, all the machinery and power of the Government were to be employed to crush out. His own ambition was to remain a minister—" a servant in the vineyard of the Lord," as he expressed it. Circumstances, instead, forced him to become a leader; to carry on what has been called the evangelical succession in the Kirk of Scotland, after it had been in the hands of John Knox, Andrew Melville, and Alexander Henderson.

Robert Livingston, the first of the American family and the youngest son of this patriot preacher, was born in the manse at Ancrum in 1654. He was educated in Holland, with the view of following a commercial career, and left that country for America about a year after his father's death. He first tried Charleston, but soon moved from there and settled in New York State, where he at once entered upon a successful career. In 1680 he became Secretary of the Commissaries at Albany, made money as an Indian trader and in practicing law, and in 1686 became Town Clerk of the City of Albany, a position he held till 1721. In 1686 he received from Governor Dongan a large tract of land on the Hudson, the beginning of the vast territorial possessions of the family, and this Colonial grant was in 1715 confirmed by royal charter from George I., a charter which conferred manorial privileges to the holder of the estate. He served in the Colonial Assembly for many years, and was once Speaker of that body. He had the Scotch " knack " of holding on to whatever he acquired, and long before he died, in 1725, he was regarded as one of the wealthiest and most influential citizens of the colony.

Robert Livingston married the widow (née Schuyler) of a minister, a member of the Van Rensselaer family, and this union brought him into social relations with the oldest and most dignified Knickerbocker families of the colony. By her he had three sons and several daughters. The eldest son, Philip, succeeded to the principal family possessions and added to them mainly by his success as an Indian trader, and among his sons was Peter Van Brugh Livingston, who was President of the New York Congress; Philip, one of the Signers of the Declaration of Independence, and William, Governor of New Jersey. It was to one of his descendants that Robert Fulton, the engineer and steam navigation pioneer, was married—a marriage to which was due the necessary financial backing to make the Clermont a success. From the second son, Robert, who acquired the estate of Clermont, perhaps the most noted branch of the family was descended. His son, Judge R. R. Livingston, was the father of the famous Chancellor R. R. Livingston, who administered the oath of office to George Washington on the latter's taking up the Presidency in accordance with the voice of the people; of Henry B. Livingston, who was one of the bravest officers in the Revolutionary Army, and of Edward Livingston, Secretary of State under Andrew Jackson, and whose services in the acquisition of Louisiana are still gratefully remembered. Edward was probably the ablest man of his family after the ancestor of Ancrum, but his life, on the whole, was too full of disappointments to be a happy one. One of his sisters was married to Gen. Montgomery of Quebec fame, another to Secretary of War Armstrong, and a third to Gov. Morgan Lewis. A score or more names of other American descendants of the persecuted Scotch preacher might be named as illustrious examples in various and honored walks in life, but enough has been said to show that the influence of the humble Scottish manse led to wonderful results in the New World. Probably no family on record ever had so many distinguished representatives within the space of a few generations as that of this branch of an ancient Scotch house.

Before leaving the Livingston family we may here recall the stormy career of Col. James Moncrieff, who was related to Gov. William Livingston and other Americans by marriage. He was born in Fifeshire about 1735 and was educated at Woolwich as a military engineer, but seems to have faced the world for himself in the capacity of Captain of a privateer. He was in New York when the Revolutionary turmoil culminated in hostilities, and it was thought that he would throw in his lot with the Colonists, but he declined to throw off his allegiance to the Crown. In 1776 he served under Lord Percy on Staten Island, and two years later was taken prisoner at Flatbush, L. I. Afterward he performed valuable services for the royal forces at Savannah, and it was he who planned the defensive works at Charleston when the British held that seaport. He was commissioned Lieutenant Colonel in 1780, and certainly deserved that recognition of his endeavors, but it is a pity that his memory should be tarnished by some grave charges which have never been satisfactorily cleared away—notably one of shipping 800 slaves from Charleston to the West Indies with the view of pocketing by the sale of these human beings. He certainly was a brave man and an able soldier, but he did not seem to impress his military superiors very favorably or to be generally well liked. Of his closing years nothing is known beyond the fact that he died in France in 1793.

On the sea the Scots in America, although by no means as numerous in number as those who took part in the stirring events on shore, won equally noteworthy records. The most famous of these, with a reputation extending over the Old World as well as the New, is Paul Jones, although a very varied estimate of his character is taken. By some he is spoken about as famous, by others as notorious, and between these extremes lie very considerable ground for argument and opinion. Briefly summed up, his career was as follows: He was born at Arbigland, Kirkcudbrightshire, in 1747, the son of a gardener named John Paul, after whom he was named. His parents were poor, but they kept him in attendance at the parish school until he was twelve years of age, long enough to give him a good rudimentary education, and then he was sent to earn his own living as a sailor. A year later he crossed the Atlantic for the first time and visited an elder brother, William, who had settled on the banks of the Rappahannock, in Virginia, and married a Virginia girl. He was welcomed there, and possibly the kindly reception he met with warmed his heart to America. He continued in the merchant service, making many voyages, among them at least two slave-catching expeditions, until 1773, when, hearing that his brother had died in Virginia childless and without leaving a will, he hastened there to settle up the estate. It was at this time that for some reason now unknown he assumed the name of Jones.

He seems to have invested his means in Tobago and to have soon lost everything by the mismanagement or dishonesty of agents there. Then he turned planter and hoped to devote his time to peaceful pursuits. But soon the rush of events brought the Colonies face to face with the mother country, and Capt. Jones, as he was called, espoused the popular cause. In defending his position he afterward wrote: "I was indeed born in Britain; but I do not inherit the degenerate spirit of that fallen nation, which I at once lament and despise. It is far beneath me to reply to their hireling invectives. They are strangers to the envied approbation that greatly animates and rewards the man who draws his sword only in support of the dignity of freedom. America has been the country of my fond election from the age of thirteen, when I first saw it. I had the honor to hoist, with my own hands, the flag of freedom the first time it was displayed on the Delaware, and I have attended it with veneration ever since on the ocean."

This raising of the flag occurred on the Alfred, one of the five ships which constituted the American Navy when the Revolutionary War broke out. Jones, on the first sign of hostilities, offered his services to the Congress, and he was appointed First Lieutenant of the Alfred. The details of his naval career are so well known, so fully recorded even in American school histories, that there is little use in occupying space with recording them here. They prove Jones to have been a most skillful seaman, an able manager of men, an ingenious tactician, and a brave man. In the course of it, however, he visited his birthplace and landed a force, with the intention, according to his own letters, of capturing Lord Selkirk and carrying him away to America as a hostage. But Lord Selkirk was not in his mansion, and the seamen had to content themselves with robbing the premises of all the silver plate they could find. This adventure is the great blot upon Paul Jones's character, and his correspondence shows that he saw a blunder had been made. He returned the plate, or as much of it as he could, after a time, and explained his motives. It stamped him, in the eyes of his fellow-countrymen at home, not as a patriot fighting for freedom, but as a pirate of the most vulgar and mercenary sort, for no one with any spark of sentiment would have wantonly carried the horrors of war to his own birthplace. Besides, he used the early knowledge he had obtained of St. Mary's Isle to rob the place of its treasure chest. However the people may have been justified in their views of the adventure or not, there is no doubt that Jones's yarn about desiring to capture Lord Selkirk is a very improbable one, for Lord Selkirk was too unimportant a personage to affect in any way the conduct of the war or to bring about any wholesale discharge of American prisoners. It seems more likely that Jones's men wanted plunder and he took them where he knew they might get some with the utmost ease, and in a place which he was perfectly aware was wholly unprotected. Then, having seen the mistake he made, he tried to remedy it as best he could. Lord Selkirk was very glad to get back as much of his property as he did, but that did not alter the complexion of the affair with the mass of the people, and Jones was regarded by his brother Scots as being a mercenary cutthroat and robber, a light in which they did not consider any of the other Scots who fought against King George in the Revolution. Jones's subsequent descents on the British coast, notably his proposed capture of Edinburgh and Leith while in command of a squadron of French ships carrying the American flag, while more legitimate under the circumstances, did not alter this popular feeling, for it was felt that he might have left puir auld Scotland alone, if he had a Scottish heart in his breast at all. However, his career was a wonderful one, and he richly earned the honors which his adopted country awarded him. On the conclusion of the war Jones attempted to establish a fur trade between the American Northwest territories and Japan and China, but the scheme fell through. In 1787, after being disappointed in hopes of active service in other directions, he accepted an appointment in the Russian service, and took a prominent part in the war with Turkey. His fortunes seemed to rise to their highest point at that time, but he was the victim of intrigue and jealousy on the part of others who favored the course of the Empress Catherine, and, weary and worn out, he ultimately resigned from her service. Then he retired to Paris, where, after a long illness, he died in 1789, in the forty-fifth year of his age.

How a man could pose as a pure devotee of freedom and unsheath his sword with equal readiness in the service of the American Congress, and of that abandoned, cruel wretch, the Empress Catherine II. of Russit, is, it seems to us, a conundrum that would require a good deal of reasoning to demonstrate. Except for office, there was nothing to attract any man to the service of the Russian autocrat, least of all one who avowed to be opposed to the tyranny of Britain. Nor can it be pretended that the campaign he waged for Catherine against the Turks had anything to do with liberty. It was simply a matter of position and pay. He forsook the Stars and Stripes and all that glorious ensign meant for the world and talked glibly of the " honor of the Russian flag and the interests of Her (Russian) Majesty."

This, however, is not the generally prevailing idea of the character of Paul Jones. A recent writer puts the popular American idea very clearly as follows:

" It is not necessary at this day to refute the slanders once current against Paul Jones; but, incredible as it may seem, within the last ten years he has been described in popular verse as a notorious pirate, in a leading American newspaper as a privateer, and in a book alleged to be for the instruction of American youth as a 'bold marauder!' This, be it remembered, applies to a man who headed the list of the First Lieutenants appointed in the navy of the Colonies on Dec. 12, 1775; who held the first Captain's commission granted under the United States, Aug. 8, 1776; who was made the commanding officer of all American ships in European waters in 1778; who received the thanks of Congress in 1781; who was unanimously elected by Congress to be the first officer of the American Navy in 1781, and who received a gold medal from Congress, similar to that given to Washington, in 1787. Moreover, he was presented with a gold sword by Louis XVI. of France, and also with the Grand Cross of the Order of Military Merit, never before given to a foreigner. He was also a Rear Admiral in the service of Russia, and received the Order of St. Anne from the Empress Catherine. Greater tributes than any foreign honor or order he received were the esteem in which he was held by Washington, and the affection felt for him by Franklin, Morris, Jefferson, and Lafayette. If they are worthy of belief, Paul Jones was an unswerving patriot, and a very great man. * * *
He served with the utmost distinction in the Continental Navy, but without pay or allowance. The British Government officially declared him a 'traitor, pirate, and felon,' and put a price of 10,000 guineas upon his head;

but he was no more a traitor, pirate, or felon than Washington was, or any other man who, born a British subject, chose to throw off his allegiance."

We fear this reasoning, even with the impartial sentiment which prevails in these later days of peace and good will, will hardly be accepted. There is a wide difference between the cases of the patriots named and the case of Paul Jones. Washington, Franklin, and Jefferson, although originally British subjects, were born in America. Morris was by birth an Englishman, Lafayette a Frenchman; yet neither of these men fired a shot against the countries which gave them birth. We cannot, reviewing the career of Paul Jones, regard him in the light of a disinterested patriot, nor hold him up to detestation as a pirate pure and simple. He was simply a maritime Dugald Dalgetty, true to whatever cause he fought for, and, naturally, uttering its shibboleths and upholding its right; but, while placing this estimate upon his worth, we cannot ignore the fact, even if we wished to ignore it, that he did grand service to the young republic in its struggle for freedom and nationality.

This doughty representative of auld Scotia's naval prowess, when all is said on the subject, has—justly or unjustly—a cloud resting on his fame, and so it may be in keeping with the fitness of things to mention one or two representatives of the thistle at sea on whose record no one has ventured to cast any smirch, for the best of all reasons—that their lives were above reproach. Few people now remember anything of Admiral Schank, although he was a man of unusual prominence in his day. He was born at Castlerig, Kinghorn, Fifeshire, in 1740, and was a cadet of the family of Shank of Castelrig, which received its territorial possessions from a grant by King Robert the Bruce. Why the Admiral changed the spelling of his name is not known; possibly simply on account of a freak, for most great men have their weaknesses. In early life he learned seamanship on a merchant vessel, but he entered the Royal Navy and passed slowly through the grades of promotion till he attained the rank of Second Lieutenant. His first position of importance was that of senior officer of the naval squadron at St. John, N. B., and when hostilities were rife he rendered good service to the Home Government. One instance of his energy that attraced general attention at the time was in connection with his ship, the Inflexible. He commenced building it at Quebec, and within six weeks from the day its first timbers were laid he had built, rigged, completed it from stem to stern, put her to sea and won a battle with it. He fitted out several armaments for employment on the great lakes, and at one time had four dockyards under his direction. He also distinguished himself in Burgoyne's campaign in 1777, when he acted in the capacity of engineer, and greatly facilitated by his arrangements the movements of the troops. When peace was declared he returned to Britain and, with the rank of Captain, enjoyed a period of leisure, which he devoted to literary studies and to the development of theories in seamanship which his experience had suggested. In 1793 he published a treatise on the sailing of vessels in shallow water by a series of sliding keels he invented, and which could be operated easily by means of some mechanical arrangements. He also contributed several valuable papers for the transactions of the Society for Improving Naval Architecture, of which he was one of the founders. He held several active appointments in connection with his profession before being, in 1805, raised to the rank of Rear Admiral, and he afterward received, in succession, the higher honors of Vice Admiral and Admiral of the Blue. He died at Dawlish, Devonshire, in 1823, leaving behind him a record, if not as brilliant, as honorable as that of any other name on the long roll of British Admirals.

There is a tradition that Robert R. Randall, the founder of the noble home for aged seamen, on Staten Island, known as Sailors' Snug Harbor, was the son of a Scottish merchant. The commonly told story is that " Thomas Randall, a thrifty Scotchman who amassed a competence as an 'honest privateersman' in pre-Revolutionary times, and whose great plantations near the then Spanish port of New-Orleans were used as the storehouses for the products of his enterprise as a bold buccaneer, followed the example of the rude forefathers of his hamlet—in short, died, leaving to his 'only' son, Robert Richard, his vast possessions and remorse." The remorse feature of the story is the only thing that elevates the character of Randall above that of the one commonly ascribed to Capt. Kidd. Gov. Trask, however, who, as the executive head of the Snug Harbor, has investigated the career of the founder's father, says that instead of being a pirate and all that the name implies, Thomas Randall was a well-known American patriot, a member of the Committee of One Hundred in 1785, one of the original founders of the New York Chamber of Commerce, and the first President of the Marine Society of the Port of New York, an organization which had for its object 'the relief of indigent and distressed masters of vessels, their widows and orphan children.' Thomas Randall was for many years intimately connected through ties of friendship and business with Alexander Hamilton, the great soldier-lawyer-financier of the Colonies, and it is recorded that Randall and Hamilton had built and fitted out, at their own expense, the vessel which conveyed Gen. Washington from Elizabethport to New York on his journey to the first inauguration.

Capt. Trask has taken a great deal of pains to solve the question of Thomas Randall's birth, but without success. "If a Scotsman," he says, "he must have come to this country when young, as at the age of twenty-five he appears to have been a shipmaster and in command of the American brigantine, The Fox!" The son, however, bequeathed his means unto a charity which has proved of practical service to the class for whom it was intended, and, in the absence of proof to the contrary, we feel justified in claiming Thomas Randall as a Scot on the strength of the tradition. Such institutions have ever been favorite ones with Scotsmen of means, and perhaps it may have been one of the dreams of Thomas Randall to found such a home, a dream made a reality by his son.

CHAPTER V.

MINISTERS AND RELIGIOUS TEACHERS.

NO class of men have done more to direct public opinion and conserve public morals in North America than the preachers of the Gospel who have settled in the United States and Canada from Scotland. In speaking of the Scotch clergy on this continent, and particularly in the United States, we generally think of them as Presbyterians. The majority of them certainly were, and are, of the Kirk of John Knox, but we also find them in all denominations, Episcopalian and Baptist, Methodist and Roman Catholic. Indeed, one of the Bishops of the latter Church in the United States who died a year or two ago was a native of Scotland, and as proud of the fact as he was of his crozier. Presbyterianism, however, is so much associated with the history of Scotland that when we speak of a Scottish clergyman in America he is generally supposed to be a Presbyterian—until the contrary is made known. Then, many Scotch preachers ordained in some one of the Presbyterian denominations in Scotland become Congregationalists when they reach America, believing that that form of Church government is more suited to the requirements of the country than any other, and many have found in the pulpit of the Reformed Dutch Church a haven from which they could preach the Word. Such changes may, of course, be made without sacrificing one iota of the preachers' early notions of the unity of the denomination and the inter-dependence of individual congregations taught in the policy and practice of the religious organization under which their fathers had worshipped, and in which they themselves had been trained for the work of the ministry.

Sometimes we read of a Scotsman who crossed the Atlantic to further the views of his denomination as a missionary, and of this the history of the Quakers has already furnished us with several examples. Sometimes the head and front of a new denomination settles in America, hoping in a new country to find men ready to change the views they had previously held, or at least so open to conviction as to hold out some hope in the way of making converts. This was the case with Robert Sandeman. He was born at Perth in 1718, and after a short university course at Edinburgh entered into commercial life in the linen trade. He married the daughter of the Rev. John Glas, minister of Tealing, near Dundee, whose views against a national church and other matters led to his deposition and to the founding of a new sect—the Glassites. Sandeman not only adopted his father-in-law's views, but reduced them to a system. The Glassites had some peculiar views on church government, and were pronounced against all State connection with religion. They did not believe that their spiritual teachers should be set apart, or that they should contract second marriages, or that prayer should be promiscuous. They had love feasts—real feasts—celebrated the Lord's Supper every Sabbath, interpreted the Scriptures literally, disapproved of eating animals that had been strangled, and adopted such minor matters as washing the feet of brother disciples and implanting the kiss of charity, and many other views which drove them apart from the other communities into which the religious world of Scotland was divided. Sandeman became what might be called the evangelist of the new church, and was instrumental in organizing in connection with it many congregations, not only in Scotland, but in London, Newcastle, and other English towns. In 1764, leaving Mr. Glas to watch over the denomination at home, Sandeman crossed to Boston and founded a church there, the body being known in America by his name—Sandemanians. He also established a church at Danbury, Conn., and congregations elsewhere, but the progress of the movement was hampered by the uncertain political conditions which began to prevail, and Sandeman suffered many disappointments. He died at Danbury in 1771. Probably not more than 5,000 persons in America could then have been regarded as adherents to Sandeman's views, and after his death that number began steadily to decrease, although, to a small extent, they are still represented in American denominational lists. During the Revolutionary War they were noted for their loyalty to Britain, and that fact alone kept them from winning the amount of attention which their earnestness, their charity, and their striving after pure Christianity entitled them.

Another worker in a new sect—a sect, however, whose purpose was to unite all the sects, with the Bible as the sole bond of union, was Walter Scott, who, it has been claimed by some of his admirers, could claim kinship with the "Author of Waverley." He was born in the now popular and pleasant town of Moffat in 1796. He landed in the United States in 1818 and became acquainted with Thomas and Alexander Campbell, father and son, two Irishmen who had the courage to think out religious problems for themselves. For Alexander Campbell, Scott conceived a warm friendship, and the views of the Disciples of Christ, as the holders of the Campbellite doctrines were called, found in him a devoted believer. As a preacher, Scott exhibited such oratorical powers that he became recognized as a leader in the new ranks, and his writings formed a feature for years in Alexander Campbell's paper, "The Christian Baptist." The sect thus founded spread rapidly over many sections of the United States, and it has churches in various parts of the world. Its vitality seems to increase with the passing of time—the great wrecker of so many sects—and it now has over 2,000 ministers and some 2,500 churches. For much of this popularity the labors of Walter Scott must receive credit, for in the work of the organization he seemed never to tire. Just before the outbreak of the war of the rebellion, as might be expected from one holding such broad, simple views of Christian life, he spoke against an appeal to arms, and in a pamphlet called "The Union," issued in 1861, a short time before his death, he uttered a ringing protest against the impending conflict. Words, however, by that time were of no avail—affairs had passed that stage, and the bombardment of Fort Sumter announced the beginning of one of the most appalling of modern wars. Scott was then in infirm health, and the grief which the news of the doings at Sumter occasioned hastened the end, and closed in gloom a life that had been spent in trying to infuse light and joy through the world. He died at Mayslick, Ky., in 1861.

Sometimes we find Scotsmen among the pioneers or active workers in fields that are neither orthodox nor established, seekers after something new, as zealous as the typical Yankee. Even in the ranks of the Mormon Eldership the ubiquitous Scot can be found, and those of them we have met have displayed the greatest earnestness in their work and expressed a most complete belief in the righteousness of the doctrines held by that people. So, too, in the circles of the Spiritualists and such-like "new-fangled" folks, Scotsmen seem to hold prominent rank. The most noted of all the modern Spiritualists was David Douglas Home, who was born in Edinburgh in 1833 and died in Paris—a lunatic—in 1886. He settled in America in 1840, and at the age of seventeen blossomed out into a medium. His life may generally be classed as that of an adventurer, with his fame as a spiritualist as its foundation, while as the prototype of Browning's study of "Mr. Sludge, the Medium," he even found a place in poetry. His spiritualistic performances were remarkable, whatever way we may look at them, and included all sorts of manifestations. Home had a career in Europe as well as in America. In 1858, while in St. Petersburg, he married a Russian lady of rank. He joined the Roman Catholic Church, but was expelled for some of his manifestations. In London he was one of the curiosities of the capital for several years, and, his wife having died in 1862, he married again—this time also a Russian lady of noble birth—in 1872. He wrote a number of works on spiritualism, and certainly made many converts to his peculiar views.

If, however, we want to measure fully the influence which Scotland's clergy have had upon America, we need look no further than to the history of Presbyterianism in the United States. It is not much more than a century ago that the first General Assembly, with its 17 Presbyteries and 180 ministers, met in Philadelphia. Now there is hardly a town in the country where at least one church belonging to the denomination is not to be found, while its array of colleges, its missionary operations, and the extent and variety of its evangelistic work, make the American Presbyterian Church, North as well as South, one of the most active agents in the modern religious world. In the early history of the country Scotch Presbyterianism was even a much more pronounced factor in its religious and moral development, despite its comparative meagreness of workers, adherents, and means, than now, and one authority says that two-thirds of the Presbyterian ministers in America, prior to 1738, were graduates of Glasgow University. In the first Presbytery meeting, at Philadelphia, in or about 1700, there were seven ministers, and two of these, Nathaniel Taylor and John Wilson, were natives of Scotland, three belonged to the North of Ireland and were of Scotch descent and educational training, and one was a native of New-England, of whose education and ancestry nothing seems to be known. Thus, six of this pioneer band of seven owed to Scotland the grit and fidelity of purpose that enabled them to assume the dangers and hardships of pioneer life. One of these Irish Scots, the Rev. Francis Makemie, a graduate of Glasgow University, is credited with being the founder of Presbyterianism in America, having organized a church at Snow Hill, Md., in 1684, with the aid of his trusted Scotch elder, Adam Spence. A claim for priority is also made for a church at Hempstead, which was founded in 1644 by the Rev. Mr. Denton, a Presbyterian preacher from England, but Denton should rather be placed under the general head of Nonconformist, and as we judge from the story of his ministry at Hempstead, the church he founded was a Congregational rather than a Presbyterian institution. Makemie not only founded one church, but four others, within comparatively easy reach of Snow Hill, and did not rest content until he had the churches he founded and those of other pioneers organized into a Presbytery, and with the organization of that body began, really, the history of Presbyterianism in America. In 1716 the first Synod, constituted by four Presbyteries, was held in the "City of Brotherly Love," and in 1789 the organization of the Church was completed by the meeting of a General Assembly. No better or more inspiring "visible sign" of Scotland's influence upon America is to be found than in the growth and present wide-reaching influence of the Presbyterian Church in all its branches on the continent.

But under whatever denominational flag the Scotch preachers in America have enrolled themselves, their influence has been, with very few and very far-separated exceptions, for good in their ministerial relations, while as citizens they have been ever active and practical in manifesting how the duties of honest, upright, loyal citizenship should be considered and performed. Even as far back as the time of the Revolution there is abundant evidence to show that they were fast in their loyalty, whether their sentiments caused them to remain faithful to King George or, as was more generally the case, their convictions impelled them to transfer their loyalty to the Continental Congress. The leading characteristic of the great majority of the Scottish-American preachers in the past seems to have been their intense earnestness, their undoubted sincerity. They had the national dourness, the argumentative disposition of many of their countrymen, and several of them were led into uncongenial positions—to change even from one denomination into another in the hope of finding more freedom for their views or more peace for the current of their daily lives; but over all, as we study the careers of these preachers, or such of them, rather, as we have been privileged to read about, we find one grand principle ever sustaining and inspiring them—that of performing faithfully the commission, as they conceived it, which the Master had given them to do. A recent writer in a religious paper has estimated that among the foreign ministers who have preached in this country from its beginning some 3,000 have hailed from Scotland. We do not know how the writer arrived at his figures, but we think his estimate rather under than above the mark. With his calculation, however, assumed as correct, it can be understood that all types of good men are contained among the host.

One of the most famous of the early Scotch ministers to visit America was the Rev. William Dunlop, who afterward became Principal of Glasgow University. He was the son of a minister in Paisley, was graduated at the University of Glasgow, and in 1679 obtained his license as a preacher. The year 1679, however, was a distracting one in the history of the Scottish Kirk, for in it were fought the battles of Drumclog and Bothwell Bridge. In May of that year Archbishop Sharp met his death by violence on Magus Moor, near St. Andrews, and the Covenanters were persecuted with the most fiendish cruelty. Dunlop, naturally, was on the persecuted side, and was active in the movements against the State enactments, and to escape from the dangers to which he was exposed he joined a party which was formed to cross the Atlantic, and he settled in South Carolina. There he resided, preaching and teaching until 1690. He was highly esteemed, and doubtless had he remained in America would have attained an influential position in the ministry, but he looked upon himself simply as an exile, his heart yearned for home, and less than two years after the Revolution brought peace to Scotland he was again in his native land. He was at once appointed by King William Principal of Glasgow University, and held that position until his death. He had married in early life Sarah, sister of the famous Principal Carstairs, "the Cardinal" of King William's Court, and she accompanied him to South Carolina, and there their eldest son, Alexander, was born in 1684. He went to

Scotland with his parents in 1690, and ultimately became Professor of Greek in the University of Glasgow, and was regarded as the foremost teacher of that language of his time.

A preacher much more actively identified with the history of Presbyterianism in America was the Rev. George Gillespie, who was born near Stirling in 1683, and, after being educated in Glasgow University, was licensed as a preacher in 1712. In that same year he arrived in Boston with a highly commendatory letter from Principal Stirling of Glasgow to Dr. Cotton Mather and was soon placed in charge of the church at Woodbridge, N. J. He remained there only a short time, as, toward the close of 1713, he was ordained minister of White Clay Creek, Del. There he became one of the busiest men in the Church, for he had several preaching stations to attend to, and he spared neither time nor labor in the faithful discharge of his duties to each. He was a noted leader in the controversies which had sprung up in the Church and which resulted, in 1741, in a memorable secession. As a writer his pen was particularly ready not only in forwarding his own views, but in advocating tolerance for the views of others. His treatise "Against Deists and Freethinkers," published at Philadelphia in 1735, was an able argument against such heresies, and in considering the events of his somewhat bitter controversial career we read with a smile his "Sermons against Divisions in Christ's Churches" when we remember that they were issued in New York in 1740, just as an impending schism was about to distract the energies of the Church—a schism which, in a manner natural in a Scotsman, he had a considerable share in bringing about. Mr. Gillespie died in 1760.

A contemporary of Mr. Gillespie who was also noted as a controversialist, but of a less bitter type, was the Rev. Alexander Garden, who was born at Edinburgh in 1685 and settled in Charleston, S. C., in 1719 as rector of St. Philip's (Episcopal) Parish. From the first he was a success in the work of the ministry, and he soon became noted as a leader in local religious circles. He brought about a series of annual meetings of the clergy in and around Charleston, and by that means alone did a great amount of practical good, but his great claim to kindly remembrance lies in the interest he took in the education and religious instruction of the negroes. In 1740 he entered into a controversy with the famous George Whitefield which attracted much attention all over the country. His arguments against the famous *Apostle of Methodism* were printed under the title of "Six Letters to the Rev. George Whitefield" and had a wide circulation, and he also published a few of his sermons—able, orthodox, and practical discourses—which are much superior to the ordinary run of such productions. Mr. Garden was a most enthusiastic Scot, and his name appears among the members of the St. Andrew's Society of Charleston, the oldest organization of that name in America. In 1754 he resigned his pastorate on account of ill-health, to the general regret of the people of Charleston, irrespective of denominational differences, and was presented with a valuable service of plate. He died two years later. His son, Alexander, who was born at Edinburgh in 1713, became famous as a physician and botanist. In 1754 he was elected Professor of Botany in Kings (Columbia) College, and maintained an extensive correspondence with European scientists, including Linnaeus, who named the genus Gardenia in his honor. When the Revolution broke out, Prof. Garden retained his loyalty, lost everything he possessed, and was glad to escape to England, where he died in 1791. As another evidence of how that war separated families we may state that Prof. Garden's son, Alexander, who was born at Charleston in 1757 and died in 1829, served in the Revolutionary Army as aide to Gen. Greene and as an officer in Lee's legion. For his services, his father's property, or most of it, was given to him, and he was justly esteemed by his companions in the army. This warrior also inherited the literary tastes so noted in his family, and his work entitled "Anecdotes of the Revolution and Sketches of Its Characters" was very popular when first issued, and has several times been reprinted.

A stormy, turbulent, unsatisfactory career was that of George Keith, a Presbyterian, Quaker, and Episcopalian, by turns, who was born in Aberdeen in 1645. It is possible that he was a brother of the Rev. James Keith, a worthy Aberdonian, who settled at Boston about 1662, and from 1664 till his death in 1719 was the honored minister of a Congregational church at Bridgewater, Mass.; but this is only a surmise, for Keiths were and are as plentiful around "the City of Bon-Accord" as blackberries on a hedge. George Keith was originally a Presbyterian, and was educated at Marischal College, Aberdeen, where he formed a strong friendship for a fellow-student, Gilbert Burnet, who afterward became famous as Bishop of Salisbury and as a historian. The two entertained the warmest regard for each other throughout their lives. After graduating, Keith left the Presbyterian fold and joined the Society of Friends. Shortly afterward he was induced by the leading Quakers in Aberdeen to emigrate to America, with the view not only of bettering his own temporal condition, but of helping to spread their doctrines in the New World. He arrived at New York in 1684, and for some four years was Surveyor in New Jersey. In 1689 he removed to Philadelphia, where he conducted a Friends' school, but that occupation was far too quiet and monotonous to suit his disposition, and he soon gave it up. He started to travel in New England, like a Quaker Don Quixote, to win people to the views of the Society, and he was at once engaged in a bitter series of controversies with Increase Mather, Cotton Mather, and others. He did not by his journey add much to the numerical strength of his adopted people, and when he returned to Philadelphia he even managed, without loss of time, to quarrel with the Friends there. This quarrel seems to have been due to his own temper, to his sense of disappointment, to his disposition to escape from the leveling tendencies of the teachings of the Society, and to some peculiar innovations he advocated, and which none of the brethren seemed disposed to listen to. Then he went to England, and laid his whole case before William

Penn, but that leader denounced him as an apostate, and Keith was excommunicated from the Society, as completely as the gentle Quakers could excommunicate anybody. Then he founded a religious denomination of his own, which he called the Christian or Baptist Quakers, (popularly called the Keithians,) and in which he had a chance for ventilating some original views he held on the millennium and concerning the transmigration of souls. The Keithians, however, did not hold long together, and in 1702 its founder was a full-fledged and enthusiastic minister of the Church of England. Here, probably because years had softened the natural contentiousness of his dispositon, or the Church itself allowed more latitude for individual views on various matters, he found peace. Nay, more, he found an opportunity for repaying the Society of Friends for its rather summary treatment of him. He was sent as a missionary to Pennsylvania and New-Jersey, with the view of converting, or perverting, as many Quakers as possible, and used to boast that in that expedition some seven hundred Friends were by his instrumentality received into communion with the English Church. Soon after his return to England he was appointed Vicar of Edburton, in Essex, and in that beautiful parish his declining years were spent in tranquillity. Keith was a man of decidedly superior cast of intellect, an eloquent and attractive speaker and preacher, an able and ready conversationist, and, but for his choleric disposition, would have lived a life of more than ordinary usefulness, and might even have attained to real power and eminence. He was a voluminous writer, and in the fifty or so volumes (some in bulky quarto) or pamphlets which we know to have come from his pen, we can trace the current of his religious views through all their changes. He appears in them all to have been singularly honest, made no attempt to conceal or belittle his own changes, and even published retractions of his own published writings. His later works were mainly taken up with what he regarded as the fallacies of Quakerism, and he attacked the Society of Friends from every point of view and with the utmost savagery and unrelenting acerbity.

It is relief to turn from the waywardness of this turbulent character to the life of quiet consistency which is exemplified in the career of one of the most useful ministers who ever occupied a New York pulpit, the Rev. Dr. Archibald Laidlie. He was a native of Kelso, and preached his first sermon in this city in 1764. He joined the St. Andrew's Society a year later, a sufficient evidence that he was not forgetful of his native land. Mr. Laidlie had previously been pastor for four years of the Scotch Church at Flushing, in Holland. The success of his ministry there induced the Dutch Reformed Church in New York to invite him to settle in that city, and it was notable that he was the first minister of that denomination in New York to preach in English. He was a most successful preacher and a man of very considerable learning, and one of the works by which he is still gratefully remembered is his translation, for use in his church, of the Heidelberg Catechism in 1770—the year that Princeton gave him the degree of Doctor of Divinity. When the time came for men to declare themselves in the Revolutionary struggle Dr. Laidlie held aloof, but had to retire from his charge, and he went to Red Hook, Long Island, where, in 1779, he passed away at the comparatively early age of fifty-two years.

It is seldom that we hear of a preacher who knows how to defend himself with his fists with the skill of a prizefighter, and the story of one is preserved in the history of the United Presbyterian Church at Oxford, Penn., one of the oldest associate congregations in America, and which still exists in a flourishing condition. It was founded in 1753 by the Rev. Alexander Gellatly, who, along with the Rev. Andrew Arnott, settled in America, from Scotland, in response to invitations from the Presbyterians in Lancaster and Chester Counties, Penn. In 1758 the Oxford church called another preacher from Scotland, the Rev. Matthew Henderson, who had been trained for the ministry in Glasgow University. He was a good, earnest man, much beloved by his people, and had many eccentricities of manner. Several anecdotes concerning him are still related at Oxford, some of which recall the stories told of many of the Old Country preachers in Scotland in the early part of the century. Among others, it is said, that once, noticing a young woman with a new calico gown moving frequently to various parts of the church, he called out: "That is the fourth time, my lass, that you hae left your seat. You can sit doon now; we hae a' seen your braw new goun." As he was journeying over the mountains to meet with his brethren in the Presbytery he halted for the night at an inn. While resting in the common sitting room, two loafers, noticing that he was a minister, persisted in trying his patience by their roughness, and finally insisted on fighting. This caused his Scotch blood to "boil." Drawing off his coat, he exclaimed: "Lie there, the Rev. Mr. Henderson, and, now, Matthew, defend yoursel'." He threw one of his tormentors through the window, the other ran away.

In the annals of Presbyterianism in America no names are sweeter than those of the Masons—father and son—who for many years were the recognized leaders in that communion in the United States. The Rev. John Mason was born in Linlithgowshire in 1734. He was trained for the ministry in the Secession Church, and was an ardent believer, as were all his family, in the views held by the Anti-Burghers in Scotland. It is well to remember this in considering Dr. Mason's work in America, for the Anti-Burgher views are generally considered to be the narrowest and most closely confined of any held by Presbyterian denominations. But from the time he settled in New York, in 1761, shortly after he was ordained, and took charge of the Scotch Presbyterian Church, on Cedar Street, he was the apostle of liberality and toleration. He saw Presbyterianism not only divided, but the sections threatening to drift wider apart, and while he recognized the existence in Scotland of political and historical reasons which almost naturally created schism and embittered feeling, he saw no reason for there being any divisions at all in the New World. With that idea, he labored with intensity and determination, and his labors were, to a very considerable extent, crowned with success in 1782, when the Associate Reformed Presbyterian Church was organized, and of its Assembly he was the first Moderator. In all the religious and charitable movements of his time in New York, Dr. Mason was a leader. He was one of the prime movers in the American Bible Society, and issued an address on its behalf which was circulated broadcast among the people. This movement he conceived to be one of the most notable ever inaugurated in the interest of Christian union. Its platform and purpose were such that all Christians could unite upon, and, indeed, except for some objections from a few Episcopalian dignitaries and others, it was accepted in the spirit of union by all denominations, and has since done a mighty work. In charitable enterprises he was equally prominent, while as Chaplain of the St. Andrew's Society, from 1785 till his death, in 1792, he was brought into the closest contact with his countrymen, and aided largely in promoting the society's mission to " Relieve the distressed."

Dr. Mason's son, the Rev. John Mitchell Mason, who was born in New York in 1770, was in many ways the most representative and admired minister America has yet produced. He graduated at Columbia College in 1789, and then went to Edinburgh to complete his theological studies. He succeeded to the pastoral charge of his father's church on the latter's death, in 1792, and he succeeded his parent as Chaplain of the St. Andrew's Society, an office he held until 1821, when he left the city to become Principal of Dickinson College, Carlisle, Penn. He returned to New York in 1824 and resumed the active work of the ministry. As a preacher he was unrivaled in his day, and it is said that when the famous Robert Hall heard him preach a discourse on " Messiah's Throne" he said: "I can never preach again." Says one writer: "His aspect was on a scale of grandeur corresponding to the majesty of the mind within. Tall, robust, straight, with a head modeled after neither Grecian nor Roman standards, yet combining the dignity of the one and the grace of the other; with an eye that shot fire, especially when under the excitement of earnest preaching, yet tender and tearful when a pathetic passage was reached; with a forehead broad and high, and a mouth expressive of decision, Dr. Mason stood before his audience a prince of pulpit orators." He died in New York City in 1829.

Old Dr. Mason quietly adopted the American side in the Revolutionary struggle, but, unlike Dr. Witherspoon, was regarded so much as an unoffensive partisan that he retained the good will of his friends in Scotland to the last. As an offset to his example we may here recall a clergyman who was an uncompromising foe to the Revolutionary movement. That was the Rev. Henry Munro, who was born at Inverness in 1730. His first acquaintance with America was when he crossed the Atlantic as the Chaplain (Presbyterian) of the old Seventy-seventh Regiment, (Montgomerie's Highlanders.) He was with that gallant body at Fort Duquesne, Crown Point, and Ticonderoga, and was not only present at the capture of Montreal in September, 1760, but preached a rousing thanksgiving sermon a day or two later on the side of Mount Royal. As one reward for his campaigns he got a bounty of 2,000 acres of land in what is now Washington County, in New York State, but this land never added to his wealth, for the troubles of the Revolution interfered with its settlement, and it was confiscated as soon as the progress of events made confiscation possible. In 1762 he settled at Princeton, and for some reason or another joined the Church of England, and in 1765 was stationed as a missionary at Yonkers. Three years later he became rector of St. Peter's, at Albany, and was active in his missionary labors among the Mohawk Indians, whose language he knew perfectly.

When the war broke out he was unsparing in his denunciations of the "rebels," and made himself so obnoxious on that score that he had to escape to the British lines. Then he made his way back to Scotland, where he died, at Edinburgh, in 1801, a broken-hearted old man whose life went out under a sense of having suffered deep wrongs. He had married in 1766 a daughter of Peter Jay, and the lady and her family were as enthusiastic in favor of the Revolution as Munro was opposed to it. She not only refused to accompany him, but retained with her their only son—Peter Jay Munro. Father and son never afterward saw each other. The lad was educated under the direction of his famous uncle, John Jay; accompanied that statesman to Spain as an attaché of the American Embassy, and then studied law in the office of Aaron Burr. He rose in time to become one of the foremost members of the New York Bar, and served in the Constitutional Convention of 1821. He died at Mamaroneck in 1833.

Few clergymen have led more stirring lives than did the Rev. William Smith, a man of broad culture, of intense energy, of more than ordinary ability, and a preacher of wonderful force. He was born at Aberdeen in 1727, and graduated from the university there. He began life as a teacher, and came here in 1752 to take charge of the seminary in Philadelphia, out of which grew the University of Pennsylvania. In 1753 he went to England and received orders in the national Church there. On his return he was an active preacher as well as a successful teacher, and when, in 1759, he revisited England his merit and ability were so widely recognized that he received the degree of Doctor of Divinity from the Universities of Oxford, Aberdeen, and Dublin. He threw himself heartily into the popular side in the Revolution, preached frequently to the troops, and did whatever he could, consistent with his position, to favor the movement for independence. His very consistency raised up several enemies, and caused even a doubt to be cast on the sincerity of his sentiments, but such doubts were utterly unfounded. In June, 1775, he preached a sermon in Philadelphia to Col. Cadwallader's battalion which created a sensation, so outspoken were its sentiments, so clearly did he proclaim the righteousness of the cause of the dissidents. Even this sermon gave rise to criticism. The bane of his career was that his personal character in many ways was not a lovable one. He had a sharp temper and a tongue that was often intemperate in its expressions of personal dislike. Then the impetuosity of his disposition involved him in countless arguments and impelled men who really ought to have been ranged among his friends to be ranked among his enemies. The sentiment against him was so bitter in some influential quarters for a time as to cause the charter of the college in Philadelphia, of which he was the head, to be suspended for ten years, and later to defeat the approval by the General Convocation of his Church of his election as Bishop of Maryland. But he continued preaching and teaching—mainly at Chesterton, Md., (where he established Washington College,) until the clouds rolled away, and his latter years in Philadelphia, where he died in 1803, were spent pleasantly and peacefully. The blemish in Dr. Smith's career was his fondness for secular pursuits, notably for land speculation, a weakness that has never yet, so far as our experience goes, added much to the popularity of a clergyman. It may safely be said, however, that his business ventures never interfered with his duties as a teacher, a Principal of a seat of learning, or as a preacher of the Gospel. He was an incessant worker, a marvel of energy. In spite of his numerous avocations he devoted a great deal of time to his study, and was a voluminous writer on religious and secular topics and a patient investigator of scientific matters. A nephew of this sturdy divine, William Smith—also an Aberdonian and a zealous upholder of the Revolutionary cause—was rector of Trinity Church, Newport, for seven years, having previously held rectorships at Stepney, Md., and Narragansett, R. I., and afterward, until his death, in 1821, at the age of sixty-seven years, was a preacher and teacher in New

York. His pupils were mainly private ones, and as a classical instructor he was regarded as the foremost in the city. He was the author of several religious works, which seem now to be unobtainable—and forgotten.

Having recalled two pro-Revolutionary ministers, the strict impartiality of this survey again impels us to consider two who were conspicuous in their own circles on the opposite side. The first of this pair was the Rev. Dr. Myles Cooper, a poet of no mean order, as well as a theologian and life-long student. The place of his birth is uncertain. He seems to have been educated at Oxford, and was a Fellow of Queen's College there. In 1763 he was elected second President of King's College (now Columbia College,) New York, and in the performance of all the duties pertaining to that office he was faithful and zealous and deservedly popular. He, however, took up such a thoroughgoing loyal stand against the Americans in the troubles with the mother country that in 1775 he was obliged to return to Britain. Dr. Cooper soon after his return was made rector of the Episcopal Church (now a Roman Catholic church) in the Cowgate of Edinburgh, and he continued in charge of that congregation until his death in 1785.

The Rev. Thomas Rankin was another refugee. He was born at Dunbar in 1738, and crossed to America as a missionary sent by John Wesley. Before that he had been preaching in various Methodist Episcopal circuits, Sussex, Devonshire, and others, and was regarded as a successful evangelist and a most devoted worker in the promulgation of Scriptural truths. He was equally successful in his work in America until the outbreak of hostilities, when his intense loyalty made him turn his abilities to keeping the clergy of all denominations fast in their loyalty to George III. He thought there was no use of preaching the Gospel to men who were arrayed in open opposition to lawful authority. "God," he said, "would not revive His work in America until they submitted to their rightful sovereign." Holding such views, his usefulness in the New World was at an end, and he returned to England, spending his latter years in missionary work in London. We may close our selection of Revolutionary era preachers by recalling the name of the Rev. Alexander Hewat, who may be classed as an inoffensive partisan. He was born at Kelso in 1745, educated at the grammar school there, and became pastor of the Scotch Church at Charleston, S. C., in 1762. He remained in Charleston until it seemed certain that war was about to break out, when, unwilling to renounce his allegiance, he relinquished his charge and returned to the mother country. His interest in America did not, however, cease when he left it, for in 1779 he published in London a valuable and interesting " History of South Carolina and Charleston," his only published work of which we have knowledge excepting a volume of sermons, which he published in 1803. Within a year after reaching America Mr. Hewat testified to his native patriotism by joining the Charleston St. Andrew's Society. That society in the early period of its career was watchful to add to its list of members all notable arrivals to the Scottish community, and among its pre-Revolutionary members we find such names as those of Gov. James Wright of Georgia, Sir Alex Nesbit, Gov. Johnston of North Carolina, Sir James Home, Gov. James Grant of East Florida, and Gov. James Glen of South Carolina. The early records are full of military names, and in one year the resident members placed on the roll the names of the Earl of Eglinton and all the officers of Montgomerie's Highlanders they appeared to have been acquainted with.

Henceforth, in this chapter at all events, we deal with men of peace—men who were permitted to carry on their spiritual work without interference from the roll of drums or the agitations of political strife. The clergy who settled in America from Scotland after Washington and his compatriots placed the United States in the list of nations accepted the situation loyally. In fact, Scotsmen generally accept a change in such respects with equanimity—when it is made for them. Even in religious matters, what in Scotland would be deemed a momentous change is accepted by the Scot in foreign lands without scruple. We have known Scotsmen who at home would have turned pale at the thought of a harmonium in a kirk be quite satisfied with the assistance of an organ in a church in America, and can recall instances of many dour opponents of the use of anything in the worship of praise except the " Psalms of Dauvit " who willingly saw spiritual beauty in many hymns by uninspired writers after they had been a few weeks in the United States or Canada.

The Rev. James Muir, Presbyterian minister at Alexandria, Va., from 1789 till his death in 1820, deserves to be held in kindly remembrance for the able manner in which he handled in at least one published volume the heresies of Thomas Paine, the sceptic, when they were enjoying more influence than they do now, or than they ever deserved. Mr. Muir was born at Cumnock, Ayrshire, in 1757, and had studied for the ministry at Glasgow and Edinburgh. He had been pastor of the Scotch Church in London, and of a church in Bermuda for eight years, before settling in America in 1788. He was a man of wide views, tolerant of all opinions which he believed to be honestly held or uttered, and thoroughly orthodox in all he himself said or wrote, as may be seen by a perusal of the volume of sermons he published in 1810. His son, Samuel, had a strange history. He was born in the District of Columbia in 1789, and in due time was sent to Edinburgh to study medicine. In 1813 he was appointed a surgeon in the United States Army. That position he resigned in 1818, when he married the daughter of the then chief of the Sac, or Fox, Indians. He settled among his wife's people, assumed their ways, and became regarded as one of their leaders. In 1828 he left the Indian settlements and earned his living again by practicing medicine at Galena, Ill. In 1832, when there was an epidemic of cholera among the United States troops, he volunteered his services. His offer was accepted, and he saved many lives by his skill, but fell himself a victim to the disease within a few months.

It is refreshing after dwelling so long among "the cloth" to turn to a lay preacher who did magnificent work for the Master in his day and generation and around whose name many fragrant memories yet linger. This was John Clark, better known as Father Clark, whose only educational training was that which he received in the school of his native parish of Petty, near Inverness. He was born there in 1758, and in early life is said to have been a sailor. In the course of one voyage he landed in America and concluded to associate his future with it. He settled for a time in South Carolina, where he taught in a backwoods log school, and then moved to Georgia, where he joined the Methodist Church and became a class leader. Desiring to revisit his native land, in 1787 he engaged to work his passage before the mast, and did so, but remained at home only a short time. Returning to America in 1789, he became an itinerant preacher in connection with the Methodist body, his travels being mainly throughout Georgia. He was a man of devout spirit, outspoken in his views and ready to denounce wrong wherever he found it, without regard to church affiliation, general policy, or self-interest. As might be expected, he was a bitter foe to slavery, and it is on record that he twice refused to accept his annual salary of $60 because the money was obtained through slave labor. Doctrinal differences at length led to his withdrawal from the Methodist Church, and he went to Illinois, where he taught school, preaching as he got an opportunity, without owning allegiance to any denomination. Then he joined the anti-slavery Baptist organization known as the "Baptized Church of Christ, Friends of Humanity," and in connection with that body he resumed his work as a traveling evangelist.

"Father Clark," as he was lovingly called, was indefatigable in his work of spreading a knowledge of the Gospel. His missionary wanderings led him far into the then unknown West and southward through Florida. We have a record of his having walked, when seventy years of age, over sixty miles to fulfill a preaching engagement, and one missionary journey of 1,200 miles was performed alone, partly on foot and partly with the aid of an old canoe. He died at St. Louis in 1833. In his wanderings and devotion "Father Clark" was the best modern prototype of St. Andrew of whom we have knowledge.

Few ministers have found it more difficult to find a congenial denomination to cling to than did the Rev. Walter Balfour, who was born at St. Ninians in the year of American independence and died at Charlestown, Mass., in 1852. Early in life he became a protégé of the sainted Robert Haldane, and was educated through that gentleman's instrumentality for the ministry. He was intended for a pulpit of the Church of Scotland, but shortly after crossing the Atlantic, in 1806, he associated himself with the Baptists. In that communion he remained, latterly much discontented, until 1823, when, after much thought and careful study into the tenets of every Christian denomination, and with much mental misgiving, he affiliated with the Universalists, and there found that entire freedom from doctrinal restraint for which he had so long yearned. In that Church he reached the height of his popularity as a preacher, orator, and as an author. His work entitled "Essay on the Intermediate State of the Dead" was long considered a model of its kind for closeness of argument, delicacy of thought, and beauty of language.

Along with the names of the Masons in the religious history of New York stand those of the McLeods in the regard and veneration of those who have studied it. The founder of the American family was Dr. Alexander McLeod, who was born in the Island of Mull in 1774, and died in New York in 1833. He settled in America when young, and was trained for the ministry, graduating from Union College in 1798. For a short time he was pastor of a church at Wallkill, N. Y., but what may be termed his life connection was the pastorate of the First Reformed Presbyterian Church in New York. During that long pastorate "Dr. McLeod's kirk" was a Scottish landmark in New York, and the fame of the preacher was carried all over the country by hosts of his countrymen, who, after sojourning in the American metropolis for a time, departed for other sections of the continent. His powers as a pulpit orator were of a high order, and his discourses were prepared with rare analytical skill. Every subject he touched was thoroughly discussed, and, while strictly orthodox, he exemplified by his pulpit ministrations that a man can be at once orthodox and original. As one of the Chaplains for many years of the St. Andrew's Society he kept in active touch with his countrymen in New York of all classes, and was beloved by them all. After his death his son, the Rev. John Neil McLeod, succeeded to his pastorate. He was an able man, as his published sermons, like those of his father, still testify, and under his care the First Reformed Church continued to be a power in the religious life of New York. He was a Calvinist of the sternest school, and was throughout his long life bitterly opposed to secret societies of all sorts or to the singing in public worship of anything except the metrical version of the Psalms of Israel's sweet singer. He died in 1874. A brother of this worthy minister had rather a strange career. He broke away from the Presbyterian fold when a young man and entered the Episcopalian. Then, like so many others in such circumstances, he went to the end of his tether—followed his changing views to their natural end—and became a Roman Catholic. For several years prior to his death, the result of a railroad accident near Cincinnati, in 1865, he was Professor of Rhetoric in a Roman Catholic college in Ohio. Xavier Donald McLeod was a man of marked ability and scholarship. Among his published writings are a " Life of Mary, Queen of Scots," a " Life of Sir Walter Scott," and at least one volume of poetry.

Another New York clergyman who was well known on both sides of the Atlantic was the Rev. Archibald Maclay, who was born at Killearn in 1778 and settled in New York in 1805. He had been a minister for a short time in Kirkcaldy before crossing the Atlantic, and on his arrival in New York he at once got charge of a small Presbyterian church in Rose street. In the course of a year or two his views on the subject of baptism so changed that he felt impelled to throw in his lot with the Baptist denomination, and in connection therewith he founded a church on Mulberry Street, (afterward in Second Avenue,) of which he continued to be pastor for nearly thirty years. In 1837 he retired from pastoral work and became agent of the American and Foreign Bible Society. In that capacity he traveled extensively through the United States, Canada, and Great Britain. In 1850 he was one of the organizers of the American Bible Union, and was elected its President. He was drawn to take the great interest he did in the dissemination of the printed Scriptures because he realized that to be one of the quickest means in the power of man for spreading into every nook and corner of the world a knowledge of the unspeakable riches of the Truth. He regarded every Bible, or portion of the Bible, as a missionary ever ready to do effective work and enjoying a closeness of communion which no merely human teacher could hope to equal. At the same time Dr. Maclay was outspoken in arguing the desirability of a new translation of the Scriptures, or the need, at least, of a revision of that which was given to the world under the patronage of King James, "the Sapient and the Sext" of Scotland. It was with this object in view that he helped to organize the Bible Translation Society of England. There is no doubt that he did good work in forming public opinion to the necessity of revision, and that it was due to him, as much as to any single individual, that the work was begun in 1870—ten years after he had passed from his labors to his reward.

Almost equally prominent during a long American career was the Rev. Dr. James Laurie of Washington. He was educated for the ministry in his native city of Edinburgh and obtained his license as a preacher in 1800. Two years later he determined, on the invitation of Dr. J. M. Mason, to settle in America, and in 1803 he was installed as pastor of the Associate Reformed Church in Washington. At first he preached in the old Treasury Building—a structure that was afterward burned by the British troops, in 1814. One of his first duties was to procure a decent church for his people. This he accomplished in 1807, after acting the part of a "big beggar man" in every quarter of the country where contributions were likely to be had. He preached and implored wherever he went, for it was a period when money was scarce and the "art of giving" was not understood as well as now. He continued to act as pastor of his church for forty-six years, and for a time held a position in the Treasury Department, closing a life of devotion to the cause to which he had devoted his pilgrimage, at Washington, in 1853. Another of Dr. Mason's protégés was the Rev. R. Hamilton Bishop, a native of Edinburgh, who settled in America in 1801, and, after preaching for several years in New York, went West as a missionary and subsequently was connected, as teacher or Principal, with several Western colleges. He died at College Hill, Ohio, in 1865.

Dr. William M. Taylor, who died at New York in 1895, in the dignified position of a "pastor emeritus" of the church to which he gave the best years of his active life, was a worthy successor to the Masons and McLeods, whose pulpits were so long lights to the Scottish dwellers in the commercial metropolis of the United States. Born at Kilmarnock in 1829 and educated for the ministry of the United Presbyterian Church, at Glasgow and Edinburgh, William Mackergo Taylor was a painstaking and brilliant student. For two years, from June, 1853, he was minister of a church at Kilmaurs, near his native town. In 1855 he went to Bootle, near Liverpool, and he remained there until 1872, when he accepted a call to the Broadway Tabernacle, New York, of which, after many years of faithful labor, he became pastor emeritus three years before his death. By his writings Dr. Taylor enjoyed the acquaintance of a wide circle of readers. His monograph on "John Knox" is the best short life of the great Scotch Reformer which has yet been written—the best for those to read who have not the patience or the time to enjoy McCrie's classic work. His books on Bible biographies have been circulated by the thousand, and his published sermons have also had thousands of readers. In 1886 Dr. Taylor was the "Lyman Beecher Lecturer" at Yale Theological

Seminary, and in connection with that appointment delivered a series of lectures on "The Scottish Pulpit from the Reformation to the Present Day," which is virtually a sketch of the ecclesiastical history of his native land. By the terseness and lucidity of his style in these lectures Dr. Taylor controverted unconsciously the oft-repeated fallacy that men who are in the habit of preaching lose the power of condensing their thoughts and arguments.

Faithful lives in the ministry, might be the words used in summing up the careers of such men as Dr. W. C. Brownlee, a native of Lanarkshire, who closed a long life of usefulness in New York in 1860; of Andrew Stark, a Stirlingshire man, who was pastor of Grand Street Church, New York, for a few years, and died in Scotland, as did one of his successors in that charge, the Rev. Dr. John Thomson; of Robert Kirkwood, once of Paisley, who died at Yonkers in 1866, after holding pastorates at Courtlandville and Auburn, N. Y., and after several years' experience as a missionary in Illinois; of Dr. John Lillie, a Kelso man, who was one of the foremost ministers at Kingston, N. Y., from 1836 till his death in 1867, and gave many evidences of the possession of ripe scholarship, notably by his translations in connection with Lange's magnificent series of commentaries; of Dr. Peter D. Gorrie, who was carried across the Atlantic in 1820, when only three years old, from his native city of Glasgow, and was a noted member of the Methodist Episcopal Church, and died at Potsdam, N. Y., in 1884; of Dr. J. Harkness of Jersey City, who was born in 1803 and died in 1878, whose birthplace was in Roxburghshire, and whose first charge was at Ecclefechan, where his son, William Harkness, the famous astronomer, was born in 1836; of Dr. Duncan R. Campbell, long of Covington County, who was born in Perthshire in 1814 and was President of Georgetown College when he died, in 1861; of David Inglis, a native of Greenlaw, Berwickshire, who, after holding various minor pastorates, became, in 1871, a professor in Knox College, Toronto, and died in 1877, while pastor of a Dutch Reformed Church in Brooklyn, and of hundreds of others—enough to make up a very respectable dictionary of representative clerical biography.

These men belonged to generations which have passed. What may be called our own generation is still adding to the list—adding, it may be said, in greater proportion than any previous one, so far as our records enable us to judge. In Canada the great majority of the Presbyterian divines are of Scotch birth or of immediate Scottish descent. In the States such men as the Rev. William Ormiston, now of California, provide us with names sufficient to show that Scotland still "leavens the lump."

Latterly we have been dealing with preachers pure and simple; with ministers who by their own merits won positions of pre-eminence for themselves in the world of theological thought, or by their eloquence made their pulpits conspicuous "above the lave," or by their sainted lives left memories which are still among the precious heritages of their own churches and denominations. In thinking over the influence which Scotland has exerted over the history of religion in America we somehow overlook, however, the ecclesiastical dignitaries who have adorned the Churches in which their lifework was done, or is being done. The bulk of Scotsmen are so accustomed to their Presbyterian, or Congregational form of Government, with the practical independence of each church and the equality in rank of all ministers, that they seldom contemplate Deans and Bishops, and an Archbishop seems to them a man who stands a long way off, so little does he enter into their calculations. Sometimes they are told that the Moderator of a Presbytery is a sort of Bishop, and that the Moderator of a General Assembly is virtually an Archbishop. But the men who have held such positions seldom, if ever, think so themselves; and if they did they would soon be dispossessed of such thoughts. Beside, they hold such offices only for a brief period and by the votes of their brethren, and after a short interval lay down their honors and fall into line once more with the rank and file unless—as is often the case—their own ability wins for them continued prominence and influence. There never was a purer form of democracy conceived by man than that which prevails in the Government of the Kirk.

But Scotland can point to a long array of Bishops—good, bad, and indifferent—and the race in America has had its influence on the Episcopal throne as well as in the halls of Assembly and of Congress. The Scottish-American Bishops, however, were—or are—all good men and true, and however we may differ from their views or standpoints, we cannot withhold from them that commendation which the sanctity of their lives, the devotion of their purposes, and their high abilities imperatively demand.

In the annals of the Protestant Episcopal Church in the United States few memories are more precious than that of Bishop James Kemp of Maryland. He was born in the Parish of Keith-Hall, Aberdeenshire, in 1764, and educated for the Presbyterian ministry at Marischal College, Aberdeen. In 1787 he crossed the Atlantic, and for two years was employed as tutor in a family in Dorchester County, Maryland. During these two years his views on Presbyterianism underwent a change and he was led to study the tenets of the Church of England, and finally to fully and loyally accept them. He devoted all his spare time to the study of theology, and in 1789 was ordained a priest in the Protestant Episcopal Church. In the following year he was appointed rector of Great Choptank Parish in Maryland. There he remained, faithfully fulfilling his pastoral duties and steadily adding to his store of learning, until, in 1813, he was elected rector of St. Paul's Church, Baltimore. By that time he was recognized as the most profound theologian in the diocese, and his ability as a preacher, his able executive qualities, and the native kindliness of his disposition, had won him hosts of friends. In these circumstances, when it became necessary, in 1814, to appoint a suffragan Bishop to aid Bishop Claggett, there was little opposition to the selection of Dr. Kemp, and he was duly consecrated. Two years later he succeeded, on the death of Dr. Claggett, to the full honors of the Bishopric, and occupied that position, as well as the office of Provost of the University of Maryland, till his death, in 1827, at Baltimore.

Bishop Kemp published during his lifetime several of his sermons on special occasions and a number of controversial tracts, but such specialties are by no means contributions to literature, and have, naturally, been long forgotten. Not so, however, the example of his life, his devotion to duty, and the manner in which he administered and discharged every trust confided to him.

The Episcopal Church in the Dominion gives us several examples of noted Scotch Bishops, for the Scot in Canada flourishes and forces his way to the front under all sorts of conditions. One of the earliest of these dignitaries was Charles J. Stewart, Bishop of Quebec. He was the fifth son of John, seventh Earl of Galloway, and was born at Galloway House, Wigtownshire, in 1775. He was educated at Oxford. Having selected the ministry for his lifework, his studies were directed toward that end, and in 1800 he was ordained a priest. His first charge was a small parish near Peterborough, England, where he remained eight years. Then, desiring to engage in mission work, he applied to the Society for the Propagation of the Gospel and was assigned to the mission of St. Armand, P. Q. There he built a church at his own expense; but his district was a wide one, and he was equally ready to preach the Gospel in a parlor, a barn, or a room in a village inn, as in the sacred edifice he had had constructed. In 1819 he became visiting missionary in the Diocese of Quebec, virtually embracing the whole of Canada, and the story of his journeys in the discharge of his duties, involving discomfort, danger, fatigue, and discouragements, would furnish themes for many romances. Bishop Mountain of Quebec died in 1825, and the faithful missionary was nominated to the see. He was consecrated in Lambeth Palace, London, and at once entered on his duties. These he performed with rare fidelity till his death, in 1837. 'He was," wrote Mr. H. J. Morgan, " a most zealous servant and soldier of Christ, a noble, disinterested being, endowed with rich qualities of heart and mind, and a mouth that spoke no guile."

Bishop Strachan of Toronto will long be remembered in Canada as having virtually ruled the Church of England there during many years of his life, and for having ruled it well. He was born at Aberdeen in 1778, graduated at King's College in that city, and afterward studied theology at St. Andrews. After a brief experience as a teacher in Scotland he emigrated to Canada in 1799, and taught school at Kingston, Ontario, for some three years. He was ordained to the priesthood in 1803, and opened a school at Cornwall, where he remained until, in 1812, he became rector of York (Toronto.) Here he commenced his career as a statesman as well as a pastor. He was nominated an Executive Councillor, took his seat in the Legislative Council, and continued to show an active and direct interest in politics until the end of his career. In 1825 he was appointed Archdeacon of York, and in 1839 reached the highest of his ecclesiastical honors when he was nominated Bishop of Toronto. Few men possessed more influence in Canada than this noted prelate. He established some fifty-seven rectories in Ontraio, and to his efforts was due the foundation of Trinity College, Toronto. The cause of education was possibly dearer to his heart than any other earthly agency, and as a successful teacher himself he knew how to appreciate success in others. Quite a large number of eminent men sat under him as pupils. In Scotland during the few years he taught there he had among his boys David Wilkie, afterward the famous painter, and Capt. Robert Barclay of Lake Erie fame. In Canada Sir John Beverley Robinson, Chief Justice Sir James B. Macaulay, and the Hon. Judge Jones attended his classes. The friendship of these men and scores like them he retained until death dissolved mere earthly ties, and Sir David Wilkie often asserted that to Bishop Strachan he owed everything. The good Bishop died at Toronto in 1867. To the end he preserved the Aberdeen dialect in all its freshness, and a stranger, hearing his accent, might have been excused for thinking he was listening to one who was fresh from the "City of Bon Accord." "Bishop Strachan," writes one who knew him, "when he came to

Canada, taught school in Cornwall, and educated some of the best men we have ever had in Canada. There are few of them left, I am sorry to say. What was curious about the old Bishop was, he never lost the Aberdeen accent, although he thought he had. I have heard him preach. In pronouncing the benediction he always said: 'The peace of God, which passeth all understanding, keep your herts.' Many years ago he had a clergyman come from Aberdeen. He asked him: 'Far dae ye come fae?' The minister said: 'Fae Eberdeen.' After asking some more questions the Bishop insisted on the clergyman getting clear of his Scotch accent, adding: 'I had some trouble in getting clear of it, but I have none of it now'; yet all this was said in the broadest 'Eberdeen' dialect."

Turning to the Roman Catholic Church, we find the Scot flourishing there as elsewhere. In the Lower Provinces few names are held in more kindly remembrance than Bishop Angus McEachern of Charlottetown, Bishop Ronald McDonald of Pictou, or Bishop William Fraser of Antigonish, Vicar Apostolic of Nova Scotia in 1821. The latter deserves to be honored by Scotsmen, for he certainly suffered much for "puir auld Scotland's sake." In fact, it was complained of him at Rome that he devoted himself exclusively to the Scotch members of his flock, for a long time hardly recognizing any others, and finally rarely journeyed outside of the Scotch settlement at Antigonish. He seemed to have a special aversion to Irish Roman Catholics.

In point of devotion to duty, liberality of views, and earnestness of purpose, no fault could be found with Bishop Alexander MacDonell, who was born at Glen Urquhart, near the shore of Loch Ness, in 1769, and is said to have belonged to the family of Glengarry. Long before he was consecrated Roman Catholic Bishop of Kingston, at Montreal in 1826, he had done rare service to Canada by inducing Highlanders to settle in its wild lands, and he had seen active service in Ireland as Chaplain in a regiment of Catholics. In fact, his services were such that he was publicly thanked by the Prince Regent.

He was a thoroughly patriotic Scotsman, and one of his earliest undertakings was the formation of a Highland Society in Ontario, of which he became President, and which was designed to be of real use to settlers and intending settlers. He built no fewer than forty-eight churches and established missions at every point. He had a profound faith in the wonderful future of Canada, and believed in building the foundations of the Church he served so loyally on a scale worthy of that future. Personally he was a kindly man, who made friends wherever he went, and his death, in 1840, while revisiting his native land, was regretted by all classes in the community.

"Bishop MacDonell," once wrote a correspondent to a Canadian newspaper, "was a very kind-hearted man. He was a great means of settling the part of Canada called Glengarry. Some of them were more than ordinary big, strong men, and the present generation of them are worthy of their sires. I never heard that he was particular to have them all Roman Catholics. There are a number of Presbyterians amongst them, and they have a good congregation in Alexandria. The good Bishop gave all the first Roman Catholic settlers in Glengarry a copy of the Holy Bible, which the Presbyterian clergyman told me they would not part with for any money.

"I have been told many good stories about the Bishop by an old French friend. I will only mention one. In the early settlement of the County of Kent the roads were very bad and there were very few places to stop at. The Bishop was exploring through the county on horseback, and, being benighted, he had to ask a farmer for lodgings for the night. After getting supper, and time to go to bed, the farmer said he would show him his bed. The Bishop said: 'Are you a Scotchman and don't take the "Book" before going to bed?' The Scotchman was ashamed to confess that he did not. The Bishop took the Bible and read and prayed with and for the family. The farmer was astonished when the Bishop told him who he was."

Bishop Gilmour of Cleveland, Ohio, who died in Florida in 1891, was born in Glasgow in 1824, and moved in early life, with his parents, to New Glasgow. He was educated in Canada. After many years spent in missionary work he was assigned to the pastorate of St. Patrick's in Cincinnati in 1857, and was consecrated Bishop of Cleveland in 1872. His administration of the diocese was most successful, and was particularly noted for the manner in which it developed the system of parochial schools.

A Catholic prelate need not be a Bishop, and the Very Rev. Monsignor Seton of St. Joseph's, Jersey City, is a case in point. Descended from the ancient noble family of Winton, Dr. Seton's ancestors came to America before the Revolution, carrying with them many historical relics of the family to which they were proud to belong in spite of its misfortunes. One of these American settlers, William Seton, (of whom Dr. Seton is the great-grandson,) was from 1766 to 1771 an officer in the New York St. Andrew's Society, and to the present day the members of the family are proud to recall the fact that their forbears hailed from " dear old Scotland."

CHAPTER VI.

ARTISTS AND ARCHITECTS.

PAINTINGS from Scotland by Scottish artists do not seem nowadays to find much acceptance in America. They are rarely found in the catalogues of the many art sales in New York or Boston or the other large cities, and in the art dealers' establishments the best-known painters of Scotland are unknown either by name or by example. In art circles, in periodicals devoted to art, and in the columns of newspapers which make a feature of artistic matters, hardly any attention is paid to collecting and presenting news from the Scottish studios, and even the gossip of American professional critics seldom troubles itself concerning what may be passing in Scotland, where so many recognized masters have gained their reputation and established a national claim to artistic recognition. The amateur lovers and professional creators of art in America talk glibly of Chalon, of Palmaroli, of Garnier, of Gerome, but of Thomson, Phillip, Macnee, MacCullough, Allan, Faed, or any of the recognized Scottish masters they seem to know nothing.

This is singular when we consider that so many other professional, as well as business and working, men from Scotland, and Scottish products generally, find such a kindly reception in America. The Scottish artisan is always welcomed in every section of the United States as a superior, thorough, and industrious workman, one with a degree of intelligence above his fellows; the Scottish farmer is hailed as an accession in each agricultural community, and it is safe to say that there is not an American steamer afloat on which the services of Scotch engineers are not in use or in demand. In the higher walks of life the influence of Scotland is everywhere seen. Scottish architecture has been closely studied, and the old Baronial style has been copied, adapted, or "applied" to the majority of American modern villas, and, in fact, along with the so-called Colonial style, was the main foundation for the exteriors of such places until recently supplanted by the nondescript "Queen Anne" and pseudo-Elizabethan styles. Even in many public buildings, although a sort of mongrel renaissance is the prevailing fad, the towers and peaks and gables of the Scottish school take the place of the "Grecian" front elevations, with their wooden pillars and impossible pediments. Scotch financiers stand above the tumults, the reactions, the bull-and-bear movements of the stock exchanges, veritable pillars of strength in a seething, sometimes repulsive, sea of dishonesty and dishonor. Scottish theology has been gratefully accepted by Americans, and not even in Scotland have the writings of such men as Prof. A. B. Bruce, Dr. Calderwood, the late Dr. John Ker, Dr. Oswald Dykes, and Dr. Buchanan more appreciative readers. Scottish poetry, too, is also in great vogue; Robert Buchanan, for instance, used to be a favorite; several editions of "Olrig Grange" were readily disposed of when that poem first appeared; Shairp's verses also found a ready sale, and even Pollok's "Course of Time" has been printed in a dozen different forms. There are a half a dozen editions of Aytoun's "Lays," and there are numerous editions of Motherwell, Montgomery, Campbell, and most of our poets, printed and sold in this country. Scots songs are sung on every concert platform, and students of Burns are as numerous as in Scotland. Indeed, probably the most ambitious edition of the works of the Ayrshire bard—six large volumes with notes, steel engravings, and all sorts of editorial paraphernalia—was published in Philadelphia only a few years ago. Of the Waverley Novels there are over twenty-five distinct editions in the market, and editions of Scott's poetry seem to grace, either completely or singly, every publisher's catalogue. One firm has printed over 300,000 copies of Barrie's works, and there is a choice of various editions of any of the writings of Stevenson or Black. Excepting art, everything Scotch, from curling to philosophy, seems to find congenial soil in America.

This lack of appreciation of Scottish art applies as much to loan exhibitions and museums and public galleries, of which better things might be expected, as to private collections and the dealers' offerings or stock in trade. In the Metropolitan Museum of Art, at New York, the greatest institution of its kind in America, not a single work painted in Scotland by a Scottish artist is to be found. Even in the large and costly collection of Miss Catharine Lorillard Wolfe, which by terms of its bequest to the museum is kept distinct from the other pictures, and which is undoubtedly the crowning artistic feature of the institution, the absence of Scottish art is equally apparent.

In the Lenox Library of New York, founded by a Scotsman and still mainly directed by a Scotsman, we find a somewhat similar condition of affairs. True, the collection there is not large, but every picture on view is supposed to be a representative one, and ought to be, if placed on exhibition in accordance with the ideas on which the library was founded. In such a collection we would naturally expect to find some Scotch examples, yet, instead, we have some rather paltry sketches by Sir David Wilkie, of no interest to the public and of little value even to art students, certainly not representative of the man; a painting of the Scottish regalia which is attributed to Wilkie, but with which he had no more to do than the man in the moon, and a couple of specimens (one of them doubtful) of Sir Henry Raeburn. These things, with a very commonplace bust of Scott from Steell's studio, but not his handiwork, and a really good bust of Dr. Chalmers, evidently modeled by Steell himself, are all that represent Scottish art in what might be or ought to be the great repository of that art in America. What has been said of these institutions may be held to apply to all the other art centres in the country. Even at the Chicago World's Fair Scottish artists were poorly represented. There were several Scotch canvases in the British section, but not one that really commanded attention. So far as art was concerned, Poland far outstripped Scotland in excellence, variety, and in the evident genius of the artists.

Scottish sculpture is no more highly regarded than the sister art of painting. Not long ago a replica of Stevenson's fine statue of Sir William Wallace, which is on the corbel over the entrance to the hero's monument on Abbey Craig, near Stirling, was unveiled in Baltimore, and the pose of the figure is laughed at in every circle that makes any pretention to art culture. The pose, they say, is theatrical, the drawn sword is too prominent a feature, the figure itself is stiff, there is nothing below the armor, and so on. Of course people who know why the figure and sword were posed as they are and the latter made so prominent will admit that the artist made the most of his original opportunity for a particular effect. But Americans do not know this, and so they criticise the figure as they find it—standing on an ordinary pedestal in the midst of a park landscape—and find much to sneer at and condemn. If they had said the pose was simply unsuited to the location in which the replica is placed, every one would have agreed with them, and an additional argument against the use of replicas would have been added to the stock on hand. But when they fail to take the change of position into account and simply condemn on general principles their criticism is not worth considering from an artistic standpoint, although, commercially, it is to be regretted. Sir John Steell is represented in America by two statues in Central Park, New York, one a replica in bronze of the figure of Scott, which, in marble, sits under the arch of the monument at Edinburgh, and the other his figure of Burns, of which there are replicas in Dundee and London. Those who know anything of the inside workings of Steell's studio while the Burns statue was in process of development will not be anxious, however patriotic they may be, to claim that statue as one of even his second-rate works, for it must be confessed that, while in parts it shows the genius of the sculptor, it certainly is, as a whole, disappointing. His statue of Scott, however, has long since passed the gauntlet of criticism, and been accepted as a masterpiece, in spite of the clumsiness of the plaid and the stiff massiveness of the whole figure. Yet in New York there is a sort of trades union society of local sculptors, which openly advocates the removal of both these figures to a less prominent place, and would not mourn were they stolen from their pedestals some night and broken up beyond hope of repair. One guide book, describing these statues says: "They are coarsely modeled by a man with a local fame in Scotland, but no artist." This criticism, it must be remembered, was written in a city which contains more atrocious examples of the sculptor's art than any other in the world, such caricatures as the bronze figures of S. S. Cox, Roscoe Conkling, Horace Greeley, W. E. Dodge, and Secretary Seward, which seek honor and recognition in the most prominent thoroughfares. Beside any of them Steell's work, even his poorest, rises as the modeling of a master.

The trouble, however, does not lie now, nor has it ever lain, with any prejudice on the part of the people against either Scottish art or artists as such. It is rather the result of a fashionable current directing the public taste toward Continental schools and a lack of enterprise on the part of the artists in Scotland themselves in not catering to the wants and whims or tastes of the people. Scottish artists residing in America have, from the very beginning of its history, really attained as much honor and success as their countrymen have won in other walks of life. The names which follow will abundantly demonstrate the truth of this assertion.

So far as we have been able to discover, the first Scotch painter to make his home in America was John Smibert, who was born in the Grassmarket of Edinburgh in 1684. He served an apprenticeship as a house painter, but his artistic ambition led him to aspire higher, and he went to London, where, after a time, he made a comfortable living by copying paintings for dealers. Then, after he had saved a little money, he went to Italy, where he studied hard, copied many of the most famous works of the old masters, and made many friends, among them Dr. Berkeley, afterward Bishop of Cloyne. In 1728 he crossed to America in the company of that divine, with the idea of becoming professor of drawing, &c., in a university which it was proposed to found at Bermuda. While the negotiations regarding that seat of learning were in progress, Smibert took up his residence at Newport. When the university scheme was abandoned the artist settled in Boston, where he acquired not only reputation, but a comfortable fortune by his art. Horace Walpole, in his "Anecdotes of Painting," describes him as "a silent and modest man, who abhorred the finesse of some of his profession." A number of his paintings are still to be seen in Yale University, in the Boston Museum of Fine Arts, and in the houses of many old New England families. He married a lady belonging to a well-known Boston family, and had two children. One of them, Nathaniel, gave promise of attaining celebrity as an artist, but he died at an early age. Smibert died in 1751.

Smibert excelled as a portrait painter. America had not in his time got as far advanced in a love of art to affect to admire efforts that were not to a certain degree utilitarian, useful, and productive of dignity, as well as being ornamental. The most famous, perhaps, of American portrait painters was Gilbert Charles Stuart, who was descended from a Scotch family and was born in Rhode Island in 1756. He went to Scotland when a lad and studied painting there, but when his teacher died he returned to America and made his living by painting portraits at Newport. In 1778 he crossed over to London and attracted the attention of Benjamin West, the greatest of all American artists, and from that time he was able to date his success in life. His own studio in London, which he opened in 1781, was a fashionable resort, and he painted portraits of King George III., the Prince of Wales, (George IV.,) and many of the most celebrated characters of the time. He also painted, in Paris, a portrait of Louis XVI., the unfortunate sovereign on whom the wrongs and misgovernment of a race of Kings were avenged at the French Revolution. Stuart settled down in his native country in 1793 and painted many of its most distinguished sons. His portraits of Washington are generally accepted as the best which have been made of that great and good man, and by them Stuart's name has been kept prominently before the people of the United States. He died at Boston in 1828.

James Smillie, who may be regarded as the American founder of an artistic family, landed at Quebec in 1821. His father and elder brother, who were with him, were jewelers, and they at once went into business in that quaint, historic town. James did the engraving and chasing for the establishment. His abilities won the notice of Lord Dalhousie, then Governor General of Canada, and that nobleman sent him to London to study. Smillie failed to get the sort of instructor he wanted, and he returned to his native city of Edinburgh, worked there for five months, and then rejoined his relatives in Quebec. In 1829 he settled in New York and established himself as a line engraver. An engraving after Weir's picture of "The Convent Gate" brought him into favorable notice, and he soon had all the work on hand he could accomplish. In 1830 he became an associate of the National Academy, and an Academician in 1851. Among his most successful engravings are "Mount Washington," after Kennett; "Dover Plains," after Durand, and "The Rocky Mountains," after Bierstadt. Mr. Smillie in his latter years lived in retirement at Poughkeepsie, where he died in 1884. There is no doubt he was the most successful line engraver of his time in America, and one of his brothers, William Cumming Smillie, was long equally recognized as a leader among the bank-note engravers of this country and Canada.

Of Mr. Smillie's sons, two have carried on to the present day the reputation he so deservedly won for the family name. James D. Smillie, who was born in New York in 1835, made his mark by his engravings of Darley's illustrations to Cooper's novels. He became a National Academician in 1876. Besides being noted as an engraver, J. D. Smillie has won much success as a painter in oil and water colors, and such works as " The Cliffs of Normandy," in oil, and " The Passing Herd," in water color, have given him a place among the most praiseworthy artists of the country. He was President of the Water Color Society in 1873 and 1878. Mr. Smillie has also shown exquisite skill as an etcher, and the best-known specimen of his work in that method is the etching of the magnificent statue of Robert Burns at Albany, the work of his friend, Charles Calverley. His brother William M. was eminent as a letter engraver, and was General Manager of the American Bank Note Company when he died, in 1884. The third son of James Smillie, George Henry Smillie, is a National Academician and a master of oil and water color, and such works as " A Florida Lagoon," " A Lake in the Woods," and " Under the Pines of the Yosemite " show that he has inherited a full share of the wonderful talent of the family.

Among landscape artists in America none have been accorded a higher position by critics and the public alike than William Hart, who died at Mount Vernon June 17, 1894, in his seventy-second year. When a boy his parents removed from Kilmarnock, and, crossing the Atlantic, settled at Albany, where William, after a brief schooling, was apprenticed to a coachbuilder. He was then instructed in the art of decorating carriage panels, and that employment awakened his artistic tastes. A severe illness made him leave the coachmaker's employment when seventeen years of age, and on recovering he opened a studio at Troy, where he did both portrait and landscape work, and by dint of patient devotion to his subjects not only earned a livelihood, but steadily added to his knowledge of his art. A visit to Scotland completed his artistic education and training, and after three years' sketching there he returned, in 1853, to America with several portfolios filled with drawings and " bits," and suggestions for future works. He opened a studio in New York, and in 1855 was elected an Associate of the National Academy. Three years later he was chosen an Academician. His works betokened careful, thoughtful, and conscientious work, and in country scenes introducing animal life he particularly excelled. There was nothing outré in his methods; no straining after mere color effects, no desire to startle by following the dictates of some of the new schools, which, now and again, in his time, as to the present day, strive to capture public attention by some royal road to excellence, which ends in bathos—the Pre-Raphaelite, for instance. Hart's excellence was the result of a careful desire to reproduce nature and show on his canvases every little detail, which, taken together, make up completeness. Among his most noted works, all of which exemplify his technique, his devotion to the highest principles of art and his mastery of that art, are: "Coming From the Mill," "The September Snow," "Autumn in the Woods of Maine," "Scene on the Peabody River," "Twilight on the Brook," "Goshen, N. H."; "Twilight," "A Brook Study," "Easter Sky at Sunset," water color; "The Golden Hour," "Morning in the Clouds," "Keene Valley," "Cattle Scenes," "Landscape with Jersey Cattle," "The Ford," "Scene on Napanock Creek," "A Modern Cinderella," and "After a Shower."

Mr. Hart was equally great in the use of water color as of oil. Indeed, the former, perhaps, was his favorite mode of artistic expression, and his love for it led him to take an active part in the formation of the American Society of Water Colorists, of which he was President for three terms, 1870-73. For many years also he was President of the Brooklyn Academy of Design.

A brother of this noted painter, James McDougall Hart, has gained equal fame in the annals of American art. Born at Kilmarnock in 1828, he, like his brother, crossed the Atlantic in boyhood and began life in the service of a coachbuilder at Albany. In 1851 he went to Dusseldorf and studied art, and on his return settled in Albany, where he opened a studio. After about four years' struggle in that good old phlegmatic Dutch town, he thought his opportunity for the future lay in New York, and there he removed, and soon won a prominent place among local artists. His pastoral scenes, especially, won him popularity, and as a landscape painter none of his contemporaries excelled him for his faithfulness to nature and the poetic glamour he threw into most of his work. Like his brother, he never tried any of the tricks which so many artists attempt to win attention, and it is noted that one can study any of the productions of this painter's easel and find the attractiveness of the subject growing as a result of that study. Such is notably the case with his " Summer Memory of Berkshire " and his " Indian Summer," both of which won deserved applause when exhibited at the Paris Salon in 1878. They are poems as well as pictures, and arouse many pleasing thoughts in the mind of the spectator who has any power of thought at all. So, too, with the masterpiece which he exhibited at the Centennial Exhibition in 1876— " A Misty Morning "—a work which stood out in bold relief among the contributions of American artists to the collection there displayed for its wonderful interpretation of one of nature's moods. Some affect to find little to praise or enlarge upon in such works as that of Mr. Hart, because they are so true to nature that they awaken nothing discordant in the mind or present anything particularly odd to attract the eye. Their very fidelity is apt to make them be overlooked in an exhibition, while a flaring canvas, with an unearthly green foreground, a wooden-like figure in a glaring yellow gown, and a sky with a series of streaks of all the colors on the palette, would attract a gaping crowd and charm the dilletantes and the newspaper art critics, the latter mainly because it would give them a chance to display their stock of artistic slang. Such paintings as that of " Cattle Going Home " are not enthusiastically praised for the same reason that the Scotch sewing woman saw nothing to admire in Burns's poem, " The Cotter's Saturday Night," because it told just what she saw done every night in her own father's house since ever she could remember. So long as Scottish art in America is represented by the examples we have named, and by such paintings as "Moonrise in the Adirondacks," "A Breezy Day on the Road," "On the North Shore," and a dozen others from the same studio, her lovers will have no occasion to "hing their heids."

Another landscape painter of note was James Hope, who was born not far from Abbotsford in 1818, and settled on a farm in Canada, along with his parents, when a boy. He was for a time a teacher in a seminary at Castleton, Vt., and it was not until 1848 that he found it possible to put into practice an ambition which had long possessed him and devote his time entirely to art. After considerable struggles to gain a footing, he took up his abode in New York in 1853, and soon found a market for his canvases. In 1865 he was chosen an Associate of the National Academy, and such works as "Rainbow Falls," "The Forest Glen," or "The Gem of the Forest," amply proved his genius for landscape painting. From 1872 till his death Mr. Hope spent his time in quiet retirement at Watkins Glen, New York.

In a purely popular sense no Scottish-American artist ever commanded so wide attention as Alexander Hay Ritchie, who died at New Haven, Conn., Sept. 19, 1895. He was born at Glasgow in 1822, and in early life removed to Edinburgh and was educated in Heriot's Hospital. He was apprenticed to a firm of machinists, but developed a taste for art, and studied under Sir William Allan, one of the most famous of the historical painters of Scotland. In 1843 he settled in the United States, after a short stay in Canada, and soon afterward took up his residence in Brooklyn, where he resided until just before his death. He quickly acquired high rank as an engraver in stipple and mezzotint, and gradually won a reputation as an original painter in oils, particularly of portraits and historic scenes in which figures predominated. His popularity reached its height by his painting of the "Death of Lincoln," and such works as "Mercy Knocking at the Gate," "Fitting Out Moses for the Fair," showed that he possessed the charms of fancy as well as the graces of art. His painting of "Washington and His Generals" proved equally popular, and by means of his own engraving of it, that patriotic group now decorates thousands of homes throughout the American continent. As a portrait painter, in which work his "Dr. McCosh," "Henry Clay," and "Professor Charles Hodge of Princeton" are notable examples, Mr. Ritchie left some particularly creditable examples of his skill, while as a book illustrator his graver was constantly employed for many years prior to his death.

Pleasing memories are recalled by such examples of pure art as "The Palisades," "Sugar Loaf Mountain," "Autumn in the Adirondacks," and other pictures of John Williamson, an artist who found in and around the magnificent scenery of the Hudson constant employment for his brush, and a perpetual incentive to attain the highest possible ideal of his art. He studied that noble stream from its source to the sea, and knew it, and could reproduce it in all its moods. Williamson was born in the very inartistic region of Tolcross, Glasgow, in 1827, and died at Glenwood-on-Hudson in 1885, nearly all of his life being passed on this side of the Atlantic, as he was taken from his native land while a child.

Another artist who had Glasgow for his birthplace was Thomas Lachlan Smith, whose specialty was Winter scenes, and who contributed two notable pictures to the collection at the Centennial Exhibition—"The Deserted House" and "The Eve of St. Agnes." Smith received his artistic training in the studio of George H. Boughton (now winning yearly successes in London) at Albany, and he opened a studio in that city in 1859. In 1862 he forsook Albany for New York, where he died in 1884, having won a recognized position among the American painters of his time.

So much for painters. We may now, having shown the merits of the Scottish-American "limners," bring forward some instances of those who have won fame with the chisel and molding tools. One of the earliest of these on our list is John Crookshanks King, who was born in the ancient and historic village of Kilwinning, Ayrshire, in 1806, and died in the historic city of Boston in 1882. He was educated in his native county, and there served his apprenticeship to his trade—that of machinist. In 1829 he crossed the Atlantic, and for a time was Superintendent of factories in Louisville and Cincinnati. It was in 1834 that he began to understand the extent of his genius for modeling, and in that year he made a clay figure which so pleased Hiram D. Powers, America's most poetic sculptor, that he advised him to devote his entire attention to such work. After a brief residence in New Orleans, King settled in Boston in 1840, and in that city most of his artistic career was spent. Among his best-known busts are those of Daniel Webster, John Quincy Adams, and Ralph Waldo Emerson. King also excelled as a maker of cameo portraits a branch of art which at present has gone out of fashion, although there are not wanting signs that it will again become a fad in the society world.

Few if the many thousands of visitors to the memorial temple which rises over the Doon, not far from the Auld Brig, as a national tribute to the memory of the genius who gave fame to that classic section of Ayrshire by his pen, know that the two figures representing "Tam o' Shanter" and "Souter Johnnie" which are shown in the grounds below are the work of a sculptor who died on a farm at Ramapo, N. Y., in 1850. James Thom, the sculptor in question, ended his career in that lonely spot a sadly disappointed man. He was born in Ayrshire, and began life as a stone mason. He acquired the art of modeling mainly by his own personal observation and practice, and in 1828 produced the two figures which, shown on the banks of the Doon, have preserved his name to the present day. In an artistic sense he never advanced any further than these statues, and such works as his figure of "Old Mortality" simply reproduced their artistic beauties and defects. It seems a pity that Thom did not have the benefit of two or three years' practical training at some of the art centres, but fate denied him the opportunity, and all his work was done in a narrow and rather primitive groove. But he was a genius undoubtedly, and lacked merely the necessary study to have been able to give full expression to the ideals he so earnestly tried to interpret with his chisel. His work was very popular with the people, but his studio at Ayr was never greatly burdened with orders, and it was in the hope of winning a more remunerative popularity that he emigrated. In America, however, there is no trace of his having had any success at all, or even of his doing any work.

A much more modern instance of a Scottish sculptor's success in America is that of Mr. J. M. Rhind, son of a once well-known Edinburgh sculptor. Mr. Rhind settled in New York from Edinburgh in 1888, and was not long in coming to the front among that city's sculptors. His most noted work—the King memorial fountain at Albany—is an elaborate and thoughtful group of sculpture, rather than a single example, and shows the artist to be a man of imagination as well as of artistic ability. Its theme is that of Moses striking the rock, and the story is completely told in the attitude and composition of all the figures, from the majestic representation of Moses to the sweet outline of the baby which is getting from its mother a draught of the blessed water flowing from the rock in answer to the stroke from the Patriarch's staff. Mr. Rhind also executed one of the magnificent bronze doors now on Trinity Church.

Visitors to New York's Central Park have admired the beautiful carved work on the Terrace and Mall—work that is now beginning to lose its sharp outline under stress of the weather changes, which in the Northern States are so destructive of outdoor stonework. A great deal of this carving was done by Robert Thomson, a sculptor of exquisite taste, who, if we may judge by his work in Central Park, was as conscientious and thorough in his attention to the most trifling and almost hidden details as to those things which were certain to arrest the public eye. For many years there stood in the same park a group modeled by him to which was given the name of "Auld Lang Syne." It represented Tam o' Shanter and Souter Johnnie enjoying a crack, with the usual accompaniments. To a Scotsman the group was more than a work of art; it was a glimpse o' hame. Every

Scot resident in New York knew each line in the group, and every new arrival in the community was taken to the nook where it stood, or was sent there soon after his arrival. After several years of exposure the freestone in which the figures were carved began to show signs of disintegration, and to save the work it was removed to the building at the Casino where the Crawford models were on view, and there it was badly damaged in the fire which laid that building in ruins. It is still stored somewhere in the Park, but too much worsted in its encounter with the flames to be attractive—even to Scotsmen, it is said. After a residence of some fifteen years in this country, spent mainly in New York, Philadelphia, and Baltimore, Mr. Thomson returned to Scotland, and, settling in Edinburgh, continued his work as a sculptor. He executed, among other things, several figures for the niches in the Scott Monument, including Jeannie Deans and the Laird of Dumbiedykes. He died in that city early in 1895. One of Thomson's pupils, Alexander M. Calder, a native of Aberdeen, has long held a noted position among Philadelphia sculptors. He cut or designed most of the carved work on the new Public Buildings, and that magnificent pile is crowned by his gigantic figure of William Penn.

George E. Ewing, the once noted Glasgow sculptor, whose figure of Burns stands in that city's famous plaza, George Square, closed a somewhat varied career in New York in 1884. He had done much good work in Glasgow and the West of Scotland, and many Scots in America were surprised when he forsook his native land and entered upon a new career in New York. Whatever expectations he had formed of America were doomed to disappointment, and his experience was a succession of failures. The fact was, he was too old on reaching America to begin life anew, and his artistic methods and ideals were too firmly cast to adapt themselves to the taste of the American connoisseurs, and so accomplish anything like satisfactory financial results. He executed some very pleasing busts, notably one of the Rev. Dr. Taylor, and one of the Rev. Dr. Omiston, both good examples of conscientious modeling, with, in the bust of Dr. Ormiston, a dash of genius which marked the artist; but these things brought no " grist to the mill." After two years' struggling in New York, Ewing went to Philadelphia, but there his success was no greater, and his life became full of sadness. When Henry Irving first visited Philadelphia Ewing called on him—they were acquainted long before. Learning of his plight, the great actor at once gave him a commission to execute a medallion portrait of himself and one of Miss Terry. To get the necessary sittings he accompanied the actors to New York and lodged at the Brevoort House. There, one morning, he was found lying dead in bed. The room was partly filled with gas from an open jet in the chandelier, and it was supposed that Mr. Ewing had either not noticed the escape when he retired to bed, or, in extinguishing the light had involuntarily reopened the jet. The remains were interred in Greenwood Cemetery, Brooklyn. Mr. Ewing virtually left nothing on this side of the Atlantic by which his ability as a sculptor can publicly be judged, a fact which is to be regretted, for he was a man of brilliant parts, with high ideals as an artist, and would have at least amply justified his Scottish reputation had a fitting opportunity been vouchsafed to him.

In the Wellstood family, which for a long series of years had at least two representatives in the foremost ranks of American engravers, we find several men of undoubted artistic ability who devoted their whole lives toward improvement of that branch of art. The family was an Edinburgh one, and is still in some of its branches active in the daily doings of that grand old city. John Geikie Wellstood was born in Auld Reekie in 1813, and settled in New York in 1830. After being in business for several years, his firm merged in the American Bank Note Company, and he remained in that concern until 1871, when he founded the Columbian Bank Note Company in Washington, of which he became President. In connection with this establishment he modeled and partly engraved the backs of all the United States Treasury notes. When all work of this class was undertaken by a Government bureau Mr. Wellstood returned to New York and became again connected with the American Bank Note Company. As a script engraver he was considered superior to any man of his time.

His brother, William, born at Edinburgh in 1819, and who was for a long term of years engaged in business in New York, devoted himself more to pictorial work, and his portraits of Longfellow, President Grant, and Florence Nightingale, were long ranked as among the best examples of the American engraver's art. High praise is due also to such works as his " Mount Washington," after Gifford, and his " Coast of Mount Desert," after William Hart. For a small engraving, an engraving in which the engraver has put his heart as much as painter ever did into his canvas, we know of nothing finer than the portrait of Hew Ainslie, the poet, with its emblematic wreath, which William Wellstood engraved after a design by his brother Stephen, for the edition of Ainslie's poems issued in 1855. James, a son of William Wellstood, who was born in New York City in 1855 and died in 1880, was an engraver of much promise, as is amply evidenced by his " Safe in Port," after the painting of that name by William Moran. The whole family, however, have been in one way or another distinguished " above the lave," and would require a chapter to themselves, instead of merely the passing notice it is within the province of a volume like this to give.

A noted example of an engraver developing into a painter—and a painter of first rank—is furnished by the career of Walter Shirlaw. Born in Paisley—the town of poets—in 1838, and emigrating to the United States with his parents two years later, Mr. Shirlaw's entire education, artistic and otherwise, has been gained on this side of the Atlantic. He learned the trade of engraving— his specialty being work on bank notes—but even when a child had inclinations for the higher branch of art, and the first picture he exhibited, at the National Academy in 1861, won such favorable comment that he decided to leave engraving alone for the future. After studying in Munich for a year or two, he returned to America, and his career since then as a landscape artist has been one of continued and increasing success. Among his most noted works have been " Jealousy," now owned by the National Academy of Design; " Good Morning," " Sheep Shearing in the Bavarian Highlands," " Gossip," and " Indian Girl." Mr. Shirlaw became an Academician in 1888, and was one of the founders and the first President of the Society of American Artists.

We would like to devote considerable space to the hundreds of Scotch architects who have been at work in this country since it began to cultivate the arts, but the subject is too great to be even more than barely hinted at at the tail end of a chapter, and that is all that our scheme will permit. So we must content ourselves with a couple of examples.

In an issue of the New York " Scottish-American " for 1888 is the following notice regarding an early architect whose name is by no means yet forgotten in New York:

" The alterations now in progress at Castle Garden reveal much of the old work of Alexander McComb, the old New York architect, who was the most prominent member of his profession in this country in the middle of last century. He was a native of Scotland, but of what county is not known, although it is generally believed to have been Ayrshire. When the old City Hall, in Wall Street, was remodeled and practically rebuilt, Mr. McComb was the architect, and a very stately building it was. McComb amassed considerable wealth, bought a large tract of land in the Adirondacks, and finally settled there, leaving his business to his son, John. His name is still recalled by McComb's Dam Bridge, in the upper part of the city.

" John McComb was born in this city in 1763, and was as successful as his father. He erected a fine house for himself in Bowling Green, which was long known as the McComb Mansion, and all the principal buildings put up in New York between 1795 and 1830 were designed by him. His greatest work, so far as we know, is the present City Hall, the cornerstone of which was laid in

1803, when Edward Livingston, the descendant of an old and aristocratic Scotch family, was Mayor. Another memorial of McComb's skill is old St. John's Church, on Varick Street, which in its day was thought to be a more perfect and comfortable church than old St. Paul's, at the corner of Vesey Street and Broadway. McComb also designed several improvements at Castle Clinton, (now Castle Garden,) some of which after being concealed by wooden erections for many years are again being exposed to view. He lived to a good old age, dying in this city in 1853, and left a name that will ever rank prominent among New York architects."

A more modern example may be selected in the career of John McArthur, who was born in Bladenock, Wigtonshire, in 1823. In 1848 he did his first public work in this country, when he designed the House of Refuge in Philadelphia. Since then he has designed scores of public buildings, such as the Naval Hospitals at Philadelphia, Annapolis, Md., and Mare Island, Cal.; Public Ledger Building. Philadelphia; Lafayette College, Easton, Penn., and for his crowning work, the new Public Buildings of Philadelphia. In 1874 Mr. McArthur declined the offer of the office of Supervising Architect of the Treasury.

It would hardly do to pass away from the architects without some mention of the men who interpret their ideas—the mechanics. In stonework, Scotch masons long held the lead in this country; wherever a stone building was being erected, Scotsmen in greater or lesser numbers were certain to be found. Every building of any size in the country, it may be safe to say, owes something to Scotch ingenuity. The Capitol at Albany, the State House at Boston, the Tomps at New York, the Metropolitan Museum, the City Hall at Chicago, and hundreds of other edifices famous over the country were reared amid the sound of the Doric. To take one notable instance, the Smithsonian Institution at Washington was built by Gilbert Cameron, a native of Greenock, who for several years was the most noted contractor in the Capital City. When the civil war broke out Cameron, then an old man, found himself in possession of a competency, and, despising all schemes for amassing greater wealth, he returned to his native country and spent his time in a house he called " Washington Cottage," at Greenock, until his death, in 1866.

CHAPTER VII.

SCIENTISTS AND INVENTORS.

IT would be singular if a country whose genius gave to the world the art of logarithms, the steam engine, the knowledge of chloroform, illuminating gas, and a host of other universally renowned inventions, discoveries, and appliances would not be represented in scientific pursuits and the higher mechanical sciences in America. We specify higher mechanical because what might be termed actual mechanical work can have no share in our inquiries. Scotch mechanics are found all over the country, and are generally held in the highest regard for their thorough mastery over their work, their intelligent manipulation of details, their readiness to grasp new ideas, even when they do not evolve them, and their conscientious devotion to whatever matter may be in hand. There is not a railway machine shop in America, or iron shipbuilding establishment, where Scotch mechanics may not be found. The same, in fact, might be said of every extensive mechanical establishment on the continent. Into the story of this great army of toilers, hard at work, every day doing something that is to aid in the further development of the country's resources or comforts, we cannot enter. We must perforce confine ourselves to the higher departments of science—to examples selected from among what may be called professional workers.

Without at all attempting to take away from any one the credit of being the first to make the science of telegraphy a success, we must claim that the first publicly to express the idea that electricity could be so utilized was a Scotsman who ended his days in Virginia. This was

Charles Morrison, a native of Greenock. Very little is known about his life history beyond the fact that he was a surgeon by profession, a man of extreme modesty, and that, unable to make a living in Scotland, he crossed over to Virginia and died there. Many efforts have been made in America and Scotland to discover some additional information about his life and death, but without avail. His claim to have demonstrated that electricity could be utilized for conveying intelligence is based upon a letter which he sent from Renfrew to the Scots Magazine, and which appeared in that once famous periodical in 1753.

The essential portion of the letter is as follows:

"It is well known to all who are conversant with electrical experiments that the electric power may be propagated along a small wire, from one place to another, without being sensibly abated by the length of its progress. Let, then, a set of wires, equal in number to the letters of the alphabet, be extended horizontally between two given places parallel to one another, and each of them about an inch distant from that next to it. At every twenty yards' end let them be fixed in glass, or jeweler's cement, to some firm body, both to prevent them from touching the earth or any other non-electric, and from breaking by their own gravity. Let the electric gun barrel be placed at right angles with the extremities of the wires, and about an inch below them. Also let the wires be fixed on a solid piece of glass, at six inches from the end, and let that part of them which reaches from the glass to the machine have sufficient spring and stiffness to recover its situation after having been brought in contact with the barrel. Close by the supporting glass let a ball be suspended from every wire; and about a sixth or an eighth of an inch below the balls place the letters of the alphabet, marked on bits of paper or any other substance that may be light enough to rise to the electrified ball, and at the same time let it be so contrived that each of them may reassume its proper place when dropped.

"All things constructed as above, and the minute previously fixed, I begin the conversation with my distant friend in this manner. Having set the electrical machine a-going as in ordinary experiments, suppose I am to pronounce the word Sir; with a piece of glass or any other *electric per se*, I strike the wire S, so as to bring it in contact with the barrel, then i, then r, all in the same way; and my correspondent, almost in the same instant, observes these several characters rise in order to the electrified balls at his end of the wires."

Any one can see that there is a big difference between the electric telegraph of to-day and that outlined in this letter, but the essential principle is the same, and surely this unfortunate Scot should receive credit for thus promulgating an idea which others took up and perfected until it has become one of the wonders of the modern world.

So, too, with the question of steam navigation. Years before Taylor or Miller on Dalswinton, or Bell on the Clyde, or Fulton on the Hudson, demonstrated its feasibility it was fully shown on the Potomac in the presence of George Washington by James Rumsey, who was born in Virginia of Scotch parents in 1754. His first really public experiment was made in 1786, and two years later he exhibited another model. One writer, Mr. James Weir, Jr., says: "He had all the native shrewdness and astuteness generally ascribed to the Scotchman. He was a man of fine presence, tall and powerfully built. While, strictly speaking, not an educated man, he was an omnivorous reader and well versed in matters pertaining to his profession—civil engineering. He was a good talker, but a better listener, and his neighbors regarded him with respect, and looked upon him as a man of undoubted genius.

"Testimony adduced before the House of Representatives in 1839 shows that Rumsey had conceived the idea of steam navigation as early as August, 1783. Laboring under very adverse circumstances, he succeeded in the Autumn of 1784 in making a test of some of the principles of his engine and propelling apparatus. In January, 1785, Rumsey obtained a patent from the General Assembly of Maryland for navigating the waters of that State. During the whole of that year he was busy in the construction of a steamboat, and in 1786 he successfully navigated this boat on the Potomac at Shepherdstown in the presence of hundreds of spectators."

We have quoted American testimony in connection with this case, as Scotsmen have often been accused of national prejudice in connection with the subject of early steam navigation.

The first Scotch scientist of any consequence, so far as we have been able to trace, to settle in America was William Douglas, a native of Linlithgowshire. He was born in 1691, and left Scotland for the American Colonies in 1716, settling in Boston two years later as a physician, a profession he had studied at Glasgow. He quickly established a large and profitable practice, but he had the knack of making enemies, and soon could number them by the score. He appears to have been a man of strong prejudices, quick in temper, and possessed of a degree of blunt outspokenness which often led him into awkward positions. He was considerable of a busybody, too, and had opinions on almost any subject, and these opinions he never concealed, even when personal policy would have inculcated silence as his best and most profitable course. He was a bitter opponent of the idea of vaccination as a preventive of smallpox, and he advocated additional stamp duties at a time when the trend of public sentiment in the Colonies was in favor of their abolition. But in spite of his marked peculiarities he was a man of the warmest heart, and had, after all, more friends than enemies. He was scrupulously honest in everything he did, and as a medical practitioner his reputation was second to none in New England. He published an "almanack" in 1744 which is yet highly valued by the curious, and his many medical publications show him to have been a fearless thinker and a diligent student. He died at Boston in 1750.

A year later than Dr. Douglas there came to America a much more lovable personage, who was destined to leave a deeper mark in the country's annals. This was

Dr. Thomas Graeme, who, as one of the founders, in 1749, and the first President of the St. Andrew's Society of Philadelphia, raised a better and more enduring monument to his own worth and patriotism than could have been constructed in marble or granite. Indeed, he seems to have been very popular among his countrymen in the Quaker City, for, after leaving the chair of the society which he had helped to found he was recalled to that honorable office, and served from 1764 until his death in 1771. Dr. Graeme was born at Balgowan in 1688 and settled in Philadelphia in 1717, at the instance of Sir William Keith, Lieutenant Governor, whom he accompanied across the ocean, and remained there until the end of his career. During most of his life he practiced his profession as a physician, and as such he attained considerable eminence, but his practice was more or less interrupted by several appointments which he held. In 1726 Dr. Graeme became a member of the Provincial Council, in 1727 he was appointed Naval Officer at Philadelphia, in 1731 he was chosen a Justice of the Supreme Court, and in 1741 became again Naval Officer, and continued in that position for twenty years. He had a marked influence on Philadelphia during his career, and his charitable disposition was shown in many ways. Besides helping, at least, to organize the St. Andrew's Society, which from its beginning has been an exponent of practical, sensible, and timely charity, Dr. Graeme took an active part in founding the Pennsylvania Hospital, of which institution he acted (from 1751) during several years as physician. Scotsmen of this stamp, and there were and are an army of them, exert a wonderful amount of good in the world, and, indeed, it may be said that the influences of their lives are not lost even in the mass of good influences which preserve the moral vitality of the world, but stand out in bold relief as instances of what may be accomplished by well thought out and kindly efforts even when not backed up by vast individual wealth.

Dr. John Linning, who, according to the records of the St. Andrew's Society of Charleston, became a member of that organization in 1731, arrived in America a year before, and soon built up a prosperous practice in South Carolina's historical city. He was born in Dundee in 1708 and studied medicine at Edinburgh. Early in his professional career he took a special interest in natural science, was fond of experimenting in physics—or natural philosophy—and when the subject of electricity first began to be broached he carried on an extensive and learned correspondence with Benjamin Franklin concerning it. Dr. Linning was the first to introduce an electrical apparatus in Charleston. His interest in his profession, however, was not lessened by such experiments or studies, and he was ever striving to keep fully abreast with the medical progress of his time, either by observation in his own practice or by reading. One evidence of this still remains, although the work is now obsolete, in his "History of Yellow Fever," the first American book on the subject. Dr. Linning died at Charleston in 1760.

The family physician of George Washington and his firm and attached friend from the day they first met, at Fort Necessity, in 1754, until the nation's hero passed away at Mount Vernon, in 1799, was Dr. James Craik, a native of Scotland, who had settled in early life in Virginia. He was born in 1731. In 1754, when he met Washington at Fort Necessity, he was Surgeon in a provincial corps, and stood by that officer's side when the body of the commander of the provincial forces, Gen. Braddock, was being committed to the grave. When the Revolutionary War broke out, Craik adopted the cause of the Colonies and saw a good deal of active service. At the siege of Yorktown he was director general of the hospital, and the skill and the devotion he showed won the admiration of all who were brought into contact with him. After the struggle was over, Dr. Craik settled near the home of Gen. Washington, and the two men enjoyed the pleasantest intimacy. When Washington was seized with his last illness, the old family physician was summoned, and held the hand of the warrior-statesman as he passed out through the veil. Dr. Craik spent his closing years quietly in his Virginia home, and he died there in 1814, when the country was in the midst of its second, and it is to be hoped its last, armed contest with Britain.

Dr. Craik was one of those quiet, useful men who do much good on their journey through the world, but who, it must be confessed, acquire eminence not so much by their own talents as by those of their friends. He was recognized as a skillful, conservative physician, but without any of those brilliant qualities which would have of themselves given him prominence in his profession or would have preserved his name and memory till the present day. His fame was not to be compared to that of his contemporary, Dr. Peter Middleton, one of the original members of the St. Andrew's Society of New York and its President for three terms, 1767-8-9. He was a native of Edinburgh, and graduated in medicine in that city. He settled in New York about 1730, and soon was regarded as the most eminent physician and surgeon in the Colony. In 1750, in company with another medical man, he made the first dissection in America of a body before a number of students, and in the matter of the education for his own profession Dr. Middleton seemed to have always taken a deep interest. In 1767 he established a medical school in New York, a school which was subsequently merged into King's [Columbia] College, of which institution he was one of the Governors from 1770 till his death, in 1781.

Equally prominent as a physician, and entitled to special remembrance as the first of the great scientific American weather prophets who have made the name of "American weather" so famous or notorious over the world, was Dr. Lionel Chalmers. He crossed the Atlantic in 1736, settled soon afterward in Charleston, S. C., and practiced his profession there for some forty years, or until his death, in 1777. Dr. Chalmers was born at Campbellton, Argyllshire, in 1715, and left Scotland for America immediately upon graduating from Edinburgh University. He published several medical books and essays, but his weather researches, notably as expressed in his now scarce "Treatise on Weather and Diseases of South Carolina," are his best claims to distinction. He made careful observations, ventured even on prophesying, and saw that study on scientific lines was only needed to reduce the weather problem to an exact science.

An amiable man, of high scientific attainments, and whose life was one of usefulness, was Dr. William Wilson, who was contented to practice his profession as a physician in a very limited circle—that of the family and friends of Chancellor Livingston—but who filled several offices with marked ability and was one of the early promoters of scientific agriculture in America. He arrived in New York in 1784, bringing with him from Scotland his newly received medical graduation papers, from Glasgow University, and letters of introduction to Chancellor Livingston. That great and good man was delighted with the new-comer, and invited him to take up his quarters at the family mansion of Clermont, which remained his home until his death, in 1828, at the age of seventy-three years, long after his patron and friend had passed away. In 1804 Dr. Wilson was appointed Judge of Columbia County, and held that office for several years. His interest in agricultural matters was increased and developed by his residence in that section of the State, and produced many useful results. One of these was the organization, by his efforts, of the Farmers' Club of Dutchess and Columbia Counties—the pioneer of the purely agricultural societies in New York.

Another scientific physician was Dr. John Spence of Philadelphia, who was born at Edinburgh in 1766 and educated at the university in that city. His first purpose when entering the classes at Edinburgh was to get enrolled in the ranks of the ministry, but his views in that respect were not realized, and he turned his attention to the study of medicine. When he took up his residence in America his first employment was as a family tutor at Dumfries, Va. He was one of the stanchest advocates in America of vaccination, and was active in spreading abroad a knowledge of its practice and its beneficent influence. He contributed largely to the medical and scientific journals of his time, and a spirited controversy which he had with the famous Benjamin Rush, and which was published in 1806 in the "Medical Museum" of Philadelphia, gave him a considerable degree of prominence. Dr. Spence died at Dumfries, Va., in 1829.

Few physicians in New York State were more honored during life than was Dr. James McNaughton, who was born at Kenmore, Perthshire, in 1809, and died in Paris, France, while on a visit, in 1874. His life from 1817 until a few months before his death was spent in Albany, N. Y., and from 1840 on he honored the office of Professor of the Theory and Practice of Medicine in Albany Medical College, while for many years he was regularly elected President of the Albany County Medical College. His birthplace is remembered in Albany by the Kenmore Hotel, named in its honor by a company in which his sons were prominent. Dr. Lawrence Turnbull (a native of Shotts) and his son, Dr. Charles Smith Turnbull, fill a large and prominent place in the medical annals of Philadelphia, while around New York such men as Prof. A. J. C. Skene, and in Boston practitioners like Dr. A. D. Sinclair are worthily upholding the fame of the motherland in the art of healing.

But we have dwelt long enough among medical men, and must now cull some examples in other walks of science.

One of the most noted of the scientific soldiers of the Revolutionary War was Robert Erskine, son of the Rev. Ralph Erskine, author of "Gospel Sonnets" and one of the founders of the Secession Church in Scotland. Erskine was born at Dunfermline in 1735. His first employment was at Falkirk, and there and in England he seems to have become thoroughly posted in the making of cannon and cannon balls. After settling in America in 1771 to become the manager of an iron works in New Jersey, he threw off, when opportunity offered, his allegiance to the British Crown and became Chief of Engineers on the staff of Gen. Washington. He died in 1780, when the conflict was at its height, and his leader honored his memory by ordering a stone placed over his grave at Ringwood, N. J.—a memorial that can yet be seen by visitors to that region.

Among the many scientific institutions of which Philadelphia is so justly proud a prominent place is held by the Academy of National Science, which is now housed in a massive Gothic building on Logan Square. It was established in 1812 by a few enthusiasts in scientific matters, one of the foremost being William Maclure, a native of Ayr. He was born in " the auld toon " in 1763. He first visited America in 1780, but his stay was short, and he returned to Britain and engaged in business in London. In 1796, having meantime acquired a competence, he crossed the Atlantic again, acquired citizenship in the young republic, and once more engaged in business, increasing his fortune. In 1803 he went to France as a Commissioner from the United States to settle the French spoliation claims, and it was while thus engaged that he became deeply interested in the then new subject of geology. He made a comprehensive study of the science, collected a large number of specimens, and determined on his return to America to devote himself solely to the study of its geology. This he did so effectively and thoroughly and with such important results that the title of " Father of American Geology " has been bestowed upon him. The first fruits of his researches were contained in an exhaustive paper which he read before the American Philosophical Society in 1809, and in 1817 he published the first geological map of the United States.

In his latter years Maclure was elected President of the Academy of Natural Science, and retained that honor until his death, although his frequent absences from Philadelphia, and even from the country, might have warranted his replacement by some other scientist. His social ideas were in many respects peculiar, and he tried in various ways to put them into practice. Thus, in 1819, he went to Spain, bought a tract of land from the revolutionary Government then in power, and endeavored to found an agricultural colony and school—mainly with the view of advancing the interests and increasing the comforts of the poorer farmers and other tillers of the soil, but the deposition of the Government vitiated the title to the lands he had secured, and he was compelled to abandon the work. Then he essayed a similar scheme at New Harmony, Ind., and it also turned out a failure, although for very different reasons.

Mr. Maclure all this time steadily prosecuted his geological studies, visiting nearly every section of the country in pursuit of data and specimens, and these he generously distributed among various societies, but his own collections, stored in Philadelphia, became wonderfully varied, and, for the time, complete. In 1827 he first visited Mexico, and was so attracted by its opportunities for study that he returned there the following year and continued traveling in its territory till his death, in 1840. By his will he bequeathed his library and the bulk of his collections to the Academy of Natural Sciences, together with $25,000, which enabled that society to erect the building it so long occupied at the corner of Broad and Sansom Streets, Philadelphia. Many of his geological specimens were given also to the American Geological Society, at New Haven, Conn.

An equally interesting and useful career was that of David Douglas, botanist, who was born at Scone, Perthshire, in 1798, and was murdered in the Hawaiian Islands in 1834. His first employment as a botanist was in the service of the University of Glasgow, and afterward, as a botanical collector for the Horticultural Society of London, he traveled over a large part of the world. He journeyed in the northern and western regions of Canada with Sir John Franklin, and was one of the early explorers of the Columbia River. In California he collected no fewer than 8,000 specimens of its flora, and wherever he went his industry and knowledge were fruitful of results. In botanical circles he is still remembered by his name being given to a species of pine—Pinus Douglassi—which he discovered, and many of the imported favorites which are now to be seen in English gardens were first carried to that country by him after some of his wanderings. Another Scot who is remembered botanically by having plants named after him was George Ure Skinner, who died at Aspinwall in 1867. While actively engaged as a member of the mercantile firm of Klee, Skinner & Co., Guatemala, he zealously pursued botanical researches in Western Mexico, Guatemala, and in the Southern United States.

In this connection we are reminded how numerous and important have been the Scotch florists who have settled in America. From the days of Grant Thorburn until the present time Scotch practical gardeners—men trained in Scotland—have always been in demand in America, and as seedsmen, florists, or overseers, working gardeners have had more to do with inspiring the American people with the love of flowers now so characteristic of the nation, than any other race. The late Peter Henderson, for instance, as a practical gardener, a vendor of seeds and plants, and as an author was better known in American country homes than any man in his business, and he did more to make gardening of all sorts—practical and ornamental—really popular than any other gardener of his day and generation. The late Isaac Buchanan, who died in 1893 at a patriarchal age, long stood at the head of New York's florists. The public park system of Buffalo owes much—if not all—of its comprehensiveness and beauty to the labors and ability of Mr. William Macmillan, a native of Nairnshire, and his assistant, Mr. James Braik; and the Botanical Gardens of Washington owe their perfection in great measure to the loving care of Mr. W. R. Smith, (a native of Athelstane, Haddingtonshire,) who has been their Superintendent for many years. Mention of Mr. Smith reminds us that gardeners—mostly, as might be expected, men of refined taste—find time to cultivate other things than flowers. Mr. Smith, for instance, proud as he is of his plants and shrubs, is also proud of his library of editions of Burns and Burnsiana, said to be the most extensive and complete in America.

The story of a life which might have grasped the highest earthly honors, which at times almost did grasp them, but failed, from some inscrutable reason, is always a sad one to read, and as we reflect on the career of David Boswell Reid it seems as if there lay in him the ability to have won for himself a famous name, but every line along which it ran seemed doomed to end in disappointment, and the whole story is a painful one. He was born in Edinburgh in 1805 and educated in the university there. His student career was a brilliant one, and four years after graduating he taught chemistry in the university laboratory. In 1833 he became one of those "Extra-Mural" lecturers whose ability and popularity did so much to preserve the fame of Edinburgh scientific education at a time when the university itself was by no means in a progressive condition. Reid built a classroom and laboratory, and for several years he had over 300 pupils at each of his sessions, a larger number than attended the chemical lectures at the university. He paid close attention to the principles of ventilation and drainage, and in 1836, at the request of the Government, he suggested many changes in the internal structure of the old houses of Parliament in London, and superintended their execution. His work was so highly appreciated that from 1840 to 1845 he was engaged mainly in London, superintending the drainage and ventilation of the present Palace of Parliament, and succeeded in perfecting these matters as fully as the plans of the architects and the nature of the site permitted. He also lectured about this time in many of the larger cities in Great Britain, and was recognized as the leading authority on ventilation and sewerage.

In 1856 Reid left Britain, and, after lecturing in many of the principal American cities, became Professor of Applied Chemistry in the University of Wisconsin, and afterward one of the Medical Inspectors of the United States Sanitary Commission. He was a man of considerable energy, a clear and fluent speaker, and an interesting writer, while his various published works and contributions to "transactions" and periodicals were valuable and widely read. He died at Washington in 1863, in what ought to have been the very meridian of his life.

In another chapter mention is made of Alexander Wilson, the ornithologist and poet, who would have been referred to at more length here did not his prominence as a writer induce the insertion of his name among those who have done something to further America's literary progress. His services to the ornithology of the United States, however, have been more generally valued and recognized than his ability as a writer, and it is with the view of recalling his earned honors in the world of books that we prefer to discuss his career among the men of letters than in this place. But his labors as an ornithologist not only had grand results in themselves, but induced in others an enthusiasm for study along the same lines. There is no doubt that Wilson's example inspired Audubon and led to the magnificent career of that genius as a naturalist.

Among others who followed in Wilson's footsteps as an ornithologist mention should be made of William Paterson Turnbull, whose work on the "Birds of East Pennsylvania and New Jersey," published in 1869, is a model of patient and accurate research and thoughtful study. Turnbull was born at Fala, Midlothian, in 1830, and was educated at the Edinburgh High School. He took up the study of ornithology at an early age, and a volume on the birds of East Lothian, which was published in Glasgow, showed that he was an observer of the closest and most painstaking type. After crossing the Atlantic, in 1851, he made his home in Philadelphia and began a thorough study of the ornithology of the country. He gradually acquired a complete library of the published works on the subject and succeeded in collecting many letters, manuscripts, and drawings of his great hero—Alexander Wilson. Mr. Turnbull was a member of the Academy of Natural Sciences, and others of Philadelphia's scientific societies, a genial, amiable man, and his death, in 1871, was mourned by a wide circle of friends.

In many respects the most extraordinary of the Scotch inventors whose ingenuity has helped to swell the business of the Patent Office was Hugh Orr, a Renfrewshire man. He was born at Lochwinnoch in 1717, and trained, probably in Glasgow, as a gun and lock smith. He settled at Bridgewater, Mass., in 1737, and started at once in business as a maker of scythes and axes, erecting in connection with his little establishment the first trip hammer ever seen near Boston. His business prospered, and his manufactures were soon found all over the New England States. In fact, for many years he was the only maker of edged tools in that section of the country, and from his employ, as time went on, men went out to various parts of the Colonies and so built up a new industry, supplanting imported goods. In 1753 Mr. Orr invented a machine for dressing flax, and in the cultivation of that plan he took a deep interest, and succeeded, in the long run, in making it a profitable agricultural industry around his home town. The subject of flax raising indeed, seems to have been his hobby, and in it he found health and change from the harassing labors of his foundry. Almost every man, philosophers tell us, requires to have a hobby of some sort, and it is well when it takes the form of something practical, something that may be of use to himself and to his fellow-creatures. But the hobby, whatever development it may take, should be encouraged so long as it is innocent and healthful. Some men take to photography, others to athletics, a lawyer may coquette with literature, a literary man may make a plaything of the law, a preacher may try gardening and a business man yachting. But, though the lawyer may make a poor litterateur and the litterateur be a tyro in law to the end of his days; though the preacher be an expensive gardener, raising potatoes at a cost of a dollar apiece, and the business man's heart may sink to his boots in a gale, such changes from the routine of men's daily lives are beneficial both to soul and body. It is rarely, indeed, that a man's hobby directs him to study out some matter that is at all likely to add to the general wealth of his fellow-citizens, and it is in this respect that Hugh Orr's flax-raising experiments deserve the highest commendation.

In 1748 Orr made some five hundred stands of arms

for the Province of Massachusetts Bay, which were deposited in Castle William, in Boston Harbor. There they were in due time seized by the British, and it is said that some of the weapons are still stored in the museum in the Tower of London. When the disputes with the mother country culminated in the Revolution, Orr threw himself into the ranks of the Commonwealth and erected a foundry for the casting of brass and iron ordnance and the making of cannon balls. He was also busily employed manufacturing small arms, and the energy he threw into all his work astonished his contemporaries. After peace had been restored Orr returned to more useful pursuits than manufacturing life-destroying weapons. In company with two Scotch mechanics, Robert and Alexander Barr, he constructed some carding, roping, and spinning machines, and he had become so thorough a Yankee as to ask for an appropriation from the Legislature to complete them, and got it. The machines were the first of their kind ever seen in America, so that Orr may be called the introducer into the United States of the "spinning jenny." He was much honored by his fellow-citizens, and served as a State Senator from Plymouth County for several years before his death, in 1798. Orr's son, Robert, was the first to make iron shovels in New England, and for a long time was Master Armorer in the United States Arsenal at Springfield.

Scotsmen are still "beating their brains" to supply the American forces with arms, and a very recent example of this is Mr. James P. Lee, the inventor of the Lee magazine gun, which in 1895 was adopted by the United States Navy. Mr. Lee was born in Roxburghshire in 1837. On leaving school he learned his father's trade of watchmaker, and in his twentieth year went to Janesville, Wis. From there he removed to Stevens Point, in the heart of the lumber region, and it was while in that place that he first began the series of experiments which culminated in the most wonderful gun that the American Navy now possesses. His first weapon was a breech-loading rifle, which was submitted to the Government during the civil war and adopted. Secretary Stanton gave Lee a contract to manufacture the weapon, and he organized the Lee Firearms Company, with a factory in Milwaukee. The company did not prosper, mainly on account of the high cost of labor, and in 1870 Mr. Lee connected himself with the Remington Company. With them he remained until the organization of the Lee Arms Company of Connecticut, with headquarters at Hartford. Despite his long residence in America, Mr. Lee is an enthusiastic Scot, and as proud of the Borderland as though he had never been fifty miles from the Tweed all his life.

Hugh Orr, as we have seen, was one of the first to start the American agricultural implement industry on its progress to become the best-known of all the manufactures of the country, and the first product of American mechanical skill to occupy a pre-eminent place in the markets of the world. One of the most noted of his successors and the first to bring about that perfection which has won general admiration was Henry Burden, a native of Dunblane, who came to America in 1819, in the twenty-eighth year of his age. He had received a good technical education, and was a thorough mechanic before he crossed the Atlantic, but his ingenuity—his genius, it might be called—was developed by the requirements of the new country, and, settling at Troy, he began the manufacture of agricultural implements. His first venture was an improved plough, which was very successful, and he sold as many as he could produce. He also introduced the first cultivator ever seen in this country, and was continually inventing new implements or improving those already in use. A machine for making horseshoes was not only regarded as his greatest triumph, but made him wealthy, and gradually his establishment at Troy became famous as one of the most extensive in the world. Mr. Burden took a deep interest in the science of steam navigation, watched its progress closely, and himself invented a " cigar boat," with which he foresaw great possibilities, but was forced for various reasons to lay aside. The invention was regarded simply as a curiosity, but Mr. Burden had no conception of concocting merely what might be regarded as a sight to astonish visitors; he was thoroughly practical in all his ideas, and, although he did not live to see his cigar boat a commercial success, its principle was not lost, and is to be found in the "whaleback" steamers now in use on the great lakes and in many of the modern models of torpedo boats. He owned patents by the hundred, and even these only represented a part of the fruits of his ingenuity. At his death, in 1871, he was beyond question the most successful inventor in the country, and he had the satisfaction of knowing that the products of his great establishment were as highly appreciated in Europe as in the markets of his adopted country.

One of the most characteristically Scotch inventors the writer of this volume ever had the good fortune to meet was the Rev. Robert Dick of Buffalo, "Brother Dick," as he was most generally called. He was at once preacher, lecturer, newspaper editor and writer, teacher and inventor, a man of the highest character, always aiming upward, and taking a deep interest in the moral elevation of the people. Mr. Dick was born at Bathgate in 1814. His parents, with eleven bairns, determined to emigrate when Robert was very young, and settled in Canada, where they died before any of the children had attained manhood. The lot of the bairns was, as might be supposed, a hard one. Robert managed to study for the ministry, and in spite of many disadvantages and hindrances—the result of poverty—managed to graduate at Hamilton College, Clinton, in 1841. Then he taught school for several years, held several pastorates, and in 1854 established at Toronto a religious paper called "The Gospel Tribune." All this time he found his relaxation in his workshop. He was always inventing, always trying to put his mechanical ideas into practice, and to devise something that would meet a popular demand. His newspaper experience finally gave him a clue, and his mailing machine not only met a pressing demand, but won for him comparative wealth. His business henceforth was devoted to these machines, their perfection, and introduction, and they became part of the indispensable outfit of nearly every large newspaper office on the continent. But he never abandoned his vocation of a minister of the Gospel, and even in the midst of his business journeys was always ready to "preach the Word" or to do something by speech, purse, or presence to advance the cause of total abstinence, of which he was a devoted advocate. His life was a useful and lovable one, he triumphed over great obstacles, he was outspoken in denouncing wrong, and even while immersed in business was ever ready to turn aside from temporal cares to talk of things celestial and say a word in season. Mr. Dick died at Buffalo, a city that had been his home for many years, in 1893.

Alexander Morton, the perfecter, if not the inventor, of gold pens, (for his claims to the latter distinction have been challenged,) was born at Darvel, Ayrshire, in 1820, and became a resident of New York in 1845. In 1851, after many experiments, he began making gold pens, and after awhile, with his improvements in pointing, tempering, and grinding, his manufacture became famous. Throughout his business career he was always improving these useful articles, and his efforts were so well appreciated that he acquired considerable wealth long before his untimely death, in 1860. Another noted inventor was William Chisholm, long head of the Union Steel Company of Cleveland, Ohio. He was born at Lochgelly, Fifeshire, in 1825, and, along with his brother Henry started the Cleveland Rolling Mill. He was constantly inventing new methods in machinery and mechanical implements, and particularly hoisting and pumping engines, and was the first to demonstrate the practicability of manufacturing screws from Bessemer steel.

Early in 1895 there died at Pawtucket, R. I., an inventor of an intensely practical turn of mind—practical, inasmuch as his ambition was to produce inventions that would save both labor and material, and because when he once got into a groove that brought him success, he continued to develop and deepen that groove all through his career. This was Duncan H. Campbell, who was born at Greenock in 1827 and settled, with his parents, in Boston, Mass., while yet a lad. When he finished his public school course he was sent to work at the shoe business, and conceived the idea of having machines do a great part of the work which he saw done by hand. Bit by bit, his inventions revolutionized the entire business and made it become the important factor it is to-day in the industries of New England. He invented pegging machines, stitching machines, a lock-stitch machine for sewing uppers, a machine for using waxed threads, a machine for covering buttons with cloth—and it is hard to recall all what, but all were in connection with the manufacture of shoes.

An equally inventive genius, and a more fortunate one, so far as financial returns was concerned, was Thomas Dickson, who died at Scranton in 1884, and whose name was for years the most prominent in that thriving Pennsylvania town, and is yet held in kind remembrance. Mr. Dickson was born at Lauder in 1822. He left Scotland when comparatively young, and his first employment was as a boy in charge of a couple of mules on the towpath of a canal at Carbondale, Penn. From that he gradually rose in life, until he was known all over Pennsylvania as the head of the Dickson Manufacturing Company at Scranton, and then he acquired a national reputation as President of the Delaware and Hudson Canal Company and as a Director in a score or more of other corporations. He also established an iron plant on Lake Champlain, and was ever ready to engage in any enterprise that promised to aid in the development of the country. Mr. Dickson's ingenuity and inventive genius kept the Dickson Manufacturing Company's products at the front all over the country, and these products covered a great variety of manufactures, from locomotives to stoves. He was a man of considerable refinement, and his elegant home at Scranton, with its magnificent library and large and well-selected gallery of paintings, was one of the show places of the city. He was an omnivorous reader, and nothing pleased him better than to spend a few hours each day in the quiet of his library, while his pictures were a constant source of delight to him and others.

For many years one of the most popular teachers of elocution in Edinburgh was Alexander Melville Bell, whose "readings" were regarded as among the most successful of each season's round of entertainments. Mr. Bell, who was born in Auld Reekie in 1819, was more than a mere elocutionist. He possessed the qualities of the poet and actor, and never gave a reading on any theme if he did not thoroughly appreciate and understand the full meaning of the author. He wrote much on elocution, and always from a scientific standpoint. He invented a method for removing impediments in speech, and as author of "Visible Speech" was the first to show how words might be framed and meanings conveyed in the absence of sound. Somewhat late in life he removed, with his family, to Canada, and became instructor in elocution at Queen's University, Kingston. His great work was his investigations among deaf-mutes, and to the end of his long life he was constantly engaged in problems calculated to break down the barriers of their isolation—to bring them into active sympathy with the rest of the world.

In spite of his useful labors, however, Mr. Bell's memory would be by this time only a reminiscence to a few personal friends and pupils were it not for the brilliant success accomplished by his son in working out ideas on the same line as his father. This son, Alexander Graham Bell—the inventor of the telephone—was born at Edinburgh in 1847, and accompanied his father to Canada. In 1872 he took up his residence in Boston as a teacher of vocal physiology, and, like his father, took a deep interest in the education of deaf-mutes. It was this that led to the romance and the fortune of his life—the invention of the telephone and his marriage. One account, seemingly by Mr. Bell himself, tells the story as follows:

"The history of the telephone has been so often written that the facts relating to its growth and development, its legal battles and patent complications, are too well known to need repetition. Few people, however, are aware that an interesting romance hides in the background. To go back to the beginning, there lived in the classic shades of Cambridge a Mr. Hubbard, who had four charming daughters. His youngest daughter, when but five years of age, was attacked with scarlet fever, which left her totally deaf. Everything possible was done for the child. She was sent to the best institutions in Europe, but her hearing was entirely gone. The rudiments of lip-reading were taught to her, as well as speaking by means of mechanical training of the vocal chords. On her return to her home her father decided to continue her education, and she was sent to an institution in Charleston. It was here she first met Mr. Graham Bell, then an instructor in the institution. The sequel was an engagement between the teacher and his pupil.

" It was while endeavoring to contrive some electrical method by which his fiancee could regain her lost sense that Mr. Bell, who was always of an inventive turn of mind, discovered the secret of the transmitter of the telephone. At first he did not realize the importance of his discovery, and it was only after much persuasion that Mr. Hubbard induced him to take out patents. The rest is well known."

The success of the Bell telephone was immediate, and Mr. Bell, with the pertinacity of his race, kept steadily at work improving it, leaving the commercial side of the invention to be managed by others. In 1892, after a long and trying series of experiments, he in a manner perfected his telephone by making it useful for any distance. On October 18 of that year he opened the first telephone connection between Chicago and New York, and its success demonstrated that distance was practically no bar to the use of the instrument. Further than this into the story of the telephone we need not go. Its history—with its triumphs, litigations, and heartburnings—belongs to the scientific story of America. At his home in Washington and his country seat at Baddeck, Cape Breton, Mr. Bell is still busy in what he calls his workshops, but the secrets of these places are carefully guarded. The possessor of immense wealth, he can afford to experiment with whatever he has on hand until perfection is attained. But wondrous stories somehow creep out, and one is to the effect that a flying machine will in time make the name of Mr. Bell as widely associated with a new era in locomotion as it has been with the transmission of recognizable sound.

Among practical mechanics, men who can design as well as themselves handle the tools which fashion their designs, no name is more prominent than that of Henry Eckford. This once famous shipbuilder left Scotland in 1791, when he was sixteen years of age, and tried to establish himself in some way of earning a living at Quebec. The opportunities there, however, were small, and in 1796 he crossed the St. Lawrence, settled in New York, and threw in his future with the United States. But he did not ignore his native land by his change of allegiance, for we find that in 1802 he joined the local St. Andrew's Society. He commenced business as a boatbuilder and did fairly well, but his great opportunity came with the outbreak of the war of 1812, when he built several vessels for the Government to engage in service on the great lakes. In 1822 he built the steamer "Robert Fulton," which made the first successful steam voyage to New Orleans and Havana, an occurrence that attracted attention all over the country. His greatest American work was done as Naval Consructor at the Brooklyn Navy Yard, an appointment he secured in 1820, for while there he built six ships of the line from his own models, and one of these, the "Ohio," was regarded at the time as the finest vessel of her kind in the world. While in New York Eckford resided mainly in a pleasant rural cottage on Love Lane, now part of West Twenty-sixth Street, and it was the scene of many joyous and intellectual gatherings. One of his closest friends was the poet Hallock, who was a frequent visitor at the cottage, with many other of the leading literary men and thinkers of the day, as well as Drake and De Kay—two young men afterward celebrated as poets —who became the Scotch shipbuilder's sons-in-law.

Eckford, as a result of a disagreement with the United States Government, left New York and readily found employment in designing war vessels for other countries. His last engagement was in Turkey. He had built a sloop of war for Sultan Mahoud, and, accepting the offer of the position of Chief Naval Constructor of the Ottoman Empire, he proceeded to Constantinople, but died soon after he reached that city, in 1832.

James Ferguson, who between 1817 and 1819 was assistant surveyor of the Erie Canal, was a native of Perthshire, where he was born in 1797. From 1819 till 1822 he was one of the surveyors on the boundary commission acting under the provisions of the treaty of Ghent, and afterward became assistant astronomer of the United States Naval Observatory, an appointment he held till his death, at Washington, in 1867. His career as an astronomical student was a very brilliant one, and he was the discoverer of three asteroids, for which he received two of the astronomical prize medals given by the French Academy of Sciences. He was a quiet, unobtrusive, lovable man, immersed in his studies, and regardless of personal labor in faithfully fulfilling whatever work he had in hand. A shallower man with more pretensions might have cut a greater figure in the world, but he had no regard for mere fame, and was satisfied with his own consciousness of work well done.

James Pugh Kirkwood, who in 1867 and 1868 was President of the American Society of Civil Engineers, had a much more varied career. He was born at Edinburgh in 1807, and learned civil engineering and measuring in that city. On taking up his residence in America in 1832 he became resident consulting engineer on several railroads. His first prominent appointment was as constructing engineer for the docks, warehouses, and other Government structures at Pensacola, and then he secured the position of General Superintendent of the Erie Railroad. From 1850 to 1855 he was chief engineer of the Missouri Pacific system, and then became its consulting engineer. From 1856 to 1860 he was chief engineer of the Nassau Water Works, Brooklyn, and from the latter date he acted as a general consulting engineer, with water works as his principal specialty. He took charge of laying the water mains on Eighth Avenue, New York, into a rock bed which was cut according to his directions, and the work at the time attracted much attention among engineering experts on account of its difficulty. His latter years were spent mainly in Brooklyn, and he was regarded as one of the leaders in his profession, and enjoyed the respect and affection of a wide circle of friends. His death, in 1877, was the occasion for a host of tributes being paid to his services and worth by societies, newspapers, and individuals.

A career which run on somewhat similar lines was that of James Laurie, who was born in 1811 at Bell's Mills and settled in America in 1832. In fact, he was closely associated with Kirkwood in considerable railroad work, and the two men entertained the warmest friendship for each other, until Laurie's death, at Hartford, Conn., in 1875. His first notable appointment was as chief engineer on the Norwich and Worcester Railroad; then he filled a similar office on the New Jersey Central Road, and later was consulting engineer in Massachusetts in connection with the Housatonic Tunnel. As Mr. Kirkwood made a specialty of water works, so Mr. Laurie, in time, made a particular study of bridge building, and was regarded as the foremost practical authority on that specialty in America, so that his services as consulting engineer on such structures were in constant demand. Among other of his achievements it may be mentioned that he built the wrought-iron bridge over the Connecticut River at Windsor Locks, the first of its kind in the country. Mr. Laurie was honored by his professional friends by being elected the first President of the American Society of Civil Engineers, an organization in the founding of which he took a deep interest.

Donald Craig McCallum was a soldier as well as a civil engineer, and during his career did much good work in both capacities. He was born at Johnstone, Renfrewshire, in 1815, and emigrated with his parents and the rest of his family in 1832. They settled in Rochester, N. Y., and soon after Donald started in the battle of life by learning the tailoring trade. That business did not suit him, and, going to Canada, he became a carpenter and studied architecture. Then he returned to Rochester, engaged in business for himself as a builder, and did fairly well. He took a special interest in railroad and bridge construction, invented what was known as the "inflexible arch truss bridge," and gradually left off his building operations to become a constructor of railroads and bridges. In 1855 he became General Superintendent of the Erie Railroad. During the war he was appointed director of the military railroads in the United States, and in that capacity he not only rendered particularly brilliant services at critical periods by massing troops at certain strategic points, but he maintained the entire service in a state of efficiency that contrasted in a wonderfully favorable manner with the disorganized condition of many of the other administrative departments of the Northern Army. His services with Sherman on that soldier's memorable march to the sea were conspicuously valuable and won the highest encomiums from all in authority. When the war was over, McCallum, who had enjoyed the rank of Colonel in the United States Army, retired from service with the honors of a Major General, and until his death, in Brooklyn, in 1878, confined his attention to civil pursuits. Gen. McCallum was more anxious to be known as a poet than a soldier or engineer, and in 1879 issued a small volume containing specimens of his muse. They are full of fine sentiment, lofty thought, sage reflection, and timely admonition, and, while no one would award their writer a position among the foremost ranks of singers, he deserves a marked place among what Mr. Stedman happily calls the "general choir." One poem, "The Water Mill," is certain to live in literature, but the authorship has been questioned by some writers, and the problem, like most others of the kind, is a vexing one. The poem, however, has generally been attributed to McCallum, although we are not aware that he ever gave personally any information on the subject; but, even if this beautiful bit of sentiment be taken away from him, enough remains of his undoubted compositions to entitle him to a very respectable place among the minor bards of America.

A fair representative of the Scottish working engineer, the men who do their work so well that their services are always in demand, and who are ready to develop into heroes or millionaires as time and chance may offer, might be found in George M. Wait, who died at Brooklyn in 1894. He was a native of Dunse, (Duns they call it now,) Berwickshire, and was born in that staid old-fashioned town in 1825. After serving his apprenticeship in a " machine shop," he developed into a railroad engineer, and then devoted himself to marine engineering. He came to America shortly before the outbreak of the civil war, and when that cloud darkened the country he volunteered his services to the Union Navy. Such offers from such men were then gladly received, and Mr. Wait found himself enrolled as chief engineer of the warship Monticello. One of his most daring acts was the cutting of the chains which the Confederates had placed across the Mississippi River to obstruct the Federal fleet in its purpose to get near enough to New Orleans to bombard it. Mr. Wait had many narrow escapes in the course of his service, but the narrowest of all came from his own side, when Gen. Butler in a moment of haste ordered Commander Braine (afterward Admiral) and Chief Engineer Wait to be hanged for disobeying his orders. The carrying out of these orders was an impossibility, and Butler fortunately recovered his temper before the sentences were carried out and came round, as gracefully as he could, to Wait's way of thinking on the matter at issue. Wait afterward became chief engineer for the Pacific Mail Steamship Company, and his last employment was on some local boats making daily excursions from New York Harbor, as he did not care about being deprived, as old age began to creep on, of the comforts of his own fireside.

CHAPTER VIII.

MERCHANTS AND MUNICIPAL BUILDERS.

IT may safely be laid down as a self-evident truth that every Scotsman in America who has gained position or eminence or wealth, or all three, has worked hard. Among the Scotch community, even in the fourth or fifth generation removed from the "Land o' Cakes," there are no idlers, no " gilded youth," no merely empty loungers on the face of the earth. We find Scotsmen and their families moving in the very highest social circles in each community—among the " Four Hundred," to use a ridiculous expression that has come into use in recent years—but they all seem to engage in business of some sort. They do not figure much, if at all, in what loves to be distinguished as the " smart set," the butterflies whose only object in the world seems to be to derive pleasure from it, pleasure sometimes innocent, sometimes brutal, sometimes silly, always extravagant, and a standing menace to the peace of the community. The main purpose in life, if there be any purpose, after all, of such creatures is to draw themselves into a class apart from the common herd, to ape the manners of the aristocracy of the Old World, and this latter purpose they accomplish in such a way as to win the disgust of every honest citizen and the contempt of every honest aristocrat.

If we designed to devote a chapter to titled personages in this book, it might easily be done. The adventures of the members of the British peerage alone in America would fill many pages and would include soldiers, statesmen, sightseers, hunters and adventurers—for even the latter class are found legitimately occupying a line, at least, in the standard peerages. Such a chapter would, however, include names like that of Lady Macdonald, who enjoys a peerage through the services which her late husband, Sir John A. Macdonald, rendered to the Empire; and of Lord Mount Stephen, who won his peerage by his own successful and eminently useful life, as well as those of many baronets and knights. It would also refer to an old title, that of Baron de Longueuil, a French title of nobility originally granted by Louis XIV., but recognized by Great Britain. The dignity was first conferred on a French subject, Charles Le Moyne, but as might, somehow, be expected, the present holder of the title, Charles Colman Grant, is more entitled to be regarded as of Scotch descent than the representative of a French family. The chapter would also chronicle the story of an old Scotch title which has been so long held by residents of this country that they pride themselves as much from their descent from Colonial ancestors as from their Saxon forbears—Saxons who were prominent in England before the advent of the Normans. The title, Baron Cameron of Fairfax, in the peerage of Scotland, was bestowed by Charles I. in 1627 upon Sir Thomas Fairfax of Denton, an Englishman. The family never had any connection with Scotland, however, beyond the title, but the name yet stands on the roll of the Scottish peers and is still called at each assemblage of these peers in Holyrood to elect their representatives in the British House of Lords. The representative of the family, the holder of this ancient title, still resides in Virginia, but so far as we can trace he and his immediate progenitors, as soldiers, preachers, or physicians, have done something to justify their existence, have pursued some recognized profession.

But all this reference to nobility is merely a digression by way of variety in the opening matter of a new department of our story. Here we have to deal with what may be called the nobility of business. To acquire eminence in trade, finance, or commerce, especially in view of the ever-watchful and sometimes unscrupulous competition which prevails in all large business centres, a man needs rare qualities, and a successful merchant is generally an individual possessing not only a clear head, but a large heart. If we could enumerate the practical charitable institutions of the world, group together the art galleries, museums, and halls of learning, we would find that successful business men, when not their founders, were their most liberal benefactors. We will get abundant evidence of this as the present chapter proceeds, and will find also that these same business, money-making, men were sterling and self-sacrificing patriots whenever occasion arose for the display of that quality. Such men are entitled to be called nature's noblemen—men who hold their patents of nobility from Almighty God.

We could place the life, for instance, of Alexander Milne, an Edinburgh man who was long a merchant in New Orleans, as a pattern—one which could be surpassed by the product of no other class. After a noteworthy and commercially irreproachable career, he became distinguished for his philanthropy, although the world never knew its extent or imagined the amount of thought and care he exercised in trying to do as much good as possible to his fellow-men. Even the good he did lived—and lives—after he had passed away, for when he died, in 1838, at the age of ninety-four years, it was found that he left most of his fortune to endow the Milne Hospital for the orphan boys of New Orleans.

In treating of the classes embraced in the title to this chapter we are more than ever overwhelmed by the difficulty of selection. There is hardly a city or township in which Scotsmen have not more or less prominently figured in its business interests. In financial circles everywhere, whether in Montreal or New York, they have held a front rank, and that might be said also of every branch of business. We can only array a few examples, selected almost at random, and endeavor to be as representative in each selection as possible.

The founder of the famous town of Yorktown, Va., was Thomas Nelson, who was born in 1677 in Cumberland, not far from the Scottish border. His parents had moved there from Wigtonshire shortly after their marriage, and the district was more Scotch in its speech, manners, and customs than English, so that, although actually born on what Scotsmen playfully call the "wrong side of the Tweed," Nelson was in reality a Scot. Indeed, after his arrival in America, about 1700, he was generally known as "Scotch Tom," and appears to have been quite proud of the appellation. He started in business, began at once to make money, and in 1705 founded the town of York—one of the few really historic towns in America—which witnessed the surrender of Cornwallis in 1781 and was the scene of a stirring conflict between the forces of McClellan and Magruder in 1862, during the civil war. Nelson died full of years and honors, in 1745, in the town he had founded and which he had been spared to see grow slowly and surely. If he did not hold high office, he founded a family which has made its mark in the history of his adopted State. One of his sons, Thomas, was a candidate for Governor of Virginia, but was defeated by the celebrated Patrick Henry, (also of Scotch descent,) and afterward for thirty years was Secretary of the Privy Council. Another son, William, was President of the Council for a long time, and on the death of Lord Botetourt became Governor of Virginia and administered its affairs for about a year, until the arrival of the Earl of Dunmore in 1771. He died a year later, leaving three sons, who all became famous. One of these sons, Thomas, who was born in Virginia in 1738, was educated partly in America and partly at Trinity College, Cambridge. As might be expected, he ranged himself on the side of the patriots, and as a member of the House of Burgesses was outspoken in his condemnation of whatever tended to abridge the freedom of the Colonies. "He was a member," says Miss M. V. Smith, in her able volume on "The Governors of Virginia," "of the Revolutionary Conventions of 1774 and 1775, and was appointed by the convention in July, 1775, Colonel of the Second Virginia Regiment, which post he resigned on being elected to the Continental Congress in the same year. H was again called to administer home affairs, and was a prominent member of the Virginia Convention of 1776, which met in May to frame a Constitution for her Government. Here he offered a resolution instructing the Virginia delegates in Congress to propose a Declaration of Independence. Having been elected one of these delegates, he had the satisfaction of seeing the hopes and wishes of his people embodied in a crystallized form, and, with unfaltering faith in its declarations, set his seal to the historic instrument July 4, 1776." In 1777 he became Commander in Chief of the forces in the State, and devoted not only his time but his means to the war. In 1781 he was chosen Governor of Virginia, but his health was then broken. He soon resigned the office, and, retiring to Hanover County, resided there in seclusion till his death, in 1789. He lost his fortune in the war, sacrificed everything he had to the State, and the State was too poor to recoup him, so his latter years were passed amidst poverty. But he never complained on that score, and awaited the last roll-call conscious that he had done everything a patriot could do to advance and establish his native land. Two of Gov. Thomas Nelson's brothers, William and Robert, were in the Revolutionary Army, and both were captured by Col. Tarleton's forces. When the struggle was over, William engaged in the practice of law until 1803, when he became Professor of Law at William and Mary College. On his death, in 1813, he was succeeded in that office by Robert, who held it for five years, or until he died, in 1818. The public services of the family were continued, as far as our records go, to the fourth generation after " Scotch Tom," for Gov. Thomas Nelson's son, Hugh, was a member of Congress for Virginia during several terms, and in 1823 was appointed by President Monroe United States Minister to Spain.

The family of Thomas Campbell, author of "The Pleasures of Hope" and of "Gertrude of Wyoming," had rather an intimate connection with America. His father, Alexander Campbell, the son of a landed proprietor, was born at Kirnan, in the parish of Glassary, Argyllshire, in 1710. He was trained to the mercantile profession in Glasgow, and in early life crossed the Atlantic and settled at Falmouth, Va., where he engaged in business for several years and acquired considerable means. There, too, he made the acquaintance of a countryman named Daniel Campbell, afterward his brother-in-law. Returning to Scotland, the two Campbells founded the firm of Alexander & Daniel Campbell and engaged in the Virginia trade. In this they amassed considerable wealth and became recognized as among the leading merchants in a trade whose very name was then regarded as synonymous with opulence. In 1756 Alexander Campbell married a sister of his partner, and had a family of eight sons and four daughters. One of these sons, it may be said, afterward emigrated to America and married a daughter of Patrick Henry, the great Governor of Virginia. Thomas, the poet, the youngest of the family, was born at Glasgow in 1777, but two years before that the outbreak of the Revolutionary War had knocked away the props of the Campbells' business and the poet's father and uncle were practically ruined, the former having lost some £20,000, the savings of a life devoted to business. We have no interest here with the personal career of the poet, except we choose to speculate how far the stories his father may have told of America influenced him to look for a theme for his muse in the traditions of the beautiful Wyoming Valley. An uncle of the poet—Archibald Campbell, an Episcopalian minister—was located for some time in Jamaica, but settled in America about the same time as his brother Alexander. He remained in Virginia after his brother left to begin a business career in Glasgow, and in time threw in his lot with the Colonists when the struggle came which welded the Colonies into a nation. He was a much-esteemed minister, and had among his parishioners such men as Washington and Lee—the famous "Light-Horse Harry" of the Revolution.

Sir William Dunbar, who appears to have belonged to the old Banffshire house of Dunbar of Durn, now represented by a family in Australia, was a noted personage in American business and political circles for many years.

He was born in 1740, and appears to have landed at Philadelphia about 1771, just when matters were approaching an interesting crisis with the Home Government. In company with John Ross, a once well known and prosperous merchant in the Quaker City, and who in 1774 was honored by being chosen as Vice President of the local St. Andrew's Society, Dunbar formed in 1773 a partnership for opening a plantation in West Florida. The affair did not seem to be a success, and Dunbar moved to Baton Rouge, near New Orleans, and finally to Natchez, Miss., where he managed to get possession of a plantation, and where he died in 1810. He led the career of an adventurer and suffered the usual ups and downs of fortune incidental to such a career, but his latter years seem to have been pleasant and prosperous. He had assumed allegiance to the Federal Government, from motives of policy rather than from any deep-seated principle, and under it held several important offices. He was an intimate friend of Thomas Jefferson, and corresponded with him at frequent intervals, and to the "Transactions" of the American Philosophical Society of Philadelpha, of which he was a member, he contributed a number of papers on various subjects, all of which were considered valuable in their day.

Among the early merchants of Virginia no name stands higher or is surrounded with more honorable associations than that of Thomas Rutherfoord of Richmond. He was born at Kirkcaldy, Fifeshire, in 1766, but was educated in Glasgow, where his family removed while he was an infant. In that city, too, he received his mercantile training, and when he reached early manhood he secured a position in the house of Hawkesley & Rutherfoord of Dublin, the junior partner in which was his elder brother. In 1784 he was sent by the firm to Virginia in charge of cargoes in two vessels, the value of the goods being placed at $50,000. He was well recommended to the local business men of Virginia, and among others he carried a letter of introduction to George Washington, which had been given him by Sir Edward Neversham, then member of Parliament for Dublin. Rutherfoord took up his quarters in Richmond, where he opened a branch establishment to the Dublin house and quickly put it on a substantial footing. After some four years spent in Richmond he returned to Ireland and was admitted as a partner in the firm to which he had proved so faithful and profitable a servant. His stay in Ireland lasted only about a year, and in 1789 he was once more in Richmond, which was henceforth to be his home. His business career was a continued round of prosperity, and he gradually became regarded as one of the wealthiest and most upright merchants of the city. His life was a pleasant one, although as general merchant, miller, importer, and exporter the daily routine of his affairs was for many years of the most engrossing description. He invested his means largely in Richmond real estate, until he was the most extensive owner of that class of property in the city, and even this reputation added to his wealth, for others, seeing the sagacious Scot sinking his money in land, followed his example, and so raised values all around. But Mr. Rutherfoord's days were not wholly devoted to business; he found time for all the interest in the affairs of the city that any true citizen should take, and his public spirit and liberality were as conspicuous as his wealth. He was bitterly opposed to tariffs or to anything that looked like an abridgment of individual, state, or national freedom, and the papers he published on such questions and on commercial matters attracted wide attention. In 1841 he was selected to draft a petition to President Tyler protesting against the imposition of tariff duties, and the Chief Executive of the Nation found in Rutherfoord a man whose sterling honesty, devoted earnestness, singleness of purpose, and native intelligence won his entire respect. Years afterward President Tyler, when lecturing at Richmond, referred to his acquaintance with Rutherfoord in words that evinced his high appreciation of the Scottish-American merchant, whose earthly career closed at Richmond in 1852.

John Rutherfoord married an American girl and left thirteen children, whose descendants are found all over the Union, although principally in Virginia. Of his children the eldest son, John, who was born in Richmond in 1792, graduated from Princeton College in 1810 with the degree of M. A. and then applied himself to the study of the law. In 1826 he was elected to the House of Delegates from the City of Richmond, and in 1830 was one of the Councillors of State. As senior Councillor, he became in 1841 Acting Governor of Virginia and served in that capacity for a year with marked acceptance. Gov. Rutherfoord died in 1866, " leaving," says one of his biographers, " the memory of a man of strong intellect and vigorous character combined with those enduring charms which ever attach to a modest, virtuous, and unassuming gentleman."

In the records of the Albany (New York) St. Andrew's Society there is a notice of the family of John Stevenson, the first President of the organization, which had been prepared by one of his descendants and read at the annual meeting on St. Andrew's Day, 1878. As it is interesting on account of its tracing a family's history from its foundation and also on account of showing how the sturdy Scots made themselves at home in America, and became regarded as part and parcel of its people, the sketch is here reproduced, with only slight curtailment:

" John Stevenson was born in Albany March 13, 1735. His father, James Stevenson, a Scottish gentleman, came to America after the ' rising ' in 1715. He was a freeholder in the city in 1720 and a friend of Robert Livingston, the possessor of large tracts of wild land on the Hudson, which by the favor of the ruling powers had been erected into a manor. Stevenson was something of a military man, and held several responsible local trusts, among which was that of receiver of taxes. James Stevenson and his son John seem to have had a taste for classical and polite literature, if the books they possessed be taken as an indication.

" James Stevenson died Feb. 2, 1769, and was buried in the church which then stood on the hill in State Street. His name appears on the still sonorous old bell, cast in 1751, which hangs in the tower of St. Peter's. Among his Scottish friends in Albany may be named Jame

Lyndsay, Esq., and Capt. Dick of the army. His son, John Stevenson, and Philip Livingston, one of the Signers of the Declaration, were tenants in common of an estate of more than 8,000 acres on the Mohawk, called Lilac's Bush.

"John Stevenson also owned other large tracts of land. He married Magdalen, sister of John de Peyster Douw, the Chairman of the Committee of Safety in this State during the Revolutionary War. He was fitted by position, education, and natural abilities for public service, but he preferred a private station. Mr. Stevenson was an early stockholder in the Bank of North America at Philadelphia, the oldest bank in this country, and also in the Bank of New York and the Bank of Albany, now defunct, and was a contributor to the foundation of Union College.

"John Stevenson died April 24, 1810, aged seventy-five years. His only son, James, lived and died in Albany. He was a patron of the Albany Academy and active in securing a supply of good water to the city. A daughter of John Stevenson married Dudley Walsh, an eminent merchant during the latter part of the last century. During the early settlement of Western New York, then called the Genesee country, he advanced to the land agent (Williamson) of Sir William Pulteney more than £25,000, and, it may also be added, had considerable difficulty in getting his money back from that eccentric, land-loving, and land-possessing baronet. Another daughter of John Stevenson married Gen. Pierre Van Cortlandt, a patriot of the American Revolution and one of nature's noblemen."

In the early commercial history of the City of New York, Scotsmen, as might be expected, were both numerous and influential. We have already in the course of these pages mentioned several, and the Livingston family, the Colden family, the Barclays, the Irvings, were all names that once were synonymous with the commercial story of the city. President William Maxwell of the Bank of New York, and one of the founders of the Chamber of Commerce, was a native of Scotland, as were several other of the founders of the latter institution. From a list drawn up by the writer some years ago of the leading Scotsmen in New York in 1789 the following is extracted:

Hugh Wallace of the Scotch firm of H. & A. Wallace was one of the charter members of the Chamber of Commerce and its Vice President, and another of the charter members was Thomas Buchanan, a native of Stirling, who used jocosely to claim that he was descended from the immortal scholar, teacher, poet, historian, and philosopher, George Buchanan. James Barclay was an importer at 14 Hanover Square, and Robert Affleck carried on business at 60 William Street. Robert Hodge, an Edinburgh man, who carried on business as a bookseller and printer at 37 King [Pine] Street, was very popular in business circles and commanded a large trade. In February, 1879, he published "The Power of Sympathy," the earliest American novel. Thomas Allen, whose place of business was at 16 Queen Street, was the representative of a number of British publishers and the first agent in America for the Encyclopedia Britannica. Samuel Campbell, whose place of business was at 44 Hanover Square, was a native of Kilbride. He reprinted Falconer's "Shipwreck" and many other standard Scotch and English works. Another Scotch bookseller was Samuel Loudon of 5 Water Street, and the first New York edition of Burns's poems was published in 1788 by J. McLean. The Scots in the early part of the century claimed Cadwallader D. Colden—Mayor in 1820—as one of themselves, although he was born in America, but his Scotch descent through his grandfather, Gov. Colden, made his heart warm to the tartan. Mayor Colden was as patriotic an American as his grandfather was loyal as a Briton, and during the three years he sat in the Mayor's chair made a grand record for honesty, usefulness, diligence, and administrative ability. He greatly aided De Witt Clinton in advocating the construction of, and in the work of building, the internal waterways of the State of New York, and was an ardent supporter of that statesman's entire policy.

An interesting sketch might be written of the career of the firm of Boorman, Johnston & Co., which for a long time ranked as one of the wealthiest and most enterprising houses in the city. Both partners landed here from Scotland about the year 1800—possibly some years earlier—without a penny in their pockets, but with plenty of Scotch sagacity and Scotch grit and perseverance. After a year or two they got on so well that they started business in South Street. The exact date of the commencement of their operations is not known, but the War of 1812 found them carrying on business, and apparently caused them no loss. They mainly imported and sold goods from Scotland, their principal article being bagging from Dundee. After some time they built up a great Southern trade, and most of the tobacco that came to this city from Richmond, Va., was consigned to them. Next they added the iron business, and had many vessels bringing them iron from Sweden and England. Their premises in South Street became too small, and they removed to Greenwich Street, where they had what was then considered a mammoth establishment.

In 1827 Mr. Adam Norrie came out from Scotland and was admitted a partner in the firm. One of his first acts on arriving was to become a member of the St. Andrew's Society, his proposer being Mr. John Johnston, the junior member of the original firm, and who had been a member since 1811. Mr. Norrie's connection with the society was a long, honorable, and useful one, as he served as a manager in 1838 and 1839, as a Vice President from 1843 to 1850, and as President from 1851 to 1861. Mr. Norrie quickly made his mark in the community. One who knew him well wrote: " New York has never seen a more energetic and intelligent merchant. Scotch to the backbone—that is, filled with ideas of stern honesty, sagacity, prudence, and determination, Mr. Norrie has never been beat. He probably was remarked for those great mercantile qualities before he left Scotland, for with them he also brought to the firm he joined a splendid connection and correspondence in the Old Country, and greatly added to the business of

Boorman, Johnston & Co." Under Mr. Norrie's direction the firm gained immensely in strength, and many of its clerks branched out into business for themselves; and it was a noticeable feature that to several of these offshoots the parent firm gave up some department of their business. Thus Wood, Johnson & Burritt got their drygoods trade, Wilson & Brown their wine importing agencies, and so on. These young firms were nearly all composed of Scotsmen. They all enjoyed the confidence and good will of their old employers, and most of them did well in after years.

Another famous old house was and is that now known as Maitland, Phelps & Co., but which in its early years was known simply as Maitland & Co. The business was commenced before the Revolution by two supercargoes in Scottish trading ships. The Maitlands were from the south of Scotland. The father of the house, as it exists to-day, was David Maitland, and the firm name when he was at its head was Maitland, Kennedy & Maitland. The office was in Front Street, and Mr. Maitland, being a bachelor, lived in rooms which he had fitted up with his own notions of comfort in the same building. He was a good type of the old Scotch merchant, enterprising yet cautious, full of dogged perseverance and indomitable courage, a man of few words, set in his ways, brusque in his manner, yet with a kindly heart and a desire to see every one get along in the world. When the opportunity came he gave up active business and retired to some property he had in Scotland, where he lived very happily. The business in New York was left to his nephew, Stewart Maitland, and he formed a partnership with Mr. Royal Phelps, a gentleman who had amassed a fortune in South America, and the firm became Maitland, Phelps & Co. On Stewart Maitland retiring his place was taken by James William Maitland, who at his death bequeathed handsome legacies to the poor in the parishes in Scotland with which the family had been connected. The history of this firm, if fully told, would fill an ample volume, and would be interesting reading, so wide were its ramifications and so clearly were its successes the result of sagacity and hard work. The business still ranks among the most respected in New York, although none of the Maitland family is connected with it.

Another old firm which is still represented in the business houses of the city, although the name is changed, is Barclay & Livingstone. The original firm was Henry & George Barclay, and the partners were the sons of Thomas Barclay, who was the first British Consul in this city. Another son, Anthony, who went in early life to Georgia to seek his fortune, succeeded so well in the South—after becoming a Colonel and marrying the wealthy widow of a Scotsman named Glen—that when he returned to New York he was made a partner. He lived in a fine house on Dey Street, near Greenwich Street, was the aristocrat of the family, and became British Consul, like his father. The Barclays of the firm all prided themselves on being British subjects. They were all born here, but their father being Consul, they claimed that his house was British territory.

Few are now living who remember the importing firm of Gillespie & McLeod, which flourished between 1825 and 1835. Both partners were Scotch, but William McLeod was particularly enthusiastic about his native land. His early life was full of promise. He was descended from an old Highland family, and inherited considerable wealth through his father, an officer in the British Army, who was killed at Waterloo. McLeod once held a commission in the army himself, but for some reason he sold out when his regiment was in Canada, and settled in New York to enter on a commercial career. For some years the firm did a large business, for Gillespie, the senior partner, was a hard-working and thorough business man, which McLeod certainly was not. He was a generous, warm-hearted fellow, proud of his birth and his Highland ancestry, careless of money, and utterly improvident. He aimed at being a fashionable leader rather than a merchant, and in this aim he certainly succeeded. For years he was one of the most popular society men about town, and had as large and varied a circle of friends as any one in it, while everybody knew him by sight. He was an arbitrator in society quarrels, and was equally ready to act as a peacemaker as to be a second in a duel. He made one great mistake in his life, and that was when he quitted the army for commerce. For the latter he was in no way suited, and, though he appeared to flourish for a time, his brother merchants shook their heads when asked about the prospects of the firm, and were very cautious in their dealings with it. Gradually the business grew smaller and smaller, until one or two wild plunges, made in the hope of improving matters, ended in bankruptcy and ruin. Mr. McLeod took his misfortune with remarkable composure. Although he lost his position in fashionable society, and found in his later days that his real friends were few, he never murmured. He continued to live in New York, and died at a good old age in the old City Hotel, which had for years been one of his favorite haunts.

The most noted, however, of the early mercantile families of the City of New York was that founded by Robert Lenox, a native of Kirkcudbright, and belonging to a family which had long been famous in the ancient Stewartry. One Robert Lenox was shot in 1685 by the notorious Grierson of Lagg, the infamous persecutor of the Covenanters, of whom no man has ever yet spoken a favorable word, although Claverhouse and others have had their defenders. Robert Lenox was a Covenanter, and " suffered " like so many hundred others for his adherence to that noble cause. Whether Robert Lenox, who crossed the Atlantic about 1778, was a descendant from the same family as this martyr or not we cannot say, but he and his son certainly showed a devotion to the cause of religion that almost tempts one to conclude that the same blood flowed through their views. Robert Lenox seems to have settled first in Philadelphia, but after a year or two removed to New York. He started in business as a general shipping merchant at 235 Queen Street, and rapidly, for those days, rose to a foremost position among New York's merchants. He married a daughter of Nicholas Carmer, a representative of an old Knickerbocker family, and so got a recognized place among the local aristocracy, while his own countrymen admired his executive ability and mercantile standing so highly that in 1792 they elected him a Vice President of the St. Andrew's Society, and its President from 1798 till 1813. Of the Chamber of Commerce he was also President for many years.

While Robert Lenox's entire career as a merchant is interesting, its most noteworthy incident was his purchase of the five-milestone farm of about thirty acres from the Corporation of New York City. The purchase money paid was, comparatively, a trifle, and as the farm lay between what is now Fourth and Fifth Avenues and Sixty-eighth and Seventy-fourth Streets, every New Yorker knows that this land is now among the most valuable in the city. Mr. Lenox was firmly convinced that this land would "improve" in value, and steadily added to its extent as opportunity offered, and in drawing up his will he bequeathed it in such a way that its sale for many years was effectually prevented. When he died, in 1840, Mr. Lenox was reputed to be among the five wealthiest citizens of New York. His only son, James, who was born at 59 Broadway, New York, in 1800, succeeded to his entire estate. James Lenox was educated at Princeton, where he was graduated in 1821. He studied law, but practiced little, if any, and went to Europe soon after his admission to the bar. While there he developed his bibliographical and artistic tastes and laid the foundation for his future benefaction to his native city of a public library. On his return he carefully attended to his property, which year by year increased in value, but at the same time he was actively engaged in thinking out those schemes of public benefit with which his name is now associated. He was a man of retiring disposition, very sensitive as to public notice, and, while he was constantly engaged in doing good, it was in such an unostentatious manner that often the recipients of the bounty were unaware of its source. His first great benefaction was the site and $250,000 toward the construction and equipment of the Presbyterian Hospital, which was opened Oct. 10, 1872. Then he gave the ground on Seventy-third Street, valued at that time at $64,000, for the Presbyterian Home for Aged Women, and in 1874 the site for a Presbyterian church on Seventy-third Street.

The other gifts Mr. Lenox gave to these institutions will probably never be fully known, but during his lifetime none of them suffered for lack of funds. In 1870 he conveyed ten lots on the crest of a hill overlooking Central Park for the erection of the Lenox Library, and built the structure which adorns that site and to which he gave his family name. To it, when completed, he presented his magnificent collection of books and pictures, and augmented since, as it has been, by the funds bequeathed by him and by other donations, notably that from the Stuart estate, it is become one of the choicest of the public libraries in America, although its individuality has been in a measure lost since becoming a part of the "New York Public Library—Astor, Lenox, and Tilden Foundations." It does not aim at comprehensiveness, but whatever branch of literature it takes up it tries to illustrate completely. Thus, of Bibles it has the finest collection in the country, from the rare "Mazarin" of Gutenberg and Faust, about 1450, to the Oxford Bibles of the present age. There is a set of Shakespeare folios and quartos, seven Caxtons, and nearly every known edition of Bunyan's "Pilgrim's Progress," Walton's "Angler," and Milton's works. The Americana is particularly large and valuable, and the collection of manuscripts is especially noticeable. The art collection is small, but includes a number of Washington portraits, and examples of Reynolds, Turner, Gainsborough, Wilkie, Stuart, Leslie, Delaroche, and other modern artists. The most conspicuous picture in the collection is Munkacsy's "Blind Milton Dictating 'Paradise Lost' to His Daughters," the gift of Robert Lenox Kennedy, who succeeded Mr. Lenox as President of the library, and who, like the present President, John S. Kennedy, was ever on the outlook to advance the importance of the institution by gift or executive ability. Mr. Lenox died in 1880. Of his seven sisters, only two survived him, and the bulk of his property was distributed so as to reach these, and ultimately his numerous benefactions. Of one thing he was very imperative in the terms of his will, and that was that no details of his life should be given for publication in any form. It is impossible to estimate what New York—the poor of New York—owe to the deeds of this family, but when we remember that thousands each year pass through the Presbyterian Hospital either as indoor or dispensary patients, we can understand slightly the good work that is being carried on by one agency established through the foresight of the father and the benevolence of the son. In this instance, too, the educated are equally benefited by the family benefactions, for the scholar and man of letters has in the Lenox Library access to literary treasures so rare and so valuable as to be nowadays beyond the reach of purchase. Surely among the things which make up the great metropolitan city of America these institutions will ever deserve a prominent place and the name of Lenox be reverently cherished, not only as that of a family of representative Scots, but of men who strove to do the utmost good to the city which had become their home.

Equal prominence as public benefactors is due to the Stuart family, which may be said to have been founded in America in 1805, when Kinloch Stuart settled in New York from Edinburgh and started in business as a candymaker. He attended closely to his establishment, and when he died, in 1826, had not only acquired considerable means, but was regarded as a substantial merchant, two reputations which do not always go together. His sons, Robert L. and Alexander Stuart, both of whom were born in New York, succeeded him and carried on the business until 1856, during which time the confections of R. L. & A. Stuart became famous all over the country. In that year they gave up candymaking and devoted themselves to refining sugar—they were the first, by the way, to use steam in the process in America —and finally retired from business life in 1872 with large fortunes. The rest of their lives were truly spent in doing good, although the performance of charity was no new hobby with them, for from 1852 they had each laid aside yearly a stated amount of their income for works of benevolence or religion. Alexander died in 1879 and Robert L. in 1882, and it has been estimated that jointly they gave away during their lives over $2,000,000. Princeton College and Theological Seminary were liberal partakers of this bounty, and the New York Presbyterian Hospital and the San Francisco Theological Seminary were enriched by munificent gifts. R. L. Stuart was long President of the American Museum of Natural History, and the early growth of that institution was greatly facilitated by his generosity, and as President for a time of the Presbyterian Hospital he did good service —service only second to that of the founder himself—to the poor of New York. No one, however, knew exactly how far the charitable hands of these brothers were extended or how many churches, missions, and agencies of good, not only in America, but throughout the world, were helped by them.

After R. L. Stuart's death the philanthropic work of his life was nobly carried on by his widow, who henceforth lived to be virtually the almoner of her own and her husband's wealth. This estimable lady was the daughter of Robert McCrea, a wealthy Scotch merchant of New York, who died in 1830. The Presbyterian Church in its various schemes was the recipient of large contributions annually, and special occasions were always certain of her assistance. To Princeton College she was a princely benefactor, founding in it, at Dr. McCosh's special request, a School of Philosophy with a gift of $150,000, and that was only one of many contributions to the institution. To the Historical Society she gave $100,000, to the Half Orphan Asylum $100,000, and so on—always generous in her contributions. She was invariably giving—and giving in secret, for she shunned notoriety or publicity, and hardly a day passed that she was not assisting in some good work. When she died, at the close of 1891, most of her means went to Princeton, to the various

Presbyterian Church schemes, and to a host of charities, for she had no near relatives. Her books and collection of paintings went to the Lenox Library, and those who perused her will saw that in the final distribution of her wealth she aimed to be as comprehensive in its disposition as possible, to aid established and tried agencies, and to spread the light of the Gospel as well as the blessings of education and charity. She used common sense throughout her life in her giving, and this good Scotch quality was never more apparent than in the instrument which contained her instructions for the disposal of her " guids and gear."

In the " Statistical Account of Scotland," Vol. I., Page 495, is the following brief notice of a Scot whose name was once well known all over the Eastern States and is still prominently remembered in horticultural circles: " Mr. Grant Thorburn, seedsman, New York, the original ' Lawrie Todd,' though a native of Newbattle Parish, where he was born on the 18th of February, 1773, lived in Dalkeith from his childhood till he sailed for New York on the 13th April, 1794. He is a man of great piety and worth, though of a remarkably lively and eccentric character. He visited Dalkeith in 1834, when he published his ' Autobiography,' which he dedicates with characteristic singularity and elegance to Her Grace the Duchess of Buccleuch."

It did not suit the purpose for Mr. Peter Steele, the gifted schoolmaster who in 1844 wrote these words, to give any indication of Thorburn's career in Scotland. Political feeling then ran very high and political resentment was very bitter, and the teacher could not, had he so inclined, say a word commendatory of Thorburn's early life without bringing upon his own head the ill will of the Buccleuch family and its adherents. So, like a canny Scot, he acted the part of the Aberdeen man's parrot, which " thocht a guid deal but said naething ava." Thorburn learned from his father the trade of a nailmaker and became quite an expert at it long before his apprenticeship was past. Like most of the Scottish workmen of the time—a time when the old order of things was fast changing and the governing powers tried to quell the popular advance and the political aspirations with trials for treason, sedition, and the like—Thorburn became deeply interested in politics, and in Dalkeith was prominent among those who advocated Parliamentary reform and a generous accession to the rights of the people to a voice in the conduct of affairs. The result was that when opportunity offered he was arrested for treason, and, after a short time in prison, was released on bail. This arrest made him a marked man and blocked any prospect of his making his way in the world, so, believing that the star of freedom blinked bonnily across the sea in the new Republic which had thrown off the yoke of the same Parliament he had protested against, Thorburn left Scotland and, settling in New York, tried to earn his living at his trade of nailmaking. It, however, did not promise much for the future, and in 1801 he started in business as a grocer at 20 Nassau Street. "He was there," writes Walter Barrett, "some ten or twelve years and then he moved to No. 22, and about the time of his removal, in 1810, he changed his business and kept garden seeds and was a florist. He established a seed-raising garden at Newark, but it proved unsuccessful, and thereafter he confined his attention to his business in New York and acquired considerable means."

From the beginning of his American career almost, Thorburn became known for his kindly heart, and he did much practical good in a quiet way, not only among his countrymen, but among all deserving people whose needs touched his sympathy or aroused his compassion. For many years his store in Liberty Street was not only a lounging place for the merchants who bought flowers, but for the practical gardeners who grew them. His place became a sort of clearing house for the horticulturists in the city, and every Scotch gardener who arrived in New York from the Old Country made Thorburn's place his headquarters until he found employment, and hundreds used to say that the advice and information they received from him at that critical stage in their careers were of the most incalculable value to them through life. In

1854 Mr. Thorburn in a sense retired from business and settled in Astoria. From there he moved to Winsted, Conn., and finally to New Haven, Conn., where he died in 1861.

Mr. Thorburn possessed considerable literary tastes, and, under the *nom de plume* of "Lawrie Todd," wrote in his later years at frequent intervals for the "Knickerbocker Magazine" and other periodicals. He gave to John Galt much of the information which that genius incorporated in his story of "Lawrie Todd; or, Settlers in the New World," and his published volumes of reminiscences, notably his "Forty Years' Residence in America" and "Fifty Years' Reminiscences of New York," still form interesting reading. So, too, does a now scarce volume published in 1848 under the title of "Lawrie Todd's Notes on Virginia, with a Chapter on Puritans, Witches, and Friends." This book is one of those contributions to American social history which will become of more value as time speeds on, although its importance may be more appreciated by the student than by the general reader.

In Walter Barrett's interesting volumes on "The Old Merchants of New York" we find the following notices of an old family of merchants, the founders of which settled in America from Inverary. Says Mr. Barrett: "Robert Bruce came out to Norfolk as a protégé of the Earl of Dunmore, who was then Governor of Virginia. The Governor was about to visit the Province of New York in an English man-of-war. 'Robert, I want you to accompany me to New York; Norfolk is too small a sphere for your mercantile operations. New York will be the great commercial city. You must anchor there,' were the kind words of Lord Dunmore to Robert Bruce. * * * Accordingly, the young Scotch merchant accompanied Gov. Dunmore to New York. Here he introduced him to Gov. Colden, who became his friend and patron ever after.

"When Robert had been in the city a few months he determined to make it his permanent home, and sent for his brother, Peter, to come over from Scotland. At that time Broadway did not extend up to where Chambers Street now is, though Peter Bruce bought a spot of ground on the southeast corner of Broadway and Duane Street. The brothers were in this city prior to the Revolution, probably about 1768. Robert was a Tory and Peter a Whig in the war times. It is a wonder to me how a merchant of that day could be anything else than a Tory—particularly in the case of Robert Bruce, who had been the protégé and had received the warm personal friendship of two royal Governors. Probably it was a little bit of policy that made Peter a Whig. After the war was over they kept their store, in 1784, at 3 Front Street, and as late as 1795, when they removed to 120 Front Street. There was a William Bruce who was in the grocery business at 129 Front Street. He was from Aberdeen. He died in 1798 of yellow fever.

"Both Robert and Peter died in 1796 within a short time of each other. In 1789 the firm of Robert & Peter Bruce owned a little vessel called The Friends' Adventure. She was commanded by Peter Parker, and traded to Shelburne. At the time John Jacob Astor arrived in New York from Germany he found Robert Bruce the richest man in the city, as Mr. Astor frequently stated." From these brothers descended a family whose representatives are now to be found in the highest circles of the representative houses, not only of New York, but in Virginia and other States.

Another family of Bruces crossed the Atlantic about the time these Inverary merchants were passing off the stage. The first of this family to settle in America was David Bruce, a native of Edinburgh, who landed in New York about 1793. His brother, George, followed him in 1795. After being employed in several establishments, the two brothers, in 1806, opened a book store and printing office on Pearl Street. They soon had a fair business, but their success really dated from the day they published an edition of Lavoisier's "Chemistry," all the work in connection with the printing of which they did themselves. In 1812 David revisited Scotland in search of matters that might extend their business, and when in Edinburgh mastered the art of stereotyping—an Edinburgh invention—and on his return proceeded to turn his knowledge to practical account. This led to the making of improvements in typesetting, and finally to the establishment of a type foundry, which at the present day ranks as one of the foremost in the United States. Their first stereotyped work—the first in America—was an edition of the New Testament in bourgeois type, and this was followed by an edition of the entire Bible in nonpareil. After a most successful career, David Bruce died in Brooklyn in 1857, and George survived till 1866, having done more to make American type famous for beauty of outline and strength of material throughout the world than any of their contemporaries.

Philadelphia furnishes us with the names of several even earlier Scotch printers, and it is worthy of mention here that the first American edition of Burns's poems was published in the Quaker City in 1788—a year after the first Edinburgh edition and a few months before the first New York edition—by Stewart & Hyde. One of the most noted of the Scotch printers and publishers in Philadelphia was Robert Aitken, a native of Perthshire. He was born in 1724, and, although nothing can be learned of his early life, he appears to have been a man of considerable education and mental capacity, and thoroughly imbued with republican principles. We first find him in Philadelphia in 1769 engaged as a printer and active in the then undefined movement which within a few years was to burst aside the bonds which united the Colonies to the old land. In 1775 he published the "Pennsylvania Magazine; or, American Monthly," but the times were not propitious for the success of magazine literature, and after issuing it for eighteen months, during which it contained many attractive and timely articles—some from the pen of Dr. Witherspoon of Princeton—he reluctantly abandoned it. A year later his enthusiasm for the cause of the young republic landed him in prison. In 1782—a most ill-advised time for such a project—he printed the first American edition of the English Bible, and lost money by the speculation. Its title page bears the imprint, "Philadelphia, Printed and Sold by R. Aitkin, at Pope's Head, Three doors above the Coffee House, in Market Street, MDCCLXXII.," and it has become a very scarce book. It is doubted if there are fifty copies in existence, and the value of a perfect one is very great. Aitkin was the author, or the reputed author, of a work on a commercial system for the United States, which was published in 1787, and of a number of pamphlets. He died in 1802, in the city which had so long been his home.

Another noted Philadelphia printer was David Hall, whose firm—Hall & Seller—printed the paper money issued by authority of Congress during the Revolution. Hall was born at Edinburgh in 1714, and thoroughly mastered what is called "the printer's art" in his native city and in London, to which place he removed shortly after his apprenticeship was over. He settled in Philadelphia in 1747, and after working at his trade for several years started in business. For a time he had the famous Benjamin Franklin as a partner, but that great patriot had then fully entered upon that public career which was to redound so nobly to his own fame and to the welfare and stability of the Nation he did so much to found, and so his partnership was of little practical use in the business, and the relations between Hall and Franklin were soon dissolved. In 1766 he formed the copartnership of Hall & Seller, a firm that continued in existence long after he had passed away, his own interest being taken up by his sons. The firm printed the "Pennsylvania Gazette," and the editorial work was done by Hall. It was a model of its kind, and typographically and editorially the publication was ahead of any of its contemporaries. Hall also conducted on his individual account quite an extensive book and stationery store, so that he must have been a pattern of industry—just the sort of man whose life ought to have been written by Dr. Smiles or included in that author's "Self Help." His death took place at Philadelphia, in 1772, just as the struggle was fairly opening that was to culminate in the political independence of the land he had made his own, and whose cause had no warmer supporter.

Possibly the pioneer Scotch printer in America was John Campbell of Boston, who published on April 17, 1704, the Boston "News-Letter," the first regular newspaper issued in the country. It was a small production looked at alongside of the mammoth "blanket" newspapers of the present day, but, small as it was, its publication involved an amount of thought and care and enterprise which stamps John Campbell as having been no ordinary man. Campbell was born at Islay in 1653, crossed the Atlantic in 1686, and became a bookseller in Boston. For many years he was Postmaster of that city, and seems to have been held in general esteem. He died in 1728.

Another enterprising newspaper was published before the outbreak of the Revolutionary troubles by Robert Wells, an Edinburgh man who, in 1754, when in the twenty-sixth year of his age, settled down in Charleston to make a fortune. One of his first acts was to get enrolled as a member of the St. Andrew's Society of Charleston, so that his own land and its associations were not to be forgotten, although he had "crossed the sea." Wells commenced business as a bookseller, stationer, and printer, and for many years his establishment was the leading literary emporium in the Carolinas. His paper, "The South Carolina and American General Gazette," enjoyed a large circulation—as circulations went in those days. When the Revolutionary movement approached a crisis he declined to throw off his allegiance to the Crown, and, resigning his business to his son, John, who had no such scruples, Wells returned to Britain and died at London, in 1794. While in Charleston he wrote for his amusement a "Travestie of Virgil," and he seems to have been a person of considerable attainments, a self-educated and self-made man.

As we have lingered so long among printers and booksellers, we may be pardoned for continuing here to write of them down to a period beyond that intended to be covered at this stage of this chapter. Having dwelt on the beginning of the business of typography, we may as well go on to see its highest development. This was brought about, it may be said, through the life-long labors and learned as well as artistic zeal of John Wilson, the founder of the still-famed Wilson Press of Cambridge. John Wilson was born at Glasgow in 1802. His parents were of humble position, his early education scant, and early in life necessity compelled him to adopt a trade, and by accident or from inclination he became a printer. Nothing shows the character of the lad better than the fact that despite his "short schooling" and the long hours which his occupation demanded, he developed into a man of very considerable learning and an adept in Greek, Latin, French, and other languages. Leaving Scotland about 1824, he went to Belfast, and there showed that he thought of more than the mere mechanism of his business by publishing in 1826 a small "Treatise on Grammatical Punctuation," a work which was afterward (in 1850) rewritten and republished in Boston, and which has since been accepted as the standard work on the subject, so much so that over twenty editions have been published since the author's death.

In 1846, after many other migrations, Wilson settled in Boston and began business for himself at his trade. Moving from the city subsequently to its suburb of Cambridge, he founded the firm of John Wilson & Son and did a large business—a business of that high class that brought into constant practical service his lingual acquirements. A great deal of his business lay with Harvard University and with the writings of its professors and instructors, and this connection gained for him, in 1866, the well-merited official acknowledgment of the degree of Master of Arts. In his religious belief Mr. Wilson was a stanch Unitarian, and wrote several volumes and pamphlets in defense of the principles of that body—of the school, rather, of which the gifted Channing was the leader.

Mr. Wilson was constantly engaged in perfecting the details of his business in all departments, and for many years no establishment could turn out more perfect work. His proofreading was a model of accuracy, and in the printing of wood cuts he was especially successful. For a long time his office was the only one in America that could print a book in Greek with any degree of accuracy, and in the classics he attempted to rival the beauty and correctness of the Foulis Press, which made his native city so famous in the annals of typography. To the end of his career Mr. Wilson was a devoted Scot, growing prouder, it almost seemed, of his native land as the years sped on and it became to him simply a reminiscence. From the moment he could read, almost, he became a student of the poems of Robert Burns; and as early as 1837, while still in Belfast, he contributed a well-written and appreciative essay on the life and character of the poet to an edition of Burns's writings printed in that city that year. He also delivered a noteworthy address on the bard in Boston in connection with the centenary celebration of 1859. Mr. Wilson closed his useful and honorable life—honorable equally to Scotland and America—in 1868, at Cambridge.

Our next illustration had to deal with books, not as a writer or manufacturer, but simply, for the most part, as a dealer, although he knew the contents of the books he sold more intimately than many who professed superior learning, and though his name appeared as publisher on the title pages of several volumes. This was William Gowans, long the most famous of New York booksellers, whose stock for variety and value was only equalled by those of some of the old-established emporiums in London or on the Continent. Gowans was born at Lesmahagow in 1803, died in New York on Nov. 27, 1870, and was buried a few days afterward in Woodlawn Cemetery, where a plain stone marks his resting place. At the funeral services the Rev. Dr. John Thomson, long pastor of the Fourth Presbyterian Church in New York and afterward a minister at Grantown, Scotland, delivered an appropriate address, in which he said:

"William Gowans, well known—few men better known—among the men of literature, not only in New

York—a city of no mean literary excellence—but also over all the land, has stood amongst us, *facile princeps*, as a peculiar man. A native of Scotland, having been born in the parish of Lesmahagow, in the county of Lanark, in the year 1803, he immigrated with the family to Philadelphia in the year 1821. In various situations he spent the succeeding years until 1830, when he began his career as bibliopole in Chatham Street, in this city. Between the little store and little stock in Chatham Street and the thronged passageways of 115 Nassau Street, tapestried—I had almost said padded and paved —with books—one will say what a change! Yes, but how many changes are embraced between two such extremes? Another generation has risen and has buried that that first patronized the bibliopole. Authors have been born and have written their names on the grand historic tablets and have since died. Authors long dead and buried out of sight have been disinterred and, silent for centuries, have spoken again, and modern life hears their speech and lives their laborious days over again, all since that young Scotsman fathered the store in Chatham Street. Since then bookselling has become a marvelous and mightily honorable trade, and one only yet in its infancy, for it has not a State or a few States, but a continent, to compass and an appetite insatiable to provide for. William Gowans was a dealer in books. Aye, so will some most pitiful dealers in money represent him and all such as he. But he was more. He was not so much a dealer *in* books as a dealer *with* books. To know them, their authors, age, spirits, range, and bearing was not his labor or life task; it was his delight and high enjoyment. Among books, old and rare, and the rarer and older the more agreeable the work for him. William Gowans was the antitype of Old Mortality among the tombstones. It was his high calling to bring out into the light of modern life what time and ignorance were fast in conspiracy to waste away."

Two more illustrations, each still nearer to our day, and we will leave the makers of books. One of these we select is Henry Ivison, whose firm was for years foremost in New York in the publication and dissemination of school-book literature. Mr. Ivison was born at Glasgow in 1808, and settled in America, with his parents, when twelve years of age. He acquired a knowledge of the book trade as apprentice to William Williams, bookseller in Utica, and in 1830 started business on his own account in Auburn. He remained there for sixteen years, and not only was in comfortable circumstances, but accumulated a little money. Then, in 1846, he accepted the offer of a partnership with Mark H. Newman of New York, and removed to that city.

The copartnership was a pleasant and profitable one from the start, and of one series of books—Sanders's Readers, the first consecutive series of school readers published in America—the sales were enormous. Of the "Primer," the first of the five in the series, never less than 100,000 copies were ordered printed at one time for quite a number of years. In 1852 the partnership was renewed, and the firm became known as Newman & Ivison, but within a year, through the death of the senior partner, the entire management passed into Mr. Ivison's hands. The firm afterward was reorganized several times, and bore the names of the partners who subsequently became associated with him—one of these partners being H. F. Phinney, a son-in-law of J. Fenimore Cooper—and it did business under the firm name of Ivison, Blakeman, Taylor & Co. in 1881, when Mr. Ivison retired, leaving his interest to his son. After retiring from business, Mr. Ivison led a quiet and happy life between his city home in New York and his country residence at Stockbridge, Mass. But his career of usefulness still continued. As a Trustee of the Union Theological Seminary, an Elder in the Fifth Avenue Presbyterian Church, and in many other directions he had plenty of scope for his energies and for the exercise of that business shrewdness which was his distinguishing characteristic throughout his career. He died after a brief illness, in New York, in 1884.

Our last "examplar" in this section, Robert Carter, was for years the leading publisher of religious—thoroughly orthodox—literature in New York, and in his earlier years he showed a degree of enterprise and of reliance on his own judgment which few religious-book publishers have shown in the history of the trade. Mr. Carter became a bookseller and publisher by force of circumstances rather than anything else, for he was designed by his parents, and the design was seconded by his own inclinations, to be a teacher. He was born at Earlston, not many miles from Abbotsford, in 1807. His own education was, it might be said, not much more than begun when in 1822 he opened a night school in one of the rooms of his father's cottage for the young lads of the neighborhood, and at the same time was applying himself diligently to a study of Latin and Greek, assisted by a cousin some years older, who had been at college. In 1827 he entered upon the battle of life by securing a position as teacher in a grammar school at Peebles. From the money earned during the two years spent in that work he saved enough money to spend a session at the University of Edinburgh. Mr. Carter landed in New York in 1831, and for over three years was engaged in teaching, latterly in a school of his own, but in 1834 he commenced his real career by leasing a store at the corner of Canal and Laurens Streets, and entering into business as a seller of books. It was a fairly successful venture, but too slow for the young merchant, and he resolved to try his hand at publishing. His first experiment was a book which it is safe to say no other publisher in America would have risked a cent of money or a moment's consideration on—"The Atonement and Intercession of Jesus Christ," by Dr. William Symington. The venture hung fire at first, but one gentleman bought 100 copies for distribution, another wrote a warm eulogy of the book for a religious paper, and gradually the entire edition disappeared.

This book brought Mr. Carter into notice in religious circles, and his business steadily increased. In 1841 he revisited Scotland in search of business connections and books to sell, and while there bought a copy of the earlier volumes of D'Aubigné's "History of the Reformation," which he republished immediately on his return, and which reached a sale of over 50,000 copies. In 1848 Mr. Carter assumed as partners his brothers, Peter and Walter, and under the style of Robert Carter & Brothers the firm moved to 258 Broadway, and in 1856 to the building at the corner of Spring Street and Broadway, which continued to be its place of business until it went out of business, after the death of its founder.

Early in his business career Mr. Carter made two resolutions to which he adhered steadfastly—to make all purchases for cash and to give no notes. Therefore, he always knew "where he stood," whatever the conditions of trade or general business. Then no book was ever published whose religious teaching was not unimpeachable. The mere fact of there being "money" in a publication was in itself no consideration, and, unless Robert Carter and his brothers were perfectly certain that a book was strictly orthodox, that its teachings were helpful, that some benefit was to be gained by its perusal, no thoughts of sale would tempt the firm's imprint to appear on the title page. Some even good men averred that in all this the Carters were too particular, and a story used to be told that Robert Carter once took home a manuscript to read, and was delighted with it, talked about its early chapters to his friends with enthusiasm, and had made arrangements to print it, but when he came to the last pages he saw some stains that led him to believe the writer had been smoking when he penned them, and as part of the story had shown the evils of tobacco he returned the manuscript at once, because he thought the writer was not an honest man.

A Presbyterian of the strictest school, accepting humbly all the canons of that denomination, even those which are most sneered and laughed at, Mr. Carter was a bitter foe of hypocrisy and cant, and was intolerant of dishonesty in any form. For, although it is the common practice to charge such men as he with narrow-mindedness and intolerance, a more unfounded error never acquired popular belief. The most intolerant, bigoted, self-conceited prig to be found in any community is the professed infidel, who always avers that he sees no good in any man's opinion which differs from his own, and is either sneering or gibing or denouncing any views held by his fellow-men which do not square with those sentiments which, generally for a fee or an advertisement, he is always proclaiming in season and out of season. The truly religious man honors all sorts of sincere belief, and this was the case with Robert Carter. He cared nothing for controversial literature—it never figured in his list of publications, but that list was wide enough to include literary examples from every evangelical denomination.

We have many examples in the trade history of New York of men achieving distinction in the common callings of life—the callings which could not be dignified with the title of professions—and it is the same in all centres of population. For many years the official time-keeper of New York, as he might be called, was a Scotsman, and in the old houses of the city no furniture is more prized than that made by Duncan Phyfe, a native of Glasgow, who was for many years at the head of the furniture-making trade in America. Even to-day his handiwork stands out as solid, as clear cut, and as beautiful as when it first left his workshop, although, for very evident reasons, undoubted examples of his skill are yearly becoming more scarce. We can easily believe, however, that he made a special study of every article he manufactured, that the workmanship, even where concealed, was honest, and everything was made to last, rather than merely to sell—as is the fashion nowadays. Duncan Phyfe was born in 1770, and, with his parents, emigrated to America in 1783, just after he had got through schooling. Where he learned the trade of a cabinetmaker is not known. It is possible he had even started to understand its mysteries before he left Scotland, but about 1796 he commenced business for himself, and continued steadfastly at work, at the bench and the designing board, until 1850, about which year he died. "In that time," says one record, "he made a vast deal of excellent and beautiful mahogany furniture, including pieces of all sorts and sizes. Chairs were his specialty. A dozen well-authenticated Duncan Phyfe chairs sold not long ago at $22.50 each. He also made card tables with richly carved tripods provided with an internal mechanism that caused the legs to spread or collapse, as desired. The simplest carving on his small chairs was wrought with the utmost care and precision, while the more elaborate carvings on the larger pieces were marvels of the art. The renovation of Duncan Phyfe's work is expensive, because of the care and time required. Phyfe was fond of introducing the figure of the lyre into his furniture. It appears in chairs, in swinging mirrors, and in various pieces, large and small. He seldom chose to mark his work, and only experts are able now to recognize it.

"As Phyfe used to employ fully one hundred of the most skillful journeyman cabinetmakers in New York, and as his furniture was of the most durable sort, there is still a great deal of his work in existence. It is seldom for sale, and when any of it is sent to the auction room it is usually disposed of at private sale. A maiden lady who died a few years ago at the age of ninety-four left behind her a full set of Duncan Phyfe furniture, the gift of her father when she was a girl of eighteen. The set was reproduced in mahogany by a German cabinetmaker, and imitations of it are to be found in some of the more fashionable stores."

Among the hundreds of Scots who have been prominent in St. Louis, probably no name stands out in bolder relief or is held in more pleasant remembrance by the older residents than that of John Shaw, who died at his residence near that city, in 1878, at the advanced age of eighty-eight years. It is worth while dwelling on Mr. Shaw's career and idiosyncrasies, because the details show how many transformations may happen in a man's life between the cradle and the grave, and because in all he said and did he was most characteristically Scotch. John Shaw was born in Edinburgh Castle, where his father, a soldier, resided with his wife in the barracks. His parents removed to Grantown, in the north, and his early years were spent there. While yet a boy he entered the army, and was engaged in the Spanish campaign which resulted in the retreat upon Corunna and the death of Sir John Moore. He obtained his discharge shortly before the battle of Waterloo, and, returning to Grantown, began an apprenticeship as a stonemason, in which business nearly all his after life was spent. When his apprenticeship expired he wandered all over Scotland and the North of Ireland to acquire experience and skill in his trade. After leading a life of this kind for some time he married and returned to Grantown, where some of his children were born.

Turning his steps westward, Shaw landed in America, and settled in St. Louis about 1842. His life there was that of an active and energetic master builder. All for whom he worked had the greatest confidence in his ability, and he soon became the head of his branch of business. Many of the best buildings in St. Louis are the result of his skill. Among others were the foundation of the old Post Office, the Mercantile Library Hall, the Old Lindell, and numberless stores and residences of all sizes. In 1862, finding himself possessed of a competency, he retired from business, and, purchasing a large tract of land in Franklin County, Mo., settled there and engaged in the quiet life of a farmer.

"Mr. Shaw," wrote one who knew him well, shortly after his death, "was a man of marked force of character, decided in his opinions, and often severe in his judgments. To a stranger he may have appeared bluff and brusque in manner, but it was merely on the surface, for any of those who enjoyed his acquaintance knew that he possessed many kindly qualities and a warm, generous heart. In enthusiasm for his native land (which he twice revisited after making his home in St. Louis) he was really 'second to none.' He was a diligent and careful reader, and, while well informed upon all subjects, he took a special interest in the history of the Highland clans, and could tell many thrilling stories of their fights and feuds. Of what he called his own clan he felt particularly proud, and jocularly claimed that he was its real chief. As became a thorough Highlander, he had a good deal of the Jacobite in his nature, and felt a genuine contempt for the memory of 'the wee, wee German lairdie.' To sum up, he was as thorough a Scotsman as if he had never left the soil. All his standards of comparison were there, and his great delight ever was to recall the scenes and memories, the history and traditions, the wit and wisdom of 'Auld Scotland.'"

Turning to Chicago, we are confronted with an array of names prominent in every walk to which a volume would hardly do justice. As a fairly representative career we select that of George Smith, who, in 1839, established the first bank in the city. Mr. Smith was born at Old Deer, Aberdeenshire, in 1808, and was intended for the medical profession. After studying two years in Aberdeen University his health failed, and, believing that an active outdoor life was necessary for his constitution, he turned his attention for a time to farming, with the most beneficial results. But he had no desire to resume his professional studies, and, crossing the Atlantic, in 1833, " went West," before that phrase became current, and entered upon a business career. Chicago was then not only decidedly far West, but it was little more than a village, yet Mr. Smith believed that its geographical position insured it a grand future. In 1834 he commenced dealing in real estate, and bought up as many lots as he could within the then limits of the city. Believing that the then newly conceived City of Milwaukee might be a close rival to Chicago, or, at all events, an equally prosperous city, he invested largely in its lots and sold out his Chicago holdings in 1836 at a considerable profit, one-quarter of the price being in cash and the rest in notes. A tide of commercial depression, however, swept over the place the following year, and, as his notes were unpaid, Mr. Smith had to resume possession of his Chicago lots. He ultimately lost nothing by the transaction, however. In 1839 he helped to obtain a charter for the Wisconsin Fire and Marine Insurance Company, which was then established with himself as President, and the late Alexander Mitchell as Secretary.

The latter really was the practical head of the corporation from the beginning, for Mr. Smith soon started the Chicago banking establishment of George Smith & Co., the pioneer of the great financial institutions which now adorn that city. His Chicago and Milwaukee interests proved veritable gold mines, and in 1852 Mr. Smith began to think seriously of retiring from business cares and enjoying the fruits of his business career free from all commercial worriments and entanglements. The first step was the disposal of his interest in the Milwaukee bank to Mr. Mitchell, whose business sagacity had raised the institution to a high eminence among the financial concerns of the Northwest, and bit by bit he steadily closed up all his other active business interests. These, however, were so many and so intricate that the task of unloading judiciously was by no means an easy one, and it was not until 1861 that Mr. Smith found himself free from all entanglements and ready to enter upon his plan of rest. He then retired to Great Britain, where he still enjoys the fruits of his years of business activity.

We may take a more recent illustration from the town of South Chicago, now a part of the big city, although it seems to preserve its individuality. John Oliver, who died there in August, 1894, was a notable figure in many ways. Born at Riccarton, Ayrshire, in 1835, he was educated in the Kilmarnock Academy, and settled in America when fifteen years of age, with no capital except his brains. He began his business career as a bookkeeper with a Chicago lumber firm, and remained with the concern for several years. Then he entered into business for himself and pegged away until he was rated among the millionaires of Chicago. After he retired from the lumber business he confined his attention to his real estate interests, and spent the evening of life in a quiet and pleasant manner, enjoying the good wishes of his friends and business acquaintances, among whom were many of the pioneers of Chicago.

We have already spoken of Alexander Mitchell of Milwaukee in connection with his one-time partner, George Smith, and it is fitting now to enter more at length into the wonderful career of that truly typical Scotsman. Mr. Mitchell was born at Ellon, Aberdeenshire, in 1817. He had two years of experience in financiering in a banking house in Peterhead, experience which was of the utmost service to him in after life. In 1839 he left Scotland, and, settling in the then "paper" city of Milwaukee, grew up with it. Not only that, for, as the manager of the Marine and Fire Insurance Company, he had a good deal to do with making the city grow. The bank early acquired a reputation for honesty, liberality, and thoughtfulness in its dealings. It entered into no wild-cat schemes, fostered every legitimate industry, pinned its faith to Milwaukee as a centre of commerce, and won. All over the Northwest the banking institution was famous, and "as sound as Mitchell's Bank" passed into a common saying. But Mr. Mitchell did not rest content with being simply a banker. He saw that the resources of the Northwest had to be developed, and this led him into railway schemes, until the magnitude of these operations eclipsed his banking interests, while at the same time they fed them. Bit by bit he became the builder, promoter, or financier of a series of railroads which was aimed to reach through the Northwest and to open new avenues of commerce, until under the general name of the Chicago, Milwaukee and St. Paul Railroad, these systems are now regarded as among the most important in America.

Mr. Mitchell served in the United States House of Representatives from 1871 to 1875, and thus acquired a national reputation, and on his retirement from political life went on calmly with what was the real business of his career—the development of Milwaukee. He died at New York City, while on a visit, in 1887.

Mr. Mitchell was one of those far-seeing men who can forecast the future successfully, who can weigh a thousand contingencies, and, having figured out their value or possibilities, hold on to that figuring with all the energy and determination which are necessary to win success even under the most brilliant circumstances. He saw that the possibilities in the way of the development of the Northwest were practically unlimited and that means of transportation were the first as well as the all-important requisites to bring about that development, and to furnishing transportation he devoted himself. Many laughed at the energy with which he threw a bit of railroad line into a practically unoccupied territory, but the business soon followed the railroad wherever it was, and justified the wisdom of its builder. In financial matters his foundation was honesty. He knew that there was no royal road to wealth, that all schemes for getting rich quickly were wrong in theory, and would, sooner or later, end in smoke. He had no patience with wild-cat banking, with financial gambling under any name, and his conservatism in this respect, sometimes galling to the "go-ahead" ideas of many of the business men of the West, leavened the whole trade of Milwaukee and made its progress more substantial than that of most Western towns. Busy as his life was, and thoroughly American as were its varied interests, Mr. Mitchell never forgot the land of his birth. To everything Scotch in his adopted city he was a liberal giver, and at the annual gatherings of his countrymen—on St. Andrew's Day or in the outdoor reunion of each Summer—he was always one of the most enthusiastic participants, and took almost a boyish delight in meeting and greeting his "ain folk," whatever their station in life might be.

In the affairs of the bank, Mr. Mitchell was assisted by Mr. David Ferguson and many others from "the Land o' Cakes," but in his latter years his mainstay was his nephew, Mr. John Johnston, a native of Aberdeen and a graduate of its university. Mr. Johnston, soon after his arrival in Milwaukee, began to take an active interest in municipal as well as financial affairs, and once, indeed, refused a nomination as Mayor of the city when the nomination was equivalent to election. Mr. Johnston proved himself to be a scholar as well as a banker, and was recognized as one of the literary lights of the city. This led to his appointment as one of the Regents of the Wisconsin State University, as President of the Wisconsin Historical Society, and to many other honors of a like nature. In the Scotch community he soon became a leader, and in such games as curling, quoits, and others that smacked of the old land he was an adept. Besides serving as President of the Grand National Curling Club of America, he was one of the founders of the Northwestern Curling Association and its chief executive officer. At his death, in 1887, Mr. Mitchell left onethird of the stock of the bank to Mr. Johnston. The business continued to increase to such an extent that Mr. Johnson felt there should be an augmentation of the board of directors. Some of his colleagues held different views, and, as a result of the variety of opinions, Mr. Johnston retired, in 1892, in the prime of life, intending to spend his time at his books or his outdoor amusements. But the financial crisis of 1893, which involved Mitchell's Bank, as so many others, called him back to his desk, and he once more cheerfully went into harness, with the most beneficial results to all concerned, and to the general satisfaction of all business circles in Milwaukee.

We may here turn, for the sake of variety, to find an illustration of the Scot in agriculture. One case in particular is peculiar, inasmuch as the individual was possessed of a competency before settling in America. George Grant, a native of Speyside, made a large fortune in London as a silk merchant. Then he desired to do something practical to benefit other men, and hit upon the device of organizing a British colony in Kansas. His first purchase was a tract of land containing 69,120 acres, to which he gave the name of Victoria. To this tract he afterward added a large number of acres. The first settlers arrived in May, 1873, and so rapid was the growth of the settlement that there was not, at the time of his death, in 1887, an acre of land for sale within ten miles of Victoria on the south. None of the settlers were allowed to purchase less than 640 acres. Mr. Grant began with a flock of 3,555 breeding ewes and 60 long-wooled English rams of the highest pedigree, and in 1874 his wool alone brought $11,700, in Boston, at 33 cents per pound. In the management of his vast concerns Mr. Grant displayed great activity, and a remarkable business aptitude. His efforts were successful in a very eminent degree, and he enjoyed largely the confidence and esteem of those who had business or private associations with him. The Scotch farmer in America is generally successful, and instances of this success might be drawn from the local histories of every county on the continent.

Monument builders are not very numerous in any country, except we include such people as build monuments to themselves, and therefore it would seem that those who erect memorials to others, mainly on patriotic grounds, are deserving of the highest meed of praise. The Scots in America have done their share in this regard if we estimate what they have accomplished compared with that of other nationalities whose numbers greatly exceed theirs. One of the most striking statues in the "Monumental City" of Baltimore, on a commanding position in Druid Park, is the huge figure of Sir William Wallace, Scotland's popular hero, which is referred to in an earlier chapter. The donor of the statue to Baltimore, Mr. William Wallace Spence, was born at Edinburgh in 1815, left his native land in 1834, and went to Norfolk, Va., where he obtained a situation with the old Scotch firm of Robert Souttar & Sons, who were then largely engaged in the West India trade. One of the local papers at Baltimore, in reviewing Mr. Spence's career at the time the statue of Wallace was presented to the city, in 1893, gave the following particulars as to his career: "While in the employ of Messrs. Souttar, Mr. Spence became well acquainted with their trade, spending several months in the West India Islands to gain additional knowledge of it. For two years he was in business for himself in Norfolk, and then, in 1841, came to Baltimore, commencing business with his brother, John F. Spence, under the firm name of W. W. Spence & Co. In 1849 Mr. John F. Spence went to San Francisco to open a house there, and in the same year Mr. Andrew Reid came to Baltimore from Norfolk and became associated in business with Mr. Spence under the firm name of Spence & Reid. The firm remained in business for twenty-five years, when both its members retired. For the past twenty years Mr. Spence has been largely interested in purely financial affairs. He was for many years President of the St. Andrew's Society, is President of the Presbyterian Eye, Ear and Throat Charity Hospital, and of the Egenton Orphan Asylum. Mr. Spence is an active member of the First Presbyterian Church, and for nearly forty years has been a ruling Elder."

But Mr. Spence is not the only Scot whose patriotism has raised a monument in America to one of his countrymen. That labor of love had a precedent in 1888, in Albany, when the Burns Monument there was unveiled through the exertions of Mr. Peter Kinnear. Mr. Kinnear, who is a native of Brechin, and was born there in 1826, came to this country in 1847, and for many years carried on business in Albany as a brassfounder, acquiring a handsome competence as a result of his labor, and then taking a warm interest in various business matters in his adopted city, as well as developing activity in municipal affairs. For many years he was active as an official in all the Scotch organizations in Albany—St. Andrew's Society, Burns Club, and Caledonian Society—in everything Scotch except curling; he drew the line at that. The St. Andrew's Society was his favorite organization, and he served it for many years as Secretary, and for several terms was its President and chief spirit. His connection with that venerable society brought him into close relations with all his country people in Albany of whatever degree, and that, coupled with his enthusiastic admiration for his country's bard, led to the erection of what had long been one of his dreams—the statue of Burns which now graces the beautiful Washington Park of Albany. The money with which the monument of the poet was set up was not the gift of Mr. Kinnear. In its erection he was simply acting as executor in carrying out the wishes of an old Scotswoman who was long regarded in Albany as a miser, but the terms of the bequest were such that Mr. Kinnear could, had he so desired, placed a marble or other tablet in the park and retained the balance of the money. But he was too honest a man to take advantage of any quibble that might be raised for any personal gain to himself, and he rejoiced that Mary McPherson's eccentricities and close-fistedness had been the means of putting it into his power to realize his desire of seeing a monument to Scotia's darling poet in the city of his adoption. So, soon after Mary McPherson died, on Feb. 6, 1886, the legal machinery in the case was fully put in operation, and in a short time Mr. Charles Calverley, sculptor, of New York, formerly of Albany, was at work on the clay model of the figure of the poet. Mr. Kinnear never for a moment concealed or thought to conceal Mary McPherson's share in the monument, but it should not be forgotten that but for him and for her reliance on his honesty and common sense she would never have made a will at all.

The statue was completed and unveiled on Sept. 30, 1888, and the day of the unveiling was a memorable one in the history of the Scotch population of Albany. The figure itself, as a work of art, fully deserved the high praise which was lavished upon it when first seen and so frequently since. Unlike most sculptors who have essayed a figure of Burns, Mr. Calverley had no previously conceived ideals or theories to work out. He simply started on his task with the view of reproducing a lifelike portrait of the man, tempered in details so as to fashion a work that would be accepted as correct in its portraiture, while satisfying the highest artistic requirements. The bases for his work were the only "originals" in existence, the Nasmyth portrait and a cast of the skull, and these were used to the utmost, with hints taken from Skirving and later engravers and artists. The result is a figure of Burns that is more satisfying—as some one put it—than any other, and which in most respects ranks superior to any of the other statues of the poet which his admirers have raised to his memory.

Among the men who have been most active in the building up of the far Western cities, Scotsmen will most assuredly and invariably be found in the very front rank. An instance of this comes before us from Portland, Oregon, where William Reid, a native of Glasgow, is regarded as prominent among those who have helped to make that city what it is to-day, one of the most prosperous trade centres west of the Mississippi. Mr. Reid was born in 1842, and after receiving his early education in his native city, crossed the Atlantic. His career in America has been eminently useful and successful, and he has combined the qualities of a literary man and financier so as to give magnificent results to Portland, the city in which he has his home. Mr. Reid organized in 1874 the Portland Board of Trade, and is credited with having been the means of investing, or causing to be invested, over ten millions of foreign capital in the industries and agriculture and development of Oregon. A pamphlet entitled " Oregon and Washington as Fields for Labor and Capital," published in 1873, was widely distributed in Britain, and was the prime factor in the establishment of the Washington and Oregon Trust and Investment Company, with a capital of $1,000,000; and in the railway, financial, and industrial interests of Oregon and Washington he has been recognized as a powerful factor.

We have already mentioned several names associated with Boston, and, did the limits of this work permit it, an interesting chapter or two, might be written headed " Scots in Boston." Such firms as Hogg, Brown & Taylor, the Gilchrists, and Shepherd, Norwell & Co., have not only led the dry goods trade in that city for many years, but from them a host of Scotch dry goods establishments has spread all through the country, even New York, itself a centre of the trade, having numbered the graduates from these establishments among its great merchants. But the Scot in Boston has flourished in all the walks of business life. For many years a notable figure in its commercial circles was James M. Smith, who was at the head of a large brewery, and had an interest in a dozen other concerns. Born at Arbuthnott, Kincardineshire, in 1832, and educated at the Montrose Academy, he commenced his business life as an apprentice in the once famous Edinburgh establishment of Duncan, Flockhart & Co., druggists. When his apprenticeship was over he went to Canada, and finally settled in Boston, where he drifted into a groove that made him a successful business man, "a man of means and substance," as the old saying puts it. No Scot in Boston was more full of patriotism than he, and his patriotism he was always ready to back up in the most practical way—by his bawbees. He was a ruling spirit in the Presbyterian Church and liberal to all its schemes. For many years he was President of the Scots' Charitable Society, and his business administration of its affairs, and wise liberality made that venerable organization take on a new lease of popularity. He revived, too, the almost defunct British Charitable Society and placed it on a substantial and useful footing, and in a hundred other ways was constantly manifesting his interest in the old land and his countrymen. Mr. Smith died in 1894, and his departure left a blank in the Scottish ranks in the "Hub" which will, we fear, long remain unfilled. The same year the grave closed over another leal-hearted Boston Scot—Robert Ferguson of the firm of Shepherd, Norwell & Co. He was on a visit to Paris at the time, traveling in search of health, and was about to leave the Continent and return for a spell to his native place, Kirkmahoe, Dumfriesshire—where he was born sixty-five years before—when the end came. Mr. Ferguson settled in America in 1855, and was employed in several dry goods houses in New York, notably that of A. T. Stewart & Co., with whom he remained fifteen years, and was regarded as one of the best buyers, always cautious, but ever ready to notice the selling value of everything brought before him. In 1870 he went to Boston to assume a partnership with the firm already mentioned, a partnership that continued until his death. In the Scots' Charitable Society he was an active and generous member, and was known for his artistic and literary tastes. He won hosts of friends in Boston, and was regarded not only as an upright and able merchant, but as an exemplary and patriotic citizen.

We have just spoken of the ramifications of the Scotch dry goods houses in America which radiated from Boston as a centre. But one might think that Scotsmen exerted a prime influence in the trade all over the country. One remarkable evidence of this is the rapid success of the Syndicate Trading Company of New York, which is a sort of dry goods exchange for its constituting members. Regarding the inception and composition of this organization, a correspondent, Mr. Donald Mackay of Worcester, sent the following intelligent account to the New York " Scottish-American " in October, 1895:

"A. Swan Brown, when a young clerk in a dry goods house in Worcester, having an instinct for enterprise and speculation, foresaw a great opportunity in amalgamating the Scottish dry goods establishments into one great syndicate. His reasoning was that, bound by national ties (and many of them on terms of personal intimacy) they would work together without friction to the advantage of the various firms involved in the enterprise. The chief aim, however, of the syndicate would be to establish an office in New York City, in touch with the markets of the world, and purchase in unprecedentedly large quantities and at cheaper prices than would be offered to satisfy those who cannot afford to buy except on a basis to satisfy a limited demand in a single establishment.

"To A. Swan Brown belongs the credit of organizing one of the greatest dry goods institutions in this or any other country—the Syndicate Trading Company, of which he is the President. It comprises the Callender, McAuslan & Troup Company, Providence, R. I.; Adam, Meldrum & Anderson Company, Buffalo, N. Y.; Sibley, Lindsay & Curr, Rochester, N. Y.; Brown, Thomson & Co., Hartford, Conn.; Forbes & Wallace, Springfield, Mass.; Denholm & McKay Company, Worcester, Mass.; Dives, Pomeroy & Stewart, Reading, Penn.; Almy, Bigelow & Washburn, Salem, Mass.; Minneapolis Dry Goods Company, Minneapolis, Minn.; Doggett Dry Goods Company, Kansas City, Mo., and Pettis Dry Goods Company, Indianapolis, Ind. Mr. Brown approached these various firms, scattered throughout the country, and the syndicate now formed is the result of his efforts. These eleven firms are among the largest dry goods houses in this country, and have experienced buyers in all the leading markets of the world. Each firm of the combine is established and managed by Scotsmen, and the employés are largely Scottish, or of Scottish descent.

"Mr. Brown has purchased a controlling interest in the Boston Store of Worcester, of which he is now President, and has removed his family from New York to a unique residence which he recently had erected in one of the suburbs of that place. He has lately exhibited an interest in the municipal affairs of this city, and it is suggested that at some not distant day he may be Mayor Brown of Worcester, Mass."

A sad break was made in one of the firms constituting this syndicate early in January, 1896, when, within a few days of each other, John McAuslan and John E. Troup of the firm of Callender, McAuslan & Troup, Providence, passed away. Both men were notable examples of Scottish-American merchants. Mr. McAuslan was born at Kilmadan, Argyllshire, in 1835. He learned the drapery business in Greenock, and in 1858 secured an appointment in the store of Hogg, Brown & Taylor, Boston. Mr. Troup was born at Old Meldrum, Aberdeenshire, in 1829, and until he sailed for the United States, in 1855, was employed as a clerk in Aberdeen. At Boston he entered the firm of George Turnbull & Co., and remained in that establishment until, in 1866, along with Walter Callender and John McAuslan, he went to Providence and opened the establishment, which, from the time it started until the present, has been the leading dry goods emporium of Rhode Island.

Recent and typical examples, and examples, too, which combine New York and Boston dry goods training, based on a thorough Scotch foundation, may be found in the careers of two brothers, Thomas and James Simpson, who, until their lives were cut short when they should have been in their prime, ranked among the leading retail merchants in their line of business in New York. They were born at Markinch, Fifeshire, and served apprenticeships to the drapery business there, and afterward gained wider experience in Glasgow. Settling in America, they secured positions in the house of Hogg, Brown & Taylor, and then, when they reached the top rung in the ladder of promotion, they, in accordance with the custom of the leading employés of that house, and with its blessing, started out for themselves. Thomas cast in his lot with Lawrence, Mass., while James went to Norwich, Conn. After a while, although both were successful, they longed for a wider sphere of business, and, an old New York house being in the market owing to the desire of the senior partner to retire, they secured the interest thus offered, sold off their respective establishments, and, removing to New York, organized the old firm into that of Simpson, Crawford & Simpson, Mr. Crawford who connected the Simpsons being the holding over partner in the old firm, and, like his new associates, a native of Scotland. The new firm was a success from the start, and its business was steadily increased until the establishment occupied many stores and gave employment to some 1,800 hands, mostly Scotch. It used to be said that it was as good as a trip across the ocean to go into this mammoth concern, a concern that was, and is, conducted with Yankee shrewdness, tempered by Scotch honesty, an invaluable combination, and hear the Doric spoken by the clerks and salesmen as fresh and pithy as though they had just come from the heather. Thomas died in 1885 and James in 1895, and both were sadly mourned.

The leading dry goods man in St. Louis is a native of Rothesay, Mr. D. Crawford. A recent article in The Mirror of that city, says that he settled there in 1860 or thereabout. " Mr. Crawford's prosperity," says that paper, " has grown with the city, but he attributes his great success to Scotch tenacity of purpose, cash payments, and printers' ink. He looks back with pride on the days of his small beginnings, and cherishes more than all the friends of these earlier days, when his great 'Broadway Bazaar' was much smaller than it now is, and when its business represented thousands where now it runs into millions of dollars. He has never forgotten his mother country, and no deserving indigent Scot ever applies to him in vain. For the last twelve successive years he has been the highly-appreciated President of the St. Louis Caledonian Society."

Mining in all its branches is an industry in which the Scots in America have taken a very prominent part, but curiously enough, miners, while hard-working men, are very modest and seldom obtrude themselves in print. They make their "pile" when they can, but do not care to "blow" about it, and are content to have the "gear" and leave the glory to others. As a result, they are difficult to get information about, although there is hardly a mineral field on the continent on which they have not been at work, and if a Scotch tourist gets among the placer mines of the Pacific slope he will not need to wander very far before shaking hands with a countryman.

One of the most intelligent and successful miners Scotland has sent to this country, Andrew Roy, a native of Lanarkshire, was the first State Inspector of Mines in Ohio, and the first in the United States outside of the anthracite district of Pennsylvania. He has been identified with mining in the State of Ohio for thirty years, and has had practical experience in other parts of the country. He is a scientific miner, a thoroughly practical geologist, and it was through his exertions that the Mining School was established in connection with the Ohio State University. Mr. Roy may, therefore, be fairly regarded as a representative type of the educated miner, and one who loves his business for its own sake rather than for the mere consideration of the money that may be in it, and that, after all, is the highest sort of representative any trade or profession can have. The man who merely bends his energy to getting rich may thrive with shoddy, wooden nutmegs or bogus clocks, just as the grocer may thrive who carefully sands his sugar, or the milkman who mathematically dilutes the fluid he sells, or the speculator who waters the stock in which he is interested. But these things have no real influence upon the world. The man who does his work—whatever that work may be—honestly and thoroughly, does something that justifies his existence, that adds to the wealth of the world, and reflects honor on his name after he has passed away. Nay, honest work is very often the most enduring monument a man can have. Old Phyfe, the cabinet-maker, is still remembered for the excellence of his workmanship, although his hand has long been at rest, while hundreds of richer makers of shoddy furniture—furniture made to sell, and that only—have been forgotten, even although during their lives they loomed up much more prominently in the public eye. But their lives were based on shoddy principles.

In the course of an interesting letter to the writer of this book in response to a request for some information concerning the Scotch miners in the Buckeye State, as Ohio is fondly called, Mr. Roy said: "Curiously enough, the native Scotch have not had a great deal to do with the early development of the mining industries of this State. They were the pioneer miners of Maryland and of Illinois and other Western States, but not of Ohio. The men who might be called the fathers of the mining industries here had in many instances Scotch blood coursing through their veins, but they themselves were born in America. Such was the late Gov. David Tod, the father of the coal and iron industry of Ohio, whose grandfather, as he told me himself, came from Edinburgh. The late Mr. Chisholm of Cleveland was, however, a native Scot, and his was the greatest success possible, though his field was in manufacturing rather than in mining. In Southern Ohio, John Campbell, the late iron king, was of Scotch blood and descent, though a native of Virginia. He was one of the pioneer miners of the Hanging Rock region.

"The Hon. Thomas Ewing, a United States Senator and a Cabinet officer, was another coal and iron miner in another part of Southern Ohio. He, too, was of Virginia birth, but a full-blooded Scot. Gen. George W. McCook, of the family of the 'fighting McCooks,' was one of the pioneer miners of Ohio. I think he was born in the State, but he was a Scot to the backbone. We have a number of native Scots in the coal and iron business of the State at present, such as Alexander McDonald, the millionaire of Cincinnati. He is of Highland birth. The Hamiltons of Columbus, John and John C. and Gen. W. B., can hardly be classed as pioneers, but rather as successful Scotch business men."

If we were to look for a Scotch colony near New York we would assuredly go to the Wyoming Valley, where we would find groups of families as Scotch as though they had newly left Scotland, speaking their native Doric in all its purity, preserving Scotch customs, even to "first fittin'," and rejoicing in all things Scotch, in the kirk, the slippery rink, and the pleasant foregathering in Summer and Winter after the day's "darg" is done. Sometimes we could find so many of one name that the different wearers of the cognomen are distinguished by nicknames—titles given without any attempt at disparaging an individual, but bestowed and used for convenience sake, and we would find these Scots in all sorts of positions, in the mines as well as in the ranks of the local tradesmen. One of the most noted of the miners of the Wyoming Valley, Thomas Waddell of Pittston, was a fair type of the rest, although he was more successful from a financial standpoint than most of his fellow-miners. But the mere possession of money made no difference to "Tam," as he was generally called, and he was hail fellow alike with sleek Senators and nabobs, mine workers, and the boys of the Thistle Band, a company of musicians that used to wake the beautiful Wyoming Valley with their beautiful rendering of Scotch music.

Mr. Waddell was born near Edinburgh in 1827. In 1850 he left Scotland to make a home for himself in this country. He first tried his fortune in Wilkes-Barre. Beginning his American career as a working miner, he worked in the coal shafts for a year or two and then went to California to try his fortune in digging for gold. He secured enough to give him a working capital, and, returning East, he bought a coal mine and continued in that business till his death, at Pittston, in 1894. It may be worthy of mention that Mr. Waddell's home town of

Pittston was the last place in America where, so far as the writer's knowledge goes, Allan Ramsay's "Gentle Shepherd" was publicly performed in an American theatre. That was in 1880. The piece was well put upon the stage and capably acted, and delighted a large and representative Scotch audience which assembled to witness it, and with its aid to renew many pleasant memories of auld lang syne.

Weaving, like mining, owes much of its prominence and perfection among American industries to the Scotch operatives who carried their skill across the Atlantic and exercised it all over New England, in Pennsylvania, and the State of New York. A fair example of how a Scotch weaver can make his mark in America is found in the career of Samuel Laurie of Auburn, who died in 1895, while on a visit, in the hope of recovering his health, at Hot Springs, Ark. He was born at Glasgow in 1834, and learned his trade of a weaver there—the best place in the world at that time to learn weaving except, perhaps, Paisley. He left Scotland for America in 1856, and, after working in mills in many places, principally in New England, went to Auburn in 1866 to take a minor position in the woolen mills there. In a short time he was superintendent, and finally became President of the company. Mr. Laurie was a thorough master of his business, an enthusiast at it, even, and was always striving how to effect improvements in the designs of the goods, the fastness or purity of the colors, or the fineness or evenness of the textures. He invented several arrangements which helped considerably to bring about these improvements and to lower the cost of production. He had one great ambition—to place on the American market tweeds equal to those produced at Bannockburn or Galashiels, and, toward the end of his business career, it was generally acknowledged that he had succeeded.

Business men, most of them, whose lives are not based upon shoddy foundations are full of charity. We have had several instances of this in the course of this chapter, but the theme is so inexhaustible, so full of scope for patriotic pride, and, withal, so pleasant and instructive, that we cannot resist the temptation of citing a few more illustrations before closing this chapter. The philanthropic love-labors of that kindly son of auld Dunfermline, Andrew Carnegie, in founding libraries, musical conservatories, and aiding all sorts of helpful objects of a general nature that are upward in their tendency, are too well known to need recital here. But Scottish philanthropists have been in America from an early age, and have invariably shown judgment in their gifts. Take the case of James Lee, who was born at St. Andrews in 1795, and for forty years prior to his death, in 1874, was a merchant in New York City. He was long noted for the warm interest he took in the New York Society Library, an institution he assisted with his money, as well as with his advice and business experience and influence. But he left a memorial of his disinterested patriotism in the Washington Monument that adorns Union Square. Few of the thousands who pass that grand memorial of the first President of the United States know that its erection was brought about mainly through the exertions of a Scottish citizen, but such was the case. James Lee worked hard to gather together the needed funds to purchase the work, and as the result of innumerable calls, bushels of letters, and pleadings of all sorts, he eventually succeeded. He used to say that he had less trouble in getting subscriptions from citizens of America by adoption than from those who were citizens by right of birth. One of these, in declining Mr. Lee's request for a subscription, said grandiloquently: "Washington, Sir, needs no monument, Sir; he is enshrined in the hearts of his countrymen." "Well," retorted Lee, "if he is in your heart he is in a pretty tight place." Active as an American citizen as he was, however, Mr. Lee was noted for his enthusiasm for his native land, and he affiliated with the St. Andrew's Society in 1822, shortly after settling in New York, and retained his membership till the end.

For true philanthropy, the name of no Scot in America stands higher than that of Archibald Russell. His father was at one time President of the Royal Society at

Edinburgh, and Archibald was born in that city in 1811, graduating in time from its university. In 1836 he settled in New York, and almost immediately after entered upon that career of kindly usefulness which has enshrined his memory in the charitable annals of America's commercial metropolis. He founded the Five Points Mission, one of the most needed, most beneficent, and most practical charities in New York, and aided in founding the Half Orphan Asylum and a dozen other institutions. During the civil war he was a member of the Christian Commission, whose noble work needs no retelling here, and even when resting at his Summer home in Ulster County, Mr. Russell was always thinking upon some scheme of kindly work, or putting such schemes into execution. Mr. Russell died in New York in 1871.

A kindly man, although of a peculiar temperament, but whose daily business life was seldom unproductive of some good deed quietly done, was Robert L. Maitland, whose death at Port Washington, N. J., in 1876, was a surprise to his hosts of friends in New York, although it was known to himself long before the summons came that his life hung by a more than usually slender thread. Mr. Maitland was born in New York, but he always claimed to be of the Scottish race, and was proud of it. His father was a native of Kirkcudbrightshire, in Scotland, and belonged to an ancient family, for which a remote kinship was claimed with the noble house of Lauderdale. His uncle established the firm of Maitland, Phelps & Co., already referred to. His mother was a daughter of Mr. Robert Lenox. His associations, therefore, social as well as business, were of a character to give him a splendid start in life, and no one could have used them to better advantage. If we were called upon to name a dozen firms in this city distinguished above all others for long standing, great energy, and enterprise, honorable principles, and a credit that never was doubted in the most troublous times, Messrs. R. L. Maitland & Co. would be one of them.

Mr. Maitland was frequently impetuous and sometimes imperious, but a good deal of this might justly be attributed to the irritableness produced by a painful disease from which he was long a sufferer. In private life few men were more considerate, gentle, and lovable. He was certainly strong in his likes and dislikes, but, his confidence once secured, he was the most faithful and devoted of friends. Like all of his race and name, he loved to play the part of a country gentleman, and he played it with genuine courteous hospitality and dignity. His establishments in town and country were filled with old and faithful servants—no slight proof of his kindness and consideration as a master. His contributions to every meritorious scheme of benevolence and religion were all on a scale commensurate with his great wealth, but were always bestowed in the most unostentatious manner. Like his kinsman, Mr. James Lenox, he loved to do good by stealth.

Business and philanthropy were also combined in a laudable degree in the career of another Scotsman's son, who, from the beginning to the end of his career, invariably reflected upon and spoke of his Scotch origin and blood with unbounded enthusiasm. This was John Taylor Johnston, who was born in New York in 1820, and died in that city in 1893. He was a son of John Johnston, a native of Edinburgh, who was partner in the once-famous importing house of Boorman, Johnston & Co., on Greenwich Street, New York, mentioned on a previous page in this chapter. While on a visit to Edinburgh with his parents in 1832, John Taylor Johnston was sent to the High School, where he remained a year and a half. He then returned to New York, and was educated for the law. He did not take kindly to legal work, however, and when twenty-eight years of age he branched off into railroad management. He began by taking the Presidency of the Elizabethtown and Somerville Railroad, then only a few miles long and struggling for existence, and he steadily developed it until, under its new name of the New Jersey Central, it covered the greater part of the State. The chief business feature of the enterprise was the cultivation of the anthracite coal trade, and part of Mr. Johnston's scheme was the construction of a vast system of wharves, basins, and docks, involving the reclamation of the greater part of the Jersey flats. In 1877, however, before that undertaking could be carried out, the New Jersey Central, in common with other railroads engaged in the same line of business, was overtaken by disaster, and had to go into the hands of a receiver. Mr. Johnston lost a large portion of his private fortune in trying to maintain its credit, but ultimately resigned the Presidency, which he had held for twenty-seven years. Mr. Johnston took the leading part, in 1870, in founding the Metropolitan Museum of Art, and was its President when he died. He contributed $15,000 to the starting of the institution, and collected personally in Europe a large number of the works of art which were first shown in it. He was for many years an active office bearer of the St. Andrew's Society, and was for one year its President. He was also a Trustee of the Presbyterian Hospital, besides being otherwise an extremely useful citizen.

Another Scotsman's son who has come to the front in financial circles, especially from the manner in which he twice came to the rescue of the financial end of the Cleveland Administration by organizing syndicates to take up its early issues of bonds, is John A. Stewart, President of the United States Trust Company. It is well known, too, that Mr. Stewart has been liberal of his means in a quiet, unobtrusive way in promoting good works. In speaking of his work in the bond syndicate in November, 1894, "The New York Herald" remarked: "It is not everybody who can go around among his friends and by a little persuasive argument induce them to form a syndicate which will pay out $50,000,000 in gold at the beck of his finger." This was exactly what John Aikman Stewart did, and the fact speaks volumes for the trust reposed in his honesty and shrewdness as a financier. "The Herald," in further commenting on this great bond transaction, gave the following particulars of Mr. Stewart's parentage and early career: "Mr. Stewart first saw the light of day on Aug. 26, 1822.

"From the land of Robert Burns came his ancestors.

His father was born on the Island of Lewis, one of the Hebrides group, on the northwest coast of Scotland. Coming to this country when quite young, he was a ship carpenter in this city for many years, then embarked in business, was for a long while an Assessor for what were then the Twelfth and the Sixteenth Wards, and was also Receiver of Taxes. Mr. Stewart's mother was born in this city, her father being a Scotchman."

Perhaps the most conspicuous example of the influence which Scotsmen have exerted and are exerting upon American progress is found in the career of John S. Kennedy, of New York, who was born at Blantyre, Lanarkshire, (the birthplace of David Livingstone,) in 1830, and settled in New York in 1856.

During his American business career Mr. Kennedy has been associated in many of the most important business interests of his time, and railroads, banks, and syndicates of all sorts have felt the influence of his guidance and judgment. He undertook the receivership of the Central Railroad of New Jersey when that road was practically bankrupt, and when he retired he handed it over to its present owners as a paying concern. His connection with the Canadian Pacific Railroad is well known, but few can appreciate the amount of work he did as Vice President and Director of the St. Paul, Minneapolis and Manitoba Railroad Company, or as Vice President of the Indianapolis, Cincinnati and Lafayette Railroad Company, or as President of the International and Great Northern Railroad Company of Texas. Even now that he is supposed to be retired from business, and enjoying his *otium cum dignitate*, he is trustee under the mortgages of various railroads to an amount approaching $100,000,000, besides being trustee or executor on many private estates involving many millions more, a Director of the National Bank of Commerce, the Manhattan Company's Bank, the Central Trust Company, the United States Trust Company, the Title Guarantee and Trust Company, the New York, Chicago and St. Louis, and several other railroad companies, and many lesser concerns.

In the affairs of the Presbyterian Hospital and of the Lenox Library, of both of which he is President, Mr. Kennedy takes more than ordinary interest. No one knows the extent of his gifts to the hospital, and to the library he is constantly giving. He is also an ex-President of the St. Andrew's Society, a Vice President of the New York Historical Society, a Trustee of the Metropolitan Museum of Art and of many other of the public institutions of which New York is proud. In the Fifth Avenue Presbyterian Church (Dr. John Hall's) Mr. Kennedy has long been a Trustee, and in several of the boards of the Presbyterian Church he is an active office holder.

Two of his offices, and of both of which he is peculiarly proud, are those of President of the Board of Trustees of the American Bible House and of Robert College, both at Constantinople—institutions which he visited when returning from a tour through Egypt and the Holy Land, a few years ago, and again in 1894. Mr. Kennedy's latest gift to New York is the Public Charities Building, at the corner of Fourth Avenue and Twenty-second Street, which cost about three-quarters of a million of dollars, and brings the various public charities of the city under one roof.

In this chapter we have said nothing of the Scot in Canada, for the reasons elsewhere stated, and because to cross the St. Lawrence in search of illustrations would simply mean to confront the entire business interests of the Dominion. We have, however, selected a few names, but merely at random, and as much for the sake of substantiating this remark as for any other purpose.

A prominent type of a Scottish merchant in Canada was the Hon. John Macdonald, who died at Toronto early in 1890. He was born in Perthshire in 1824. His father, who was a native of Knockoilum, in Stratherrick, Inverness-shire, was a Sergeant in the Ninety-third Highlanders. He accompanied his regiment to Canada in 1837 and took his son along with him, the lad's mother having died the day before the vessel sailed. John received his education at Dalhousie College, Halifax, and then went to Toronto. His first connection in business was as a clerk in a store at Gananoque, and in 1849 he started in for himself and founded the firm which afterward became noted throughout Canada as that of John Macdonald & Co., wholesale dry goods dealers and importers. Its credit was unlimited, its warerooms were magnificent, and the Toronto Scots pointed to the imposing pile as evidence of what Scotch grit can accomplish in Canada. But Mr. Macdonald was more than a mere merchant. He was a philanthropist, a patriot, and a public-spirited citizen. He was a member of the Canadian House of Commons and afterward one of the Senators of the Dominion. In church and temperance work he was most assiduous, and in the Toronto School Board, in the university, and other educational institutions he was prominently identified for years. To the young men in his establishment he was more than an employer, and his will showed that they were in his thoughts when they little imagined it. The life of such a man is blessed not only to himself, but to the community in which he dwells, and to every one who is directly or indirectly brought under its influence, and it may well be imagined what regret was felt in Toronto when it was known that this career of usefulness and beneficence was closed.

The annals of the Scot in Montreal would probably keep us, were they studied, almost always closer to the top of the tree in all departments of commerce, industry and finance than those of our countrymen in any other city on the American Continent. Take as a solitary case the career of Sir Donald A. Smith, whose gifts to the Victoria Hospital in Montreal alone have amounted to a quarter of a million sterling. He is a native of Morayshire, and went out to Canada while a youth and entered the service of the Hudson's Bay Company. Rapidly rising to the head of that corporation, he was the last resident Governor of that body as a governing corporation. During Riel's rebellion he was Special Commissioner in the Red River Settlements, and was thanked by the Governor General of Canada for his many services. Sir Donald has taken a foremost part in such large commercial undertakings as the Canadian Pacific Railway and the Bank of Montreal, of which he is President. It was he who drove in the last spike of the Canadian Pacific Railway, nearly twelve years ago, at Craigellachie, in the Eagle Pass. In Canada his name is a household word, while in Scotland, as the proprietor of the historic estate of Glencoe, he occupies a prominent place among the county magnates of Argyllshire.

One more illustration, and then we leave this long and honorable record. It is that of William Walker, who, after a stirring and honorable career as a merchant and statesman, died at Quebec, in 1863. He left Scotland in 1815, when twenty-two years old, and went at once to Montreal, where he became a partner in the firm of Forsyth, Richardson & Co. of Montreal, and Forsyth, Walker & Co. of Quebec. He was part owner of the steamer Royal William, the first steam vessel that crossed the Atlantic from British North America. He was first President of the Quebec and Riviere du Loup Railroad Company, President of the Quebec Board of Trade, and a Director in nearly all the financial institutions of that ancient city. He was a bit of a soldier, too, and raised and commanded the Quebec Volunteer Rifle Corps. But, with all these occupations, he attended closely to his main business, and in 1848 was enabled to retire with a handsome fortune. In 1839 he was appointed a life member of the Legislative Council by royal mandate, and in that capacity did much good work for the Dominion, as well as for his own province of Quebec. His later interest, however, centred in the University of Bishop's College, Lennoxville, of which he was the first Chancellor, and his benefactions to it, as well as his influential labors, were such as to stamp him as one of the most thoughtful workers on behalf of higher education in Canada.

We would fain dwell yet a while across the St. Lawrence, but the work has been done already by loving hands, and we have now lingered too long with this branch of our theme—not too long to exhaust it, but longer than was necessary to demonstrate how much America owes to the Scottish merchants who threw in their lot with the New World.

In Glasgow they generally estimate the good qualities of a man by figuring up how much he is worth. That basis of merit we have generally avoided in the preceding pages. But it may not be out of place to say that the fortune of Mr. George Smith, the pioneer Chicago banker already mentioned, is now believed to amount to about $50,000,000. With it he is doing much practical good, for, besides founding several bursaries in the schools of Old Deer, he gave $5,000 last year to Aberdeen University towards its new buildings.

When Alexander Stuart of New York died he bequeathed his entire estate, valued at $2,000,000, to his brother, Robert L. Stuart, his sole legatee. When, later, Robert L. died, he left his fortune, estimated at over $5,000,000, to his wife. In spite of her many benefactions, Mrs. R. L. Stuart left $5,000,000 when she died, nine years after her husband. After making liberal provisions for distant relatives and a few personal friends, she bequeathed nearly $4,500,000 to religious, benevolent, and educational institutions.

CHAPTER IX.

EDUCATORS.

IF a Scot were asked in what direction the influence of his native land was most plainly and characteristically to be seen in America, he would undoubtedly answer in the direction of education. In surveying the entire scholastic field—primary, grammar, and collegiate—in America, we are struck by the fact that the underlying theory of the whole is that promulgated by John Knox when he proposed an ideal system for Scotland, but was defeated by the greed and treachery of the Scottish nobility—including even those who were with him in the struggle against the old Church. In brief, his system called for at least one grammar school in every parish, a burgh or high school and, where possible, a collegiate institution in every town, and a university in the principal cities, besides " bairn schules " in connection with each kirk. His theory is that the education of the youth was part of the legitimate business of every State, and his wish was that that education should be as liberal as possible. Education, the education of the masses, has always been since Knox's time one of the ruling principles of Scottish life. It was carefully fostered by the Church; the management of the schools long formed part of the most important business of every General Assembly, and their visitation and supervision were regarded as not the least among the duties of the clergy. It was only within a comparatively recent period in Scotland that the State stepped to the front in educational matters, and the Church gradually released its hold, until now the entire management, even of the universities, is professedly secular. This change—this separation of education from religion—it has always appeared to us, is one of the things that the Old Country has learned from America, where scholastic training from the beginning of the national history of the United States has been secular, except where particular religions have founded schools or colleges of their own.

In speaking of the Church having control of the schools in Scotland, however, it must be remembered that that control sprang from a different source from that which actuates most Churches in educational matters. There never was, there never will be, a more perfect system of republican government, a more complete democracy, than that devised for the Kirk by John Knox and his associates. In that system the basis of everything was the Kirk meeting, in which every one, every head of a family, had a voice and a vote; from that popular meeting came the session, from the session the Presbytery, from the Presbytery the Synod, from the Synod the General Assembly. The last being thoroughly representative in its complexion, was for many generations the real parliament of the nation, and thus it was the voice of the Scottish people acting through their regularly and honestly chosen delegates that inspired the zeal for the cause of education throughout the country and maintained it.

Although the educational system of the United States, the system made compulsory by State laws, is as perfectly secular as can be devised, yet it should be remembered that the earliest American teachers were either the clergy or that the early schools were founded under the auspices of some Church. The Presbyterian, as the representative Scotch denomination, for a long time was as active in establishing schools as churches. Thus, in the early history of the Carolinas, we find that one Synod admonished all the Presbyteries under its control " to establish within their respective bounds one or more grammar schools, except where such schools are already established," and the early Presbyterian records all over the Colonial settlements are full of such references, where the records are found to exist. One of the most famous of the early educational institutions in the Carolinas was the Innis Academy, founded in Wilmington by Col. James Innis, a native of Dunse, who incorporated the school in 1783. He had been an officer in the British Army, and distinguished himself in the expedition against Carthagena, in South America. The University of North Carolina, too, was established in 1795 by the Rev. Joseph Caldwell, an educational pioneer of Scotch and French descent. Before that, however, in 1685, the Rev. James Blair, a Scotch missionary, founded William and Mary College, in Virginia, the most ancient of the American colleges, and which still carries on its good work to the present day, and we have seen in the course of this work, by the labors at Princeton of Witherspoon and other early Scotch teachers, how active the pioneer Scots in America were in the cause of higher education.

Among the most prominent of the early Scotch teachers, whose life story has been preserved to us mainly because he became as active as a patriot and a legislator as an educator in his adopted country, was Peter Wilson, a native of the little parish of Ordiquhill, Banffshire. He was born there in 1744, and, after attending Aberdeen University for several sessions—long enough to graduate, for in Scotland they used to enter college at an age when the children of the present day are only half way through the grammar schools—he left Scotland and landed in New York, in 1763. Wilson soon received an appointment as a teacher in Hackensack Academy, New Jersey, and served there as Principal for many years. His labors appear to have been interrupted by the Revolutionary War, and the movement for independence found in him one of its most devoted adherents and promoters. From 1777 to 1783 he served in the New Jersey Legislature, and afterward took a prominent and exceedingly useful part in codifying and revising the laws of that State. In 1789 he accepted the professorship of Greek and Latin in Columbia College, and remained there till 1792, when he resigned to become Principal of Erasmus Hall Academy, Flatbush, N. Y. That office he vacated in 1797, when he returned to Columbia College as Professor of Greek and Latin and of Greek Antiquities, and taught until 1820, when he retired on a pension. He died five years later, at New Barbados, N. J., and was buried in Hackensack Churchyard, where a stone was erected to his memory on which his career was summed up in the words: "A zealous and successful patriot and Christian, and exemplary in all the public, social, and domestic relations which he sustained." Dr. Wilson published several textbooks, each of which bore evidence to his scholarship, but they are now forgotten, for old textbooks, like old almanacs, seem to be neglected and cast aside as soon as they have served their day.

A representative Scot, whose life story, however, is rather a painful one, was James Hardie, an Aberdonian and a graduate of Marischal College, Aberdeen. He was born in 1750, and after graduation became an inmate of the domestic circle of Prof. James Beattie ("the Poet of Truth," as he has been called,) as secretary, or tutor, or both. Beattie possessed influence enough and heart enough to have advanced his protégé's fortunes in a material way, but there were several matters which caused the philosopher and poet to believe that Hardie's interests would be best served by his removal from his associates and accustomed haunts, and by beginning life anew in a far country. He, therefore, advised him to emigrate to America, and the advice was taken. Hardie settled in New York, and from 1787 till 1790 was employed as a tutor in Columbia College. He then lost his employment on account of his dissipated habits, for he did not "mend his ways" in the new land, and, after drifting aimlessly along in the current of life for several years, picking up a precarious livelihood one way and another, he obtained a minor position in connection with one of the city departments. His salary was small, barely enough to keep body and soul together, and he eked it out by doing hack work for the publishers when he got the opportunity. In this way he became the author of quite a number of books, the most curious of which are "An Account of the Yellow Fever in New

York," (1822,) and a descriptive account of the same city, issued the same year. He also completed a Biographical Dictionary, which was issued in 1830, and proved that he could be industrious and painstaking when he liked. Hardie died in New York, in 1832, leaving behind him nothing of real value to the world beyond the awful example of a richly endowed life wasted.

We get a much more noble illustration of the Scot abroad in studying the career of another Aberdonian, John Keith. Born at Achlossan, in 1763, he graduated from Aberdeen University in 1781, and soon after, before he had even attained full legal age, was admitted a member of the Royal Society of Edinburgh. In his twentieth year he emigrated, and, after spending a year or two in Virginia, finally settled in New York. He secured employment as a teacher in Columbia College, and soon after became one of the Faculty of that institution by accepting the Chair of Mathematics. In 1795 he was transferred to the Chair of Geography, History, and Chronology, and proved a most devoted teacher. But he was more than a teacher. He was a public-spirited citizen, and took an active interest in matters far from akin to his profession. For instance, the desirability of a system of internal waterways through the State of New York, which was first suggested by the old Scotch Governor, Cadwallader Colden, was a burning question early in the century. The problem of the feasibility of such waterways was keenly debated, and De Witt Clinton, their great and unswerving advocate, found no more logical, determined, or efficient supporter than Prof. John Keith. The latter readily foresaw the immense advantage these waterways would be, not merely to the State, but to the entire continent, for he believed they could be connected so as to open up communication with the Mississippi. He advocated their construction as a matter of practical necessity, and his position as a professor in Columbia College gave great weight to his words. In 1810 he visited Lake Erie to examine into the feasibility of the proposed Erie Canal, and made private surveys and calculations, with the result that he fully demonstrated the entire practicability of the waterway long before any authoritative survey had passed judgment upon the scheme. It is a pity that he was not spared to see the great work fairly entered upon, but he died in 1812, when the whole scheme was in that stage of all great American measures when it was simply a football for politicians.

Among the names of the early professors in Princeton College none is more highly cherished than that of John Maclean, who became Professor of Chemistry and Natural History in that young institution in 1795, the year after President Witherspoon had passed to the rest he had craved and the reward he had earned, and been succeeded by his son-in-law, President Stanhope Smith. Dr. Maclean was born at Glasgow in 1771, and studied medicine in Edinburgh, London, Glasgow, and Paris. His travels and reading, and his own personal observation of European Governments, had made him become a thorough believer in a republican form of government, and led him, when his studies were completed, to throw in his lot with the United States. He settled in Princeton in 1791, and, with the encouragement of Dr. Witherspoon and the then limited Faculty, commenced lecturing on chemistry before becoming a member of the professorial staff. He continued to fill a chair in Princeton till 1812, when he resigned to accept the Chair of Natural Philosophy and Chemistry in William and Mary College. That post he resigned in the course of a year on account of ill-health, and he died in 1814. His memoir was written by his son, John Maclean, who was born at Princeton, in 1798, and graduated from the college there in 1816. The story of this man's life was bound up with that of the college of New Jersey, and to his enthusiasm and learning, as well as to his industry as a professor and executive ability as its President, it owed much of its renown as a seat of learning. He became President in 1854, and continued to fill the office until 1868, when he resigned the dignity into the hands of Prof. McCosh, but the remaining years during which his life was prolonged (he died in 1886) were devoted to advocating the interests of the college in every way that lay in his power. President Maclean's name is yet one of the most honored on the roll of Princeton's teachers.

Another of the early professors of Princeton of whom mention might be made was Walter Minto, who was born at Coldingham in 1753, and after graduating from Edinburgh University became tutor in the family of George Johnstone, once Governor of West Florida, (see page 80,) and traveled with his charges over the Continent of Europe. When that position could no longer be retained, Minto became a private tutor of mathematics in Edinburgh, but his prospects were not inviting, and he emigrated in 1786, hoping to find some opportunity in the New World. A year later he was appointed to the Chair of Mathematics and Natural Philosophy in Princeton, and filled that position with much brilliancy until his death, in 1796. Professor Minto received in 1787 the degree of LL. D. from Aberdeen University, and was the author of several interesting works, the best remembered of which is "An Account of the Life and Writings of John Napier of Merchiston," which was published in 1787, and professed to be written in conjunction with Lord Buchan, a celebrated amateur scientist and would-be patron of learning of the time.

Reference has already been made to the Scotch founder of William and Mary College. But many more Scotch founders of institutions devoted to higher education could readily be named. Dalhousie College, in Halifax, was organized mainly through the exertions of one of the holders of that peerage, and Morrin College, Quebec, was founded by a native of Dumfries-shire, who had long practiced medicine in that historic city. Bishop John McLean of Saskatchewan, a native of Portree, founded Emmanuel College, of which he became Warden, and held that office, as well as its Chair of Divinity, at his death, in 1886.

Judging by results, one of the most noteworthy, if not the most noteworthy, of Scottish college founders was James McGill of Montreal, to whose wise philanthropy

that city owes the great seat of learning which bears
his name and of which it is so justly proud. McGill was
born at Glasgow in 1744. After settling in Canada, he
engaged in the fur trade for a time, but afterward made
his home in Montreal, where he entered into business as
a merchant. He was successful from the start, and
quickly won a large fortune. For several years he represented Montreal in the Parliament of Lower Canada,
and became a member of the Legislative and Executive
Councils. His whole life was an example of patriotism,
and was devoted to the advancement of the highest interests of the city in which he had his home, and in
which he had risen to the most honorable eminence.
Connected by marriage with one of the most aristocratic
of the old French families in the city, he had the social
entrée to both the English and French speaking circles,
and was held in the highest esteem in these exclusive
sets, as well as by all classes in the community. His patriotic instincts even induced him to apply himself to
military matters. He became an officer in the militia
service, and in the War of 1812 rose to the rank of Brigadier General. Throughout his life, Mr. McGill was
prominent in Montreal for his charitable gifts. He was
noted for his practical ideas in connection with his giving, but the most conspicuous proof of this was given
when, after his death, on Dec. 19, 1813, it was found
that he had bequeathed over £30,000 in property and
£10,000 in cash for the foundation of a great university
in Montreal. The bequest was not at once made available, for litigation—that bane of will-making all over
America, and which has so often upset from trivial
causes many kindly intentions—interfered, and it was
not until 1821 that the obstacles were cleared away and
the institution established, with full university powers,
by royal charter. The real estate left by Mr. McGill
steadily continued to increase in value, and when the
magnificent mission of the institution began to become
apparent, many of Montreal's citizens liberally contributed to its resources, either by contributions or bequests. Thus, Miss Barbara Scott bequeathed $30,000

for a Chair of Civil Engineering, Major Mills $42,000 for a Chair of Classics, Mr. David Greenshields $40,000 for a Chair of Chemistry, and Mrs. Andrew Stewart $25,000 for a Chair of Law. Writing in 1884, Mr. S. E. Dawson said: "The latest large benefaction which it has received is the Peter Redpath Museum, which was erected by the Scot whose name it bears at a cost of about $120,000, and contains very valuable collections, more especially in geology and mineralogy. The university has four faculties—of Arts, Applied Science, Medicine, and Law. Being non-denominational, it has no theological faculty, but it offers advantageous terms of affiliation to theological colleges, whereby their students can have the benefits of its classes and degrees, and it has already four such colleges, representing four of the leading Protestant denominations. * * * Its buildings are pleasantly situated in grounds laid out in walks and ornamented with trees at the foot of the Montreal Mountain, and, though most of them are unpretending in exterior, they are substantially built of stone and are well adapted for the purposes of education. It has an excellent philosophical apparatus and collections of models in mining and engineering, and also good chemical and physiological laboratories. It has a library of 25,000 volumes, in addition to its medical library, and, though these libraries are not large, they include an unusually choice and valuable selection of books. Though the university has existed since 1821, and its endowment since 1813, its actual history as an important educational institution dates from the amendment of its charter and the reorganization of its general body in 1852. It is thus a comparatively new institution, and is, perhaps, to be judged rather by indications of vitality and growth which it presents rather than by its past results. It has, however, already more than 1,200 graduates, many of them occupying important public positions in Canada and elsewhere."

Among the colleges affiliated with McGill University are Morrin College, of which mention has already been made, and the Presbyterian College of Montreal. This latter institution was founded in 1865 for the training of ministers and missionaries in connection with the Presbyterian Church in Canada. Its origin was very humble, but in 1893 its endowment was valued at $16,000, it owned property worth $225,000, and its annual income was $12,600. "The college," according to Mr. Dawson, "has found many generous benefactors. Among them are Mrs. Redpath, who endowed one of the chairs with $20,000, and the late Mr. Edward Mackay, who gave $40,000 to the endowment in his lifetime. The sum of $10,000 was bequeathed by Mr. Joseph Mackay for the same purpose."

It is impossible to estimate the amount of good, not merely in the education of young men, but in the cause of patriotism of the purest sort, that year after year is accomplished by the single agency begun by the thoughtful bequest of James McGill. Such institutions stand for much more in a community than merely advanced schools or degree-conferring establishments. They foster a national spirit much more potent and far-reaching than a standing army and they develop a sentiment of pride in the present progress toward nationality and hope for its perfect realization in the near future. Without such institutions as McGill University, Toronto University, Knox College, and the other institutions of higher education with which Canada is so plentifully supplied, it would still be in the colonial stage. With them it is a nation in all but in name, and that name will undoubtedly be willingly given to it as soon as its races become a little more blended together, if the sentiment of the nation does not induce it to remain, as now, an integral and honored factor in the British Empire. No one who knows Canada believes it will ever consent to be obliterated by annexation.

While we are across the border and dealing with colleges founded there by Scotch benefactors, it may not be out of place to mention a few representatives of the thousands of teachers which Scotland has given to the Dominion. There is not a college or university in Canada where at least one "son of the heather" is not to be found in some capacity, and the entire educational system of the country, from primary school to university, is more indebted to the Scottish section of the commnuity than to any other. It is the Scotch element, in fact, that has made education become the prime factor in Canadian public life, so important an office in the general and provincial Governments, it is to-day.

Daniel Wilkie was born near Hamilton in 1777. He was the youngest of twelve children and was left an orphan in early life. His education was undertaken at the expense of his elder brothers, who designed him for the ministry, and with this object in view he went to Glasgow University, after passing through the grammar school of Hamilton. In 1797 he entered the Divinity Hall and won the first prize, a medal for an essay on the Socinian controversy—a controversy that then and for more than half a century afterward seriously troubled the Kirk and which still bobs up now and again. In 1807 Wilkie crossed over to Canada, and in the same year was licensed to preach by the Presbytery of Montreal. He was sound and orthodox in his pulpit ministrations and might have passed his life in the work of the ministry, or he might have confined himself to literature, for as editor during three years of a Quebec newspaper he won many high encomiums for his work. But teaching was his real mission, his hobby. For over forty years he was engaged in teaching in Quebec, and in that respect was one of the most successful in Canada. Hundreds of pupils passed through his hands each year, and toward the close of his career he could point to his "old boys" occupying positions of distinction or prominence in every walk of life throughout Canada. Probably the happiest day of his life was that on which the High School of Quebec was opened, and thus was realized a dream he had long cherished. This was in 1843, and as rector he hoped to enter upon a new and extended lease of usefulness, but ill-health compelled his retirement within a year and the remainder of his days were spent in privacy, sometimes in gloom, for toward the end his mind gave way. As the night was falling he forgot everything save the words of Divine truth. When he had forgotten all about the classics he could still read and quote Scripture, and as the end drew nearer every feature of his once varied and aggressive character seemed to disappear excepting that of love. Dr. Wilkie was buried in Mount Hermon Cemetery, Quebec, and his grave was marked by a handsome monument erected by a number of his old pupils.

The funeral discourse that was delivered over the body of the dead teacher was one of the most beautiful of its kind ever heard in Canada. Its speaker was the Rev. Dr. John Cook of Quebec, himself a teacher of note, as well as one of the most influential divines of his time in Canada. He was a native of Dumfries-shire, and had studied at Edinburgh under the great Dr. Chalmers, settling in Canada in 1836. In the divisions which entered the Church in Canada consequent upon the Disruption in Scotland, Dr. Cook took a prominent part, not only counseling adherence on the part of the Canadian Presbyterians to the old Church, but after the schism did take place striving hard to effect a reunion. In the foundation of Queens College, Kingston, he took a deep interest. He was one of the delegation that went to Great Britain to obtain its charter, and afterward became one of its trustees. Urged in 1857 to act as Principal of the college, he agreed to fill the office until the faculty could secure the services of some one else, and he continued as Principal for two years, during which time he taught the divinity class. Then he was succeeded by the Rev. William Leitch, a native of Rothesay, and who was minister of Monimail when he was summoned to Kingston, (where he died in 1864.) It was through Dr. Cook's influence that the Quebec High School was founded in 1843. For years he was the backbone of the institution, and to him more than to any one else was it indebted for triumphing over its many early difficulties and developing into one of the foremost institutions of its class in Canada. In connection with Morrin College, Dr. Cook's name was also conspicuous.

Another name which stands out prominently in the history of education in Canada is that of the Rev. Dr. Michael Willis, Principal of Knox College. He was born in Greenock, where his father (afterward of Stirling) was for many years a minister. For twenty-five years after leaving college Dr. Willis held pastoral charges in Scotland, in the old Secession Church, and threw in his lot with the Free Church when that denomination sprang into existence. It was by a vote of the Colonial Board of that Church that he was selected to the Chair of Divinity in Knox College, and though the change was stoutly opposed by his congregation in Renfield Street, Glasgow, he felt that duty and conscience called him "over the sea." His long connection with Knox College, as teacher and Principal, was a very valuable one to the Church in Canada, and he not only aided greatly in giving to the students the thorough teaching which made a Knox College graduate so acceptable to the ranks of the ministry, but he infused into every one of his pupils a catholicity of taste and a non-sectarian spirit which led them to place the simple truths of Christ's teaching above all creeds or denominational barriers. He was a determined opponent of any union between Church and State and spoke and wrote against it on all occasions, but so honest were his utterances and so lovable was his character, that his outspokenness raised him no enemies even among those who were as zealous in the opposite direction.

Treating of Knox College recalls a flood of Scotch professors, among whom we will mention only one, Dr. Robert Burns, who from 1856 till 1864 occupied its Chair of Church History and Apologetics. Dr. Burns was born at Bo'ness in 1798 and for some thirty years preached in Paisley, from the same pulpit that had once been occupied by Dr. Witherspoon. At the Disruption he "came out" and, crossing to Canada, became minister of Knox Church, Toronto, and remained there until he entered the faculty of the college. He was a man of great learning and culture and an amiable and thoroughgoing preacher. Outside of the ministry he took a special interest in poor-law matters, and wrote much on that and other subjects. Dr. Burns will, however, be best remembered by his carefully edited edition of "Woodrow's History of the Sufferings."

Many other names crowd upon us, such as that of Vice Principal Leach of McGill College, Montreal, a native of Berwick on Tweed; Dr. Inglis of Charlottetown, a native of Montrose; Principal McVicar of McGill College, and his brother, Prof. Malcolm McVicar of Toronto. But we must cross the St. Lawrence again, or the rush of Canadian teachers demanding notice would swamp this chapter.

One of the most industrious and painstaking of scientific students of whom we have record was Granville Sharp Pattison, who was for many years teacher of anatomy in the University of the City of New York and was engaged in that capacity at the time of his death, in 1851. He was born near Glasgow in 1791, and was for a time lecturer on anatomy in the Andersonian College, in that city. After settling in America he became Professor of Anatomy in the Medical College at Baltimore. After many years' residence in the Monumental City he enjoyed a short vacation in Europe, and then took the Chair of Anatomy in Jefferson Medical College, Philadelphia. He was recognized there as one of the ablest men in his profession, a particularly painstaking demonstrator, and won the confidence and respect of the students who attended his lectures. His contributions to medical literature in the shape of pamphlets and papers in transactions were highly praised in their time, but they have long since served their day and generation and been relegated to the honorable condition of scientific curiosities like most medical works after a very brief season of popularity or usefulness.

In the annals of education in the United States no name stands out more boldly not only for his knowledge of the science of pedagogy, but for the manner in which he advocated its highest interests and directed public opinion in its advancement than that of William Russell, who, besides understanding the theory of teaching, was himself a practical and successful instructor. Born in Glasgow in 1798, he settled in Savannah, Ga., in 1819 and took charge of Chatham Academy there. After a few years' experience in Savannah, he removed to New Haven, and taught in the new Township Academy and the Hopkins Grammar School, the latter one of the schools founded by Edward Hopkins, an English trader, who died at London in 1657, and whose gifts to the cause of education in America have done more to keep his memory alive than the important position he held in New England for many years.

All this time, while teaching, Mr. Russell had been studying the entire science of pedagogy, and the fruits of this were seen in the masterly manner in which for some four years, 1826-29, he conducted the "American Journal of Education." Removing in 1830 to Philadelphia he took charge of a ladies' seminary. In 1838 he returned to New England and devoted himself to the teaching of elocution in Boston and Andover, lecturing at frequent intervals to teachers through New England and in New York. In 1849 he organized a teachers' institute in New Haven and removed its headquarters to Lancaster, Mass., where he remained until his death, in 1873. For the last ten years of his life he lectured frequently before teachers' institutes throughout Massachusetts and was recognized as one of the leading and most successful instructors of the day in his own specialty, that of elocution. He was the author of many popular and highly practical schoolbooks, including "The Grammar of Composition," "American Elocutionist," and a dozen others.

One of the best-known educators in New York for many years was Charles Murray Nairne, who from 1857 to 1881 was Professor of Moral Philosophy in Columbia College. He was born at Perth in 1808, graduated from St. Andrews in 1832, and afterward extended his studies at Edinburgh University. For a short time he was associated at Glasgow with Dr. Chalmers, but in 1847 he left Scotland, and soon after reaching the United States found a position as teacher at College Hill,

Poughkeepsie. Then he opened a private school in New York City, and continued to conduct it with every success that can attend a teacher until he became connected with Columbia. He retired into private life with the dignity and title of an emeritus professor of Columbia in 1881 and died a year later at Warrenton, Va.

Another noted New York teacher was David Burnet Scott, who died in 1894. " He had been connected," said one of the newspapers which recorded his death, " with the public school system of New York City from its beginning, and as a teacher, a successful schoolbook writer, and a public speaker prominently identified with the great political movements of his day, he was a well-known and highly respected man." Prof. Scott was born at Edinburgh in 1822 and educated at the High School with the view of being sent to St. Andrews University. Circumstances, however, compelled his father to emigrate, and the family settled near Hartford, Conn., where young Scott worked for a time with his father as a tailor. He kept up his studies, however, while working " on the board," and in time obtained a position as instructor of classics in Hartford High School. In 1845 he settled in New York, and for many years was connected, as teacher and Principal, with the public schools. In 1870 he became Principal of the introductory department of the College of the City of New York and afterward was transferred to the Chair of English Literature, which he filled till his death. He was the author of three school histories of the United States and other works which enjoyed a wide circulation and were, and still are, eminently useful.

Prominent as he was in connection with his duties as a teacher, Prof. Scott became more widely and popularly known by the force he exerted in public affairs, by the boldness and originality of his views on social economy and by the brilliant manner in which he gave expression to them. He was an ardent and uncompromising Abolitionist and aided in the formation of the Republican Party. Afterward, when he thought that party had fulfilled its mission, he desired to see another movement come into operation, and he found what he wanted in the single-tax theories of Henry George. In 1886 he threw himself heartily into Mr. George's candidature for the Mayoralty of New York. This movement started in a very half-hearted manner, speedily assumed great proportions, and ended in a magnificent run on the part of Mr. George. That gentleman was defeated, but his large vote surprised even his friends and demonstrated that there was a very large body of citizens who cared little for either of the two predominating parties. To this end, Prof. Scott signally contributed by his voice, his pen, and his example, and thereby earned the thanks of all interested in improving the system of municipal government not only in New York, but throughout the United States.

A friend recently sent us the following cutting from an American paper, which is interesting at least for the many brilliant names it contains, apart from the record it gives us of a Scot who devoted the best years of his life to the cause of education in America:

"The Rev. Dr. R. A. Paterson, late President of Binghamton College and founder of the first women's training college in America, has returned (1894) to Edinburgh, Scotland, his native city, to resume the pastorate after forty years' absence in this country. He and Baron Playfair, Prof. P. G. Tait, the first scientist in Edinburgh, and the late Prof. James Clark Maxwell, the foremost scientist and Professor of Experimental Physics in Cambridge, were all boys in Edinburgh together in the forties, and Paterson, Tait, and Maxwell were university classmates under James Forbes, Christopher North, and Sir William Hamilton. Dr. Paterson came to this country in 1852, to be the tutor of the Hon. Charles Ellis and the Hon. Edward Ellis, now proprietors of the Schenectady Locomotive Works."

We have reserved, as a fitting name to close this chapter, the name of William Wood, not only because of his grand services to education, but because his services were in reality typical of the devotion to that cause of thousands of Scotsmen who have no connection with teaching as a profession and devote themselves to promoting it because its advancement is one of the intuitive duties of their race, and because by spreading broadcast the blessings of education they are thereby advancing the best interests of their adopted country. Thousands of Scotsmen in America have served upon boards of education or as regents or trustees of universities or colleges, and thereby performed one of the highest services which patriotism can inspire.

Pre-eminent among such public benefactors must linger the memory of William Wood. He was born in Glasgow in 1808 and belonged to that Dennistoun family which has given its name to one of the sections of the Western Metropolis of Scotland. He was educated at the Universities of Glasgow and St. Andrews, and at the latter place had for one of his teachers Dr. Thomas Chalmers, a fact of which he was very proud and never tired of recalling in his public addresses.

Throughout his long life he remained a diligent student. President Hunter, of the New York Normal College, said of him: " In 1870 he got out of the Board of Education to study up on his Greek because he felt he was a little rusty. His memory for poetry was marvelous, and I have heard him repeat verses by the hour. His favorites were Wordsworth, Coleridge, and Southey."

Mr. Wood came to America in 1828 and begun his commercial career. After several years' American experience he returned to Scotland, remaining there till 1844, when he once more settled in New York as a partner in the firm of Dennistoun, Wood & Co. This partnership continued till 1868, when Mr. Wood retired from business. The first year Mr. Wood saw New York he joined the St. Andrew's Society, believing that to be a duty, and he served it in many capacities—two years as President—and for some time prior to his death was its oldest member. He was a regular attendant at the St. Andrew's Day celebrations, and very frequently responded to toasts, the last occasion being in 1893, some ten months before his death, when, visibly failing, he made a reminiscent speech in response to " The day and a' wha honor it." He spoke of the many similar meetings he had attended, and then, as if conscious that that was to be the last, he closed by quoting Tennyson's famous "Crossing the Bar":

> "Sunset and evening star,
>   And one clear call for me,
> And may there be no moaning of the bar
>   When I put out to sea.
>
>   *   *   *   *
>
> For tho' from out our bourne of Time and Place
>   The flood may bear me far,
> I hope to see my Pilot face to face
>   When I have crost the bar."

With these words the old man left the banqueting room and virtually closed his public appearances. These had been many, for Mr. Wood was a magnificent speaker, and a popular man, and when in the hey-day of his strength his services were often in demand at gatherings of all sorts. Possibly the most noted of these occasions was in Central Park, at the unveiling of the Scott statue, on Aug. 15, 1871, when he delivered an oration which was regarded as the best example of Scotch eloquence ever heard in America. His public career may be said to have commenced in 1869, when he was appointed a Commissioner of Public Instruction. He continued for the rest of his life to have a potent influence on the education board in the city, even in the intervals when he was not connected with it as its President or as a member. He also served for a time as one of the Dock Commissioners of the city. In 1888 he retired from official life, and was publicly thanked for his services to New York by the then Mayor, A. S. Hewitt. From that time until his death, in 1894, Mr. Wood spent his days in pleasant retirement, taking a keen interest in passing affairs, holding fast to old friends, but seldom going beyond the limits of his own immediate circle.

CHAPTER X.

STATESMEN AND POLITICIANS.

WE enter upon the subject-matter of this chapter with fear and with trembling, and would fain dismiss it altogether, pass its theme by, as it were, but for the sake of the completeness of our survey of the Scot in America. The subject is practically an inexhaustible one. From the beginning of the Colonial history Scots have been prominent in public affairs, and at the present time it is safe to say there is not a Legislature or municipality in the country that cannot produce one or more members who are able to trace Scotch blood in their veins. The connection of the Scots with America, in fact, began long before the Colonial period, and has steadily waxed in importance and numerical strength ever since. Sometimes, we must confess, the claim of Scotch descent is decidedly infinitesimal, but the claim, even when made on the slenderest grounds, is a compliment to the "Land of the Heather."

However that may be, there is no question that a complete survey of the story of the Scottish race in America, even within the limitations imposed by the title to this chapter, would bring us face to face with the task of writing a tolerably complete American dictionary of biography. Thomas Jefferson, James Madison, James Monroe, Patrick Henry, Andrew Jackson, Thomas Benton, John C. Calhoun, James Buchanan, J. C. Breckinridge, U. S. Grant, R. B. Hayes, Chester A. Arthur, and James G. Blaine, all claimed descent from Scotland, and so did Robert Fulton, the steamboat pioneer; C. H. McCormick, of thrashing machine fame;

Davy Crockett, the fighter; Joseph Henry, the scientist, and if the student of this subject were to incorporate, as he would have a perfect right to do, the legion describing themselves as of the Scotch-Irish race, he would be confronted with an appalling task. Even George Washington had a little mixture of Scotch blood in his composition—so it is said.

In these circumstances it is absolutely necessary to draw the line somewhere, and instead of attempting anything like a complete survey, to rest content with selecting a few instances from early times until the present day. Of course many who might claim a place in this chapter have already been spoken of in other connections, and so we must pass over a large number of names which would add greatly to the brilliancy of the present record.

One of the earliest of the minor Scotch office holders in the history of the continent was Thomas Gordon, who was born at Pitlochry, in the parish of Moulin, Perthshire, in 1650. In 1684 he settled at Scotch Plains, and in 1698 was elected Attorney General of the Eastern district of Jersey and Secretary and Registrar in 1702. Despite these legal appointments, it was not until 1707 that he was licensed as an attorney, and the same year he was elected to the Legislature and served as Speaker of the Assembly. These appointments and elections show that he must have enjoyed considerable popularity among his fellow colonists. But he rose still higher when he was appointed Chief Justice of the Province, and, later on, its Receiver General and Treasurer. He died at Perth Amboy in 1722, having a record as an office holder that would have won for him the envy of a modern politician had he lived in later times and been as successful. But, unlike the majority of modern instances of success in that regard, old Thomas Gordon's good fortune was undoubtedly due to his honesty and ability, two qualities which do not figure very largely in the qualities of our contemporary office seekers.

A man who loomed up even more prominently in the public eye of his day was Andrew Hamilton, who was called by Gouverneur Morris "the day star of the American Revolution." There is a good deal of mystery about the early career of this man. He was born, it is believed, in Edinburgh about 1656 and settled in the American colonies in 1695. Of his family or history until landing in America nothing is certain. For some reason or other he never referred to such matters. It is known, however, that when he first settled in the Colonies he bore the name of Trent, although he soon discarded it for Hamilton, which is believed to have been that of his family. Probably he was concerned in some of the Covenanting troubles and his own strict religious views would seem to warrant this suggestion, for when he settled in Philadelphia he was received into communion by the Quakers and was one of the most strait-laced of that sect, although a lawyer. His first resting place in America was in Accomac Parish, Virginia, where he got a position as steward on an estate and added to his income by conducting a classical school. After a while the owner of the estate died and the widow became the wife of Hamilton, who thereby not only became a landed proprietor, but at once got a standing in social life which started him in a signally favorable way toward the success which he afterward attained. He entered upon the study of the law with all the zeal of a determined Scot, and in due time was admitted to practice. Then, seeing that the opportunities of the profession lay in the large cities, he removed to Philadelphia, and as the saying goes, "hung out his shingle." This was some time prior to 1716. In 1717 he became Attorney General of Pennsylvania, and in 1721 a member of the Provincial Council. He became Recorder of Philadelphia in 1727, and the same year was elected a member of Assembly from Bucks County. He continued to be a Representative until 1739, and was several times Speaker of Assembly. It is worthy of note that the ground on which Independence Hall in Philadelphia stands was bought by Hamilton for the purpose of the erection of a suitable building to accommodate the Legislature and the courts, these public bodies having previously been sheltered in private houses, and, though the scheme was not completed until after Hamilton's death, it is curious to know that a spot so famous in the history of the country and so sacred to every lover of freedom was once in the possession of one whose country has been famous for its struggles on behalf of liberty.

Notwithstanding his public duties, Hamilton continued zealously to practice his profession, and gradually advanced to the front until he became the undisputed leader of the Pennsylvania bar. His fame had extended far beyond the boundaries of his own State—and fame did not travel as quickly then as now—and he was noted not only for his fearlessness in maintaining the rights of his clients, but in his adherence to what he perceived to be the rights of all citizens and the inherent liberties of the Colonies. All this gave him the opportunity which has won him a place in American history and caused Gouverneur Morris to characterize him by the proud title with which we began our reference to him, a title which any American family would be proud to possess among its ancestral glories.

A printer in New York—John Peter Zenger—had printed in the columns of the "New York Journal," a little newspaper issued by him, some strictures on the then Chief Magistrate, Gov. Crosby. The strictures were very unpalatable, mainly because they were for the most part true, and as a warning to others, as much as for his own offenses, Zenger was arrested. It was proposed to deal summarily with the prisoner, but public interest was aroused in his case, and it was seen that if he was convicted all hope of free speech would, for the time at least, be gone. As the public became interested the authorities became determined and harsh. In pursuance of his rights Zenger's counsel made an objection to the Judges who were to try the case, and they were promptly disbarred, while a lawyer was assigned by the court to carry on the defense. All this time public sentiment had been forming and consolidating, and the "Sons of Liberty," as representatives of the spirit of liberty among the people, took a hand in fighting the Executive and in defending what they regarded as the inalienable rights of all freemen—that of free speech and discussion. When Zenger was finally called on to face a jury, the authorities were confident of making short work of his case and of establishing a precedent which would crush out what they deemed "sedition" in the future. It was not known to them that Zenger's friends were doing any practical work on his behalf, but they were better enlightened when the court was open and Andrew Hamilton walked in and announced that he had been retained as counsel for the prisoner. The fame of the venerable attorney, his standing at the bar, the prominent offices he had held, and his position as a member of Assembly forbade his being treated in the summary fashion of Zenger's earlier counsel, and the representatives of the prosecution could do nothing but submit. They had great hopes from the jury, and, besides, they knew that the Judges were with them.

The prosecution held that all the jury had to determine was whether the publication which was scheduled as libelous had appeared, and that they had nothing to do with the truth or falsity of the libel. Hamilton demurred from this, saying he was prepared to admit the publication of the strictures and to prove their truth, leaving the issue to the jury to be whether truth was a libel or not. He was overruled by the Court on the inferred ground that anything reflecting on the King was a libel. Hamilton then denied that the King's representative had the same prerogatives as the sovereign himself, and claimed the right of proving the truth of every statement that had been made in Zenger's paper. This the Court again overruled, and Hamilton confined his attention to the jury and made a glowing speech on behalf of personal liberty and the right of free criticism, which still ranks as one of the masterpieces of American legal eloquence. His speech was productive of effect far beyond the limits of the courtroom in which it was delivered, or the case in which it was used. It started a train of thought which fired men's minds and did more than anything else to give expression to the popular desire for freedom—for the freedom which the people deemed their birthright as British subjects—for independence was not then thought of, though it was the natural and unavoidable result, as men's minds and men's experience then went in Britain and in America. He practically admitted again the publication of the words deemed libelous. "Then the verdict must be for the King," broke in the prosecuting attorney. But Hamilton proceeded to contend that the words must be considered by the jury as to whether they constituted a libel or no, and quoted texts of Scripture to show how even they might be considered as libelous, by a zealous lawyer, against the then government of the Colony. Therefore he urged the jury, even though the Court might decide otherwise, to consider the words for themselves, and put their own construction on them. In concluding he said: "You see I labor under the weight of many years, and am borne down by many infirmities of body; yet, old and weak as I am, I should think it my duty, if required, to go to the uttermost part of the land where my service could be of any use in assisting to quench the flame of prosecutions upon informations set on foot by the Government to deprive a people of the right of remonstrating and complaining, too, against the arbitrary attempts of men in power. Men who oppress and injure the people under their administration provoke them to cry out and complain, and then make that very complaint the foundation for new oppressions and prosecutions. * * * The question before the court is not of small or private concern. It is not the cause of a poor printer nor of New York alone which you are now trying. No! It may in its consequences affect every freeman that lives under the British Government upon the main of America. It is the best cause; it is the cause of liberty; and I make no doubt but your upright conduct this day will not only entitle you to the love and esteem of your fellow-citizens, but every man who prefers freedom to a life of slavery will bless and honor you as men who have baffled the attempts of tyranny, and by an impartial and incorrupt verdict, have made a noble foundation for securing to ourselves and our posterity and our neighbors that to which nature and the laws of our country have given us a right—the liberty of both exposing and opposing arbitrary power in these parts of the world, at least by speaking and writing truth."

The prosecution replied, and the Court charged against the prisoner, but Hamilton's eloquence was irresistible, and the jury, after a few minutes' deliberation, acquitted Zenger, much to the disgust of the powers. But the public delight was unbounded, and Hamilton became the hero of the hour. The next day he was entertained at a public dinner, received the freedom of the city from the corporation, the certificate being inclosed in a gold box purchased by private subscription, and he was escorted by a large crowd to the barge which was to carry him back to Philadelphia. Hamilton died in Philadelphia, in 1741. His son, James, became Governor of Pennsylvania.

Sometimes, in the course of this work, we have traced the fortunes of a family for two or three generations, mainly for the sake of showing how the qualities which distinguished the founder have not been lost in his descendants. Another instance of the same sort may be recorded in this place in connection with the Auchmuty family. The first of the name to settle in America was Robert Auchmuty—born in Fifeshire, in 1670. His American experiences seem to have been confined to Boston, where he appears to have arrived in 1699, and at once assumed a prominent position as a lawyer. He was active in local affairs, and was held in general esteem. In 1741 he was sent to England as agent for the Colony of Massachusetts, an appointment that is sufficient testimony to his standing as a citizen and his honesty as a man. He died, in Boston, in 1750. His eldest son succeeded to his law business, and carried it on in Boston until 1776, when, being an intense loyalist, he left the country and went to Britain, where he remained till his death.

A younger son, Samuel, born in Boston in 1722, was

educated for the ministry, and became assistant rector of Trinity Church, New York, becoming rector in 1764. The Revolution brought him into a sea of troubles. As intensely loyal as his brother, he continued to read prayers for George III. long after the Revolution had broken out and the rule of monarchy was declared at an end. When ordered by Gen. Alexander, titular Earl of Stirling, to discontinue such loyal petitions, he closed the church and left the city. New York was at that time in possession of the Continental troops, and when, by a turn in the tide of war, it fell again into the hands of the British, in 1777, Dr. Auchmuty returned to his post of duty, only to find his beloved church in ruins and its records destroyed. The shock was too much for him, and he died, broken-hearted, in March, 1777. His son, Samuel, born in New York in 1758, entered the British Army and served in it during the Revolutionary War. Obtaining a Captaincy, he served in India from 1783 to 1796, and in 1800 was in Egypt under Abercrombie. In 1803, for his services, he was knighted, and soon after proceeded to South America, where he distinguished himself by his skill and bravery. In 1811 he reduced Java, and was regarded as one of the best officers in the service. Returning to Britain, he was commissioned a Lieutenant General in 1813. He died at Dublin, in 1822, while Commander in Chief of the forces in Ireland, leaving behind him the record of a long and honorable career, unmarked by reproach or blame.

In the history of the City of Richmond, one of the most prominent of its residents in civil life during the Revolutionary War, and for many years after it had become reminiscent, was John Harvie, a native of the Parish of Gargunnock, Stirlingshire. He was born about 1740, and is believed to have emigrated to the Colonies shortly after reaching his majority. He settled in Albemarle County, Va., and began the practice of law. In this he was eminently successful, and his ability was so generally acknowledged that in 1774 he was commissioned by the General Assembly to make a treaty with the Indians, a task that was always reckoned a delicate one, requiring unlimited diplomacy, cool judgment, and the utmost firmness. He also threw himself devotedly into the cause of the Colonies against the motherland, and in 1775 and 1776 represented Augusta County in the Virginia Conventions of these years. Then he was sent to Congress, where he served during two eventful years, and he afterward held several State offices, including that of Secretary of the Commonwealth of Virginia. His latter years were spent in Richmond, and he took an active part in every movement designed to add to the importance and beauty of that city. Indeed, it was while superintending the erection of a handsome new building which he intended to be an ornamental landmark that he met with the accident which, in 1807, caused his death.

Another Indian-treaty-making Scot was David Brodie Mitchell, a native of Paisley, who crossed the Atlantic in 1783, in his seventeenth year, to take possession of some property in Georgia which had been bequeathed to him by his uncle, David Brodie. He took up his headquarters in Savannah, and the work necessary to enable him to acquire his property led to his devoting himself to the study of law, and in due time he was admitted to the bar, having assumed citizenship in the young Republic. His studies were so well directed to acquiring the mastery of his profession that he soon enjoyed a widespread reputation as a lawyer, and, in 1795, was chosen to be Solicitor General of Georgia. A year later he was elected to the State Legislature, and he was afterward elected several times Governor of the Commonwealth, and each term justified the public confidence by the executive qualities he displayed. In his dealings with the Indians he was ever just and humane. In any treaty negotiations he tried to be honorable in his claims and concessions, and his treatment of these people won for him their regard. Gov. Mitchell also took a deep interest in educational matters, and did much to extend their progress in the State he had adopted, and which he loved and served so well.

A curious instance, for America, of a man eminently

fitted for public life, yet utterly regardless of its honors—a man with ability to have reached and retained a high position in the service of the country, yet who preferred the pleasures of home life to the allurements of office—is afforded by a consideration of the career of John Greig of Canandaigua. Born at Moffat, Dumfries, in 1779, and educated at Edinburgh University, he settled in America in 1800, and applied himself to the practice of law. He in time acquired a competency, and, though often urged to run for Congress, he steadily refused, excepting once. He had hosts of admirers, and the graceful hospitalities which were so marked a feature of his home life made him even better understood and more endeared to his associates and friends than though he had met their wishes and embarked on the stormy and uncertain, sometimes dirty, sea of politics. Among others of his guests was the illustrious Lafayette, the "patriot of two hemispheres," as he has been called, who was entertained by Greig on his triumphal return visit to the States in 1824. In 1825 Greig accepted the office of Regent of the State University, hoping thereby to do some service to the cause of education, and he attended to the duties of the office with all the zeal they gave opportunity for. He was induced to stand as a representative of his district for Congress, and was elected in 1841, but he served only one term, having no taste either for life in Washington or the duties and requirements of a Congressman. So he gladly retired when the term for which he was elected had expired, and returned to his home and his law practice. In 1845 he was made Chancellor of the State University, and that position, of which he was very proud, he retained until his death, at Canandaigua, in 1858.

It may have been noticed in the last few cases mentioned, and in several others in the course of this volume, how easily and naturally many Scots on settling in America turned to the law as a profession. Another and conspicuous instance of this was Judge Mitchell King. He was born at Crail, Fifeshire, in 1783. In 1805 he began his long connection with the City of Charleston by securing an appointment as an assistant teacher in Charleston College, having been a teacher for a short time before leaving Scotland. While attending to his duties in the college and prosecuting the studies necessary to advancement in the teaching profession, he saw that there were more possibilities in the practice of law, and in 1807 he began its study. Three years later he was admitted to the bar, and gradually won a front rank. In 1819 he became a Judge of the Charleston City Court, and served on the bench many years. Throughout his career Judge King took a deep interest in what is now called " higher education." He founded, in 1809, the Philosophical Society of Charleston and lectured before it frequently, and he was the author of many treatises on scientific and agricultural subjects. An exemplary American citizen, Judge King seemed to grow more and more enthusiastic over his native land as time cast it deeper into the shadows of remembrance, and his nationality was always with him a matter of pride. In 1808 he joined the Charleston St. Andrew's Society, and served it in many ways, notably as its President for several terms. In 1829, when that organization celebrated its centenary, he delivered an oration which is a model of its kind. Judge King continued to take an active part in the work of the society, and so to do something for puir Auld Scotland's sake, until his death, at Flatwick, N. C., in 1862, when his adopted country was in the throes of the great civil war.

Hugh Maxwell of New York, one of the best known and, in some quarters, best hated, of the public men of that city in his day, was equally conspicuous during his life for his prominence in Scottish circles. The older he got, the closer Scotland came to him, although in his case the love was purely sentimental, as he was carried from his native city of Paisley when very young. He was born there in 1787. His early schooling was in one of the grammar schools of New York, and he studied at Columbia College with the view of engaging in the practice of law, and passed successfully. He began business as an attorney soon after he attained his majority, and in

1814 was appointed an Assistant Judge Advocate General in the United States Army. In 1819 he was elected District Attorney of New York, and won a flattering reputation in his administration of that difficult and unenviable position. He so won the confidence of the public that he was again elected to the office, and continued to hold it until 1829. He was truly a terror to evil-doers, uniting the cleverness of a detective to the genius of a lawyer, and leaving no effort undone to bring the guilty to book. But he never, like so many modern prosecuting attorneys, rejoiced in a conviction for the sake of conviction alone. He shielded the innocent as determinedly as he crushed the guilty, and, unlike some of his successors, never used his office to aid a "pull" or to defeat the majesty and power of the law. He took a particularly active part in the prosecution of the so-called "conspiracy trials," which created a great amount of excitement at the time. Mr. Maxwell's work in this connection raised up for him many enemies, among them Halleck, the poet, who held him up to ridicule in some rather commonplace verses.

Mr. Maxwell's last public office was that of Collector of the Port of New York, which he held between the years 1849 and 1852, covering the terms of the Administrations of Presidents Taylor and Fillmore. In the St. Andrew's Society, of which he became a member in 1811, he passed through the office of manager and the Vice Presidential chairs to the Presidency, which he held in 1835 and 1836, and at the time of his death, in 1873, he had long been the oldest living member, having paid dues into its treasury for sixty-two years.

A public man of a stamp not too common in America, one who united the shrewdness of a lawyer, the breadth of a statesman, and the humble piety and aggressive zeal of a true Christian, must be the verdict of every one who, after a study of his career, passes judgment on Walter Lowrie, for many years Secretary of the United States Senate. Born in Edinburgh in 1784, he settled with his parents in Pennsylvania in 1791. He was brought up on a farm owned by his father, a man of sincere piety, who, although unable to give his son a thorough general education, took care that his religious training was as full and deep reaching as though he were designed for the ministry. This was, in fact, the utmost legacy the Scottish farmer could give his son, but it was enough, as a foundation, to carry him safely through life and exalt him to high places.

When eighteen years of age, Lowrie resolved to study for the ministry, but after a time he abandoned the idea and determined to enter the legal profession. When twenty-seven years of age his neighbors, with a high appreciation of his character, elected him as their representative in the Senate of Pennsylvania. After serving in that body for seven years, he was chosen as one of the Senators from his State to the United States Senate, and when his term expired, in 1824, he was elected Secretary of the Senate, and held that important office for twelve years, when he voluntarily retired, to the regret of all the members of that body.

The rest of Mr. Lowrie's life was spent in doing good, and the influence he exerted, even upon Congress, was very great. He founded the Congressional prayer meeting, and was active in the formation of the Congressional Temperance Society, and, although these institutions have now long been abandoned, they did much good in their day, and some time in the future their influence may be revived. In 1836 Mr. Lowrie was elected Corresponding Secretary of the Western Foreign Missionary Society, and in the following year was called to a similar position in the Board of Foreign Missions of the Presbyterian Church, which latter office he held for thirty-two years. He was particularly interested in the evangelization of the American Indian tribes, and spent much time in visiting the red men on their reservations and throughout the West. It is impossible to calculate the full value of this man's life work. Wherever he went, his thoughts were always directed to noble ends, and his blameless career as a politician stands out in pleasant relief in the somewhat muddy atmosphere of American practical politics. Several of his sons, emulating his example, became missionaries of the Gospel in foreign lands, and his eldest son succeeded him in the Secretaryship of the Presbyterian Foreign Mission Board, after preaching the Gospel in India for three years, and so having practical experience in that noblest of all the outcomes of Christian practice and teaching.

In 1765 there arrived in Boston from Dornoch, Sutherlandshire, a Scotch crofter-fisherman named Adam McCulloch. He settled at Arundel, afterward known as Kennebunkport, in Maine. He joined in with the Revolutionary movement and accepted citizenship in the young Republic with equanimity, and, if he did not wax rich, he at least became comfortable in his circumstances through his own exertions, although the life of a pioneer in Maine in those days was one of much hardship and danger. His son became a ship owner, and when the War of 1812 broke out was one of the largest merchants of the ship-owning class in New England and in a fair way to becoming one of the recognized wealthy men of the northern seaboard. The business interests of Maine, however, suffered sadly in the war, and the ship owner sustained such losses that his operations had, temporarily, to come to a complete standstill. His son Hugh—the grandson of the Scotch crofter—who had been born at Kennebunk in 1808, had been entered a student at Bowdoin College, but his health gave way, and this, together with the condition of his father's financial affairs, caused him to leave the institution long before the usual course was completed.

At seventeen years of age, Hugh McCulloch began to earn his own living by teaching school, and continued at that occupation until 1829, when he commenced the study of law. That study he completed in Boston in 1832, and a year later he went to Fort Wayne and entered upon the practice of his chosen profession. But it was soon discovered that his talents were those of a financier rather than a lawyer, and he entered on his real career, when, in 1835, he became manager of one of the branches of the State Bank of Indiana. A year later he became one of the Directors, and finally, as President of

a great banking company, became known as one of
the financial authorities in the West. He entered public
life in 1863, when he accepted from Secretary Chase the
position of Controller of the Currency, and in 1865 he
became himself Secretary of the Treasury, with a seat in
President Lincoln's Cabinet, and he continued to hold
the office under President Johnson. When his term expired he retired from official position, until, at President
Arthur's request, he again returned to the Cabinet as the
head of the Treasury. From that time he lived mainly
in retirement, enjoying the glorious sunset of a busy
life, until his death, in 1895.

Hugh McCulloch was by no means what is commonly
regarded in the States as a politician. He had no political fences to keep in order, no wires to manipulate, no
leaders to conciliate, or heelers to propitiate. Every
public office he held came to him unsolicited, and he
cared nothing for intrigues or for personal popularity.
He did simply what he thought was right; he had no
motive in any of his acts as a public man beyond serving the best interests of the country. In the Cabinet
councils his cool, practical, common-sense view of whatever topic came up for discussion proved of incalculable
value, and his shrewdness and sterling honesty were always conspicuous. In the Treasury Department his
policy was always regarded as safe, and his reputation
as a financier was of infinite value to the country, especially immediately after the war, when so many wildcat
schemes were on foot. His innate Scotch practical nature showed him clearly that there was no royal road to
national wealth, no sidetracks from the strait path of
national integrity.

An equally noteworthy exponent of Scotch industry,
honesty, and common sense was James Gilfillan, who
from 1869 till his death, in 1895, was, with the exception
of a short interval, Chief Justice of the Supreme Court
of Minnesota. Judge Gilfillan was born at Bannockburn in 1829, and was brought to this country in his
childhood. He received his early education in New
York City, studied law at Ballston Spa and Buffalo, and

in 1850 was admitted to the bar at Albany. He practiced at Buffalo for some seven years, and then removed to St. Paul, Minn., which became his home city thereafter. When the civil war started he joined the Seventh Minnesota Regiment, and in 1862 was commissioned as Colonel of the Eleventh Minnesota. He commanded that regiment until it was mustered out of service at the close of hostilities, in June, 1865. He then settled down again to the practice of law at St. Paul. In 1869 he was appointed Chief Justice of Minnesota, to fill a vacancy, and held a seat on the bench until the next election. In 1875 he was again appointed temporarily, but at the election that year he was elected to it by the votes of the people, and his subsequent re-elections demonstrated their satisfaction with his services. During his long term on the bench not a whisper was ever heard reflecting on his impartiality, and his thorough knowledge and grasp of the law, national as well as State, was conceded. His opinions and judgments were models in their way. They were couched in plain language, and terse in their expression and so written that they could be clearly understood by whoever chose to read them, a quality which is seldom characteristic of legal documents of any kind. It seems essential to the extreme sentiment of trades unionism which prevails in the legal profession to clothe everything with a disheartening and unmeaning mass of verbiage, as well as to multiply forms and procedures, and, of course, costs. This brings grist to the legal mill, but is of no service for any other purpose in the world—certainly not for any purpose of right or of justice. Some day this extraneous mass of legal cobwebs will be swept away by a disgusted people, and then Judge Gilfillan's clear-cut decisions may be taken as models of what such judicial utterances ought to be—terse, sound, logical, and conclusive, and thoroughly understandable by any man possessing mere common sense.

A jurist with an even more national reputation was (or is, for he still lives in honorable retirement,) Arthur MacArthur, who in 1887 retired from the bench as Associate Justice of the Supreme Court of the United States under the act which permits judicial retirement after the occupant of the bench has reached the allotted span of threescore years and ten. Judge MacArthur was born at Glasgow in 1815, and settled in America when very young. In 1841 he was admitted to the bar in New-York, and began practice at Springfield, Mass. In 1849 he removed to the then new city of Milwaukee, resolved to "grow up" with it, and two years later was elected its City Attorney. In 1855 he was elected Lieutenant Governor of Wisconsin, and acted as Governor for a time. His first appointment to the bench was in 1857, when he became Judge of the Second Judicial District of the State, and was re-elected in 1863. He was called to the Supreme Court in 1870, and in that position his merits as a jurist became recognized all over the country. With the exception of serving as one of the United States Commissioners to the Paris Exposition of 1867, Judge MacArthur has held no other public office, confining himself mainly to the pursuit of his profession, and, as a recreation, to the study of literary and historical subjects. As an orator he held high rank in Wisconsin, where his principal efforts in that line were made, and his services as a lecturer were for many years in constant demand. In the St. Andrew's Society of Milwaukee he was long a leading figure, presided over it for several terms; and at its banquets on St. Andrew's Day, or in connection with the Burns anniversary celebrations, his presence and speeches were for years regarded as prominent features.

Another noted figure in public life, who began his career as a lawyer, was James Burnie Beck, for many years United States Senator from Kentucky. He was born in Dumfriesshire in 1822, and settled with his parents in Lexington, Ky. He was elected to the lower house of Congress in 1867, and served until 1875, (through four terms,) and was then chosen one of the representatives of his adopted State in the National Senate, and so continued till his death, in 1889. He was noted in public life as an authority on financial and currency matters, and was devoted in his adherence to free-trade principles. His honesty was admitted on every side, and his addresses on any question were listened to with marked attention, for his ripe judgment and wide range of information made his utterances well deserving of careful consideration. He had a contempt for such legislative pranks as filibustering, or talking against time, and, although pronounced in his own opinions and zealous in every cause he adopted, he never stooped to tactics that were unworthy of his high legislative position or derogatory to the assembly of which he was a member. Scotsmen in the lower house of Congress have been plentiful enough all through its history, and in the Fifty-first Congress, for instance, there were no fewer than five Congressmen—D. B. Henderson of Dubuque, Iowa, a native of Old Deer, Aberdeenshire; David Kerr of Grundy Centre, Iowa, a native of Dalry, Ayrshire; J. M. Farquhar of Buffalo, N. Y., a native of Ayr; W. G. Laidlaw of Ellicottville, N. Y., a native of Jedburgh, and John L. Macdonald of Shakopee, Minn. This, considering that Scotsmen do not take professionally to politics, like their Irish cousins, seems to us a pretty fair showing.

CHAPTER XI.

AMONG THE WOMEN

IN the course of the present work we have several times mentioned the name of women who have, for some laudable reason or other, acquired publicity or deserved remembrance. But even with the mention of these, scant justice has been done to the claims of "the lassies" to a share in all that has made the Scottish name honorable in America. It may not therefore be inappropriate to make the ladies the text for one chapter in this book, and in the few names we will mention we are sure it will be seen that the fair sex has not been behind the other in good deeds and kindly ways. It is, of course, difficult to get information regarding women's work, for most of them prefer to do what good they can without attracting publicity, and in the quiet of the domestic circle many matters have been suggested and planned and projected which have done grand work in the world. The Scotchwoman is naturally a housewife, bending her energies to the care of the home in which she is recognized as queen, and planning and contriving day out and day in for the comfort of those who look to her for all the pleasures which are associated with domestic life. If she be blessed with children her whole heart goes out to them, and in the development of their minds, their physical and mental progress, as well as their material welfare, she devotes herself with a degree of self-abnegation which is one of the highest and grandest tributes to the real majesty of her sex. But for having been left a widow, with a young family totally unprovided for, it is questionable if Mrs. Grant of Laggan would ever have aspired to the honors of authorship or emerged from the happy obscurity of her own fireside. That wonderful and irrepressible production of nature and art generally called " a woman with a mission " has her representatives in and out of Scotland, but as a general rule Scotswomen who have become famous have become so by force of circumstances bringing into action their innate sentiments of patriotism, charity, and love. Outside of the people of the stage and concert platform, and, of course, outside of the woman with the aforesaid mission whose vanity is the cause of all her silliness, we never yet heard of a Scotswoman who started out in life or cut out a career for herself with the idea of becoming famous or of even acquiring undue publicity. The fame which has come to so many of them has been the result of work well done, of service to God and humanity faithfully rendered, and of simple, trustful devotion to duty in whatever sphere and circumstances they happened to be placed.

From a historical standpoint, the most famous of all the women of Scotland who have had a home in America was Flora Macdonald, the noblest of all the heroines whose name comes down to us with that of Bonnie Prince Charlie. She was a simple, honest Highland girl, with wonderful strength of mind, fertility of resource, rigid devotion to whatever she deemed to be right; a brave heart, with all a woman's modesty and grace. Judging her by the portraits which have come down to us, she was by no means a beauty; her features were interesting rather than prepossessing, but she had a wonderful pair of eyes that lighted up her countenance, and the vivacity of her conversation, the charm of her smile, and the sprightliness of her slim figure more than compensated for mere beauty of features. She played a difficult part, under peculiar circumstances, and in company with a man whose love for the fair sex often overcame his sense of duty and interfered even with the progress of his life ambition, yet against her personal repute no whisper has yet been raised, and she emerged from the ordeal of her life as simple and honest a Highland lass as she was before she ever risked her liberty and reputation to save the head of the young Chevalier.

Flora Macdonald, the daughter of Macdonald of Milton, in South Uist, was born there in 1722. Her father, who was what was known as a tacksman—a farmer of means apart from the income of the land he leased—died when Flora was a child, and her mother some years afterward married Macdonald of Armadale, in the Isle of Skye, who, during the rebellion, was on the side of the Government and commanded one of the militia companies raised for King George's service by Sir Alexander Macdonald. At the same time it must be said that, though arrayed against Prince Charlie, Flora's stepfather not only wished no harm to befall the Prince, but once at least aided very materially in his escape. Flora was in her twenty-fourth year when she entered on her romantic task and the details of her wanderings with the " King o' the Highland Hearts " are too well known to need recapitulation here. The whole episode lasted only a few weeks, but during that time Flora's services won for her a niche among the heroines of Scotland and a place in the hearts of the Highlanders only second to that of the Wanderer, for the disclosure of whose identity a fortune was offered without effect.

After the Prince had escaped, Flora was arrested and carried to London a prisoner, but her treatment was of the most lenient description. After receiving attentions that might have turned the head of any young woman less endowed with strong common sense than herself, after being, in fact, one of the pets of a London season, she was permitted to reside under a sort of parole in the house of a private family in the metropolis until after the passing of the act of indemnity in July, 1746, when she was formally set at liberty and returned to her beloved Highlands. In 1750 she married Alexander Macdonald, younger, of Kingsburgh, a family that had much to do with the escape of Prince Charles.

In 1773 Macdonald, like many other Highlanders, hearing of the ease with which large tracts of land were acquired by settlement in the New World, determined to emigrate, and a year later found him and his devoted wife and family settled at Fayetteville, North Carolina.

Around that place at that time there were hundreds of Highlanders, many of whom had settled in America after Culloden, and it is said that Gaelic was very generally spoken in six counties, with Fayetteville as a centre. We can imagine with what enthusiasm the Highland chief and his heroic wife were received on their arrival. They afterward resided at Cameron Hill, not far from Fayetteville, and Macdonald was preparing to settle down to his new way of life when the grumblings which presaged the Revolution drove an element of uncertainty into Colonial life. When hostilities opened, Macdonald drew his sword as loyally to support the Government of King George as ever Highland sword was drawn for the Stuarts, and accepted a commission in a detachment raised among the Highlanders of North Carolina in 1775 to form part of the Royal Highland Emigrant Regiment. This command was made up of veterans, mainly in Canada, and its headquarters were there. Drawn from various settlements, the men had great difficulty in getting to their rallying place on the banks of the St. Lawrence, and the detachment to which Macdonald belonged, besides the fatigue of the weary miles that separated Canada from Carolina, had to face armed resistance to their progress, and finally were forced to break up into small parties, and reached their destination by various routes. Macdonald saw much active service in Canada, was in Quebec when it was defended against Arnold and when the American leader Montgomery fell, and took part in various minor enterprises.

In 1783, when hostilities were over, Macdonald, who had attained the rank of Captain and could have obtained an extensive grant of land in Nova Scotia, preferred to return to his native land on half pay. On the journey across to Scotland the vessel on which the Macdonalds were was attacked by a French privateer, and in the encounter Flora's natural courage asserted itself. She refused to seek safety below, and remained on deck, animating the seamen and rushing from place to place where a word might do good or a little assistance help matters. In the course of the fray her arm was broken, but she had the consciousness of having aided in winning a victory. After many other adventures the party reached Skye in safety and never afterward left it. Flora died in 1790 and was laid to rest in the burial ground of the Kingsburgh family, at Kilmuir, and in 1796 her husband was laid beside her. They had a family, says Dr. Carruthers, of five sons and two daughters. "The sons all became officers in the army and the daughters officers' wives." None of the family became conspicuous excepting Lieut. Col. John Macdonald. He was born in Skye in 1759 and entered the service of the East India Company, attaining the rank of Captain of Engineers. His scientific attainments were very great, and he was a frequent contributor to the transactions of learned societies, while on military matters he was an advanced critic, and the many works on that science which he published during his career were judged to be of the highest practical value by those qualified to estimate. In 1800 he was appointed Lieutenant Colonel of the Clan Alpine regiment, a command of Highlanders raised by Col. Alexander Macgregor Murray and enrolled at Stirling in 1797 for service in any part of Europe. Col. Macdonald served with this regiment in several parts of Ireland, and continued its active head until it was disbanded at Stirling, in 1802. In his later years he paid great attention to the science of telegraphy in its relation to the military and naval services especially, and published in 1816 a Telegraphic Dictionary of some 150,000 words, phrases, and sentences, which was regarded as a model of ingenuity and usefulness. He died at Exeter, full of years and honors, in 1831.

In the whole gallery of notable and noble women of the world no figure stands out in more beautiful relief than that of Isabella Graham of New-York as an example of constant endeavor in doing her Master's work, in the accomplishment of much practical good, and for her own sweet, blameless life. She knew what it was to suffer, she had to face the world as a breadwinner for her family, she felt what it was to be poor, yet she never lost her faith and never was so poor that she had not something to give to those whose necessities were even greater than her own. Much of what she accomplished still remains actively at work in the city which was so long her home and with which her memory is most identified, and, although her name is now almost forgotten by the passing throng, the influence she exerted upon the community is year after year bringing forth fruit.

Mrs. Graham was the daughter of John Marshall, a farmer in Lanarkshire. She was born at Heads, in the Parish of Glassford, in 1740, and soon afterward her parents removed to a farm at Elderslie, near Paisley, where she spent her early years and received her education. Dr. Witherspoon, afterward President of Princeton College, was at that time a minister in Paisley, and under his teaching the maiden so grew in religious knowledge and conviction that she was admitted to the communion table in her seventeenth year, an early age in Scotland at that time. As Scotchwomen often say, her troubles began when she was married. In 1765 she was wedded to Dr. John Graham, a surgeon in Paisley. He was soon afterward appointed Surgeon in the Sixtieth Regiment, and two years later the young wife accompanied him to his post of duty at Quebec. Mrs. Graham was not altogether displeased with Quebec, but her heart yearned for " hame." She did not in particular like the idea of attending a Presbyterian service in a Roman Catholic church. The images, altars, pictures, etc., seemed out of place in a house of worship, but as she grew to take no notice of them she hoped that " the Almighty, who knows the heart, would not be offended at our being there." From Quebec the regiment went to Montreal, thence to Niagara, and in 1774 to the Island of Antigua. There Dr. Graham died of fever, and his widow, with three little daughters and a baby son, was left almost penniless.

She managed to return to Scotland, and, finding her father a widower and poor, she supported herself and little ones by establishing a small school in Paisley. This was so successful that she was soon able to remove to Edinburgh, where she opened a boarding school, and prospered exceedingly. As her means grew she took an active part in charitable work, to which she scrupulously devoted a tenth part of all her earnings. She organized a Penny Bank to encourage the very poor to save, and out of that institution grew the Society for the Relief of the Destitute Sick, which is still actively carrying on its blessed work in Auld Reekie. We need not mention Mrs. Graham's career in her native land further than to say that she earned a living for herself and little ones as a teacher, did much good among the poor, and raised up for her household many friends.

Among these were Mrs. Scott, (mother of Scotland's great novelist and poet,) and the sainted Lady Glenorchy, whose story is one of the many refreshing bits of biography of which the lives of Scottish religious women have been so productive. Lady Glenorchy had the warmest admiration for Mrs. Graham, and entered into her charitable and religious schemes with much zeal. She took her daughter, Joanna, to her home for a time, and then sent her to Rotterdam to complete her studies. Mrs. Graham attended this Christian lady during the illness which ended in her death, and was by her will the recipient of a bequest of £200.

In 1789, at the request of Dr. Witherspoon and other friends in New-York, Mrs. Graham, with her bairns, settled in New-York. Soon after she landed she opened a school, and within a month had fifty pupils. Until 1798, when she retired, she ranked among the most successful teachers in the American commercial metropolis. But, deeply interested as she was in the cause of education, she delighted more than all things else in " going about doing good." She wrote her own religious experiences and thoughts and had them printed in tract form from time to time, and these she distributed with her own hands in the houses of the very poor, hoping that her practical sympathy for them in their sorrows and sufferings would cause them to take to their hearts the higher message she brought. A tenth of her income, as in Edinburgh, was still regularly distributed in relieving the distressed, and as her goodness and gentleness and patient tenderness became understood and appreciated, this brave, God-fearing Scotchwoman entered harmlessly, and was even welcomed into places—they could hardly be called homes—where many men would not have dared to penetrate. Her pastor, the Rev. J. M. Mason, was amazed at her courage, and reproached her for her temerity, but she never faltered in carrying on her self-appointed work among the poor. Remembering her own forlorn and helpless condition when her husband died, she was especially interested in cases where the bread-winner of a family had been removed, and by her kindly sympathy softened the blow of many a bitter bereavement.

In her school work Mrs. Graham was very effectively aided by her children, but her main reliance seems to have been on her daughter Joanna. The school, it may be said, from the first was a financial success, the Grahams were soon in fairly comfortable circumstances, and were welcomed into the best and most refined society in New York.

As might be expected in a girl who had enjoyed the care of such a mother as Isabella Graham, and the friendship of a woman like Lady Glenorchy, Joanna was, from her earliest years, animated by a deeply religious spirit. When she settled in New York, in her nineteenth year, her sentiments were as fixed as ever. One gentleman—an Irishman—who was paying her attentions, said that when he married her he would take her where she would never hear the sound of a church bell. That settled his case. Her next wooer was a wealthy merchant, but she declined his proffers for some reason. Then Divie Bethune, at that time a young merchant on Broadway, near Wall Street, without a superabundance of means, laid siege to her heart, and in proposing, according to her story, "adverted to his poverty and talked much of living by faith." She construed this to mean that Divie was not in circumstances to support her, and so refused him. But Divie had a stanch ally in Mrs. Graham, who thought him one of the best men in the world, and so, when the young woman told her mother of the interview and its result, the good old lady simply said: "Joanna, if he has asked you in faith, he'll get you in spite of your teeth." Divie did not take "no" for an answer, and in July, 1795, the two were married.

From that time Mrs. Graham and Mrs. Bethune and her husband were united in every good work—a glorious trio whose highest aim was to do good through the spirit of the Saviour, and until death stepped in and, one after the other, carried them off to a higher sphere, the life story of the three run on the same lines.

Mrs. Bethune's active career in well-doing commenced with her marriage, and here it may be said that a happier union than that of the Bethunes, during the twenty-nine years it lasted, could hardly be imagined. During part of that time old Mrs. Graham was a member of the household, and the warmest affection animated every one in the home. Mrs. Graham and Divie Bethune were hand in hand in all good works, and Divie had a theory that women understood the practical workings of benevolence and Christian endeavor better than men, and so was ever willing to follow the lead of his wife and his mother-in-law.

Divie Bethune was a native of Ross-shire, a Presbyterian, and an honest, conscientious, God-fearing man. He had fairly prospered in business, was not rich by any means, but had established a trade that promised steady and increasing, if not extravagant, returns. He was active in Scotch matters, for he was an enthusiast in all things pertaining to his native land, and in the cause of religion he was noted from his arrival in New York for his earnest and faithful work. He appointed himself a missionary among the poor, and gave away hundreds of Bibles and good books while relieving the pressing necessities of each case of actual poverty with a liberal hand. No wonder that the heart of Isabella Graham warmed to this typical Scottish merchant as soon as she became acquainted with him, and that it was with peculiar satisfaction she witnessed his marriage to her daughter Joanna. While Mrs. Graham lived she and her son-in-law were associated in many Christian enterprises, and

Divie Bethune revered her. In her later years, especially, Mrs. Graham mainly made her home "at Divie's," and nowhere was she more warmly welcomed. We hear a good deal of mothers-in-law. They are credited with causing much trouble and any amount of fun, and an incredible number of silly jokes have been concocted at their expense. In this case, Mrs. Graham loved her son-in-law as a mother loves her son, and he looked up to her with truly filial affection. A day or two before her death, in 1814, she penned the following tribute to his worth in a letter to a friend: "According to knowledge, observation, and even investigation, Divie Bethune stands, in my mind, in temper, conduct, and conversation, the nearest to the Gospel standard of any man or woman I ever knew as intimately. Devoted to his God, to his Church, to his family, to all to whom he may have opportunity of doing good, duty is his governing principle."

In 1796 Divie Bethune was one of the managers of the St. Andrew's Society, and had personally to attend to the distribution of its charity along with the other managers, for these officials at that time were the almoners of the organization. Bethune, of course, had to refuse relief from the funds to many worthy applicants whose cases did not come properly within the province of the society, and Mrs. Bethune at once saw the necessity for a general organization which would help the most pressing at least of such cases. Woman-like, her heart went out to the widows with young children, and, besides helping such cases as her means permitted and collecting aid for them among her acquaintances, she set about the formation of a society which would more systematically do the work. She found able coadjutors in her husband and in her mother, and in the same year the Society for the Relief of Poor Widows with Small Children was organized, and it exists to this day.

Thus the influence for good of the St. Andrew's Society was shown in a direction which its members never anticipated; but it was destined to bear still further fruit. When the widows' society had been in operation for a few years it was seen that its scope was not broad enough to enable it to assist orphan children; so in 1806 the Orphan Asylum of New York was organized, mainly by the efforts of Mrs. Graham and her daughter, Mrs. Bethune, and it is still one of the most active charities of this city. Divie Bethune called the meeting which led to the organization, and while he lived spent much of his Sundays in the asylum and was ever ready to help it. For half a century Mrs. Bethune was active in the work of superintending the asylum, and only retired from her labors when advanced age incapacitated her. It is curious to think how these two societies—the one for widows and children and the other for orphans—really owed their origin to the election of Divie Bethune as a manager of the St. Andrew's Society.

In 1801 Mr. and Mrs. Bethune visited Scotland, and one result was the real beginning of the Sabbath school movement in this country. The first Sabbath school in America of which we have record was founded by Quakers in Philadelphia in 1791. In 1792 Mrs. Graham organized a Sunday school for young women in New-York. While in Scotland Mrs. Bethune saw the importance of such schools, as we now understand them, for religious instruction, and began at once an effort to have the same missionary spirit at work among the children here that she saw in her motherland. Ill health, family cares, and the amount of work already on hand prevented her from making headway with her project, and the war of 1812 put an end to it altogether apparently, but Mrs. Bethune never relaxed in her purposes, and even when the project seemed hopeless continued in correspondence with friends in Scotland so as to keep posted on the varying phases of the Sabbath school movement there. At length, in 1816, by the organization of the Female Sabbath School Union of New-York, the real foundation of the present system in this country was laid, and by her work in this connection Mrs. Bethune fairly earned her title of "Mother of Sabbath Schools in America."

Divie Bethune died in 1824 and his widow survived until 1860, and until the infirmities of years compelled her to stand aside she continued her interest in all good work.

It is impossible in this place to enter into details regarding other spheres of Joanna Bethune's usefulness, of her work in Church matters, in infant schools, in industrial schools, and in practical benevolence of all kinds. She was not a "woman with a mission," but a woman with a dozen missions, and her whole life of ninety years may justly be said to have been spent in doing her Master's work. Busy as she was, her home duties were never neglected, and few men had a happier home than Divie Bethune, and few children had more of a mother's care than did her own beloved little ones.

It is hardly possible to imagine a life more pure, more holy, more devoted to doing good, more self-denying, more full of humble faith, than that of Isabella Graham, and the same may be said of her daughter Joanna. Both women had their share of the trials, vexations, and sorrows of this life, yet they never faltered in their devoted trust or in their implicit faith that all things are ordered for the best. The life of Mrs. Bethune, like that of her mother, showed that sectarian differences are, after all, divisions in name only, and that religion and good works break down the barrier of the issues which have arisen to distract Christianity from the pre-eminence of the real message of the Gospels. Mrs. Graham rejoiced to see that her lifework was certain to be carried on by her daughter, and the daughter in her turn saw her son preaching the Gospel with much acceptance and fruit.

That son, the Rev. Dr. G. W. Bethune of Brooklyn, was born in New York in 1805, and after being educated at Dickinson College and at Princeton, became in 1828 pastor of a Dutch Reformed Church at Rhinebeck, N. Y. His next charge was at Utica, and in 1843 he went to Philadelphia. In 1849 he was called to take charge of a newly organized congregation in Brooklyn, and remained there ten years, when he went to Italy in search of health. He returned after a time, resumed his pastoral labors in Brooklyn, and made a notable public appearance and eloquent oration at a meeting held in New York to advocate the maintenance of the Union on April 20, 1861. Shortly afterward his health again gave way and he returned to Italy, where he died suddenly, in 1862. He was eloquent as a preacher, faithful in the administration of his pastoral work, and won the love of every congregation to which he ministered. His published writings were many, and his prose works were noted for their chaste diction and the clearness and crispness of their style. As a theologian he was not only profound, but had the happy art of stating even the most profound truths in language that a child might understand. But it is as a poet that he will be remembered in connection with literature, and his " Lays of Love and Faith " stamped him as a writer of rich fancy and one possessing true poetic insight and sentiment. In his poetry, too, we find the true patriotism of Isabella Graham and his father and mother reproduced and perpetuated, for it was the hallowed influence of Divie Bethune's fireside that inspired in after years his son to pen that most popular, and to the Scot abroad most dear, of modern Scottish lyrics:

> " O! Sing to me the auld Scotch sangs,
>   I' the braid Scottish tongue,
> The sangs my father loved to hear,
>   The sangs my mither sung
> When she sat beside my cradle,
>   Or croon'd me on her knee;
> An' I wadna sleep, she sang sae sweet,
>   The auld Scotch sangs to me."

A very pronounced type of the woman with a mission, but so earnest in her mission that she had none of the peculiarities which inspire contempt or arouse amusement for that class, was Fanny Wright, after whom, in the early anti-slavery days, so many abolitionist societies were named. She was born at Dundee in 1795, and in early life made a special study of Smith's " Wealth of Nations " and other works on political philosophy. She developed into a close and original thinker on such topics, and her earliest publication was a defense of the doctrines of Epicurus.

From 1818 till 1821 she resided in the United States,

mainly engaged in travel and paying particular attention to the social and religious communities then in existence, and to the slavery question in all its bearings. Then she returned to Europe and traveled over the Continent, gathering new ideas and adding to her store of knowledge as she journeyed. In 1825 she determined to turn her accomplishments to some practical purpose, and accordingly returned to America to wrestle with the slave problem. She bought some 2,500 acres of land in Tennessee as a place for the residence of emancipated negroes, so that, dwelling together in a compact colony, they might not only acquire a sense of independence by earning their own livelihood, but be sufficiently under her control that she might readily put into practice several theories she had formed for their advancement. The colony, however, turned out a failure. The time was not ripe then for such an attempt. Though disheartened greatly at the upshot of this well-meant endeavor, she did not abandon the cause of the slave, and by her lectures and speeches did much to foster and strengthen the sentiment against the accursed traffic, which was then becoming a live issue in public affairs in the Northern States. It is singular that, though retaining her Scotch accent, she had no difficulty in rousing her audiences, the very earnestness of her manner making all else be forgotten while she occupied the platform.

Becoming acquainted with Robert Dale Owen, Miss Wright adopted many of that dreamer's ideas and tried to aid him in his work at the settlement at New-Harmony, Ind. She edited the " Gazette " there, and worked hard to make the experiment a success, but her nature and that of Owen were not congenial, and she abandoned the enterprise. Crossing the ocean again, she took up her residence in Paris and married a Frenchman named D'Arusmont, but marriage is never a happy state for a woman with a mission, and this union was not a fortunate one. The pair separated, and, making her home once more in the United States, the gifted Scotchwoman entered upon a busy career, writing and lecturing on social and religious topics, and advancing often such extreme and outré views as to subject her to persecution, ridicule, and sometimes opprobrium. She was a voluminous writer, although little that came from her pen now survives. But such books as her "Views on Society and Manners in America" and "Lectures on Free Inquiry" were much read and discussed in their day. She essayed poetry also, but it has passed away into the misty sea where nearly all literary efforts, with the exception of a comparatively few, sooner or later find their way, and even her tragedy of "Altorf," which was produced at the Park Theatre, in New York, in 1817, has long since been forgotten. She died at Cincinnati in 1852. She was a woman whose thoughts were constantly directed away from self to doing good in the world, and, while we may regard her energies and endeavors to have been to a great extent wasted, and her life to that extent a failure, we should not forget her efforts in behalf of the slave, exerted at a time when such efforts were comparatively few, and to believe that she in that respect at least did much good and aided very greatly in the progress of the movement which, once started, could have no other termination than equal rights in free America for all men, black or white.

CHAPTER XII.

PUBLIC ENTERTAINERS.

SCOTTISH entertainments and entertainers have from a very early period been remarkably popular in America. When the country had grown populous enough to give the drama a foothold, Scotch actors were very numerously represented among the followers of the Thespian art who ventured to cross the Atlantic and find a new field for their talents. While, like most pioneers, they did not themselves fare very well at the hands of fortune, there is no doubt that they started the American stage on a high level, so that it is to-day the equal of any stage in the world, not even excepting those of London and Paris. Scottish music, too, has invariably been popular here, and, although they seem unable to grasp the delightful smoothness of the grand old Doric, a privilege only vouchsafed (except in a few instances) to a native, many American amateurs sing the songs of the "Land of the Kilt and Feather" with a degree of taste and with so thorough an appreciation as to warm the heart of even the most obdurate of Scottish listeners. Of course, a Scotsman would any day prefer to hear his country's songs sung by a native, but the perfection attained in the singing of these by those who are not natives, and especially by non-natives who are of the tender sex, is gratifying at once to his patriotism and his musical sentiments. At times, too, one who is not a native struggles so successfully with the vernacular that it is difficult to detect a false accent, and, to take an illustrious instance, it may be remarked that Sims Reeves when singing a Scotch song presented the Doric so faultlessly as to give the Glasgow folks a chance for ventilating a tradition that the greatest of English tenors used in his younger days to act in a booth on the Green, Glasgow's historic public park, and that he there learned how to sing!

One of the first of really great Scottish singers to try his fortune on this side of the Atlantic was John Sinclair, a native of Edinburgh, where he was born in 1793. He made his first appearance in America in the old Park Theatre, New-York, in 1837, when he appeared as Francis Osbaldistone. An old Scot who was present on that evening has left on record a statement that he had never before, not even in "Auld Reekie," heard "The Macgregors' Gathering" sung with more fire, or "My Love Is Like a Red, Red Rose" with more sweetness. Possibly this was because absence from home had sharpened his sympathies, and the sentiments which arise when a wanderer's thoughts turn back to "Auld Lang Syne" usurped the ordinary powers of criticism so natural in a Scot. However this may be, Sinclair before visiting America had earned the reputation in Scotland of being the best living interpreter of his country's songs, and his memory is still kept green in the musical history of his native land. He captured his New York audience from the moment he first appeared, and his engagement was in every way a most successful one. He repeated his success shortly afterward at the Chestnut Street Theatre, Philadelphia, as well as, later on, in Boston. At that time, by the way, a success in Boston was as gratifying to an artist as was one in Edinburgh.

"Sinclair," once wrote John Forbes Robertson of London to David Kennedy, "was a frank, genial fellow, ["the leddies' bonnie Sinclair," he used to be called,] and among his Scottish songs were 'Hey! the Bonnie Briestknots' and one of his own composition, 'Come, Sit Ye Down, My Bonny, Bonny Love.'" One of Sinclair's daughters married Edwin Forrest, the famous tragedian, and the union gave rise to one of the most notable divorce trials ever held in America. Forrest, by the way, claimed to have descended from Scotch ancestors, and asserted that Montrose was their old home. Sinclair returned to England, and died there in 1857.

The next vocalist from Scotland to visit these shores, and the grandest of them all, was John Wilson, who was born at Edinburgh in 1800, and at ten years of age was sent to learn the printing business. When his apprenticeship was over he became a proofreader in James Ballantyne's printing office, and is said to have been one of the few to whom the secret of the authorship of the Waverley Novels was made known. During this time, however, he was studying music and training his voice to speak as well as sing, and, in spite of the protestations of his friends, he made his first appearance on the stage, at Edinburgh, in 1830, assuming the character of Henry Bertram in the opera of "Guy Mannering." His success was complete. Wilson determined, in the height of his powers, to make an American tour, and he landed in the New World in 1838, and remained for two years. He was beyond question one of the most accomplished vocalists of his time, and, though he had made a brilliant reputation on the operatic stage, and had won laurels as a writer and as a composer, he was never happier or better than when singing the sweet and simple songs of his "ain countrie." His entertainments, such as "A Nicht wi' Burns," or "Bonnie Prince Charlie," proved wonderfully popular wherever he gave them, not merely among the Scottish auditors, whose enthusiasm knew no bounds, but among educated Americans and lovers of music of all classes. That he raised Scottish song to a high degree of popularity goes without saying, and he paved the way for the more complete financial success, long afterward, of the entertainments of the same class given by the late David Kennedy.

In 1849, accompanied by his wife and daughter, Wilson entered upon another American tour. While at Quebec, he was seized with cholera on July 7, and died two days later. His last wish was to be buried in a Scottish grave, but the circumstances of the case forbade that wish being carried into effect, and the great singer was laid at rest in Mount Hermon Cemetery, Quebec, and a handsome memorial was erected over the spot by his admirers. "Although far from his dearly beloved 'North

Countrie,'" wrote Gen. James Grant Wilson of New York long afterward, " Wilson is surrounded by men of his own race, on whose tombstones may be seen Mackenzie and Macdougall, Campbell and Grant, Fraser and Forsyth, Ross, Turnbull, and other ancient Scottish names, many, if not most, of them the sons and grandsons of the 672 gallant fellows of Fraser's Seventy-eighth Highlanders, who followed Wolfe up the steep and narrow escalade to the field where he met his fate."

So far as America is concerned, Wilson's great successor as a singer of Scottish songs was David Kennedy. He was born at Perth in 1825, and died at Stratford, Canada, while on a professional tour, in October, 1886, and for some forty years he was before the public as a singer of Scotch songs. He sang the ballads of his native land round the world, visiting India, Africa, Australia, as well as every section of the United States and Canada.

While Kennedy's programmes were modeled on those of Wilson, and to a great extent presented the same songs, there was a wide difference in the style of their entertainments. Wilson was a faultless singer, a student of music, and as firm a believer in the sweetness, power, and melody, native to Scotch music, as is the modern American dilettante in the genius of Richard Wagner. Kennedy was by no means so grand a singer as Wilson; he never claimed to be so, in fact; but he had the knack of getting, as it were, into the heart of a song, and making every shade of its meaning become perfectly clear to his audiences. He was in many ways the best modern representative of the old Scotch minstrel we can imagine. Nobody ever excelled him in the telling of an old Scotch story, for he did not merely repeat such tales, he acted them, and filled the stage or the platform with their personages, and there was that strong personal magnetism about the man which is so indispensably requisite to public success on the concert or lecture platform.

The wonderful success of Wilson and Kennedy induced many Scottish singers, singly or in groups, to " cross the pond," and since they illustrated the fact that there was money in an auld Scotch song, there has rarely been a season when we have not had the pleasure of listening to native talent of various degrees of ability. The Fraser family of Paisley won, as they deserved, more reputation than any of them, and the Fairbairn family were also successful for a time. Phillis Glover, wife of Thomas Powrie, the once-famous Rob Roy, sang in New York for a season in 1875, and might have done well had not domestic trouble prevented her from taking advantage of her opportunities. William Gourlay, one of the Edinburgh family of that name, essayed a season in New York in 1877 with his "Mrs. MacGregor's Levee," but failed. Hamilton Corbett would have made a fortune had he been gifted with as much strength of will as beauty of voice, and that might, too, be said of a score of others whose names need not be repeated here. We cannot, however, forbear a line to the memory of Jeannie Watson, one of the sweetest female singers of Scottish songs we ever listened to, and who, after a life of misfortune, now lies at rest in the burial plot of the St. Andrew's Society of Toronto. She was a brilliant successor to such singers as Miss Reynolds and Miss Sutherland. The latter, who made her American bow at a ballad concert in New York on July 16, 1857, won high rank as a ballad singer, and was especially a favorite in Scottish circles. She described herself, or her managers described her, as "the Scottish Nightingale," and in that respect she was the forerunner of a host of "Scottish Nightingales," "Queens of Scottish Song," and so on, good, bad, and very indifferent.

Turning to theatrical records, we are met at the outset by the difficulty of stage names concealing the nationality and identity of many whose birth and talents ought to have given them some mention in these pages. The well-known antipathy which so long prevailed in Scotland against "play actors" led most of the Scotch aspirants to footlight fame to conceal their family names more closely than those who adopted a stage name for the sake of its appearance, as Melfort looks better on a programme than Hodgkins. But both Scotch plays and

Scotch players have won more than ordinary popularity in America.

In the early dramatic history of the United States the play that appears to have been the most general favorite was Home's now almost forgotten tragedy of "Douglas." Probably more American amateurs made their first bow before the public as professionals in the character of Norval than in any other up to the close of the first half of this century, and in early American playbills it constantly held a place. The best Scotch personator of the character here was Henry Erskine Johnston, who made his first American appearance in the National Theatre, New York, in 1838, in the character of Sir Pertinax in the still popular play of "The Man of the World." Johnston was a good and painstaking actor of the old school, and his Norval won thunders of applause in all the principal cities of the country, North and South. He played in the States only one season, and returned to Britain, dying there shortly after, in 1840.

Roderick Dhu was another Scotch character which was a favorite with the public, but it was only in the large theatres that the necessary scenic and spectacular display could be made to warrant the production of its play, "The Lady of the Lake." It was placed upon the stage, however, in Boston and New York, and J. H. Wallack, especially, made a great hit as the irate Highland chieftain. Of "Rob Roys" the American theatres were at one time full, and the Bowery boys used to be as familiar with the wrongs of the Macgregors as were the laddies in "Auld Reekie." None of the great Scotch Robs ever came here, but among its first delineators, if not the very first, was an actor from Edinburgh named Bennett, who had been a member of the company in that city, playing minor parts, under Murray. He made his opening bow as Rob in the old Chestnut Street Theatre, Philadelphia, in 1831, and was fairly successful. A much more able representative of the great cateran, however, was Thomas F. Lennox, a Glasgow man, who appeared in the character in the Chatham Theatre, New York, in 1838, and made a great hit. His personal appearance exactly suited the character. He had a powerful yet not unpleasant voice, and every time he started in to denounce the Sassenachs he made the gallery howl in chorus. Lennox was a good all-round actor, and a great favorite wherever he appeared. He died at Memphis, Tenn., in 1849.

Quite a different sort of a Rob was John Henry Anderson, the "Wizard of the North," as he called himself in his advertisements and showbills. He first visited this country in 1851, and besides giving exhibitions of his really wonderful skill as a magician produced "Rob Roy" at Castle Garden, this city, with himself in the title rôle. Its merit may be understood from the remark of one of the most competent American critics of the time, that "Anderson was a very good magician, but a very bad actor."

In one way or another the redoubtable "Rob" has had his name kept pretty well before the American public, possibly because Sir Walter Scott's novel of that name has enjoyed a larger American circulation than that of any other of the romances of "The Author of Waverley." The novel has appeared in nearly all the popular "series" of "standard works," without which no American publisher's catalogue seems complete, and in all other sorts of cheap series with which the United States market is flooded. Even James Grant's story of "The Adventures of Rob Roy" has been issued in editions of thousands, and in more than one instance it has been given as a "supplement" to a Sunday newspaper.

But perhaps the most curious illustration of the popularity of the name was when it was used as the title to a comic opera in which the genuine cateran did not appear at all. It was written by a gentleman named Harry B. Smith, and from a historical point of view contained more sheer nonsense than possibly any other stage arrangement seriously or humorously founded on history. Its leading character was Rob Roy MacGregor, a Highland Chief, although the cateran was not a "chief" at all, and the cast describes him as a follower of Prince Charlie, although the real Rob died in 1738, when Prince Charlie's ideas of Scotland were the primitive ones of youth. Then we had the "Mayor" of Perth, who was an Englishman, and who seemed to have been the depositary of the ready money which the Government intended to spend in subduing the forces of Prince Charlie. There were all sorts of odd situations in the play, one of which showed us Prince Charlie as a prisoner in Stirling Castle, from which he was liberated by the efforts of Flora Macdonald, and the whole affair wound up with the marriage, or the arrangements for the marriage, of that young lady—who, by the way, was dressed throughout in a Highland male costume—and the Prince.

But lest some of our readers might think we are exaggerating the bundle of improbabilities and absurdities thus presented, we reprint here the synopsis of the play which appeared on the official programme:

"The story of 'Rob Roy' is very interesting, inasmuch as it is founded on that romantic story of Sir Walter Scott's which deals with the escapades of Prince Edward Stewart the Pretender and his faithful follower, Rob Roy Macgregor. At the opening of the first act a party of Highlanders make a raid upon the house of the Mayor of Perth and appropriate a sum of money intrusted to that worthy for English troops. The Mayor has a fair daughter, Janet, who is secretly married to Rob Roy. Owing to the Mayor's desire to keep on good terms with both the English and the Scotch, he compels Janet to declare herself the wife of first an old Scotchman and then a young English officer. As a mere declaration constitutes a Scotch marriage, Janet finds herself the wife of three husbands belonging to opposing factions. Throughout the first act the romantic interest is maintained by Prince Charlie and his sweetheart, Flora Macdonald, whose adventures have historical foundation. At the end of the act Janet deserts the two husbands provided by her father and escapes to the Highlands with Rob Roy. The scene of the second act is laid in the Highlands, when the Scotch are in hiding after the battle of Culloden. Janet, as a Highland shepherd, is waiting for the return of Rob Roy, who is fighting at Culloden. The greater part of the act is devoted to the machinations of the Highlanders to prevent the capture of their bonnie Prince Charlie. The act ends with Flora Macdonald giving herself up for the Prince. The third act, which shows the exterior of Stirling Castle by moonlight, with the English troops in bivouac, sees everything happily arranged."

Amusing as this production was on account of its silly distortion of historical matter, a distortion which was not even required by the story, it was infinitely more respectable than a rendering of " Rob Roy " which was given in Chicago in 1895. We did not see this production, fortunately, but the following advertisement of its glories will sufficiently indicate to the reader its unique character: "'Rob Roy' will be given in the great amphitheatre, Burlington Park, Saturday, Aug. 3, 1895, under the auspices of the Scottish Assembly. Twelve special acts will be presented in tableaux and pantomime. Sham battle—Highlanders and Zouaves vs. First Regiment, I. N. G. Thrilling and exciting conflict. Cannon roar, volley after volley fired, terrific fusillade; with great confusion the enemy is routed amid the applause of 10,000 spectators. The bold chieftain is free! The park will be on blaze during the evening with electric lights, so that the presentation of the soul-stirring drama will be produced with all the magnificent splendor possible."

But we must return to the players themselves, and dwell among a few names which are more or less representative, although most of them are now forgotten, for nothing is more fleeting and perishable than a player's stage reputation.

Mr. and Mrs. Marriott, who came here from Edinburgh in 1794, made the old John Street Theatre be crowded to the doors each time they appeared in " The Fair Penitent," and they repeated that success in Philadelphia and Boston and in whatever city they performed.

In 1810, in the same New York theatre, a Dundee man named David Mackenzie made an equally great hit as Flint in the now long-buried play of " The Adopted Child." He afterward made a very successful tour through the country, but for some reason now unknown he ended his life by suicide at Philadelphia toward the close of 1811.

One of the greatest favorites of the Bowery stage around 1826 was a Fife man named James Roberts, who was born in 1798, and died at Charleston, S. C., in 1833. In melodrama, either as a villain or as a hero, he was considered to have no equal. As much, at least, might be said of Richard L. Graham, a Glasgow actor, whose first appearance was made at the National Theatre, Philadelphia, in 1840, and who continued on the American stage until his death, at St. Louis, in 1857.

Another Scotch actor who was a great favorite in his time in New York was John Mason, a native of Edinburgh, who made a hit on his first appearance in America at the old Park Theatre as Rover in "Wild Oats." He afterward studied medicine, went to New Orleans, and built up there a large and lucrative practice.

P. C. Cunningham, a Glasgow man, visited America first in 1835, and made his first appearance that year in the Warren Street Theatre, Boston. He was especially noted for his excellence as a player of Irish characters and for his rendering of old men's parts. He closed his first season in America at Mitchell's Olympic, in New York, and then went back to Britain, where he acted successfully throughout the provinces. He returned several times to this country, being always certain of a hearty welcome on account of his merits as an actor. One of his last appearances was in 1852 at the opening of the Arch Street Theatre, Philadelphia, when he took the part of Gibby in "The Wonder."

Many in the States and Canada will remember the tour of Sir William Don, a native of Berwick, in 1850, and the artistic success he won. Losing his fortune in the course of the process known as "sowing his wild oats," he turned to the stage as a means for earning his livelihood, and acquired a fair degree of popularity on the boards. He was the descendant of an old Scotch family, and on the female side was the representative of the Earls of Glencairn. His father for some time represented Roxburghshire in Parliament and was an intimate friend of Sir Walter Scott. In his younger and palmy days Sir William was an officer in a regiment of dragoons, and held the appointment of an aide de camp to the Lord Lieutenant of Ireland. In 1845 he found himself so financially embarrassed that he had to resign from the army and adopt the stage as a profession. His course was deeply deplored, naturally, by his noble friends, but the public admired his independence in earning his own living rather than settling down as a paltry pensioner on whatever his relatives might allow him. In 1857 he married an actress, and together they made several successful tours through Britain. Sir William remained on the stage until his death, in 1862, and retained his popularity to the end. His widow, Lady Don, visited America in 1867, and was very successful in comedy and burlesque parts.

Robert Campbell Maywood may be regarded as a good representative of the Scots (and there have been many of them) who have held the reins of theatrical management in this country. He was born at Greenock, it is said, in 1786, and in 1819 appeared at the New York Park Theatre. In 1832 he became manager of the Walnut Street Theatre, Philadelphia, and he continued to manage theatres in that city until 1840, when he took a grand farewell benefit and retired from the stage. He died at Troy, N. Y., in 1856, from paralysis. It used to be said that whenever he was short of an attraction he invariably put "Cramond Brig" on the stage, and as invariably made a success of it.

The most noted, however, of the Scotch managers in America was Col. John A. McCaull, who, after a life of varied successes and misfortunes, died at Greensboro', Ala., in 1894, and was buried in Baltimore, Md. He was born at Glasgow in 1830, and was, when a child, taken by his parents to Virginia. When the civil war broke out he joined the forces of his native State, and served under General Mahone in the Confederate Army. When it was over he was for a term in the Virginia Legislature. But it was in connection with the stage that he became known to fame.

As an operatic manager he introduced more stars than any other man in America, but his fortunes declined in his closing years, and on Feb. 11, 1892, a monster benefit was given for him in the Metropolitan Opera House. It netted $8,000.

Among the Scottish actresses who won distinction on the American boards, besides those already named, the most famous in many respects was Mrs. Joseph Wood, who made her transatlantic début in 1833 in the Park Theatre, New York, in the operetta of " Cinderella." She was born at Edinburgh in 1802, and received her musical training under the patronage of the Duchess of Buccleuch. Under her maiden name, Susannah Paton, she made her first bow to the public at concerts in her native city, and quickly became popular, her sweet voice and winsome appearance securing for her hosts of admirers. In her case, critics and public were unanimous in their praise. In 1820 she esayed the highest rank of her profession by appearing at the Haymarket, London, as Susannah in " The Marriage of Figaro." Her success in the British metropolis was also complete, and for three or four years her life was full of happiness. She was courted by Lord William Pitt Lennox, a younger son of the Duke of Richmond, and was married to him in 1824. Lord William, soon after their marriage, began treating her cruelly, and after a while she found it necessary to separate from him. Their domestic troubles created a great sensation at the time, but amidst all the talk the young actress retained the sympathy of the public, and every one was glad when she obtained a decree of divorce from the titled brute, and resumed her place on the stage. In 1828 she married Joseph Wood, a popular actor and operatic singer, and both maintained for many years a front rank on the British stage. Mrs. Wood's American experiences were of the most pleasing description, and she was magnificently received wherever she appeared, which was in all the large cities of the continent. She died at Wakefield, England, in 1864.

Few lives have been more full of sunshine and shadow than that of Agnes Robertson, wife of Dion Boucicault, the actor and playwright. Born at Edinburgh in 1833, she became in early life famous as an actress in Scotland, and was regarded as one of the most beautiful women in the country. Her marriage to Boucicault, in 1853, brought her more prominently than ever before the public, and the same year she made her American début at Montreal. In North America she was a prime favorite wherever she appeared, and, whether in Scotch or Irish drama or in society plays, she proved herself to be a finished and accomplished actress. The story of her later domestic troubles and her retirement from the stage are painfully familiar to people interested in theatrical matters, but amidst all the recriminations and lawsuits, and variety of stories which were circulated at the time, she never lost the respect of the public.

Among musicians and composers the Scot in America has also made his mark, and as a producer and interpreter of high-class music his efforts have made him conspicuous. His quality as a producer is fairly shown in the career of William Richardson Dempster. This genius of song was born at Keith in 1809, and was apprenticed to a quillmaker in Aberdeen. He was from his boyhood devoted to music, and applied all of his spare time to its study. In early life he crossed the Atlantic and was naturalized as a citizen of the United States, devoting himself to teaching music and to public singing, for his voice and ear were equally gifted. He gradually became known as a composer, but his efforts in that direction were not generally recognized until he published his setting for Tennyson's "May Queen," which at once became very popular wherever Tennyson's poem was known. Subsequently he composed music for many of the songs scattered through the works of the great Poet Laureate, and his latter years were spent pleasantly and at equal intervals on both sides of the Atlantic. In private life Mr. Dempster was much respected as a rigid moralist, a good man in all that men hold honorable, and a conscientious citizen, and his death, at London, in 1871, was regretted by hosts of friends in the United States, as well as in the motherland.

CHAPTER XIII.

MEN OF LETTERS.

IN the gallery of Scottish-American men of letters no name stands higher, no personality was more impressive, no life was more useful, than that of James McCosh, the gifted President of Princeton College, N. J. He settled in America in the fullness of his powers, and from the day of his arrival gave himself up wholly to it. He not only strove to place Princeton among the world's great seats of learning, but he gave to America a system of philosophy, based upon the old common-sense school of Scotland, which, if followed out and studied with the closeness it deserves, will give a new trend to American thought and scholarship, and to American metaphysical study an individuality of its own. His administration of Princeton was a model one. During his tenure of office he reorganized the whole routine at the college, extended its curriculum, rebuilt most of its halls, and when he laid down the Presidency it was second in point of equipment, number of students, standing of Faculty, and moral tone to no university establishment in America. Considered simply as a man of letters, Dr. McCosh by his writings did much to advance American scholarship, and his two volumes on " Realistic Philosophy " and the one on " First and Fundamental Truths " are probably the most important contributions yet made to higher American thought. " The time has come for America to declare her independence in philosophy " formed part of one of the opening sentences of the former work, and the foundation of such a system was the purpose of his later writings—the work of all his closing years. But, full of American fervor as he was, he never lost his devotion to his native land, and what Scot abroad ever sent back to the country of his birth a grander memorial of his love than did Dr. McCosh when he published his invaluable history of "Scottish Philosophy"? As he well said in its preface: "This work has been with me a labor of love. The gathering of materials for it and the writing of it, as carrying me into what I feel to be interesting scenes, have afforded me great pleasure, which is the only reward I am likely to get. I publish it as the last, and to me the only remaining, means of testifying my regard for my country—loved all the more because I am now far from it—and my country's philosophy, which has been the means of stimulating thought in so many of Scotland's sons." To understand Dr. McCosh's life work, too, it must not be forgotten that he was a zealous and devoted minister of the Gospel. That fact he himself not only never forgot, but he placed its duties above all others. In the preface to his "Gospel Sermons," published in 1888, he sufficiently enunciated this when he said: "Hitherto my published works have been chiefly philosophical. But, all along, while I was lecturing and writing on philosophy, I was also preaching. I am anxious that the public should know that, much as I value philosophy, I place the Gospel of Jesus Christ above it."

Dr. McCosh was born in 1811 at Garskeoch, Ayrshire, and was the son of a farmer. After studying for the ministry at Glasgow and Edinburgh, he was licensed to preach in 1834, and soon after became minister of the Abbey Church, Arbroath. Three years later he became minister of Brechin, and there he labored until the Disruption, when he formed one of the noble band who "came out" with Chalmers, Cunningham, Candlish, and Guthrie. For a time he was an itinerant preacher, going hither and thither throughout Angus and Mearns, gathering the people into congregations and explaining the position of the new Free Church. Finally he settled down as minister of the East Free Church, Brechin, and gave himself up to study. It was there he commenced his lifelong inquiry into philosophical matters. One of the first fruits of that study was a volume on "The Method of Divine Government, Physical and Moral," and its publication led to his receiving the appointment of Professor of Logic and Metaphysics in Queen's College, Belfast. This appointment met with a good deal of opposition in Ireland.

The new professor speedily showed, however, that he was an acquisition to Ireland, although his earnest advocacy of a system of education in that country on national principles met with the most bitter opposition of the Roman Catholic clergy and laity. Indeed, his views and those of Mr. Gladstone on this question were diametrically opposed to each other, but he cordially indorsed, as might be expected, that statesman's movement for the disestablishment of the English Church in Ireland. His studies in metaphysics were diligently prosecuted in Ireland, and the outcome was several works which advanced his position in the world of letters and thought—notably his volume on "Intuitions of the Mind." In 1866 Dr. McCosh paid a visit to America, mainly for the purpose of studying the educational equipment of the country. Two years later he was offered the position of President of Princeton, and accepted it after considerable hesitation. From that time until the weight of years, in 1888, impelled him to resign the Presidency, his whole life was devoted to Princeton, and the devotion had magnificent results. His students loved him, the friends of Princeton had confidence in him, and he constantly was adding new names to the long list of the benefactors of the institution. But, wrapped up as he was in Princeton, Dr. McCosh took a keen interest in passing events and in the literary movements of his time. He had a profound contempt for the theory of evolution, and discussed it in print with its great apostle, Tyndall, and whatever looked like an approach to materialism found in him an inveterate foe. He had no patience with anything that paltered with the great truths of life, and if he hated an infidel he had nothing but contempt for an agnostic, or even for what might be called a "trimmer." Religion must either be wholly true or wholly false.

There was no middle way, no room for real argument except on the one side or the other. But he was no believer in the theory that religion can take care of itself. He regarded it as the duty of all men who professed religion to advance it and strengthen it at every point. Hence the interest he took in the movement for the union of the various branches of the Presbyterian Church—a union he advocated until his death, in 1894.

National predilection might tempt us to regard Dr. McCosh's greatest work as his volume on "Scottish Philosophy," but undoubtedly the book which has had and will continue to have the greatest influence upon the thought of this country is that in which he unfolded his scheme of realistic philosophy—the American school, as he liked to call it. There can be no doubt that that work has already exerted a very considerable influence in America, but we believe its influence is only in its primary stages, and that sooner or later the system laid down by the grand old man of Princeton will be fully adopted as America's own—modified, of course, by the inevitable new lights which time and circumstance will bring to bear upon it. But time and circumstance will not change the groundwork, and in Dr. McCosh's foundation we see a system founded on a rock—the rock of truth, for, after all, that is the keynote of the system he proposed. By it he hoped to make American philosophy healthy—different altogether from the vague, unsatisfactory speculation, the sickly sentimentalism, and the cowardly agnosticism of so many of the recognized European schools. His system was not altogether untried, for it is really, as we have already said, a development of the old Scotch common-sense school, and it squared in every point with natural and revealed religion. To America the life of Dr. McCosh was a grand one, and had Scotland contributed no more than that one life to the agencies which are building up and developing the highest and holiest interests of the United States, it would have deserved the kindliest recognition from American scholarship.

A very similar case is that of Dr. Daniel Wilson of Toronto—Sir Daniel, as he was called in the twilight of his life. Like Dr. McCosh, he settled in America in the fullness of his powers, and after he had established his literary reputation, and he continued at work in his transatlantic home until the inevitable summons called him to the majority. Born at Edinburgh in 1816, a nephew of "Christopher North," he early showed a predilection for literary work. His education was received mainly at the historic High School of his native town—the school of Drummond of Hawthornden, Robert Ferguson, Law of Lauriston, Boswell, the biographer; Henry Mackenzie, the "Man of Feeling"; Lord Brougham, and a hundred other notables—and at the university in that city. After graduating, he spent some years in London, mainly engaged in literary pursuits, and then returned to Scotland, where he began that thorough study into the archaeology and antiquities of the country which was destined ultimately to give him a high place among her historical writers. He became Secretary to the Royal Antiquarian Society of Scotland and contributed many valuable papers to its "Transactions." His chief study at that time was the romantic city in which he was born and in which he resided, and the result of his studies—the "Memorials of Edinburgh in the Olden Time," published in 1847—established his reputation as a writer and archaeologist. His greatest contribution to historical literature, however, was his "Prehistoric Annals of Scotland," a work which not only directed inquiry on a rational basis into a subject which had previously been treated as a romance or a series of fables, but continues to be a standard authority, notwithstanding the researches which have since been made into the subject. In 1853, through the influence of the Earl of Elgin, Wilson accepted an invitation to become Professor of English Literature and History in the University of Toronto, and thereafter made his home in Canada. From that "Queen City" he issued, in 1862, his magnificent volumes on "Prehistoric Man: Researches into the Origin of Civilization in the Old World and the New," thus grouping his American as well as his European studies of a theme that was to him of the most fascinating description. We have not space, however, to mention all of the literary work which this diligent student performed after his lines were cast in Canada. If gathered together his contributions to the Journal of the Canadian Institute and to periodicals of various descriptions would fill a goodly array of volumes. All his work was conscientiously done; every line he wrote bore the hall marks of the scholar. Dr. Wilson was a poet, too, and published a small volume of his verses under the title of "Spring Flowers" in 1875, but no one can read his prose works without feeling in them even a deeper poetical sentiment and insight than in the volume in which he uttered his thoughts in verse. His was a beautiful old age. Elevated to the Presidency of his college, honored by his sovereign with knighthood, and enjoying the respectful admiration of thousands of friends in both hemispheres, he continued in harness to the end, doing good by word, thought, and deed until the night came that ushered him into the sunlight.

The first literature that is issued in connection with a new country is generally topographical and descriptive, and in respect to the New World the ubiquitous Scot is represented among those who wrote of the American Colonies while even most of the seaboard was in a state of nature. This advance guard of a long line of litterateurs of all ranks had an early representative in John Lawson, a native of Aberdeen. He was born in that city about 1658, and in 1690 was appointed Surveyor General of North Carolina. He appears to have begun his work in America a year later, and to have applied himself to its duties with all the determination and energy so characteristic of his race. The best evidence of this extant is his volume, published at London in 1700, entitled "A New Voyage to Carolina, Containing the Exact Description and Natural History of that Country; Together with the Present State Thereof; and a Journal of a Thousand Miles Traveled Through Several Nations of Indians, Giving a Particular Account of Their Customs, Manners, &c." This work proved so popular, was recognized as so perfect an authority on its subject that it was reprinted in 1709, 1714, and in 1718, and it had the honor of being reproduced, at Raleigh, N. C., as recently as 1860. In 1712, in the course of one of his surveying trips, Lawson was made prisoner by Tuscarora Indians and was put to death in a manner that brought into operation all the fiendish cruelty for which that people were distinguished.

A better-remembered name is that of George Chalmers, one of the most prominent literary antiquarians of Scotland. This man, whose wonderful " Caledonia " remains a storehouse for writers on Scottish historical matters, was born at Fochabers in 1742, and bred to the legal profession. In 1763 he sailed for America with a relative who was anxious to recover a large tract of land in Maryland, which had been in the possession of an earlier member of the family. Making his headquarters in Baltimore, Chalmers studied the legal practice of that city, and finally determined to settle there and carry on his profession. There he remained, until the troubles of the Revolution broke out, and when he saw that separation from the mother country was inevitable, or that military rule was to be necessary to keep the country loyal, he determined to leave it. Settling up his affairs as best he could, he crossed over to London and began his career as a man of letters. It is singular that Chalmers's American experiences proved unproductive of literary result. He published in 1782 the first volume of " An Introduction to the History of the Revolt of the Colonies," but the volume was quickly suppressed at his instance, and no more appeared in print. A volume of " Opinions on Interesting Subjects of Public Laws and Commercial Policy, Arising from American Independence," issued in 1784, and a few tracts, complete his literary connection with the United States. Scotland, however, was possibly the gainer by his devotion to themes and studies peculiarly her own, and his editions of her ancient poets, his " Caledonia," his " Life of Mary, Queen of Scots," and many other works of like importance give him a high place among the literary students of the country.

In the case of James Thomas Callender we have the

first instance of a Scot whose entire literary life, almost, was given up to the United States, and was developed by the influences at work in the country. He was also one of the pioneers, if not the pioneer, of that style of American journalism which uses declamation and denunciation instead of argument, which is distinguished by the bitterness it displays toward opponents, and seems never happier than when engaged in sneering at and belittling, if not vilifying, whatever does not square with the writer's notions or interests, in Church or State, in religion, manners, or morals. Callender was born at Stirling in 1758. Of his early life little is known until, in 1792, he published at Edinburgh a pamphlet entitled "The Political Progress of Britain." It was a time when the authorities, aroused by the success of the French Revolution and the feeling of dissatisfaction with political conditions which generally prevailed, were keenly bent on suppressing anything that looked like sedition, and Callender's work was judged to fall under that category, and was seized. A warrant was issued for his arrest, but he evaded it by escaping to this country.

Callender reached America in 1793, and settled in Philadelphia. There he published the "Political Register" and the "American Register," but neither appear to have added much to his worldly fortune. Removing to Richmond, Va., he established the "Richmond Recorder," which became somewhat of a power in politics. Callender was bitterly outspoken in his opposition to the Administrations of Washington and Adams. His beau ideal of a statesman for a long time was Thomas Jefferson, but toward the end he opposed that patriot's policy as vehemently as he did those of the early Presidents. A man engaged in newspaper work has little time for anything else than to fulfill its demands, but Callender managed to publish several volumes—"Sketches of American History" being the most noteworthy—all of which show him to have been a writer at once forcible and graceful and possessed of a thorough knowledge of and a keen insight into the passing affairs of his time. His character, however, was not a lovable one. His temper was soured—perhaps by his outlawry in early life—and his work in this country seems really to have been of little passing, and certainly of no permanent, value. He met his death, by drowning, in the James River, near Richmond, in 1813.

A much more amiable career, and one still popularly recalled on both sides of the Atlantic, is that of Alexander Wilson, "the Paisley poet and American ornithologist," as he has been described. He was born in Paisley in 1766, educated at the grammar school there, and in due time was apprenticed to a weaver—the trade of his father. He did not take kindly to the loom, and after his apprenticeship was over he sighed for some other employment, which would give him an opportunity to study nature in all her moods. He early began to dabble in literature, and, at all events, to have aspirations for literary work, and one of his many biographers, Dr. Grosart, seems to regard it as probable that in 1786 he made a pilgrimage to Kilmarnock to make the acquaintance of Robert Burns, and that he succeeded in his mission. After several years spent as a journeyman weaver in Paisley, Queensferry, and other places, during which time his muse was busy, he determined to see his country thoroughly and at the same time support himself by "carrying a pack"—that is, by becoming a peddler. In this way he not only traveled into sections of his native land which otherwise he might never have seen, but his poetical qualities wonderfully developed, and such compositions as "The Loss of the Pack" are still recited in Scotland. His delightful prose style also formed itself about this time, and the journals of his travels and his letters are to this day delightful reading. While journeying he secured subscribers for a volume of his poems, which ultimately appeared in 1790 and gave him a more than local standing as a poet. The volume is, however, very unequal in its contents, and shows that the author lacked the services of a critical adviser when preparing or selecting its contents for the press. The most popular of all his poems, "Watty and Meg," appeared in 1792 as a penny chapbook, without any author's name, and was at once attributed to Burns—the highest compliment which it was possible for the people of Scotland to pay it.

In 1793, like nearly every young man then in Paisley, Wilson fell under the ban of being suspected of nursing seditious sentiments, and, as he avowed the authorship of several poems thus libeled, he was sent to jail. After his release he made up his mind to try his fortunes in the young republic over the sea, although the very idea of parting with Scotland cost him a severe pang, for America was much further away from Scotland in those days than now.

When Wilson landed in the New World he was ready to accept a job at anything that presented itself, and in time he was a helper in a copperplate printing establishment, a weaver, a peddler, and a schoolmaster. In the last-named employment he won considerable success, and his appointment as teacher in an institution at Kingess, about four miles from Philadelphia, seemed to bring him the opportunity for putting into practice a determination he had formed during his wanderings over the country, that of making a descriptive and pictorial work about the birds of America.

Wilson's fame in America rests on his "Ornithology," the first volume of which was issued in 1808. In his letters and diaries he has given us wonderfully graphic pictures of his adventures in search of material for this work, of the hardships he had to endure, of his wanderings through unknown regions and of his many hairbreadth escapes on land and water. As he journeyed he canvassed for subscribers for the work, and he has told us of his successes as well as his rebuffs in this connection with a species of humor that is thoroughly national in its alternate modesty and grimness. It was a great work to be undertaken singlehanded by a man whose sole capital, besides his fitness, was his enthusiasm, but he kept steadily to his task, overriding all sorts of obstacles, and in fairly rapid succession saw seven of its goodly volumes on his table and in the hands of his subscribers. The eighth volume announced his death, and the sad event was directly brought about through his eagerness to perfect the work. The story is then told: "While he (Wilson) was sitting in the house of one of his acquaintances enjoying the pleasures of conversation, he chanced to see a bird of a rare species, for one of which he had long been in search. With his usual enthusiasm he ran out, followed it, swam across a river over which it had flown, fired at, killed, and obtained the object of his eager pursuit, but caught a cold, which ended in his death." The end came on Aug. 23, 1813, and the poet-ornithologist was buried in the little God's-acre surrounding the old Swedish Church, Philadelphia, where the birds still sing over his grave. The spot is marked by a flat stone appropriately inscribed, and is the foremost Scottish shrine in the "City of Brotherly Love." Wilson's memory is still cherished in the land of his birth and the land of his adoption. Not far from the ancient Abbey of Paisley a splendid bronze statue of him has been erected, showing him, not as a poet, but as a wanderer in an American forest in search of illustrations for his great work, and that work has given him a place in American literature which is not only unique but has won for him the title pre-eminently of "The American Ornithologist."

In many respects the greatest name in Scottish-American literature is that of Washington Irving, who was born in New York City in 1783. His father was a native of Orkney, and traced descent back to the Irvines of Drum. He settled in New York in 1763, and became a successful merchant, but had to leave the city during the Revolutionary struggle, having adopted the Colonial cause. After a couple of years, however, he returned, and quickly made up his losses. He was a sturdy Presbyterian, a good citizen, and a stanch admirer of the first President of the country, and so named his youngest son in his honor.

Washington Irving was carefully educated, although he never attended college, and in due time entered a law office. He was attentive to his law studies, but literature had a greater attraction for him, and the business of his life was sadly interrupted—fortunately for literature—

by delicate health. This led to frequent country journeys, in the course of which he thoroughly explored the Hudson River, and in 1800 was the cause of his first trip across the Atlantic. After rambling over the Continent for two years, he returned to New York, was admitted to the bar in 1806, but did not seem to get much practice. In fact, with the exception of a short time when he managed the business which his father had bequeathed to the family during the illness of his brother Peter, his life was that of a man of letters. Even the office of Secretary of the American Legation in London, which he filled from 1829 to 1832, and the post of Minister to Spain, which he occupied from 1842 to 1846, were really subservient to his many literary studies. His career was an uneventful, and, on the whole, a happy one. He never married, and the story of the declining years of his life from 1846 until he was laid at rest in Sleepy Hollow, in the closing days of 1859, forms one of the pleasantest records of the sunset of a literary life of which we have knowledge. His fame has steadily increased year after year since then; and Sunnyside, his home, is now one of the Meccas of lovers of American literature.

Irving's first literary work—a series of articles contributed, in his nineteenth year, to the "Morning Chronicle," a newspaper published by his brother, Peter Irving— showed cleverness and versatility, and as much may be said for his "Salmagundi" papers. They were what might be called apprentice-work, the work which every beginner in literature must struggle with before essaying higher flights, or adding anything to the real literary wealth of his country or the world. Irving's first real contribution to literature was his "History of New York by Diedrich Knickerbocker," which was published in 1809. Taking the outlines of the early and vague history of the city as a foundation, he filled these outlines up with sketches of real men and women, and infused into every page such playful humor, and, here and there, such delightful satire; and, withal, such an appearance of a determination to present the exact truth in every line, that people at first did not know what to make of it.

The descendants of the old Knickerbocker families voted it a caricature and denounced it as such; others accepted it as a veritable history, and a few sat down to enjoy its perusal purely as a literary treat. It at once became popular, and has since become a classic, and we have admitted Wilhelmus Kraft, Wouter Van Twiller and Peter Stuyvesant—Peter the Headstrong—to our gallery of heroes of romance. But such is the power of genius that Irving's " Knickerbocker," without any real pretensions to be a veritable history, has taken its place among historical records to such an extent that no one would now dream of investigating the early history of New York or writing about it without studying more or less Irving's pages. We could not draw a pen picture of Gov. Stuyvesant, for instance, without his aid, for it is Irving's portrait of that one-legged hero that has been accepted as the true one, and, in the public esteem, whatever does not conform to it cannot be correct or worthy of consideration. In Scotland it is Sir Walter Scott's " Jeannie Deans's Duke " that people think of, not the historical character who figures in the annals of Great Britain as the second Duke of Argyll.

This work fully established Irving's fame on both sides of the Atlantic, and, what probably delighted him more, led to the writer's receiving a warm welcome at Abbotsford, when afterward on a visit to Scotland. "The Sketch Book," with its inimitable paper on " Rip Van Winkle," added to the popularity of Irving; but, although " Bracebridge Hall " was received kindly, it did not add much to the prestige of its author. In the " Life of Columbus," published in 1828, Irving fairly entered the arena of European literature, and that work at once became recognized as the standard biography of the great discoverer. Its diligent research, its clear array of facts, its skillful handling of details, and the beauty of its literary style were at once recognized as the work of a master, and it has since remained without a rival in popular favor.

His last work, his " Life of George Washington," was undoubtedly his greatest and his best, and gives us a picture of the great American hero which, it is safe to say, will never be surpassed for truthfulness or power. He gives way to no theories why Washington did this or did not do that. He indulges in no philosophy, and follows his hero from the cradle to the grave with a fullness that leaves no doubt in the mind of the reader as to what kind of a man Washington really was; and this, it seems to us, is the very highest form of biographical writing. When the work was passing through the press Irving began to feel that the night that falls upon all men was quickly drawing its shadows around him, and it was only a few months before the clouds closed in that he had the happiness of seeing the completed work on his table, and of rejoicing in the knowledge that all united in saying it was well done. He died on November 28, 1859, and three days later was buried in Sleepy Hollow, in the midst of a country that received from his pen some at least of the halo which Scott threw over his own beloved Borderland.

Had Washington Irving not written "Astoria" it is probable that the recognized authority, the literary genius of John Jacob Astor's expedition to Oregon would have been Alexander Ross, who from a pioneer hunter developed in his later years into a writer of books. His "Adventures of the First Settlers on the Oregon or Columbia River," "Fur Traders in the Far West," and "Red River Settlement" are good books of their kind, full of adventure and description, written in an easy, attractive—sometimes fascinating—style, and eminently truthful even in the slightest detail. Ross was a native of Nairnshire, and went to Canada in 1805, when in his twenty-second year. For a time he taught school in Glengarry and elsewhere, and found the employment fruitful of usefulness to the children and the community, but barren of results to himself. In 1810 he joined the Astor expedition to Oregon, and until 1825 was a hunter and fur trader in the Astor Company or that of Hudson Bay. In 1825 he removed to the Red River Settlement, and became its Sheriff and a member of the Council of Assiniboine. He survived till his seventy-third year, in spite of all the hardships and sufferings of his early life, and died at Winnipeg, beloved and honored, in 1856.

Pleasant memories yet linger in Charleston, S. C., of the Rev. Dr. George Buist, who settled in that city to take charge of an academy or college—the words at that time appear to have been used synonymously—and remained there till his death, in 1808. He was born in Fifeshire in 1770, was educated at Edinburgh University, and there called to the ministry. He was one of the earliest Scotch students of philology, and that subject, ever changing and progressing, and constantly opening up new fields of thought, remained his favorite study throughout his long and useful life. He was one of the contributors to the Encyclopaedia Britannica, abridged Hume's History of England for schools and ordinary readers; and a volume of his sermons, published after he had passed away, was prefaced by a brief memoir in which the example of his beautiful life was fittingly placed before the reader. The volume is now very scarce.

One of the most curious characters in all American literary history—and no literary history is so full of curiosities—was John Wood, author of a "History of the Administration of John Adams," which James Parton, the American biographical writer, has characterized as a lot of lies. This characterization seems, unfortunately for Wood's memory, to have been perfectly correct. To sum up his literary work in the most general and gentle manner, we might say with truth that he was one of the most unreliable and fact-regardless writers who ever lived in America. Wood was born in Scotland in 1775, and emigrated to America in 1800. He engaged in such literary hack work as he could find, and never really rose above the stage of such composition. This was due more to the lack of literary opportunity, the country not then being far enough advanced to foster any of the higher arts to any great extent, than to any lack of ability on the part of Wood, for he seems to have really been a man of superior intellect. For several years he edited a sheet called "The Western World," in Kentucky. In

1817 he took up his abode in Washington, and had the editorial charge of the "Atlantic World." He cultivated the friendship of the most noted politicians of his time while sojourning in the national capital, but their friendship did not advance his interests in any material way, and he died at Richmond, Va., a poor man, in 1822.

We gladly turn from the memory of such a personage as Wood to the honored name of John Galt, one of the most distinguished annalists of the Scotch peasantry and one of the most voluminous and instructive writers of his time. A few years ago he was named as second only to Scott as a delineator and illustrator of Scotch humble life, and, although time and the varying moods of public taste have removed him from that high pedestal, he yet holds a foremost place among the Scottish novelists who have written of their own people. Such works as "The Annals of the Parish" and "The Ayrshire Legatees" still retain their popularity, and are alone sufficient to keep their writer's memory green in the hearts of his countrymen. Galt was born at Irvine, Ayrshire, in 1779, and had made his mark in literature before crossing the Atlantic in 1824. "He came to Canada," writes Mr. H. J. Morgan, to whose writings we have been greatly indebted for information on many points, "as Commissioner of the Canada Land Company, an association in which he took great interest and used his best efforts to advance; and it may be said that to his indefatigable energy and ability may be in part ascribed the present [1862] high position the company enjoys. Indeed, we know of hardly any one who did so much for it as Mr. Galt. During his stay in Canada he took a great interest in the upper province [Ontario] and in colonizing and settling it; and the country is indebted to him for some of the best improvements, both on land and water, it possesses. He founded the town of Guelph, in the County of Wellington, and the town of Galt is named after him. But differences having arisen between him and the company, he resigned in 1829 and returned to Britain that same year, where shortly afterward he was obliged to take advantage of the Insolvent Debtors' act. He returned to his literary labors with renewed zest and energy, and during the remainder of his life he produced a number of works, principally novels and miscellanies, some of which range high in the estimation of literary men and belong to what is called the ' standard ' series of English literature." Galt died at Greenock, in 1839.

Two of Galt's sons went to Canada before his decease, in search of fortune, and of one of these, the late Sir A. T. Galt, the story of his public career is really a part of the history of the Dominion. The other son, Thomas, was long one of the Judges in Canada's Court of Common Pleas.

A pathetic story of promise, failure, and disappointment, of a blasted life slowly dragging on to its end and finally going out, alone, in the very depths of poverty and despair, is furnished by a study of the life of Alexander Somerville, the once-famous " Whistler at the Plough." He was born at Springfield, in Oldhamstocks Parish, Haddingtonshire, in 1811. His parents were poor, and when Alexander went to work as a cowherd at sixpence a day his father's earnings were only six shillings a week. The boy got considerable schooling, however, in parish schools, for no matter how poverty-stricken they may be, Scotch parents invariably strive to give their children some education, even at the cost of privation. As he grew to manhood, while earning a scanty income as a common laborer, Somerville took a deep interest in the political movements which then [1831-2] agitated Britain, and naturally his entire sympathies were with his own class. In 1832 he lost his employment on account of the dullness of trade, and, as nothing seemed likely to turn up to give him a livelihood, he enlisted in the Scots Greys. That regiment was then arrayed, not against the enemies of Britain, but against the people of Britain. The men did not like the work. Many of them sent letters to the War Office stating that they would not use their weapons to interfere with a public meeting or to hamper the people in the peaceful prosecution of their rights, and one of these letters was traced to Somerville. It was determined to make an example of some one, and he was tried by court-martial for a manufactured offense, found guilty, and ordered to receive one hundred lashes. The horrors of this punishment were graphically described long afterward by his own pen. The flogging, however, had far-reaching results. When Somerville left the hospital after his stripes had healed he found that the matter had been a theme of newspaper discussion, and he became a hero in the eyes of his comrades. He gave in a letter to a newspaper an account of the real cause of his flogging, the simple fact that he had dared to give expression to his thoughts, and this letter, although it disgusted the authorities, was suffered to pass without notice simply because in the condition of public opinion they were afraid to repeat the dose they had formerly administered. Meanwhile a subscription was set on foot, Somerville's discharge was purchased, and with £300 in his pocket he returned to Scotland, helped his parents, started in business—and failed in six months. He next took service with the Spanish Legion in the Peninsula, serving two years. Returning to Britain, he helped to warn the people against foolish revolutionary measures, and in that way did more service to the working classes than though he had, as many desired, become one of their aggressive leaders. He commenced his literary career as a correspondent of the "Manchester Examiner," and published, among other things, an account of his adventures in Spain. In 1852 his famous letters, signed by "One Who Has Whistled at the Plough," appeared, and afforded him an opportunity for utilizing the information he possessed of political movements, and his views on the betterment of the working classes, as well as reminiscences of his travels, and comments on all topics then interesting Britain. These letters created a wide interest, and the author was more talked about than any other journalistic contributor for a year or two. His autobiography (issued in 1848) also enjoyed a wide sale.

In 1858 he went to Canada, and for a time was editor of the "Canadian Illustrated News." His clear, vigorous English, the lucidity of his arguments for any measure he advocated, and his knowledge of the world were visible in everything he wrote. But he never seemed to "catch hold" in Canada. He wrote in praise of it to many of the home papers, told of its resources and possibilities in glowing language, and did, honestly, everything that lay in his power to help to build it up. Yet his career there was a slow but steady descent into poverty—poverty of the most abject description. He published several books in Canada, but they yielded no return, and his latter years were spent in neglect; often, indeed, in actual want. The man outlived his friends, and, lingering on the stage, had been relegated to the rear, and was unnoticed and forgotten. The last time the writer saw him, in the streets of Toronto, his apparel was that of a beggar, a collection of remnants of clothing that had seen better days, and his conversation was of the most despondent description. It is difficult to account for this man's fall. Faults he had, as have all men, but his abilities ought to have made his life comfortable, should have kept his lines in pleasant places. His career, even outside of his literary labors, was a useful one, and he ought to be remembered, if for nothing else, as the one whose sufferings led to the final abolition of flogging in the British Army. He died at Toronto, under painful circumstances, in 1885.

Returning to the United States after this sad record of a Canadian litterateur's career, we take up a beautiful, lovable Christian life, the life of one who was a man of letters and at the same time a hard-working and devoted minister of the Gospel. This was Robert Turnbull, who for twenty-four years was minister of the First Baptist Church at Hartford, Conn. He was born, in 1809, at Whitburn, Linlithgowshire, and graduated at Edinburgh University. He studied theology under Dr. Chalmers, and, becoming convinced of the truth of the doctrine of immersion, he became a Baptist, and, after being admitted to preach, he traveled a good deal through Scotland and England, occupying such pulpits as chance directed. In 1833 he emigrated to America, and, after brief pastorates in Danbury, Detroit, Hartford, and Boston, he returned to Hartford and spent there the active years of his life. For a long period Mr. Turnbull was joint editor of "The Christian Review." He edited an edition of Sir William Hamilton's "Discussions in Philosophy," and wrote several works worthy of a better fate than the neglect which has apparently overtaken them. In 1851 he resigned his pastorate and served as Secretary of the Connecticut Baptist State Convention, filling in his time with literary work, and preaching in various places as occasion offered. His closing years were full of peace and hope, a beautiful sunset, and his death at Hartford, in 1877, was really for him a victory.

This is hardly the place to estimate the value of Dr. Turnbull's religious writings from a purely theological point of view, but the statements in all his books that come under that class are so clearly laid down, their language is so precise, that even a layman is never at a loss in following his arguments, while their thoughts are ever impressive and elevated. Of his secular books, we regard his "Genius of Scotland" as the best, possibly because national prejudice may affect our judgment, possibly because we really feel that he threw his whole heart into that particular work. We know no book which somehow answers the home-cravings of the Scot abroad so well as this, none that is more enthusiastic in its praise of the old land, without running at the same time into platitudes of extravagance. There is not a line in it that is not the result of observation or personal reminiscence, its sentiments are always pure and exalted, and it not only recalls the story of the land and describes its scenery and its personages—historical or noteworthy—but every page seems bathed in that spirit of poetry which has given to Scotland the title of "Land of Song."

The State of Massachusetts has, as the historian of its share in the civil war, William Scoular, a native of Kilbarchan. Born in that once quaint village in 1814, Scoular settled in America in 1830, and for a time worked at his trade of a calico printer. From that he drifted into journalism, and from 1841 to 1847 was editor and proprietor of the Lowell "Courier." Then, for some five years, he resided in Boston as editor and part proprietor of the "Daily Atlas." The years from 1853 to 1858 he spent in Ohio, mainly as one of the editorial staff of the "Cincinnati Gazette." In 1857 he was chosen Adjutant General of Ohio, and he was placed in the same office in Massachusetts after his return to the Old Bay State, when he settled in Boston as editor of the "Atlas and Bee." Four times he was elected to the Massachusetts House of Representatives, and once was returned to the State Senate, and these honors may fairly be regarded as indicative of his personal popularity and of the trust reposed in him by his fellow-citizens. On leaving the Adjutant General's office in 1866 he occupied himself mainly with the compilation of his volumes on the "History of Massachusetts in the Civil War," which were published at Boston in 1868 and 1871. Soon after the completion of this important work, Mr. Scoular passed away—in 1872—at West Roxbury, Mass.

An enthusiastic, kindly Scot, whose name, we fear, will soon be barely remembered, was Robert Macfarlane, who for seventeen years was editor of the New York "Scientific American," and was the author of a treatise on "Propellers and Steam Navigation," which was published in 1851 and was reprinted in 1854, and who edited Love's "Treatise on the Art of Dyeing" for a Philadelphia concern in 1868. Such works rarely bring a man much posthumous fame, and Mr. Macfarlane's best work really was done in the columns of the "Scottish-American Journal," to which he was for a long time a steady contributor. To its pages he contributed a series of paper on the "Scot in America," and one on "Scotland Revisited," which were read with delight wherever that newspaper circulated. On Scottish history, manners, customs, and family tradition he had a wonderful store of information, and he freely communicated it as a commentary on anything that occurred to him in the form of letters and articles, week after week, for many years. For a long time Mr. Macfarlane carried on business as a dyer in Albany, and while in that city was a "Scot of the Scots," and took a very active interest in carrying on the work of its St. Andrew's Society. But the climate of that good old Dutch town with a good old Scotch name did not agree with his health, and his closing years were spent in pleasant retirement in Brooklyn, where he died in 1883. He was born at Rutherglen in 1812, and always used the name of his birthplace as a nom de plume in his communications to the press. It seems a pity that a selection, at least, of his writings has not been published. Such a volume would have proved acceptable to many readers, and been the best monument that could be raised to his memory. Peace be to his ashes. He sleeps in the beautiful Rural Cemetery of Albany, with many a once well-kenned, leal-hearted Scot lying at rest around him.

A conspicuous illustration of how the Scot can press upward from the humblest walks of life is afforded us by a glance at the career of the Rev. Prof. James C. Moffat of Princeton, who died in that academic town on June 7, 1890. His father was a shepherd at Glencree, and there the future teacher and author was born in 1811. His first employment was as a shepherd's boy, and his education was scanty. At sixteen years of age he apprenticed himself to a printer, as much for the sake of being in a way to get access to books as for the remuneration, although that, of course, was an important consideration. He so well improved his time that in a few years he had attained considerable mastery over Latin, Greek, Hebrew, French, German, and other tongues. He had a special fondness for Oriental languages, and made a particular study of that written and spoken in Persia. In 1833 he emigrated to America and managed to enter Princeton College, where he graduated in 1835. After a year or two's experience as a tutor, Mr. Moffat, in 1839, was appointed Professor of Classics in Lafayette College. In 1841 he transferred his services to Miami University, Ohio. While in that Commonwealth he was licensed to preach. In 1853 he returned to Princeton as Professor of Latin and History, and he held various professorships in the college and Theological Seminary there until he retired, in 1877.

Dr. Moffat was a poet, and had all the delicate **fancy,**

grace of language, and brilliancy and originality of thought which mark the possessor of the essential qualities of a son of song. His most ambitious essay, "Alwyn, a Romance of Study," is handicapped by its title and the fact that the current taste does not favor a serious work—a work extending through seven long cantos. Still, it is a really meritorious poem, a work deserving of study, and one that is certain to hold the attention of any reader with the slightest taste for poetry who fairly enters into its spirit. An earlier poem, "A Rhyme of the North Countrie," is more of a story, and some of its passages—notably those descriptive of arctic scenes—are equal to anything which is to be found in American poetic literature. Some of Dr. Moffat's shorter pieces, especially those of a religious cast, have been very popular and been reprinted over and over again in various forms.

But it is as a prose writer that Dr. Moffat claims attention in this place. In 1853 he published at Cincinnati a memoir of Dr. Chalmers, a good piece of literary workmanship, inasmuch as it tells its story completely and evinces a thorough knowledge and appreciation of the subject's character and of the principles which governed and directed his career. His best-known work is his "Comparative History of Religions," in two volumes. In this he brings to bear his profound scholarship, his keen logical analytical spirit, and exemplifies in every page his desire to be just—to maintain his self-appointed position as a judge—without at the same time sacrificing one iota of his own convictions. Indeed, the work tends to show the correctness of these convictions and demonstrate the truth and inspiration of the faith consecrated at Calvary. As a mere compendium of the leading points in the various beliefs treated, the work holds a valuable place in religious literature. Its statements are everywhere to be relied upon, and the concise and clear form in which they are presented make the volumes of value not only to the student, but to the general reader. In 1874 Dr. Moffat published an account of a ramble through Scotland, a work which was read with much interest by his countrymen in America. It was another delightful tribute to the motherland from a Scot abroad, and is to a great extent written in the manner of Dr. Turnbull's "Genius of Scotland." The spirit which prompted both books and is felt throughout their pages is certainly the same.

An industrious worker in Scottish literature, and especially in the field of Burns literature, is John D. Ross, LL. D., of Brooklyn. Dr. Ross was born at Edinburgh in 1853, and settled in New York in his twentieth year. His first volume was a collection of "Celebrated Songs of Scotland," an extensive work, copiously annotated, and soon after appeared an interesting volume on "The Scottish Poets in America," to which the present writer has been under considerable obligation in connection with these pages. A volume containing a selection of poems by various authors, entitled "Round Burns's Grave," next attracted attention on both sides of the Atlantic, and speedily ran through two editions. Since 1892 Dr. Ross has published an annual volume of "Burnsiana," an invaluable work to lovers of Scotia's great bard, and he has also issued a number of other books having the "high priest of Scottish song" as their theme. Besides his book work, Dr. Ross is a regular contributor to many American newspapers. Another volume on Scottish poets in America will also appear soon from his pen, and he seems inclined to make a complete study of the writers who can come under that head.

Among men of letters, newspaper writers are surely entitled to a place, even although their work, being mainly anonymous, passes away with the fleeting hour and becomes at best only a memory, like the impersonation of life and character on the stage. The American newspaper press owes a great deal to the labors of Scotsmen, and they are to be found in all ranks, from the case to the sanctum. They have had a full share of the prizes in the profession, too, and in the United States and Canada have been numerous enough and prominent enough to encourage the hope that in the near future some one will make a special study of their lives and writings and influence.

In this work we cannot even pretend to do justice to the claims of this vast army, and must rest contented with adducing a few instances to indicate its extent and place in the history of the literature of the continent.

The trouble is to know where to draw the line that separates the man of letters from the newspaper man pure and simple. In fact, it cannot really be drawn, for the true newspaper man is a ubiquitous sort of fellow, and has the knack of bobbing up and sailing to the front in all sorts of directions.

The late James Lawson of Yonkers is a case in point. He might, with justice, have been given a place among the poets or among the business men as in connection with the newspaper workers, yet his long connection with the press of New York would seem to warrant newspaperdom as being the sphere which really prompted all his other work and dictated the leading events in his long and honorable career. Mr. Lawson was born at Glasgow in 1799, and settled in New York in 1815. In 1827, after a thorough apprenticeship in commercial pursuits, he turned his thoughts toward literary work, and became one of the founders of the now long-defunct " Morning Courier " of New York. Two years later he retired from this publication and joined the forces of the " Mercantile Advertiser," in which he did some of his best work. After several years, Mr. Lawson re-enlisted in business, and as an agent for marine insurance became widely known and implicitly trusted by the merchants of the city. But newspaper work continued his amusement, and almost till the end of his career, in 1880, he was a constant contributor of news, criticisms, essays, and poems to the press of New York. His fugitive poems were gathered together in 1857 in a volume intended mainly for private circulation, and in 1859 he printed his most ambitious and important work, a tragedy under the title of " Lidderdale; or, The Border Chief." So far as we know, it was never acted, and it seems to us rather a composition to be read than to be placed on the stage. This is singular, considering that Mr. Lawson made the theatre a special study for years. A play written in early life—"Giordano"—was placed on the boards of the old Park Theatre in 1832, or thereabout, but proved a failure, mainly because the poet predominated over the playwright in the composition of the work.

The most conspicuous example of the newspaper man pure and simple in the history of American journalism was undoubtedly James Gordon Bennett, who was born at New Mill, near Keith, in 1795. Possibly the life of no American newspaper man has been so often and so completely told or is more generally known among people who take an interest in biographical writings. He received his education at a Roman Catholic institution in Scotland, his parents being of that faith. In 1819 he began life in the New World at Halifax, N. S., as a teacher. A few months' trial of this work proved disappointing, and, proceeding to Boston, Mr. Bennett secured employment as a proofreader, and also tried to establish a reputation as a poet. After a brief experience in Charleston as a journalistic writer he settled in New York, and newspaper work became the business of his life. He became a typical Bohemian, owning a short-lived sheet at one time, and at others picking up a living as a reporter and space writer, excepting for a brief experience as an editorial writer. The man, by these changes and ups and downs, was really serving his apprenticeship, and it was only completed when, on May 6, 1835, he issued from a cellar in Wall Street the first number of the "New York Herald." Most of the earlier issues were written mainly by himself, and he infused his vitality into every line. The history of that newspaper belongs to the history of American progress—of American civilization, it may be said. It was from the first a medium of news, and the enterprise shown in obtaining intelligence of every description earlier than did any other sheet, the striking arrangement of the news matter, and the sacrifice of merely literary style to get a story before the reader without loss of time and in the most interesting manner possible soon made it the most-talked-about newspaper on the continent. As his means progressed and opportunities arose, Mr. Bennett seemed to develop in enterprise and liberality and in the keenness of his foresight for news. He dropped, apparently, all desire to be recognized as a man of letters, and his ambition was to be known as the editor of the greatest and most talked of American newspaper, and that ambition he fully realized long before his death, in 1872.

Foremost in the ranks of Canadian journalism was George Brown of Toronto, editor of the "Globe," and a statesman who occupied a prominent place in the councils of his party, and for years was a power in the politics of the Dominion. He inherited most of his journalistic ability from his father, Peter Brown, of Edinburgh, who was once engaged in business in that city as a bookseller. Financial reverses induced the latter to leave Scotland in 1838, and, settling in New York with his family, he became editor of the "Albion," then and for a long time after the recognized organ of British thought and interests in America. After four years of this work, the "Albion" then being the property of Dr. Bartlett, British Consul at New York, Mr. Brown started an opposition sheet, "The British Chronicle." The "Albion," however, was too powerful and popular to be then easily crushed—indeed, it long after died a lingering death of pure inanition—Mr. Brown had not sufficient capital to sink into his enterprise to insure its success, and after some eighteen months of existence it quietly passed away. In 1843 the family moved to Toronto, and Mr. Brown became editor of a weekly paper called "The Banner," then started under the auspices of the Free Church Party in Canada. He died in that city, in 1863.

George Brown was born at Edinburgh in 1821, went with his father and the rest of the family to Toronto and became the publisher, and was regarded as proprietor of, the "Banner," of which Mr. Peter Brown was editor. That office did not afford him much scope for his energies, and his opportunity came in April, 1844, when the first number of the "Globe" was issued as the organ of the Reform Party in Canadian politics. Under his direction it became one of the leaders of public sentiment throughout the country. Mr. Brown aimed to make the

"Globe" a perfect mirror of the world's news, and he accomplished his aim. As a mere newspaper it soon held a high rank in contemporary journalism, and its wide circulation showed that its merits as such were fully appreciated by the public to whose wants it catered. But it is questionable if it could have attained the influence it long afterward enjoyed—and still enjoys—had not George Brown personally obtained a prominent voice in the councils of his party. In that respect his career really belongs to the history of Canada, and need not be dwelt upon here, except to state that he was a member of Parliament from 1851 till 1861, and was so much recognized as the leader of his party that he was asked, in 1858, to form a Ministry, with himself as Premier, and did so, although his Ministry was a short-lived one—lasting only two days. Mr. Brown continued to direct the destinies of the "Globe"—"the Scotsman's Bible," it was often called—until his death in Toronto, in 1880. In that city a statue has since been erected to his memory.

Another conspicuous example of the intimate union of journalism and politics in Canada was John Neilson, who was born at Balmaghie, Kirkcudbrightshire, in 1770, and became editor, in 1797, of the "Quebec Gazette." In 1818 he was elected a member of the Quebec Assembly, and was at one time Speaker of that body. In 1840 he sat in the Canadian Parliament, and exerted an active influence in public affairs until his death, at Quebec, in 1848. A much less satisfactory, and far more stormy and disappointing career, was that of John Lesslie, a Dundee man, who died at Eglinton, Ontario, in 1885. He settled in Canada in 1820, when only eleven years of age, and for over ten years prior to 1854 was editor and proprietor of the "Toronto Examiner," which ultimately was purchased by Mr. George Brown and incorporated with the "Globe." The quieter, but none the less useful, aspects of Canadian journalistic lives are well represented by such careers as those of Mr. George Pirie, editor of the "Guelph Herald," who was born at Aberdeen, in 1799, and died at Guelph, in 1870, and of Thomas McQueen, editor of the "Huron Signal," a native of

Ayrshire, who died at Goderich, in 1861, in his fifty-eighth year. Both these men had poetic tastes, both gave at least one volume of poetry—poetry of more than average quality—to add to the wealth of Canadian literature, and both were distinguished throughout their lives for their enthusiasm on every matter pertaining to the land of their birth.

But this theme of Scottish-American journalism, as we contemplate it, seems really inexhaustible, and, gratifying as it is to our natural pride, we must content ourselves with closing the record with the few, but representative, names so far adduced.

We would like to enlarge upon the careers of the two Swintons—William and John—of New York, of John Dougall of Montreal, of Whitelaw Reid of New York, of George Dawson of Albany, of Andrew McLean of Brooklyn, of Donald Morrison, once of Toronto and afterward of New York; of Dr. A. M. Stewart, editor and owner of the New York "Scottish American," and a galaxy of other names which are more or less prominent in the history of American newspapers, past and present, but the subject is too interesting to form the close of a chapter, and with this brief mention or acknowledgment we must leave it. Surely, in view of what has been written, it will be acknowledged that Scotsmen have at least done their full share in shaping and building up the literature and thought of the New Hemisphere!

CHAPTER XIV.

AMONG THE POETS.

FOR a variety of reasons, it is a difficult matter to reflect in a single chapter any true idea of the variety and value of the contributions which Scotsmen in America have made to the poetic wealth of the continent. We hold that, even though the Scottish poets domiciled in America continue to write in their native Doric, and though their utterances are redolent of Scotland, it is American literature that is enriched by their song. Time has shown that it is seldom the song uttered on the soil of the New World is carried back across the sea; indeed, the instances of that could be counted on the fingers of one hand, and the Scot in America who commits the sin of rhyme has mainly to look to the land in which he lives for a clientage, and for that meed of praise which he regards as his due.

Scottish-American singers have been, in proportion to their numbers, as plentiful as their brothers at home, and, while for none can be claimed the possession of the very highest gifts, yet there are not a few whose songs have added to the pleasantness of life and the brightness of the world; and by the Scottish-American writers of the passing day there are many songs being contributed to the national anthology which will live for, at least, some years after the singers have laid down the harp and joined the silent realms—to us—of the great majority. We do not join in the cry against mediocre poets and poetasters and the like. Every honest effort, no matter in what direction, ought to be encouraged rather than sneered at, and even if a man's song does no more than soften and mellow his own heart, or afford a glint of happiness to his ain ingleside, the song has not been written in vain. By constantly tuning the harp a song might be evolved, even by chance, to which the world will listen; but, if not, there is an exalted pleasure in the work for the worker. Men who even " dabble " in poetry are rarely found in any ranks but those who are earnestly striving to make the world better. Even when they are not, the moral of their fall is so evident that the life-story is of some value to the world.

Except for the fact that he wrote one song—" Rural Content "—which is still a favorite in the south of Scotland, Andrew Scott would doubtless have been forgotten long ere this. But he was a sweet singer whose whole life was cast in hard lines. Born in 1757, in the parish of Bowden, Roxburghshire, a shepherd's son, he died, in 1839, an agricultural laborer, although his appointment as church officer, or " minister's man," in his later years eked out his scanty means a little and recognized the worthiness of his life. When he grew to manhood, Scott got tired of herding sheep and waiting on cattle, and enlisted in the Eightieth Regiment. Before this, however, he had begun to rhyme, the desire thereto being inspired by a copy of Ramsay's " Gentle Shepherd " he had managed to buy, and with which he beguiled many an hour in the fields. Soon after he enlisted he accompanied the regiment to the fighting Colonies in America, and while in camp on Staten Island, Scott's poetical abilities became generally known among his comrades, and he was ever ready to weave a rhyme to express their sentiments, or compose a song to lighten their hearts. He served in five campaigns, and was with the army that surrendered under Lord Cornwallis at Yorktown in 1783. On retiring from " sodgerin'," Scott returned to Bowden, and there passed his remaining years, the monotony of life being varied by the publication on three occasions of a volume of his poems, all of which were favorably received and won him many friends, but yielded no alleviation of the hardships of his condition; yet he never grumbled, and continued singing to the end of his journey.

Mrs. Anne Grant of Laggan, by her " Memoirs of an

American Lady," has won a place in American literature that undoubtedly is permanent, for her descriptions of American life before the Revolution are so vivid and so full of character that their value will remain, no matter how much literary fashions may change. Mrs. Grant was the daughter of Duncan McVicar, an officer in the British Army. Although born in Glasgow, in 1755, Mrs. Grant's first impressions were of America, for, having been sent to the Colonies with his regiment, McVicar's family followed him across the Atlantic when Anne was only some three years of age. Quick in observation and unusually receptive in her studies, the young girl's early education was sufficiently attended to by her mother and by a Sergeant in her father's company so that she lost nothing by the want of ordinary school facilities, and during the years in her girlhood when she resided with the Schuyler family at Albany—of whom she afterward wrote so lovingly—she acquired not only the usual accomplishments and graces of young women of her time, but became an adept in the Dutch tongue, then generally spoken among the grandees of Albany society. Ill health compelled her father to return to Scotland in 1768 with his family, even at the cost of sacrificing some land he had purchased, for it remained unsold, and was confiscated when the Revolution broke out. In Scotland he secured the position of Barrackmaster at Fort Augustus, and it was while residing there that Anne met her future husband, the Rev. James Grant, the military chaplain of the fort. Shortly after their marriage, in 1779, Mr. Grant became minister of Laggan. There his wife's happiest years were spent. She acquired a knowledge of the Gaellic tongue, was beloved by her husband's people, and her own large family idolized her as they grew to appreciate her tenderness and devotion. Her happy home, however, was broken up by the death of her husband, in 1801, and, past the meridian of life, Mrs. Grant had to face the world and enter upon a struggle for existence, with eight children depending on her for support. She secured the lease of a small farm, and, with it as a standby, commenced her literary career in 1803 by publishing a volume of her poems. This was so well received that it enabled her to pay off all her debts and purchase several necessary articles for the farm, and by this much her anxieties and troubles were lessened. Her " Letters from the Mountains," published in 1806, soon passed through several editions, and gave her a place among contemporary writers that henceforth made her depend solely upon her pen. In 1810 she settled in Edinburgh, where her home became a literary centre, and Henry Mackenzie, Walter Scott, and the Scottish literary lights of those days were among its visitors. Every work which she published deepened the hold she had upon the reading public, especially in Scotland, for, as Sir Walter Scott once wrote: " Her writings derive their success from the Scottish people; they breathe a spirit at once of patriotism and of that candor which renders patriotism unselfish and liberal." But their great charm is that it is always an educated, refined woman who speaks, one who knows the world and is full of shrewd common sense and of that sympathy for others which is inseparable from the highest type of womanhood. In 1825 Mrs. Grant was awarded a pension from the Crown of £100 per annum, and that, with the income from her books, made her last years free from pecuniary care, and the sunset of her life had no shadows except the kindly ones of the gathering night. She died, in 1838, when in her eighty-fourth year, and her faculties remained unimpaired to the end.

Mrs. Grant will be remembered by her prose writings rather than by her poetry, though at least one of her lyrics, " O Where, Tell Me Where," has won a place in all the collections of Scottish song and in the popular anthologies. Her " Memoirs of an American Lady " has run through many editions here, and is still reprinted. Its sale in America far exceeded that it enjoyed in Scotland, as might naturally be expected, but from that sale she failed to realize a dollar. That may be natural and legal, but it is not honest.

Few men outside of the fighting professions have had to undergo more changes in their lifework than did John Burtt. The peculiarity about his career is that it is sharply divided into two parts, the one in the Old World being a constant scene of trouble, ignominy, and despair, while in the New his path was one of quiet usefulness and dignity. He was born at Knockmarlock, near Kilmarnock, Ayrshire, in 1790, and after receiving the usual country school education was apprenticed to a weaver in "Auld Killie." His few spare hours were devoted to supplying the deficiencies of his scholastic training, or, rather, to carrying it beyond the point at which the village teacher was forced by circumstances to stop, and what Burtt accomplished during these leisure hours in the way of study was really wonderful. When sixteen years of age he was "pressed" into the navy while on a visit to Greenock, and compelled to serve his sovereign at sea for five years. Then he managed to escape, and, making his way back to Kilmarnock, he worked at the loom for a while, and then taught school there and afterward in Paisley.

Soon after settling in Paisley, Burtt became prominent among the local Radical leaders, and his position among them was, in time, so marked that for his own personal safety, to say nothing of his welfare, he determined to leave Scotland and try to win fortune in the young Republic. He arrived in America in 1817. After studying theology at Princeton, he was licensed to preach, and became minister of a Presbyterian church at Salem, N. J. In 1831 he edited a religious newspaper at Philadelphia, and two years later he moved to Cincinnati, where he continued his ministry and edited a religious paper called the "Standard." After a year or two spent as professor in a theological seminary at Cincinnati, he took pastoral charge of a church at Blackwoodtown, which he held until 1859, when he retired on account of his advancing years. He returned to Salem, and resided in that village till his death, in 1866.

Burtt published two volumes of his poetry. The first was issued at Kilmarnock in 1816, and the second appeared at Bridgeton, N. J., under the title of "Horae Poeticae: Transient Murmurs of a Solitary Lyre."

A name now almost forgotten, that of John Beveridge, for many years Professor of Languages in the College of

Philadelphia, deserves remembrance for his own abilities as a Latin scholar and poet as for the indirect influence he had upon the shaping of the career of Robert Burns. He was born in the south of Scotland, and taught school in Edinburgh and other places. Among his pupils was Thomas Blacklock, and Beveridge took a particular interest in directing the blind lad's thought to poetry, thinking that the pleasures of fancy might atone, in some degree, for his deprivation of sight. It was Beveridge who first brought out and fixed in Blacklock's mind the poetic impulse that made him cling to poetry as the solace of his life, and it was this poetic impulse that carried Blacklock to write the letter commendatory of Burns's writings which turned the thoughts of that brilliant genius from Jamaica to Edinburgh. In 1752 Beveridge emigrated to New England, and, after drifting around for several years, settled in Philadelphia in 1757 as a teacher. He could hardly be called a success in this profession, for he was a poor disciplinarian, and his short stature, shabby dress, and awkward manners made his pupils feel anything for him but reverence. Yet he turned out some excellent scholars, and he was always willing to encourage and applaud their efforts, although sometimes his good intentions in this regard were thwarted by his own unintentional indiscretions. Thus, in 1765, he published at Philadelphia a volume of his Latin poems, with English translations by his pupils. In the preface he announced: "They [the translations] are done by students under age, and if critics will only bear with them until their understandings are mature, I apprehend they are in a fair way of doing better." The pupils might be proud to see their efforts in print, but their pride would certainly receive a sharp fall when they read these apparently contemptuous words.

Literary theorists who are fond of asserting that the poetic spirit, or, rather, the faculty of giving expression to it, never descends from a father to his children would do well to consider the history of the humble Paisley family of Picken. The father, Ebenezer, was a poet of more than ordinary ability, and some of his lyrics rank among the indispensables in every Scottish collection. His son, Andrew B. Picken, inherited all his father's genius; his muse even essayed higher flights, but its full soaring was unquestionably retarded by the vicissitudes of his life. Poverty undoubtedly chained him to the earth, while his fancy might have been roaming through the spheres. In 1822, when in his twentieth year, he was induced to take an interest in a silly expedition to Poyais, on the Mosquito Coast, and his sufferings and adventures in that unfortunate episode formed afterward the themes for a series of vivid sketches in poetry and prose from his pen. From that scene of desolation Picken made his way to the West Indies, and, after getting employment there for some time, saved enough money to convey him back to Scotland, in 1828. But even there the fates were against him, and two years later he sailed for the United States. His fortunes did not improve by the change, and he suffered dire vicissitudes, and tried his fortune in many cities. His last field of operations was Montreal, and there he earned a fairly decent livelihood as a teacher of drawing until his death, in 1849. In poetry, Picken's best work is his "Bedouins," a production running through three cantos, which ought to be better known than it is at the present day, while his "Plague Ship" shows that he was a graceful, forceful, and interesting writer of prose. During the latter part of his life he was a regular and welcome contributor to Canadian newspapers and magazines.

Picken's footsteps were directed to Montreal by the fact that an elder sister resided there, supporting herself by teaching music, and doubtless it was her influence that induced him to settle down in that beautiful city and give up his weary wanderings. Joanna Belfrage Picken was born at Paisley in 1798, and arrived in Montreal in 1842. She was a writer of verses of at least respectable merit, and was a regular contributor to the "Literary Garland" and other publications. Her writings were never gathered together and issued in book form, although there was some talk of this being done shortly after her death, in 1859.

One of the strongest personalities in Scottish literary history of the eighteenth century was James Tytler, better known to readers of Scottish poetry, probably, as "Balloon Tytler." He was born in 1747 at Fern, Forfarshire, of which parish his father was minister. He studied medicine, made two voyages to Greenland, tried to build up a practice in Edinburgh, and finally became a literary hack, and in that capacity compiled, abridged, and wrote many books, and prepared others for the press, although he is now remembered mainly as the writer of a couple of fairly good songs. He was a most ingenious man, invented several mechanical contrivances, and had invariably on hand some grand scheme by which his own fortunes, or those of the world in general, were to be improved. He was also a busy man; always devising, always writing, and always in extreme poverty. Sometimes he was glad to seek refuge from his creditors by confining himself within the limits of the debtors' Sanctuary at Holyrood, although it seems impossible to imagine how the most optimistic creditor could even dream of ever recovering money from him. While in Edinburgh, in the Winter of 1786-7, Robert Burns formed the acquaintance of Tytler, and was frequently thrown into his society. In 1792, when the latter issued the prospectus of a newspaper, to be called the "Political Gazetteer," and which was intended to show up the shortcomings and denounce the repressive policy of the ruling powers against the people, the poet wrote to him: "Go on, Sir; lay bare, with undaunted heart and steady hand, that horrid mass of corruption called politics and statecraft."

The prospects for the issue of the "Political Gazetteer" did not pan out very well, and that same year Tytler tried to arouse the people to a sense of their wrongs by a manifesto addressed to them. The publication of this handbill was very obnoxious to the Government. Its language was impassioned and intemperate, and its sentiments were clearly seditious, as the laws of sedition were then interpreted. A warrant was at once issued for his arrest, but he escaped prison by flying to Ireland, and when his case was called, in his absence, for trial on January 7, 1793, he was outlawed. From Ireland Tytler managed to sail to America. We first hear of him in the New World at Salem, Mass., where he edited the "Salem Register." He turned his medical skill to account by publishing, in 1799, a "Treatise on the Plague and Yellow Fever," but the newspaper was his mainstay, and he continued to edit it until his death. This took place in 1804, and was the result of an accident. He was making his way home one dark night, and fell into a clay pit, where his body was found the next morning. Surely his was a career strange and wayward enough to form a basis for a dozen romances. Except for his few years in America, life was, at best, but a desolate road for him, and had he not been buoyed up by strong sentiments of hope, we can easily understand how the gloom might have caused his descent into the most abject poverty and defiant sin.

An even sadder story is that of John Lowe, who may be called the foremost of Scotland's single-poem poets. There are doubtless in Tytler's career many things which command our respect, for he was so much the victim of circumstances, so much a product and victim of the ill government of his times, that we can pity his misfortunes while we admire his undoubted genius. But in the case of John Lowe there is no room for pity, and all the misfortunes which came upon him he richly deserved. He was born at Kenmure, in Galloway, in 1750. His father was a gardener, and, like most of the Scottish peasants, desired to see his son engage in the ministry, and denied himself so that the necessary education might be provided. In due time young Lowe graduated, and found his first employment in the family of Mr. MacGhie of Airds as a tutor. The family included several beautiful daughters, one of whom captured the heart of the young tutor, or thought she did. He certainly captured hers. Another of the young ladies was engaged to be married to a young gentleman named Miller, and it was the news that Miller had been drowned at sea that inspired the song which has given Lowe a prominent place in the ranks of Scotland's song writers. Like every other heartless man, he could pour out any amount of sympathy for other people's sorrows, but had none to spare for woes of which he himself was the cause. He tried hard to get a church in Scotland, but somehow failed, and despairing of obtaining either position or preferment in his native land, he resolved to seek them in the American Colonies. With the fondest vows, and professions of undying affection, he parted from his love at Airds and sailed for America in 1771. So far as can be seen, he forgot all about his plighted love very soon. Settling at Fredericksburg, Va., he tried to earn his living by teaching, but was only moderately successful. Then he fell in love, or professed to fall in love, with a Virginian lady, but she would have nothing to do with him, and married another. Her sister, however, seemed to have an attachment for him, and he married her out of gratitude. Meanwhile he had taken holy orders in the Episcopal Church, and was established as rector of a congregation at Fredericksburg, but he did not prosper in a worldly way. He speedily tired of his wife, she discovered he was by no means the angel she had believed him to be before marriage, and her conduct was certainly not conducive to his comfort, to say nothing of his happiness. Everything went wrong with him, somehow, and to soothe his misery, like many a fool, he took to drink. Then the end came rapidly, and he laid down the burden of life at Windsor Lodge, Va., in 1798, leaving behind him as his most useful legacy only the moral of a shipwrecked life—a life which would not have been shipwrecked if truth had only been its rudder. Lowe wrote several poems, but they are all forgotten with the exception of " Mary's Dream," yet that alone is sufficient to give him immortality.

A pathetic memory is that of John Graham, once well known in New York as the " Blind Scottish Poet," but of whose career little can now be gathered. Some of the old Scotch residents of whom the writer made inquiries in the seventies remembered him well, and spoke kindly of him, but their recollection was simply that of a respectable old man, a man of quick intelligence, who earned a scanty living by selling books, especially those compiled or written by himself. He was blind, but made no complaint on that score or sought charity on account of his affliction, and his features were readily aroused into expressive play from the usual placid repose of total blindness by any reference to Scotland or mention of anything pertaining to Scotsmen. So far as could be gathered, he was a native of Stirlingshire, and settled in America in early life. How or when he lost his eyesight is not known. He resided in New York, making a livelihood of the poorest sort, until 1850, when he migrated to the vicinity of Albany and managed a small property which had been bequeathed to him, and there his later years were spent in comparative comfort. He died about the year 1860.

One of Graham's principal works was published in 1833, and, under the title of "Flowers of Melody," gave a capital selection of Scottish songs. The notes, critical, biographical, and illustrative, with which he graced the work stamped him as being a man of taste, research, and intellect. It is a valuable book, and capable of ranking with later and more pretentious publications. With another of his works, however, we have more to do. This is his "Scottish National Melodies," published in 1841, with music. Although his verses were pleasing, we cannot rank Graham very highly as a poet. His rhythm is far from perfect, while his imagery is commonplace or tame. But throughout the whole there runs a deep patriotism which forces us to admire the writer and read his productions with great interest.

Another intensely patriotic poet, whose connection with America was, however, exceedingly brief—he crossed the Atlantic only to find a grave—was Robert Allan of Kilbarchan. He was born in that poetically famous Renfrewshire village in 1774, and was by trade a muslin weaver. He commenced writing verse in early life, and his inclinations in that direction were much encouraged by the friendship of Robert Tannahill and Robert A. Smith. The latter not only inserted several of Allan's songs in his "Scottish Minstrel," but set most of them to music. Allan also contributed several poems to Motherwell's "Harp of Renfrewshire," and a volume of his writings appeared at Glasgow in 1836. In his edition of Tannahill (which is full of references to Allan) the late Mr. David Semple wrote: "The reception the volume met with greatly disappointed the author. He supposed his merits as a poet had been overlooked, and, brooding over the disappointment, he became irritable in his temper and gloomy in appearance. Some of his friends had emigrated to America and succeeded, and he was determined to follow them. As he was in the sixty-seventh year of his age, several of his acquaintances remonstrated with him, but without success, and he sailed on 28th April, 1841, from Greenock for New York. All went well until the ship reached the Banks of Newfoundland, where the vessel was detained eight days by foggy weather, and the poet during that time caught a cold. He landed on the 1st and died on the 7th June, 1841."

From the consideration of such lives as Tytler, Lowe, and Allan, with their inevitable sadness, we turn, for the sake of the change, to the happy and perfectly rounded career of the Rev. Dr. George Scott, one of the many sacred singers whom Scotland has given to America. Dr. Scott was born at Langside, Glasgow, in 1806, studied for the ministry, mainly in Glasgow, and emigrated to America in 1832. Two years later he became pastor of a church at German Valley, and afterward had charge of the First Reformed Dutch Church at Newark, N. J., where he remained till his death, in 1858. He received the degree of D. D. from Lafayette College in 1844, and in 1848 published a keenly critical and decidedly able dissertation "On the Genius of Robert Pollok." The labor of his life, and latterly its greatest earthly solace, was his lengthy poem of "The Guardian Angel," which saw the light of print about the time of his death. "It is," says the author, "in the form of a dream, a series of conversations concerning the invisible state, the existence and ministry of holy angels, as well as their guardianship over men, held by persons who met accidentally at different places, connected by a slender thread of story." This is not a promising theme for a poem; one would need the genius of John Bunyan to build a popular work on such a foundation, and the poem as a whole is, it must be confessed, rather tedious. But it is full of many fine passages, and breathes throughout a deep religious feeling—the phase of religious feeling which, somehow, possibly because it is a true interpretation, inspires hope and peace in the heart of the reader. Religious poetry, it must be confessed, except it be brief productions in the nature of hymns or Sabbath school recitations, or work of surpassing genius like "Paradise Lost," seems to be soon forgotten. All between these extremes appears to serve its day and generation—the generation that knew that writer—and then quietly to pass into the shadows of neglect. There is one peculiarity of this poem, however, which should in this place be pointed out. It is the result of thoughts conceived in Edinburgh and enlarged and extended at such places in America as Niagara Falls and the Mississippi, and therefore owes its inspiration directly to both countries—a true Scottish-American production.

Beyond question the sweetest and best of all the Scottish-American lyrists was Hew Ainslie, who died at Louisville, Ky., in 1878. His "Ingleside" has long been a favorite in America, and the lines beginning "It's dowie in the hint o' hairst" have been popular among all classes in Scotland, especially since they were introduced so pathetically in Dr. Norman Macleod's beautiful story of "Wee Davie." Ainslie was born at Bargeny, Ayrshire, in 1792, his father being a farmer. After being educated at Ballantrae, he was put to work on the Bargeny estates for the benefit of his health, and when eighteen years of age became apprenticed to a lawyer at Glasgow. But he had become enamored of the life he had been leading in the woods, and to escape beginning his apprenticeship he fled from his father's house and took refuge with some relatives at Roslin, near Edinburgh. There his father soon followed, and took up his own residence. Young Ainslie's first employment was that of a bookkeeper in an Edinburgh brewery, and then he got a position as copyist in the General Register Office in the Scottish capital. He also married about that time, and soon was busy solving the oft-attempted puzzle in human life of supporting a wife and weans on a small salary. A short season employed as amanuensis to Professor Dugald Stewart was a pleasant interlude in a life which seemed to carry nothing but gloom in its future, and then, in 1821, Ainslie made up his mind to emigrate to the United States. Before doing so, he paid a farewell visit to Ayrshire in company with two friends, and the story of the trip was told in a little volume—his first—entitled "A Pilgrimage to the Land of Burns." It appeared in 1822, and was reprinted in the memorial volume, containing Ainslie's memoirs and a selection from his writings, published at Paisley in 1891. The work has some fine descriptive prose passages and a few good songs. Shortly after its publication Ainslie bade farewell to Scotland, and settled on a small farm in Rensselaer County, N. Y. A year later he was joined by his wife and children. In 1842 he moved to New Harmony, Ind., as he had thrown himself with all his heart into Robert Owen's social schemes, and thought he saw in the settlement at New Harmony the beginning of an earthly paradise. The practical working of the scheme did not, however, come up to his expectations, and after a while he removed to Shippensport, Ohio, where he established a small brewery. After brief residences in various towns, he finally settled in Louisville, which became his home in 1829, and was regarded as such until the end. In 1852, however, he visited New York at the invitation of the Wellstood family, (the well-known engravers already referred to,) and continued with them for over ten years. In 1862 he revisited Scotland, and spent there two very happy years among scenes that had long been but a memory. He was warmly welcomed on every side, and carried back with him over the Atlantic a host of fresh reminiscences and the good wishes of many new as well as old friends, which made Scotland dearer to him than ever. Soon after returning, he settled again at Louisville, and his declining years were tempered by the devoted care of his family, then all grown up and "weel-daein.'"

Ainslie will ever hold a place among the poets of Scotland—not in the foremost rank, certainly, but along with Beattie, Wilson, Motherwell, Rodger, and others in the second circle. He wrote much, and often carelessly, but sufficient came from his pen to make a volume of verse excellent enough in quality to give him a recognized position as a poet in any literature. He delighted in the use of the Doric; his years of toiling and excitement and worrying in America seemed to make it dearer to him as he advanced in life, and it uplifted his muse out of the levels, for everything which he wrote which was not "in guid braid Scots" seems flat and tame and little else than rhymed prose—prose that would have been better expressed had it not been hampered by rhyme. "Mr. Ainslie," wrote Dr. John D. Ross in a memoir in hi valuable volume on "Scottish Poets in America," "was a poet in the truest sense of the word. His love for Scotland, no doubt, stimulated his muse to sing forth her praises in songs which will ever retain a place in the hearts of his countrymen, but apart from this he has left us numerous ballads and lyrical pieces which we could not willingly let die. Many of these are of a very pathetic nature, and, in addition to their being very beautiful, they contain excellent sentiments expressed in the simplest of words." Three editions of his poems were published in this country during his lifetime, and contributions from his pen appeared in "Whistlebinkie," and selections from his writings in all modern collections of Scottish poetry or song.

William Wilson, bookbinder and bookseller, Poughkeepsie, N. Y., is still remembered as a pleasing writer, some of whose songs will long keep his memory green and give him a place in American literature. He was born at Crieff in 1801. His father having died in infancy, William began, at the age of seven years, the hard battle of life by being sent to help in herding sheep, and when fourteen years of age was apprenticed to a "cloth lapper" in Glasgow. He afterward removed to Dundee, where he varied the tedium of his trade by contributing to the local papers. Then he went to Edinburgh, where he was enabled to start in business as a dealer in coal. In 1833 he emigrated to the United States, and, a year later, settled in Poughkeepsie, where he conducted a book business successfully until his death, in 1860. His son, James Grant Wilson, has done good literary work as editor of several important publications, as well as by much original writing.

William Wilson's poems have twice been published, and received very considerate treatment at the hands of the critics. One of them wrote: "He was a genuine son of song, and his genius is deserving of even wider recognition than it receives at present. Simplicity and kindness are his greatest characteristics, and are shown in every line he writes. He is earnest and direct in his teaching, and whether singing the praises of his native land or the glories of the land in which he died, whether mourning beside the grave of a loved one, or warbling 'Stanzas to a Child,' the hearty, whole-souled character of the man shines clearly forth."

A truly gentle life was that of Mrs. Margaret Maxwell Martin, who died a few years ago at an advanced age at Columbia, S. C. She was born at Dumfries in 1807, and crossed the Atlantic with her parents in 1815. They settled at Columbia, S. C., and there Margaret not only received her education, but married William Martin and spent her many years of useful life. For over seventeen years she managed and taught a female seminary at Columbia, and she published many volumes of poetry and prose, among which her "Religious Poems" (1858) and "Scenes and Scenery of South Carolina" (1869) must hold a prominent place.

A man of much promise, full of poetic spirit and rich fancy, but which, however, never developed at all in keeping with early hopes, was William Kennedy, who is better known to readers of Scottish poetry as the friend of William Motherwell than for anything he contributed to the minstrelsy of his native land. He was born at Paisley, or near it, in 1799; contributed, with Motherwell, to the "Paisley Magazine," and published in 1827 a volume of poems, which was flatteringly received. He afterward removed to London and entered upon the career of a man of letters. Although fairly successful, he gladly accepted an offer to accompany Lord Durham, Governor General of Canada, to his post in the capacity of private secretary. When Lord Durham's term of office expired Kennedy was appointed British Consul at Galveston, Texas, and held that office for many years. His observations at this pleasant post were published in two volumes, at London, in 1841, under the title of "Rise, Progress, and Prospects of the Republic of Texas." In 1847 he left America, and, with the aid of a Government pension, took up his residence near London. He died in 1849. His best-known poem is one he wrote after a visit to the grave of Motherwell, in the Glasgow Necropolis, and a set of stirring lines to Scotland, written on leaving it. One or two of his songs, notably "The Serenade" and the "Camp Song," were once very popular in the United States, and are still favorites in Texas.

It seems a pity that the exacting jealousy of journalism should have kept David Gray, long editor of the Buffalo "Courier," from devoting time to poetical composition; otherwise, there seems no reason to doubt he might have obtained a foremost place among the world-renowned poets of America. But a man must live, and the thousand and one cares and anxieties of journalistic life are not conducive to the peace which permits the muse to essay lofty flights. So what we have to show for the poetic gift in Gray is mainly fragmentary compositions, "verses of occasion," although here and there his soul fairly gave itself up to the reign of fancy and, in the case of the verses called "The Last Indian Council on the Genesee," we have something that arrests attention, that carries us with the spirit of the author into realms beyond the veil, something that is bound to hold a place in literature. Gray was born at Edinburgh in 1836, and settled in America when a boy. In 1859 he secured a position on the Buffalo "Courier," and in 1867 became its editor in chief. He held that position until 1882, when his health compelled his retirement. Afterward he acted as secretary to the Niagara Park Commission, and in that capacity did good work in restoring that great example of nature's mighty handiwork to a condition as free from evidences of the commercial instincts of mankind as possible. But his health continued poor, and in 1888, when he had just started on a proposed journey to Cuba for rest, he was killed in a railroad accident near Binghamton, N. Y. Soon after that sad accident two elegant volumes, containing his life, letters, and poems, were published at Buffalo, and sufficiently indicate how valuable was the life thus summarily ended. Gray was proud of his Scotch birth and parentage, and took an active interest in Scotch affairs in Buffalo. As a journalist, he was the equal of any man of his time, while in private life his home was long one of the literary centres of Buffalo—a city of which literature is by no means one of its distinguishing features.

At the principal of the many enthusiastic celebrations, in January, 1859, of the centenary of the birthday of Robert Burns in New York Henry Ward Beecher, then in the very zenith of his marvelous power as an orator, was selected to deliver one of the speeches. There was some dubiety in many minds as to how he would treat the memory of the bard as a whole, and how he would view some of his shortcomings. At that juncture before the centenary festival came off, the following lines formed part of a poem which appeared in one of the New York papers and created considerable discussion:

> "His few sma' fau'ts ye need na tell;
> Folk say ye're no o'er guid yoursel;
>   But De'il may care:
> Gin ye're but half as guid as Rab,
>   We'll ask nae mair.
>
> "A century hence, an' wha can tell
> What may befa' yer cannie sel'?
>   Some holy preacher
> May tak' the cudgels up for ane
>   Ca'd Harry Beecher."

Mr. Beecher did the poet all the justice that his fondest admirers could desire. The history of the poem did not cease, however, with the event which suggested it. It appeared at irregular intervals and in a desultory fashion until Mr. Beecher and his old friend Theodore Tilton had their memorable struggle in the law courts. Then some one remembered it. Several expressions in the verses quoted were deemed peculiarly applicable, and it was felt that the prophecy of the poet had been realized within a quarter of the century she had allotted for the need to arise for a defender of the preacher. So the lines were then reprinted in nearly every paper in the land and sagely commented on. Very little seems to be known of Mrs. J. Webb, the authoress, except that she was a resident of New York, frequently contributed to the poets' corners of the New York papers, and died in this city about 1862. She was a woman of undoubted genius, a true poet, and every one of her effusions we have seen are of more than ordinary merit.

A contemporary of Mrs. Webb's in New York City, and who was well known not alone as a writer of poems, but as a sculptor, was George W. Coutts, a native of Edinburgh, who settled in New York about 1856. He was one of the early members of the Caledonian Club, and not only took a deep interest in its welfare, but executed several exceedingly lifelike and skillfully modeled busts of its prominent members. During the visit of the Prince of Wales to America Coutts published a volume of his poems, which he dedicated to the Prince, and of that transaction he was very proud. He did not prosper in America for various reasons, and early in 1870 returned to Scotland. His death took place at Colchester, Essex, in 1895.

Many years ago a family of musicians used to give entertainments throughout the United States, in Canada, and long were general favorites. The Fairbairn Family was known all over the continent, and clever they all were—the father and two, perhaps three, daughters. But the style of their programmes did not vary much, and the craving for something new that possesses the amusement world—Scottish as well as other sorts—drove them to the wall. Their last appearances in New York—in the seventies—were dismal failures, although every one admired the cleverness displayed, and soon after they left that city they got stranded somewhere in the upper part of the State of New York, and were finally heard from as living quietly—from necessity—on a small farm they had secured or bought in Canada. The father of the family, Angus Fairbairn, was an undoubted man of genius, and had he only possessed some share of business tact ought to have made a fortune by his own talents and those of his family. But life seemed to be for him a continual struggle, a constant present disappointment, with plenty of hopes, however, in the future—only they always remained there. He was born near Edinburgh in 1829. While comparatively a young man he began his career as a lecturer and vocalist in London, and the success of his efforts led to his making a tour through the United Kingdom, giving similar entertainments, combining lecture and music, as Wilson, the "king of Scotch vocalists," and which were afterward introduced all over the world by David Kennedy. In 1868 Fairbairn published in London a volume of his verses under the title of "Poems by Angus Fairbairn, the Scottish Singer." Very soon afterward he removed to Canada and commenced the career of public entertainer which ended in the melancholy and unsatisfactory manner which has been related. Poor Fairbairn was worthy of a better fate. He was a warm-hearted man, full of national enthusiasm, and possessed a rich vein of fancy—a vein that colored his whole life and gave him many glints of sunshine in spite of the clouds that hovered around him from the dawn to the darkness.

In 1872 the Scottish community at Montreal was startled by news of the death by accident of John Fraser, better known among them as "Cousin Sandy" the poet. He had been on a visit to Ottawa, and while enjoying a ramble among some rocks near the Parliament Buildings fell into the river and was drowned. He was a native of Portsoy, Banffshire, where he was born in 1810. A tailor by trade, he early imbibed pronounced political opinions, for the tailor's " board " was then often transformed into a forum, and Fraser became a Chartist. He also began writing for the press, and such publications as "Reynolds's Newspaper," "The Northern Star," and "Lloyd's Weekly" received his contributions gladly. But somehow things went against him, and he concluded, in 1860, to settle in Canada, where his father had taken up his abode some years previously. He arrived at his father's home at Stanstead, P. Q., only to find that his parent had died a few days before. He started in business as a tailor, and did very well, but he got tired of life in the country and removed to Montreal, where he became traveling agent for a bookselling and publishing concern. In that capacity his business took him all over Canada, and he made friends everywhere. In 1870, after being known for many years as a poet by his contributions to newspaper and periodical literature, he published a volume of his poems, a slender volume, printed on only one side of each page and entitled a "Tale of the Sea," the name of its opening and lengthiest piece. He sold the volume as he went along on his journeys, and the edition, which met with a very kindly reception at the hands of the newspaper critics, was soon exhausted. Fraser might have held political office but for his known advanced Radical opinions, and for the fact that in his poems he mercilessly ridiculed whoever or whatever displeased him—whatever he thought was wrong—in party or individual, statesman or politician. He was by no means a great poet, and he expended too much of what ability he had in merely passing themes, though it is easy to see that his ability was great enough to have won for him a higher and more popular position in the ranks of Canada's poets than is now even likely to be accorded to him. His principal poem, the "Tale of the Sea," contains many stirring—even beautiful—passages, its story is graphically told, but its theme hardly becomes the dignity of poetry. So, too, with much of his political pieces, their "snap" and vitality have departed with the causes which inspired them.

There died in Brooklyn on May 12, 1894, a Scottish poet and song writer who had long enjoyed considerable popularity on both sides of the Atlantic and been awarded a prominent place among the lyrical writers who have given to Scotland the richest body of song in the world. This was Thomas C. Latto, one of the original "Whistlebinkians," who for many years prior to his death led a life of comfortable leisure amid the companionship of his books, and beguiling the days to the end by adding to his own literary work. Latto was born at Kingsbarns, Fifeshire, where his father was schoolmaster, in 1818. After studying law for five sessions at St. Andrews he went to Edinburgh, where for some time he was employed in the office of the late Sheriff Aytoun. He also resided in Dundee for a time, and for two years was engaged in Glasgow in a commission business. From the time he went to Edinburgh he became known as a poet, and his contributions were everywhere welcomed, as was a volume of his collected pieces which he ventured upon publishing. His "Whistlebinkie" songs and several pieces that appeared in Blackwood's Magazine showed he had caught the public taste, and a bright literary future in Scotland seemed to be within the grasp of the young writer. But fate ordained otherwise, and in 1854 he crossed the Atlantic to begin life anew under strange conditions. Settling in New-York City, he soon made hosts of friends among his countrymen, and so high was their appreciation of his genius that it was in his interests the company was formed that started the Scottish American Journal in 1857. Latto was editor, and the business management was intrusted to William Finlay, another Scotsman, a newspaper man of much enterprise, who afterward died under distressing circumstances in Canada. The two men were ill matched, and the paper soon passed into other hands, and ultimately won a high rank among American weeklies. Mr. Latto finally moved to Brooklyn, and for a long time was connected with the "Times" of that city. A volume of his poems was issued in 1892 at Paisley under the title of "Memorials of Auld Lang Syne," but while it met with a flattering reception at the hands of the critics, it failed to command public interest. It really contains some of his best work and deserved a wider degree of popularity than seemed to be its fate. About the same time Mr. Latto issued a substantial volume containing a memoir and selection of poems of his old friend, Hew Ainslie, and it enjoyed a wide sale.

In a memorial tribute to Latto, published soon after the poet's death in The Edinburgh Scotsman and other papers, Dr. John D. Ross, who probably knew more of his latest literary work and aspirations than any one else, said: "As a man of letters his place at present may simply be among the minor poets of his country, but he has left poems in manuscript superior even to those acknowledged immortal effusions of his which have already been published, and these will ultimately procure for him a high position among the prominent Scottish poets of the nineteenth century." However this may be, we can simply judge by the record before us, and we can only say that the memory of Latto and his other works will be kept alive by his lyrical pieces, rather than by anything else from his pen which is now before the world. Such pieces as "When We Were at the Schule," "Sly Widow Skinner," "The Kiss Ahint the Door," and one or two others will always hold a place in the literature of his country and in the hearts of his countrymen.

The late Rev. Dr. Robert L. Kerr, for over sixteen years a minister in the Congregational Church in this country, was the author of at least one volume of poems and several volumes of a devotional cast. He was born in Kilmarnock, and for a time was minister of a church in Forres. For seven years he was pastor of the Congregational Church at Wakefield, Kan., and then accepted a call to Tomah, Wis., and died in 1895, shortly after entering on his duties there. A volume of poems, mostly in his native Doric, was found in his desk ready for publication, but it has never appeared. Dr. Kerr was a man of superior ability, but never seemed to rise in life in accordance with his deserts.

There was a vein of true poetic sentiment in the mental equipment of Donald Ramsay of Boston, who died at Liverpool while en route to Scotland, in 1892. He was born at Glasgow in 1848, and started the business of life by becoming a printer in a valentine-making establishment. When he died he was managing Director of the Heliotype Printing Company of Boston. Leading an active business life, Mr. Ramsay found little time to devote to the muses, but whatever he permitted to appear in print testified to his gracefulness of diction and the delicacy and exuberance of his fancy. He was proud of Scotland, and, like so many others, when the muse was with him his heart was across the sea. It seems a pity that he did not gather his poems into a volume before his untimely death. They are, most of them, too good to be forgotten, and that seems now likely to be their fate, scattered as they are through all sorts of publications.

In many respects the most thoughtful, the most richly endowed, of all the Scottish American poets was Alexander McLachlan of Amaranth, Ontario, who died suddenly at Orangeville on March 20, 1896. Somehow his genius never seemed to find the heights into which most people acquainted with the poet deemed it capable of reaching, and though he had a wide circle of readers, it was mainly limited to Canada, and he failed to win that general meed of approbation and popularity which has been so often accorded to men who did not possess one tithe of his ability. Circumstances, seemingly, were against him; how or why we cannot exactly determine, but in reviewing the career of this man we cannot help from thinking that circumstances, or, to put it flatly—luck—have as much to do with molding and shaping a man's life career as have his own abilities and resplendent virtues. Of course, this is rank moral treason, according to the Samuel Smiles school of biographers, but no man who has had much practical knowledge of the world will gainsay its truth or be unable to point to more than one illustration in its support.

At all events, McLachlan's life was passed without the recognition it deserved, and in a constant fight with poverty, until, in his old age, the generosity of a number of his benefactors cleared his farm at Amaranth from mortgage and debt, and so made his closing years pass on to their fruition without the perpetual worriment about making ends meet, which had for so long before been painfully in evidence in connection with his literary and business plans.

McLachlan was born at Johnstone, Renfrewshire, in 1820. Like most of the bards of Renfrewshire, that county of poets, he was born and reared in humble circumstances, but from his earliest years he imbibed that sturdy sense of independence which is so marked a feature in the Scottish character. When young he learned to be a tailor and worked for a time at that trade in Glasgow. He was a studious young man, according to his opportunities, and developed into a stanch adherent of Chartism. Glasgow and Paisley at that time were strongly stirred by the political movement that promised to enlarge citizen freedom, (and did enlarge it, in spite of Peterloo massacres, prisons, hulks, and other weapons of contentment,) and as a result the flood of oratory on such places as Glasgow Green and the Braes o' Gleniffer was something extraordinary. Among others, young McLachlan caught the art of public speaking, and was always listened to with attention because his words were carefully thought out, and he was a perfect master of every question on which he aired his views, a compliment that cannot be paid to many political orators.

In 1820, seeing no chance for improving his condition in Scotland, McLachlan emigrated to Canada, and soon after his arrival settled on a farm. That occupation was the basis of his career thereafter, but he was known a few years after settling there as a lecturer on literary topics, and in poetry and prose was a frequent contributor to the periodical press of the country. In 1862 he revisited Scotland on a mission to speak upon the advantages of Canada as a field for immigration, and his lectures on that theme were eagerly listened to all over the country and attracted general attention. His reception in his native country was an exceptionally flattering one. He was welcomed on every side, received with many marks of honor, and presented with quite a number of valuable tokens of love from admiring friends.

In 1855 he published his first volume of poetry, and it was followed by two others at short intervals, while in 1875 a collected edition of his writings appeared in Toronto. All these volumes were very highly praised by the press and by critics, but not one of them added much, if anything, to the poet's financial resources. His lecturing expeditions had made him well known all over Canada, and he had friends in every section, but for the last ten or twelve years of his life he confined himself mainly to the farm, beguiling the tedium of each long wintry season by his pen. He continued to woo the muse to the last, and age did not seem to weaken his fancy or to lessen his love for the beautiful in nature. Latterly he soared into realms of thought at which most poets, even the most gifted, enter with dread—the why, wherefore, and whither of life; its mystery, its recompense; the meaning of its signs, its promises; the present and the future, and if he did not succeed in unraveling any of the secrets, if he did not succeed in piercing the veil that separates the seen from the unseen, he at least gives us the impression of one whose whole soul was in the quest of a solution of the mystery of life; that of an intellectual pioneer of a giant mold piercing through the forest and brushing aside all that seemed to obstruct his view of the land that lay beyond, dimly shimmering as at the end of a long and narrow vista among the trees.

In connection with the singers we may be pardoned here for departing from a rule hitherto pretty generally observed so far in this volume, and make reference to a few of those who, in America, are still weaving their lays and adding, in greater or less degree, to the poetical anthology of the land of their adoption. Sons of song are seldom, somehow, overburdened with their store of this world's goods, and as they are all doing something, or honestly trying to do something, to add to the pleasures of existence, attempting it may be to lift men from the contemplation of the mere things of this life to the sweeter realms of fancy, or the still more practical purpose of developing the good that is in them, calling into play, as it were, the exercise of their higher nature, it may be not out of place to gratify some of them at least by a slight reference here. In view of this, some notice of the "living choir" may close his chapter. All those mentioned, and others who might be mentioned if space permitted, will be acknowledged as sweet singers, even if it be admitted that they have "missed the highest gift in poetry," as a recent reviewer aptly put it in estimating the value of the poetic gifts of the late Bayard Taylor.

The venerable "Bard of Lochfyneside," Evan McColl, still resides in Toronto, enjoying the beautiful sunset of a life that has been passed in comparative quiet, and broken by no ambition save recognition of his poetic merits, an ambition that was fairly gratified many years ago. McColl was born at the clachan of Kenmore, Argyllshire, in 1808, and received as liberal an education as the parish of Inveraray afforded. By his twenty-third year he had become famous throughout the Highlands for his poems in the ancient language of that region, his mother tongue, which continued to be the tongue of his thoughts throughout his career. His English writings, beautiful as most of them are, are but translations, after all, from the Gaelic in which they were conceived and fashioned and clothed.

In 1836 he published his first volume, a collection of his English as well as Gaelic poems, under the title of "The Mountain Minstrel." It was very heartily received, and the author felt encouraged in 1839 to issue a volume, "Clarsach nam Beann," solely devoted to Gaelic productions, and it widened the measure of his fame in the north, while his other volume made him known to readers unacquainted with the language spoken in the Garden of Eden. In 1839 he became a clerk in the Customs Service at Liverpool, and ten years later paid a visit to Canada for the purpose of seeing his relatives. To his native land he never returned. He secured a position in the Customs Service at Kingston, Ontario, and there he remained until he was, by dint of long service, permitted to retire on a small pension. He soon became a prominent member of the Scottish colony at Kingston, was active in the work of the St. Andrew's Society, and for many years honored it by acting as its bard, and in that capacity seldom allowed a festival to pass without hailing the occasion with a song. In Canada he has several times published a volume of his poetical compositions, and to the newspapers of the Dominion he has been and is a frequent contributor.

Alexander H. Wingfield, a resident of Hamilton, Ontario, since 1850, is the author of at least one poem—"The Crape on the Door"—that will live long after he has passed over to the land where the poets never cease singing. At one time it was thought that many gems might be added to the poetry of the continent by his pen, but somehow these high hopes have not been realized. Mr. Wingfield has done some creditable work, and some of his lines, such as "A Shillin' or Twa," are not only far above the average, but stamp him as a true poet; yet he seems to us to have frittered away his gifts on themes that were unworthy the attention of any but the most commonplace poetasters. He was born at Blantyre, Lanarkshire, Dr. Livingstone's birthplace, in 1828, and was early sent to work in a cotton factory in Glasgow. In 1847 he settled in the beautiful town of Auburn, N. Y., and three years later removed to Hamilton, where he secured employment as a mechanic in the shops of the Great Western Railway. In 1877 he received an appointment in the Canadian Customs Department, and in that vocation his days are still passed.

For many years E. N. Lamont, a native of Argyllshire, was one of the best-known writers on the New York press, and for a time was one of the editors of the "Inter Ocean" of Chicago. A graceful, fluent writer, full of humor and strange conceits, he had the happy art of telling a newspaper story with those little indefinable touches of gracefulness in style and appositeness in thought which is not generally regarded as appertaining to the rush and excitement of newspaper work. As an essayist pure and simple Mr. Lamont was without an equal while in harness, but he has for some years been living a life of placid retirement in Guernsey, one of the Channel islands. During his years of newspaper activity Mr. Lamont was wont to woo the muse as a relaxation from the vexations and heartbreaks incidental to such a career, and many of his verses have been frequently reprinted, often without his name.

Mr. D. M. Henderson, bookseller, Baltimore, is another writer who has done much to make beautiful the strains of the Scottish-American harp. Born in Glasgow in 1851, Mr. Henderson settled in Baltimore in 1873, and found employment as clerk until he was able to enter into business for himself. In 1888 he published a volume containing a selection of his poetical writings, and was gratified at the kindly treatment it received from the critics, as well as its ready acceptance by the public. One of the sweetest of the living Scottish-American poets is Mr. Robert Whittet, one of the best-known citizens of Richmond, Va., and a gentleman whose assistance has often been evoked by the writer of this work in connection with many individuals. Mr. Whittet was born at Perth in 1829, and was long engaged in business as a printer there. In 1869, although his business was fairly successful, he desired a change, and he crossed the Atlantic. Purchasing some four hundred acres of land near Williamsburg, Va., he essayed an agricultural career, but after a time he realized that "there was nothing in it," and he removed to Richmond, started again in his old trade, and now is at the head of one of the best-equipped printing plants in the South. In 1882 he published a volume of verse under the title of "The Brighter Side of Suffering, and Other Poems," which met with a large sale and stamped him as a poet of no ordinary merit.

Mr. D. MacGregor Crerar, ex-President of the New York Burns Society and its Secretary for over twenty-five years, is a writer of no mean ability, whose lines display a fullness of thought, a carefulness of diction, and a concentration of sentiment which are the very essence of poetic composition. Beyond a poem on "Robert Burns," printed at the request of the Burns Society, Mr. Crerar has published nothing in book form, although often re-

quested to do so, especially since he appeared as one of
the poetic heroes in Mr. William Black's novel of "Standfast, Craig-Royston." Possibly his strongest pieces are
his sonnets, although in such lyrics as "Caledonia's Blue
Bells" he touches the heart of every reader who possesses
even a spark of sentiment, while his lines entitled "The
Eirlic Well" and "My Bonnie Rowan Tree" are classical in their beauty. But whatever this author writes has
a certain standard below which he never falls, for he believes that the muse is one of the best gifts heaven vouchsafes to men, and that for the gift men should in return
clothe its utterances with the utmost care. He is a native
of Amulree, Perthshire.

Dr. J. M. Harper of Quebec, one of the best-known
educationalists in Canada, is also one of that country's
poets. He was born in Johnstone, Renfrewshire, in 1845,
and has been not only a frequent contributor to the press,
but the author of a number of historical and biographical
works, while as a lecturer he has won many hearty encomiums. All his poems, whether Scotch "or otherwise," betray a keen sense of the human heart, an intense
love for nature, and a hearty appreciation of all that is
beautiful and true. He sings frequently of Scotland and on
Scottish themes, but his muse is mainly cosmopolitan, and
deals with humanity irrespective of land or clime. It
might be said that he judges the world through Scotch
spectacles, but if that be a fault, this work is not likely
to admit it. There is not a namby-pamby line in all Dr.
Harper's verses, nothing that is not worth reading for
its thought and sentiment, and nothing that will not elevate the reader.

Mr. James D. Crichton of Brooklyn, who was born in
Edinburgh in 1847, is a writer very similar in his tastes
and sympathies to Dr. Harper. A man of superior intellect, widely read, and investing every subject on which
he writes with a peculiar charm, the reading public have
a right to expect more from him than has yet appeared.
He has not written much, but what he has written is full
of melody, and confirms in us the impression that in him
poetry—song—is a natural gift, which the world has a

right to expect to see utilized to its fullest extent. Another Brooklyn poet who has not written as much as he should have written is Andrew McLean, editor of the "Citizen" and for many years managing editor of "The Brooklyn Eagle." He is a native of Dumbartonshire, but has resided in America since his fifteenth year, and his devotion to journalism has checked his inclination to wander into other fields in which he might have made his mark in literature. Mr. William M. Wood is also a Scotch Brooklyn journalist whose abilities as a poet have never been fully cultivated. As editor of "The Brooklyn Daily Times" his days are fully occupied, but what he has written has stamped him as undeniably capable of yet higher flights. Mr. Wood is a native of Edinburgh and started in life as a printer.

Robert Reid, ("Rob Wanlock,") the "laureate of the Scottish moors," has resided in Montreal for several years and has won an honorable position in Canadian as well as in Scottish literature. It cannot be said that the Dominion has influenced his muse to any extent. He lives in Canada, but his heart is in Scotland, and when his muse is stirred it is by a breeze wafted from the old green hills and dim gray muirs of his ain countree. Born in the pleasant village of Wanlockhead, right on the boundary between the counties of Lanark and Dumfries, it is of the South of Scotland he sings, and the scenery and landscapes of that section give to his lines their peculiar color, just as Argyllshire has colored the Scottish landscape in the poems of that older bard, Evan McColl. Mr. Reid is one of nature's poets, that is to say, he finds his best themes in the lilt of the laverock, the wild cry of the whaup, the brown heather, and the simple affections of the heart, and to read his lines is to get, as it were, a fresh and delightful glimpse of the land he loves so well.

Andrew Wanless, bookseller in Detroit, has published several volumes of his poetry and won a wide circle of readers. He was born at Longformacus, Berwickshire, in 1825. In 1851 he settled in Toronto, where he engaged in business as a bookbinder, but was burned out and lost his all. In 1861 he removed to Detroit, and slowly but surely recovered his losses. He is not only a poet, but an authority on poets, particularly Scotch, and he discusses their merits with rare critical acumen and with a fund of story and illustration which makes him a delightful conversationalist. All his own poems are Scotch, and he handles " our mither tongue " with the ease of a master.

James Kennedy, a native of Forfarshire and many years a resident of New York City, has published a couple of volumes of verse and written much that has appeared in fugitive form. His best effort, " Noran Water," is a pure idyll, redolent of the Scottish countryside and evincing a wealth of imagery that delights the reader. Another New York poet is John Paterson, a native of Inverness, most of whose productions have appeared only in newspapers, where they have attracted marked attention and been frequently reprinted, and Mr. H. Macpherson, a younger bard hailing from the Highlands, has also won recognition as a poet from his efforts in Gaelic as well as in English during his residence in New York.

Mr. W. C. Sturoc, who was born in the auld toon of Arbroath in 1822, has written a large number of verses which speak plainly of the goodness of his heart, the depth of his affection for his native land, and the ripe scholarship and Christian spirit which direct his daily thoughts. An estimable man in every way, a loyal American citizen, and a leader in the society in which he moves, Mr. Sturoc is passing through the sunset of life in his home at Sunapee, N. H., in a way that proves the truth of the promised reward that comes from a well-spent youth and manhood. His poems are equally divided between the old land and the new, and every line he has written shows how equally dear both are to him. John Imrie of Toronto has published two volumes of his poems, and several of his songs, set to music, have become justly popular. He has the lyrical genius strongly developed, and is equally felicitous in his Canadian and Scotch themes. William Murray of Hamilton, Ontario, a Breadalbane Highlander, is a ready and pleasant writer of Scottish verse, mainly on historical themes, which have made his name known far beyond the confines of the town in which he has his home. Mr. William Anderson of Auburn, N. Y., a native of Duntocher, has written several stirring songs, one of which, "Old Glory," has become very popular. An industrious writer is Mr. J. Porteous Arnold of Quebec, and so is William Lyle, too industrious to give his rhyming qualities an opportunity to rise to the heights they seem capable of attaining.

The Rev. William Wye Smith of Newmarket, Ontario, a native of Jedburgh, has become known on both sides of the St. Lawrence as a writer of hymns, as well as of tuneful verses. He is also an adept of the Doric, and probably no man in America has given the language of Robert Burns more patient or critical study. Mr. J. D. Law of Philadelphia is another writer who has a firm grasp of the Doric and can use it with remarkable facility. He is a poet of no mean order, and soon after his arrival in the Quaker City, in 1886, became noted among the Scots resident there for his rhyming gifts. Since then he has become more widely known, for his volume of poems, issued in Paisley a few years ago under the title of "Dreams o' Hame" won golden opinions from the press both in Scotland and America, and the edition was speedily disposed of. Mr. Law is a native of Lumsden, Aberdeenshire.

As an example of a purely Scottish-American writer, that is to say, of a writer born in America of Scottish ancestry, we might mention Wallace Bruce, who for several years was United States Consul at Edinburgh, and even now, although his home is again in America, holds the office of Poet Laureate of Canongate Kilwinning Lodge, Edinburgh, in succession to Robert Burns, the Ettrick Shepherd, and other well-known Scottish poets. Born in Columbia County, N. Y., Mr. Bruce was educated at Yale University, and afterward traveled over Scotland, England, and a goodly part of Europe. Then, on his return, he ascended the lecture platform and gradually rose in popularity until he was regarded as one of the most brilliant orators of the lyceums. Such themes as "Robert Burns," "Walter Scott," and "Washington Irving " showed that the bent of his mind leaned toward the land of his ancestry, and from time to time the poems which appeared from his pen in various periodicals proved that Scottish literature had been made by him a special field of study. The success which his various volumes of verse—" Old Homestead Poems," " Wayside Poems," " In Clover and Heather " among the number— has met with is satisfactory assurance to his many admirers and friends that his poetic merit is generally appreciated.

This theme, however, might easily be extended through a number of chapters, but a limit must be made, and it is as well to close with the gifted son of song whose merits we have just discussed. It seems hard to pass over with brief mention such undoubted singers as James Linen of California and New York, P. Y. Smith of Wilkinson, Mass.; William Murdock of St. John, N. B., and a score of others; but perhaps the entire subject will some day receive full and fitting attention and treatment.

What has been written, however, imperfect as it is, is sufficient to prove the theory with which the chapter started—that the Scots in America did not leave their harps behind them when they crossed the Atlantic, and that they are as busy helping to build up the literature of America as they are in building up all its other interests.

But the Scot at home has also had a great deal to do with molding and shaping American literature. No poet not a native of the soil is more studied or appreciated than Robert Burns, and nowhere are the lesson of his life and the significance of his mission better understood. Hundreds of editions of his works have been printed in America, and in such compilations as the annual volumes of " Burnsiana " and the monograph on Highland Mary, and in the tributes of such men as Whittier, Longfellow, Emerson, Holmes, and Beecher the national love and reverence for the great poet of the Scottish people has found fitting expression. Every Scotch poetical work of eminence from the days of Ramsay has been reprinted in the States, and sometimes, as in the case of Motherwell's collected writings and Pollok's " Course of Time," the number of American editions exceed those of the old land. Sir Walter Scott's writings in prose, as in poetry, are as thoroughly familiar on the banks of the Hudson as by the side of the Clyde, and, indeed, in reviewing a list of American reprints of Scotch poetical works recently the writer was almost forced to think that the United States had simply adopted the modern poetical literature of his native land and quietly appropriated it as her own.

So, too, with Scotch songs. "Auld Lang Syne" is as much the popular anthem of America as of Scotland, as much adopted and naturalized as though it had passed through a dozen courts of record, and the same might be said of several other lyrics. America as yet has hardly produced a native minstrelsy, but there is no doubt that gradually some volkslied peculiar to herself will be evolved, and we may be sure also that it will be more after the manner of the songs of Scotland than any other. No songs can charm even a cultivated American audience like the simple ditties that first awoke the echoes on the north side of the Tweed, and "Annie Laurie," "Bonny Doon," "The Lass o' Gowrie," "O' a' the Airts," and "Robin Adair" are as great favorites in America as though they were indigenous to the soil. Indeed, the only approach to a native minstrelsy in America was that introduced by the minstrel troupes—now going out of fashion—and their melodies, on the authority of George Christie, the founder and greatest of all these singers, were most popular when they were re-echoes of, or reminiscent of the songs which were and are the favorites of the people in the Land of Robert Burns.

CHAPTER XV.

SCOTTISH-AMERICAN SOCIETIES.

IT is difficult to estimate how many Scottish societies of one name or another there are in the United States and Canada. They far exceed, considering the relative population, those of Ireland or England, and there is hardly a place on the continent where there are half a hundred Scots settled where they have not organized a society—sometimes two. Possibly the reason for this is a desire of having an outlet for patriotic sentiment, or a wish to preserve the memories of auld lang syne, or an impulse to keep "shouther to shouther" in a strange land, or possibly all three. The underlying reason, however, it seems to us, is an unconscious survival of the old spirit of clanship, which causes Highlander and Lowlander, Mearnsman and Whistler, Gleskie chap and Paisley body to shake hands and fraternize when they meet under a foreign sky with a degree of friendship and sentiment which would never evolve from their inner consciousness were their feet treading their native heath. Then, too, this feeling of clannishness, this making a real live thing of a latent sentiment, becomes more intense, more outspoken, more precious, more demonstrative, the further the Scot is removed from his native soil. On the Pacific coast the Scottish gatherings are generally the most thoroughgoing Scotch affairs in the world, and everything must be redolent of the heather. On the Atlantic seaboard, especially around New York City, where Scotland is only a question of a week's sail, they are not so demonstrative, but even there they are more Scotch— more old-fashioned Scotch—in their gatherings than are the Scots at home. As a rule, more wearers of the Highland costume used to be seen at the annual games of the New York Caledonian Club than at most similar gatherings in the Land o' Cakes, and many a Scot has confessed that he never understood what the word *perfervidum* meant when applied to Caledonia until after he had been a short time in the New World. In Scotland, St. Andrew is accepted as a figurehead, possessing the same amount of usefulness as the figurehead on an old ship; but in America he is a very real personage, and thousands of acts of thoughtful kindness are done year out and year in under the inspiration of his name.

The Scottish organizations in America cover almost every field in which the Scot abroad takes an interest—charity, patriotism, sociability, and mental or physical improvement. There are the St. Andrew's Societies, Caledonian organizations—clubs or societies—Order of Scottish Clans, Order of Sons of Scotland, Burns clubs, curling clubs, and various others. When a Scot cannot find any of these to his taste, or when he is not numerous enough to form some one of them, he expends his energy in the kirk—which, after all, according to the Reformation dictates, ought to be a complete and perfect club for the requirements of any man. In it the Scot can dispense charity, and when he pushes ahead the Presbyterian standard his patriotism is flattered by a knowledge that in his own sphere he is carrying on the work the foundation of which was laid by John Knox and Andrew Melville, and which was doubly consecrated by the struggle for Christ's Crown and Covenant, which has made Scotland one of the world's landmarks for religious liberty.

The oldest existing Scottish society in America is the Scots' Charitable of Boston, which was founded in 1657, and to which reference has already been made in a previous chapter. It is now virtually a St. Andrew's Society in all but the name. Doubtless there were Scottish organizations in the Colonies before it, but, if so, they have passed away and left no sign, and its precedence in point of age is undisputed.

The St. Andrew's Societies of Charleston, S. C., Philadelphia, New York, and the North British Society at Halifax, N. S., are all over a century old. Many wonder what the early members of these organizations got to orate about as each anniversary came around. They indulged doubtless largely in such sentiments as "Charity," "The Leal Heart," and "Patriotism," and they toasted places, like—"Iona, Where Religion and Learning Found Refuge in the Middle Ages," but they could not drink to the genius of Robert Burns or glorify Walter Scott. They knew nothing about the steam engine, or the Free Kirk, or the battle of Waterloo, or Dr. Livingstone, or Adam Smith, or Mungo Park, or the Cardross case, or Carlyle's ideas of heroes and hero worship. Of course, they could talk about Bruce and Wallace, the fight at Largs and the battle at Bannockburn, John Knox and the Reformation, the Union of the Crowns, and a lot of other things. To us these seem to be too far back in the mists of history to evoke much wild enthusiasm, but still the earlier sons of St. Andrew were able to make the air re-echo with their cheers as loudly as do their descendants at the present day. The Scot of 1657 and the Scot of the passing day were alike in one respect—and in so much are they bound together—in pledging with enthusiasm "The Day an' a' wha honour it." Our ancient as well as our modern orators on "The Day" claimed that everything on the earth, above, below, or under the earth which is at all worth thinking about, looking at, or having, was either made by a Scotsman or that a Scotsman "bossed the job."

The oldest organization in America bearing the name of St. Andrew is the society at Charleston, S. C., which was founded in 1729. It seemed to fill a want from the first, and its membership roll fully represented the Scotch element in the population. From a historical sketch written by Judge King we quote the following: "In 1731 they were joined by twenty-eight new members, among them being his Excellency Robert Johnston, the Royal Governor, and Robert Wright, Chief Justice of South Carolina. In 1732 they elected eighteen new members, and among them were James Michie, afterward Speaker of the House of Representatives, and who died Chief Justice, and the Rev. Archibald Stobo, who, providentially saved from a fearful hurricane, was long the pastor of the Congregationalists and Presbyterians worshipping together in the same building, and was probably the first who collected the Presbyterians of Charleston into one church. * * * On the death of Mr. Skene, [first President of the society and a member of the Legislative Council,] in 1740, the Hon. James Abercrombie, believed to be of the house of Tulliebody, was elected President. The Hon. John Cleland, a member of the Legislative Council, succeeded him, and on his death, in 1760, Dr. John Moultrie of Culross, one of the original founders of the society, the ancestor of the Moultries in South Carolina, was elected to the Presidency. On the death of Dr. Moultrie, in 1771, the Hon. John Stuart, Superintendent of Indian Affairs, was elected President. He retained the office until the War of the Revolution interrupted the regular meetings of the society. He had been an officer in the army and had distinguished himself by his conduct at Fort Loudon, in the war with the Cherokees, in 1760. * * * His son, Sir John Stuart, a native of Charleston, inherited the talents of his father, and at the battle of Maida, in 1806, showed what the inexperienced and raw troops of his father's country can achieve over veteran soldiers." After the war was over, the society began its active work again. One of its first enterprises was to establish a public school, which continued in active operation through its aid until the State put its educational system in operation in 1811. In that same year it was resolved to build a St. Andrew's Hall, and in 1815 the edifice was inaugurated. It proved to be one of the popular gathering places in the city, and in 1825 it was the headquarters of Lafayette when in Charleston. Bit by bit the hall was adorned with pictures and engravings of general interest, besides portraits of prominent members and it had many treasured articles, such as a snuff mull mounted in silver and covered with cairngorms; a magnificent ram's head, with generous horns, and a presiding officer's mallet made out of a bit of Wallace's oak at Torwood, with a handle from a piece of the cedar that first shaded the tomb of Washington. Except for the usual work of distributing charity and the holding of the yearly festivals, the society continued to flourish without much incident to record until Dec. 11, 1861, when its hall was totally destroyed by fire. The paintings, ram's head, snuff mull, mallet, and records were saved. The paintings were afterward sent in haste, when the civil war broke out, to Columbus, Ga., for safe keeping, but were lost when Sherman's troops sacked that city in February, 1865. The other articles, however, were preserved during that trying time, and are now in the possession of the society.

Some years ago an effort was made to write the biographies of the most noted of the early members of this society, but after a while the attempt was abandoned. This is to be regretted, for such a compilation would give a vast amount of information about many of the early Scots who held high places in the service of the Colonies. It would also introduce us to some very curious characters, a knowledge of whose careers is worth preserving. In the list of names of those who organized the society we find, for instance, that of Sir Alexander Cuming, one of the most curiously compounded mortals who ever lived. He was the head of the family of Cuming, or Comyn, of Culter, and descended from the old Earls of Buchan. He was born in 1700, at Culter, and studied the legal profession, but for some reason got a pension of £300 a year from the Government, and gave up all idea of advancement at the bar, or even of continuing practice. The pension, however, was withdrawn in 1721. He married an English lady who was as flighty as himself, and it was in consequence of a dream of hers that he determined to proceed to America and cultivate the acquaintance of the Cherokee Indians. He reached Charleston in 1729, the year the society was formed, and lost no time in making himself known to the Indians. In the following year he was crowned King and chief ruler of the Cherokees. Soon after, with six of his tributary chiefs, he sailed for England, and on June 18, 1730, had an audience with

King George II., presented his chiefs, and laid his crown at the King's feet, making his followers also kneel in homage. Sir Alexander, even at the time of his visit, found considerable dissatisfaction existing in the Colonies against the mother country, and proposed as a means of securing their perpetual dependence a series of banks in each of the provinces, these banks to have a monopoly of business in their respective territory, and in turn to be entirely dependent upon the British Treasury and accountable only to the British Parliament. The British Government would not listen to his scheme, though it must be confessed that there was some solid sense in it, for, if the entire finances of a country could be throttled, as he proposed, there would not be much chance for a successful revolution. But in brooding upon the project Sir Alexander went over the narrow line which some assert is all that separates genius or wisdom from madness. He was a zealous student of the Scriptures, and, in the course of his reading, conceived the notion that he was alluded to in several passages as the appointed deliverer of the Jews. Then he opened a subscription with a gift of £500 from himself for the purpose of starting his scheme of American banks and for settling 300,000 Jewish families among the Cherokees. Probably he did not bother himself as to how the Cherokees liked the proposal or whether the Hebrews would care to fraternize with the Indians, for that was too commonplace a detail for his thoughts. The subscription failed ignominiously, and in disgust Sir Alexander turned his thoughts and energy to the study of alchemy. This frittered away what was left of his means, and he not only became deeply involved in debt, but for some time had to subsist on the charity of his friends. Finally he was admitted a pensioner in the Charterhouse, London, where he died in 1775.

The St. Andrew's Society of Philadelphia was organized in December, 1749, by twenty-five Scottish residents of the "Quaker City." For some reason or another, these patriotic and kindly men were afraid lest the purposes of their association would be misunderstood by their fellow-citizens, and to guard against this they issued a long "advertisement" setting forth the objects their society had in view. It read, in part, as follows: "The peculiar benevolence of mind which shews itself by charitable actions in giving relief to the poor and distressed has always been justly esteemed one of the first-rate moral virtues. Any persons, then, who form themselves into a society with this intention must certainly meet with the approbation of every candid and generous mind, and we hope that it will plainly appear by the rules which are to follow that the St. Andrew's Society of Philadelphia was solely instituted with that view."

Having thus defined their position, these philosophic Scots compiled their by-laws and commenced their work. The first application for relief came from an unfortunate countryman named Alexander Ross. According to his story, he was a native of Galloway and a surgeon by profession. He had been captured by the French and Spaniards five or six times, and escaped to America from some Spanish prison. His American reception was not the most hospitable, as it seems, when he made application for relief, he was confined as a debtor in the Philadelphia prison. His prayer was attended to, and 40s. were awarded him. In 1750 the society paid £5 9s. for a "strong box" to hold books, money, and other possessions. The box is still in existence, and is a good, substantial, serviceable article. It is deposited in the Fidelity Trust Company's vaults with the old records of the society. In the same year a curious case came up for consideration which may be related here, as it illustrates the glorious uncertainty of the law which prevailed in those good old times just as much as it does in the present day.

In 1732 Janet Cleland was induced to leave Scotland and take up her residence with her uncle, John Gibbs of Maryland. That individual had pressed her to cross the Atlantic, and promised to make her his heiress, besides agreeing to support her in good style during his lifetime. Relying on these promises, Janet, before she left, like a good, kind-hearted girl, made over to another uncle, a brother of the one in Maryland, a small patrimony which she had in her native land. After her arrival here Janet continued to reside with her uncle, and acted as his housekeeper until he died. The old gentleman appears to have been a peculiar sort of character, one of those personages who, for want of a more fitting name, would nowadays be styled a "crank." He had a terrible temper, and sometimes it so far overcame him that his niece had to leave his house for a few days until its violence subsided. Then, when it had cooled off, she used to return, to his great delight, for he invariably expressed his regret at the cruel treatment and harsh words which had compelled her to seek refuge away from his home. To most of his friends and close acquaintances he often acknowledged his intention of leaving Janet all his possessions, and at one time, in presence of his attending physician, he made a formal will in which he bequeathed everything to her. Finally, in 1747, he died of an ulcer in his head, which, according to the testimony of the medical man who attended him, deprived him of his reason for quite a while before the end. While in this condition the negro slaves, in the absence of the doctor and nurse, used to give him large quantities of rum. By some means or other they prevailed upon him to sign another will. In it he cut Janet and all his relatives off without a cent, made his negroes free, and divided his property among them, with the exception of his plate, which went to comparative strangers, along with a few other legacies. Thus Janet was left penniless, and applied at length to the society for assistance. The last-made will appears to have been offered for probate, and she began a lawsuit to have it set aside. The society, considering her sad case, gave her a donation of £7, and recommended the members to give her all the assistance they could. It appears, however, that Janet lost her suit, and the last will made by her uncle was allowed to stand.

During the Revolutionary period the society probably did little more than maintain its existence, owing, as was reported on one occasion, to "a number of members being out of town, or more particularly on account of the convulsed and unsettled state of the times." The minute book covering the interesting period between 1776 and 1786 has been lost, if it ever was in existence, which may be regarded as doubtful. The subsequent history of the society is a prosperous one, and may be summarized in the old words " dacin' guid an' gatherin' gear." On its long roll of members we find the names of two of the signers of the Declaration of Independence—James Wilson and Dr. John Witherspoon, President of Princeton College. The members took an active part in the erection of the monument to this great clerical statesman which now graces Fairmount Park. The roll also contains the names of two Governors of the State—Hon. James Hamilton (President of the society for several terms) and Hon. Thomas McKean—and three Mayors of the city, Peter McCall, Morton McMichael, and William B. Smith. The roll is also graced with the names of several of the Revolutionary heroes, chief of which is that of Gen. Hugh Mercer, referred to in a previous chapter. The remains of this brave soldier were interred in Laurel Hill Cemetery, Philadelphia, and there a fine monument has since been erected to his memory. The society took the most active part in carrying on the movement for this memorial, and when it was dedicated it occupied a place of honor during the ceremonies.

The St. Andrew's Society of the State of New York was founded in 1756. The intention of the promoters was simply to form a charitable organization, and that feature has really continued to be the prevailing one ever since. These kindly Scots, however, did not forget that under St. Andrew's banner patriotism, as well as charity, could work together, and their constitution provided that a dinner should take place on the 30th of November in each year. Since then these meetings have been held regularly, except during the War of the Revolution.

Among the members enrolled in 1757 we find the name of Col. Simon Fraser, eldest son of Lord Lovat, who was beheaded on Tower Hill, London, in 1747. When the Rebellion of 1745 broke out he was a student at the University of St. Andrews, but was withdrawn by his cunning old father to be placed at the head of the clan. He surrendered himself to the Government in 1746; but, as he had never shown any sympathy for the cause of the Stuarts, and was known to have been influenced solely by affection for his father, he was released in the course of the following year. Refusing military rank in the French service, he raised, in 1757, two battalions of 1,800 men, in command of which he proceeded to New York, and on his arrival he joined the St. Andrew's Society. He served with great distinction at Louisburg and Quebec, and afterward in the War of the Revolution. In 1774 the family estates were restored to him, but the attainder was not removed until 1854, when the old title of Lord Lovat was again placed on the roll of the Scottish peerage.

The titular Earl of Stirling, one of the Revolutionary heroes, filled the office of President from 1761 till 1763. John, fourth Earl of Dunmore, Governor of New York in 1769, was elected President in 1770. His term of office was, however, very short, for in the same year he proceeded to assume the government of Virginia. In 1773 he was succeeded by Lord Drummond, son of the claimant to the attainted earldom of Perth, who came to this country as an officer in the army. A few years later he was taken prisoner by the Americans, but was released by Washington, and permitted to return to New York. His failing health obliged him to proceed to Bermuda, where he died, unmarried, in 1781.

Besides these titled personages, the society has had many members to whom it can point with pride. Some of them, such as the Coldens, Hamiltons, and Livingstons, have left their mark upon the early history of the country, and in the long roll of membership may be found the names of the most prominent Scottish merchants and professional men who have resided in this city from the inception of the society until the present time.

Whatever funds the society had prior to the Revolutionary War were dissipated by it. With the return of peace, however, it again exerted itself, and renewed its career of usefulness. Between the years 1787 and 1791 it had bank stocks worth $4,000, which were sold in the last-named year. A site was then purchased where 10 and 12 Broad Street and 8 and 10 New Street now stand, for the erection of a St. Andrew's hall. The price paid for the ground was $4,600. But the building scheme was dropped for some reason or other, and the property was sold in 1794 for $6,750. In 1803 the funds of the Dumfries and Galloway Society, then being wound up, amounting to about $2,300, were transferred to it. The financial standing of the society has since continued steadily to advance, and at the present time its permanent fund amounts to about $80,000. Besides, it owns three beds in hospitals and a plot in Cypress Hills Cemetery.

Very few persons, even after perusing the numerous details furnished in the reports of the society's operations issued every year, can form anything like a just appreciation of the nature, extent, and importance of the charitable work performed by the officers. The number of persons who have fallen into destitute circumstances, through no fault of their own, in a large city like New York, must necessarily be always very great. They include the aged, the blind, the sick, the widow, and the orphan. So numerous, indeed, are such cases that even with the resources at their command the officers are unable to be as generous as they would wish. Still, the aid they give is always timely and welcome, and helps wonderfully in throwing a gleam of kindly light upon darkened lives. By means of the beds at their disposal in the Presbyterian and St. Luke's Hospitals the officers are able to secure proper treatment and the best of medical attendance for many of the sick. The burial plot belonging to the society in Cypress Hills Cemetery, with its exceedingly beautiful and substantial shaft, the gift of Mr. John S. Kennedy, one of the ex-Presidents of the society, tells its own sad story, and shows how the thoughtful kindness of the society, besides ministering to the wants of destitute Scots in life, tries to gratify the last wish of every one by giving his remains a respectable interment.

There is another class to whom the assistance of the society is rendered, and whose cases are often pitiable. This is the immigrants, or transients, as they may more properly be called. The old story is well known of people crossing the Atlantic in search of work, finding none, and landing penniless in the streets. The cases are also common of people who leave places in the interior and come to New York with the idea that employment can be had here for the asking; and there are hundreds of other causes which somehow end in making able-bodied men become idle wanderers in the great city. A moment's reflection will tell us what this means—it is poverty, hunger, despair, and degradation. The society tries to help these cases by providing temporary shelter, by furnishing the means for cleanliness, and in many other ways.

Like the societies at Boston and Philadelphia, the North British Society of Halifax, N. S., started, in 1768, with a strong box, and determined to fill the box with money as soon as possible and keep it filled, so that it might help along those among them who fell into poverty or who arrived in their midst in a state that needed a little assistance. The members also resolved to celebrate St. Andrew's Day, and the quarterly meetings were St. Andrew's festivals in miniature, for they appear to have at them mingled pleasure, charity, and patriotism in a marked degree. The society also had another purpose—that of seeing to it that each member should have what the survivors deemed a respectable funeral. For this purpose, one of the articles in the first constitution reads as follows:

"That in case of the death of any member, the charge of the coffin, pall, grave, and attendance shall be taken out of the Box. Six scarves, six hat bands, six pair of black gloves, and six pair white gloves shall be purchased out of the Box as soon as circumstances will allow, and likewise as much as can be afforded to be given to the widow and children of the deceased member for their assistance, the scarves and gloves to be returned to the Box." The record of the society since its foundation has been one continued story of charity, varied by St. Andrew's dinners of all sorts, from the semi-public festival at "the house of Widow Gillespie" to the grand occasion when, in 1794, they reveled in splendor because their principal guest was no less a personage than the Duke of Kent, the father of Queen Victoria. It has also celebrated the centennials of Burns and Scott, and came to the front on all occasions when a Scottish society could exemplify its patriotic and charitable spirit. Its long roll of officials includes the names of the most noted Scots in Halifax, and its history all through is one of which not only new Scotia, but auld Scotia, may justly be proud. Its charity has been liberal, yet thoughtful. One notable gift deserves to be noticed. In 1868, when celebrating in grand style its own centenary, it founded a scholarship in Dalhousie College. The only other instance of a like benefaction on the part of a Scottish society in America of which we are aware is the St. Andrew's Scholarship, given by the society of that name at Fredericton to the University of New Brunswick.

The St. Andrew's Society of Montreal was established in 1835. It is one of the most active societies of its name in Canada, and yearly accomplishes a wonderful amount of good through its St. Andrew's Home or direct charitable agencies. In a discourse preached to the members by the Rev. J. Edgar Hill, on the occasion of the jubilee of the society, the following reference to the early history of the organization was made: " Previous to 1835 there had been no organized brotherhood of Scotchmen in the city, and therefore no systematic care of immigrants from the old land. From 1835 to 1857 the society had a name, but no place of habitation. Good work it had done, but it would do better. Accordingly, in the early days of June, 1857, St. Andrew's Home was opened, so that those who had left a home endeared to them by many tender associations should, in the new land across the sea, at once find a home provided for them till they had made a home for themselves. The idea was a brilliant one, and the time as well as the place was marked by an obvious leading of Providence. For, while the home was opened on June 11, the most pathetic appeal that has ever been made to the St. Andrew's Society, and the most severe test to which her philanthropy has been subjected, was made on the 27th day of the same month, when the 'Montreal' was burned to the water's edge a few miles below Quebec, on her passage to this city, and nearly 400 persons either perished in the flames or were drowned in trying to make their escape. The survivors, of course, lost their all. Many of them were widows and orphans, and all of them were sorrowful strangers in a strange land, under circumstances which evoked the sympathy of every tender heart. Most of these were Scottish immigrants, and at once the St. Andrew's Society undertook most loyally to provide for every Scot among them. 'How much money do you want?' was the almost invariable question the collectors were met with—a splendid example of the characteristic Scotch way of answering questions by putting another. Funds flowed in from Scotsmen all over Canada, for Scottish hearts were bleeding for their suffering brothers and sisters."

St. Andrew's societies have probably existed from the time that the Scot abroad first began his travels. In the earlier stages of their history they were merely temporary organizations for the celebration of the anniversary of the patron saint. The Scots' Guards in France rejoiced in a better dinner than usual on the 30th of November, and in our researches into the history of our countrymen on the European Continent we find many evidences that St. Andrew's Day was fondly kept in remembrance. Afterward, when men got settled and Scotch colonies began to arise, the regular society, as we have it now, was commenced. Originally the societies were simply patriotic in their aims, but afterward charity was added, and both of these grand qualities have combined to strengthen the organizations and make them useful as well as sentimental. In Scotland, the few St. Andrew's societies there are simply kept alive in the interests of patriotism and are nearly all modern affairs, with no history of any great interest to any one outside of their own little circles.

If a Scotsman wants to see his patron saint suitably honored he must leave Scotland and sojourn in America, where undoubtedly the kindly memory of the good old missionary is cherished with the fires of loyalty and love. If we were to believe the orators on the closing night of November in each year, in the United States and Canada, we would regard Andrew as the champion saint in the calendar, " the king o' a' the core," and Scotland as a land flowing with milk and honey, whose men are the very cream of humanity, and whose lassies are genuine queens of Parnassus, who have just come down to earth for a little change and relaxation. Patriotism runs high on such nights. Scotland is Scotland and no mistake, and woe be it to any wight who dares to gainsay it. But such a wight never appears, and the next day the highstrung patriot becomes a canny Scot once more, and for the remaining 364 days in the year his patron saint is a quiet, but none the less generous, distributor of charity. There is no more generous Scot to be found anywhere than the one who backs up his nationality with his siller, and while " Relieve the Distressed " is the accepted motto of the societies, " Patriotism and Parritch " would be more pertinent and comprehensive.

Clubs or societies organized under the name Caledonian can be traced back in this country for about a century. In the early times they were simply social combinations of Scotsmen who got up some festival, such as a ball, during the Winter, and for the remainder of the year remained in a condition of suspended animation, somewhat after the fashion of many of the Burns clubs at the present day. The oldest existing Caledonian organization in the Dominion is that of Montreal, while in the United States that of Boston claims to be the senior in point of age. But neither of these organizations would have survived for half a decade had they not been organized on definite plans and for specific purposes, and had these purposes not met, or anticipated, a public want. All the clubs or societies which have proved successful have been, to a certain extent, business enterprises, and just as much as they have been managed on business principles so much has been their measure of success. In Scotland the parish or village games have been in vogue from time immemorial, and have generally been held on, or in connection with, a local holiday. It was the reproduction, by the originators of these clubs, of such local holidays with athletic games as a central attraction that caught the fancy and made them popular among " oor ain folk." Americans, too, always noted for their admiration for manly sports, thronged to the gatherings in such numbers that the promoters of the earlier games were often surprised at the crowds which attended them, and the substantial amount of the gate receipts.

The main objects of the Caledonian organizations as at present existing are twofold—first, the encouragement and practice of Scottish games, and, second, the encouragement of a taste for Scottish literature, poetry, and song. These objects are generally stated in their by-laws, not, perhaps, in these identical words, but in others having the same purport. The rules of many of the clubs make it imperative that public games should be held at least once each year, and in the open air.

So far as the first of these objects—the encouragement and practice of games—is concerned, the Caledonian societies of this continent must be credited with having achieved a wonderful amount of success. They have made the old-fashioned Scottish games not only very popular, but the Scottish rules are really the basis on which all athletic contests here are conducted. But even this success has latterly proved so far detrimental to the clubs that their games are not, from a pecuniary point of view, so remunerative as they formerly were. All over the country, during the season, games are held under the auspices of local athletic clubs, and these games are nearly all very similar to those which might be witnessed at Hawick or Inverness. Most athletic clubs have weekly meetings, frequent tournaments with sister clubs, while now and again an amateur " star" goes on a record-breaking tour among them. The result is that these local organizations push the Caledonians into the background, and their frequent meetings seem fully to supply the demand, so far as the public are concerned. There are many other reasons for this. In the athletic world a Caledonian record is regarded with suspicion, even if it should be honored with any regard at all, which is very seldom. The system of handicapping, too, which is so generally adopted in athletic societies, has served to bring a succession of bright young men into the arena year after year, while at Caledonian gatherings it is usual to find the war horses of ten years ago war horses still. The true theory of Caledonian athletes originally was to develop the skill, strength, and agility of their own members, and had this theory been carried out in practice a more satisfactory condition of things would have existed to-day. But one club wanted to have its athletic records as good as another. If a hammer was thrown 90 feet at Yonkers, for instance, the Poughkeepsie folks wanted it thrown as far, if not further, at their games. And so commenced the nuisance of traveling professional Caledonian athletes. These men, of course, were members of sister societies, and from a sentimental point of view were entitled to equal privileges with the members of any club they might favor with a visit. This was all very well for a while, but some of the clubs were not very particular who they received into membership while the athletic craze was strong. The result was that the Scotch games were crowded with such Caledonian athletes as " Mr. Maloney," " Mr. Euth," " Mr. Sullivan," " Mr. McCarthy," and the like. The most advanced club in this connection was that of Philadelphia, which opened its " Caledonian " games to all comers without distinction of creed, nationality, or previous condition of servitude. The result was that those who, in the Quaker City, went to see *Scotch* games saw a general scramble for the prizes by negroes, Irishmen, and Germans, as well as Scots.

All these things combined to make the Caledonian games wane in popularity, and it is to be feared that they will never again gain their old measure of success. In fact, the quality of the games as athletic events has vanished, and, while the annual field days of the various clubs may be kept up, they will be more useful for drawing the Scots in their various localities—for making a Scotch holiday, as it were—than for anything else.

As regards the encouragement of Scottish literature,

poetry, and song, it must be confessed that the Caledonian clubs have not added much to the national wealth. In Philadelphia for many years a series of literary meetings has been held each Winter. These assemblies are well attended, and at them a Scotch song can always be heard well sung, but the purely literary element is very meagre. This fact is to be deplored, and even wondered at, for in a cultured city like Philadelphia it should be an easy matter to arrange for a short lecture or talk upon some Scottish theme at each meeting. In Montreal a good series of sociables is given each Winter, and the Hallowe'en entertainment is generally the best of the kind on the continent, but such meetings, or the innumerable socials held by other organizations each Winter, do little or nothing for literature. In New York they have lectures and a very commonplace debating organization; in Boston such matters seem to be severely passed by without an effort to produce them. In Chicago the effort has been made, but without success. The fact is, the literary element in the clubs is grasped in too half-hearted a way to insure success. If the Caledonians copied the Welsh, and offered prizes for the singing of auld Scotch songs, or if they offered prizes for essays on distinctively Scottish subjects, if they organized scholarships in the colleges for the benefit of students of Scottish birth or descent, if they gave prizes in the local schools for the study of Scotch history, if they subsidized a lecturer who could speak on Scottish themes before popular audiences, if they helped a Scottish poet to place his productions before the American public, then they might be credited with doing something in furthering the second of the purposes for which they were primarily established.

The wearing of the Highland costume at public gatherings has been a feature of all Caledonian organizations, and by their activity in this matter they have certainly succeeded in making the " garb of old Gaul" familiar throughout the Northern and Western States and Canada. By frequently giving prizes for the best costume, they have inspired a kindly spirit of rivalry, until at the present time we have on this side of the Atlantic many costumes as complete and as perfect as any that could be seen in Scotland. It is singular, however, that while the Highland dress is thus patronized, the music which is associated with it should be comparatively neglected. Bagpipe playing is neither fostered or regarded by the clubs. Of course, they must have pipe playing, but any one who can " blaw " and use his fingers as though he was manipulating a penny whistle is deemed good enough for any occasion. Real good playing, such as is common at the Braemar, Strathallan, or other gatherings in Scotland, is seldom heard in America, and when heard is not sufficiently appreciated.

In this country and Canada, Caledonian clubs and societies have, in spite of their shortcomings and failures, in the past accomplished much good. They have made many pleasant Scottish holidays; brought Scotsmen and their families into closer friendship with each other, and by their kindly charity and fraternal aid have lightened the load of many a wanderer. They have made Scottish games become the delight of the youth of America, and the laws they have established for the guidance of such sports are generally accepted as the best as well as the most just that could be framed. Their record, on the whole, has been a creditable one, and, while we believe that they will require to seek new fields of operations if they are to maintain their popularity, we believe that in good time these new fields will be entered upon. If athleticism be played out, literature is not, and by cultivating that, and dropping all idea of mere financial success, these Caledonian organizations, clubs, and societies may yet attain a degree of influence and accomplish an amount of good which will make the past, even with all its triumphs, seem trifling in comparison.

While athletics may be regarded as the basis of Caledonian Clubs, insurance is undoubtedly the foundation of the Order of Scottish Clans. This order has passed through the trials of infancy and youth and is now in robust manhood, and claims and takes it place as one of the most useful of Scottish societies in America. It was organized in St. Louis in 1878. For some time its schemes were confined to that city, but after a year or two it was taken up by a number of Boston Scots, and a "boom" was started on its behalf which still continues as vigorous as ever. As the advantages offered by the order became known, clans commenced to spring up all over the country, until at present there are over 100 of these, and several in course of formation. Four or five clans are located in Canada, but across the border the order has not progressed as was at one time expected.

When the Order of Scottish Clans was started the idea was to institute a grand federation of Scotsmen in America, which, by united effort and a display of the truest fraternal spirit, was to combine sentiment and patriotism with more practical matters. The members were to unite in insuring their lives, sick benefits were to be provided, and a helping hand extended to any overtaken by misfortune. The fraternity was to be a secret one, that is, it was to meet with closed doors and have signs and passwords after the fashion of the Odd Fellows. It was to have all the social features which distinguished the Caledonian societies, and, if need be, it would give public exhibitions of old Scottish games. It was to be a complete organization, offering to fill all the requirements of Scottish-Americans, only that its benefits were to be confined to its own members, possibly on the theory that all Scotsmen should be on its rolls.

The original ideas which guided the organization, while well enough for a local society the members of which were known to each other, were too crude to be successfully worked in a large fraternity the members of which were scattered throughout the country. The insurance scheme, that of each surviving member paying a dollar on the death of one of their number, seemed the very essence of simplicity, but experience had demonstrated in other societies that the plan was not so effective or so equitable as it appeared on the surface, and after a few years of the existence of the order doubts on this point began to be entertained by many of its warmest adherents. This, however, might have been expected. In insurance matters no society was ever organized at once on a perfect basis. Experience is the great requirement of them all, and, until that experience has been gained, mistakes are certain to be made. Such societies require to be watchful, to put into practice one year what they learned during the year before, to make changes after consideration and practice shows the necessity for change, and to be constantly strengthening the organization at every point, no matter how trivial. This policy has characterized the leaders and workers of the order during the past few years. They have proved themselves thoughtful, progressive, and capable, and the fraternity has advanced in a surprising manner, as a result of their work. They have had to encounter opposition, sneering, grumbling, and fault-finding; but they have kept on doing their patriotic work, until the full assessment is paid to the relatives of a deceased member. Fault finding does not amount to very much, but $2,000 is a happy, tangible fact.

The great necessity for the welfare of all such institutions is the want of Government, or, in some sections, State supervision. If the law compelled assessment insurance companies to apply for permission to trade, if their promoters were made to give bonds to the State for the honorable carrying out of all their agreements, if the policies were issued with the sanction of the law advisers of the State, and the business books were liable to be examined by some competent officer at irregular intervals, we might regard assessment insurance as being as safe as any other. Fewer companies would then be organized, but those which fulfilled all the requirements would possess stability. The management of this order has been clean. It has paid every debt as it has arisen. Its officers, except the Secretary, receive no emoluments, and its membership is selected with care as regards nationality, moral character and physical health.

The question of grading assessments according to age, which was a theme of much discussion among the brotherhood for several years, has been equitably and amicably adjusted, and, so far as one can see, there is no obstacle in the way to prevent the order from steadily increasing until every Scottish workman in the country shall be enrolled on its books. In the States it has practically no opposition to its work, excepting from what is called the American Order of Scottish Clans, which, however, is not numerically strong.

The insurance feature of the order might be that of any society, but in the subordinate clans the Scotch element comes to the front. The membership is confined to Scotsmen and their immediate descendants, and the moral character of each applicant is carefully enquired into. The ritual which is used in the initiation of candidates is founded on Scottish history, and when intelligently rendered is both impressive and instructive. The sick allowance in most of the clans is $5 a week, with free medical attendance, and these benefits, as well as the working expenses of the clan, are provided by the monthly dues of the members. Many of the clans, too, have a funeral benefit of $50, which is paid at once on intimation of death. The meetings are generally well attended, and are managed with both order and decorum, two qualities which are not characteristic of other societies that might be named. Open social meetings at which the relatives and friends of members are invited are frequently given, and the public balls, concerts, and anniversary festivals have generally been successful. Some of the clans have given games, but this feature, although one of the objects laid down in the constitution, has not been attended to as it should have been. Each clan has its regalia, in which its own particular tartan predominates, and the appearance of the members of the order on public occasions, dressed in their costume, is one of the most gratifying spectacles which a Scotsman in America can see.

In many respects the Order of Sons of Scotland, a Canadian organization, runs in much the same grooves as the Order of Scottish Clans in the States. It is economically managed, the meetings of its camps are not only interesting but thoroughly patriotic affairs, and its operations are yearly extending all over the Dominion.

A Burns club or society, properly speaking, is quite a

different description of organization from any of which we have already treated. It is organized for but one purpose—that of honoring the memory of Scotia's darling poet. It is eminently a social and literary association, and its entire horizon is bounded by that filled by the Ayrshire bard. But that is sufficient to infuse vitality and enthusiasm into any body of men, particularly if they are Scots or descendants of Scots.

There is another difference between the Burns and St. Andrew's and Caledonian societies, or clans. The latter are all essentially Scottish, and membership in them is more or less confined to natives, or the immediate descendants of natives, of Scotland. Inasmuch, however, as the fame of Burns is no longer simply confined to Scotland but has spread over all the world, so membership in clubs bearing his name is generally open to all who reverence his memory or admire his genius. It is felt that if these clubs are to be gatherings of lovers of the poet, the members should admit into their circles men of any nationality who recognize the worth of the "High Priest of Scottish Song." This is as it should be. All who acknowledge our bard as the poet of humantiy, freedom, fraternity, and love should be welcomed into such clubs, and be received all the more heartily because they do not belong to our nationality, and have to contend with difficulties in the study of the poet which do not fall to our lot.

The great night of the year for any Burns Club is the 25th of January, and care is generally taken that it be celebrated in a manner that will really honor the memory of the poet and reflect credit on his native land and on his countrymen at home as well as abroad. The most usual form for the celebration to assume is that of a public dinner. This is often very pleasant for those who are present, and it brings to the front quite a crowd of speakers, and eulogies of Burns without number, and often without common sense or discrimination.

The dues in a Burns Club, outside of what the annual celebration costs, are trifling. There is, indeed, no primal necessity for a fund, and what is over at the end of each year in the Treasurer's hands should be handed to the nearest St. Andrew's society to be dispensed in charity. This would be fully in keeping with the teachings of Burns himself and redound to the credit of the organization. Should the members be willing to assess themselves a little more than is absolutely necessary there are many ways in which their money might be invested. They might purchase copies of Burns's poems and give them as prizes each year in the public schools, or they could offer a bonus for the best poem on Burns or for the best essay on his life or genius. These are not extravagant undertakings, and quite within the reach of almost any club member, yet we do not know any better means that could be suggested for making the memory of our bard even more beloved throughout the American continent than it is at the present day.

The game of curling has made rapid strides in this country since its introduction, but though it be "Scotia's ain Winter game," and though Scotsmen have naturally been prominent in it, it really sets no national requirement in connection with its membership, and prefers to win success simply as a game—the only purely amateur game in existence. Therefore it claims no extended notice here beyond simply alluding to it as one among the many favors which Scotland has bestowed on the New World.

So, too, might Scotland's share in American Free Masonry be dismissed in a few words were it not for the fact that its history on this side of the Atlantic goes back to a much earlier period than that of curling, and there are many historical facts in connection with it which should not be passed over in a volume of this kind, especially as a claim has been made that the mysteries of the ancient order were first carried over the sea by brethren who owed allegiance to the Grand Lodge at old Kilwinning.

So far as can be traced, Freemasonry in legitimate lodges having their authority from some Grand Lodge, was first introduced into America by warranted lodges working under the jurisdiction of one of the Grand

Lodges in the United Kingdom. The records of these Grand Lodges are very defective, especially those of Ireland, as most of its papers were destroyed by fire. The English records appear to have been purposely kept in an indifferent manner, probably from an idea which once prevailed that as little as possible should be committed to writing concerning Masonry and its doings—even the doings of subordinate lodges. To this erroneous notion is due much of the defective information we have concerning many matters of interest in the general history of the craft.

Among the early lodges in this country which held warrants from the Grand Lodge of Scotland were:

1755—St. Andrew's Lodge, Boston.
1756—Lodge No. 82, Blandford, Va.
1760—Union, No. 98, South Carolina.
1763—St. John's, No. 117, Norfolk, Va.
1767—Moriah Lodge, in Twenty-second Regiment, afterward in New York.
1771—King Solomon's Lodge, No. 7, in New York, had a charter indirectly from the Grand Lodge of Scotland, for there is no record of the Grand Lodge of Scotland ever having issued a direct warrant to any lodge in New York, whether as a colony or a State.

The most noted of these lodges, that of St. Andrew's, Boston, still survives, the wealthiest Masonic lodge in the United States, if not in the world.

The earliest military lodge in the records of the Scottish Grand Lodge was granted, according to Mr. D. Murray Lyon, Grand Secretary, in 1743, by recommendation of the Earl of Kilmarnock, upon petition of some "Sergeants and sentinels belonging to Col. Lees' Regiment of Foot." This regiment has been given the number, Forty-fourth. This regiment was raised in 1741 in England, and had its first experience in actual warfare in this country in 1758. It took part in the expeditions against Ticonderoga, Fort Duquesne, and Fort Niagara, and the engagements of Long Island and Brandywine.

What is supposed to have been the outcome of another regimental lodge was that in the Twenty-second Regiment, which received its warrant from the Grand Lodge of Scotland in 1767. The regiment was in this city in 1781, and was known as Moriah Lodge. It was one of the five which formed the New York Grand Lodge, but outside of that importatnt bit of service it does not seem to have had much to do with the progress of Masonry in this State. The regiment soon afterward was ordered away from New York to another scene of usefulness— or carnage.

The most prominent lodge, however, which, in 1781, took part in the formation of the New York Grand Lodge, was that known as "Lodge No. 169," under the warrant of the Grand Lodge of Scotland, the lodge which afterward adopted the name of "St. Andrew's Lodge," and continued to be active in New York Masonry until 1830, when its charter was surrendered.

The origin of this lodge is not exactly known, but it very likely was in one of he regimental lodges. It is not known even where it got its original charter, and some Masonic writers often mix it up with the St. Andrew's Lodge of Boston. On July 13, 1771, it had obtained a warrant from the Grand Lodge of England with the title of "Lodge No. 169," and it took the name of Scotland's patron saint officially, so far as we know, in 1786. It is asserted by some writers that the lodge met under its numerical designation in Boston, but this is doubted, and certainly there is nothing on record to prove it, and the general consensus of opinion among Masonic antiquaries is that its first settled home was in New-York.

On the roll of the Grand Lodge of Scotland there is record of a lodge—St. John, No. 169—at Shettleston, near Glasgow, receiving a warrant in 1771. It is a question whether this had any connection with the Lodge No. 169 which met in Boston, and whose warrant was dated the same year. Gould, in his "History of Freemasonry," says: "No 169 was established in Battery Marsh, Boston, 1771. This lodge, which is only once named in the records of the Massachusetts Grand Lodge, accompanied the British Army to New York on the evacuation of Boston in 1776." Another authority says it is not improbable that the Scottish warrant granted for Shettleston was transferred to an army lodge and Lodge St. John became in time St. Andrew. Another matter which is regarded as very probable is that the origin of the St. Andrew's Lodge of New York was this same regimental warrant held in the Forty-second Regiment, the famous "Black Watch."

The Scottish regiments in New York from 1770 to the evacuation of the city were the Forty-second, which came here in 1776 for a short stay, returned in 1780, spent a Winter here, had their headquarters most of the time in Albany, and were in this city some months before the evacuation, Nov. 25, 1783, when they went to Halifax. The Seventy-first (old) was in this city in 1777 and then went South. They had a stirring career in the Colonies until they surrendered with Cornwallis at Yorktown. The present Seventy-first Regiment was never in this country. The Seventy-fourth (old) was represented in this city by a grenadier company in 1779, but after a short stay they were ordered to Charleston, and took part in its siege. The Seventy-sixth (old), or the Macdonald Highlanders, were stationed between this city and Staten Island in 1779, and from here left for Virginia, to surrender in the end with Cornwallis. So far as we have been able to discover, this completes the list. Doubtless many temporary commands were sent over to take part in the great struggle, but such commands would not be likely to apply for or to receive a warrant from any Grand Lodge.

Whatever the early history of St. Andrew's Lodge here, it seems to have soon held an important position in the craft. The first meeting to organize what is now the Grand Lodge of New York State was held in its meeting-room, and its master, the Rev. William Walter, was the first Grand Master, and was subsequently reelected twice, relinquishing it only when duty called him to another field of labor. "For a time," McClenachan says, "the history of this lodge seemed to be that of the Grand body, and it stood pre-eminent under the title of St. Andrew's, No. 3, on and after June 3, 1789. In time the Grand Lodge became stronger and was enabled to walk alone; the Grand officers were more widely distributed, and, although No. 3 continued in its constancy, its excessive influence waned."

The first lodge in Maryland of which there is record was organized in 1750, and its first Master was Dr. Alexander Hamilton, and its first Senior Warden the Rev. Alexander Malcolm. In the course of his oration at the centennial meeting of the Grand Lodge of Maryland, Past Grand Master Carter said: "Tradition says there were other and earlier lodges in Maryland, including one called St. Andrew's at Georgetown, now in the District of Columbia, formed by the Scotch settlers some time prior to 1737." One of the early Grand Masters of that State (the fourth) was David Kerr, who was born in Scotland on Feb. 5, 1749. He came to this country when in his twentieth year, just when the Revolutionary movement was beginning to make headway, and took sides with the Colonists. After independence had been won he settled at Easton and prospered in business. He died in 1814, leaving a family which upheld the credit of his name throughout the State.

The Grand Lodge of the State of New York was organized, as we have seen, in the meeting-room of St. Andrew's Lodge in 1781. Its charter was signed by the Duke of Atholl, as being then Grand Master of "the Ancients." This popular Scotch peer was born June 30, 1755, and succeeded his father as fourth duke in 1774. He died in 1820. He was a public-spirited nobleman, raised once a regiment of soldiers—the Atholl Highlanders—for the service of his sovereign; but, except in Masonry, he sought no public honors.

The warrant or charter issued in 1781 authorized the Masons in New York to congregate and form a Provincial Grand Lodge in the City of New York. In 1783 the independence of the United States was acknowledged, and with that independence the provincial lodge became a sovereign Grand Lodge. Of the first Grand Master, Mr. Walter, little is known, save that he was a chaplain in one of the regiments; that he was Master of St. Andrew's Lodge at the time of his elevation, and that he resigned his high office because duty called him to another place. That he was highly respected is shown by the many offices to which he was elected by his Masonic brethren, and by the resolutions of regret which expressed their sorrow at the necessity of parting with him. In this sovereign Grand Lodge there must have been quite a strong Scotch element, if we may judge by the names of its officials. James McCuan (McEwan) was Deputy Grand Master, James Clarke Grand Secretary, Archibald McNeill Grand Steward, etc. McCuan was succeeded in 1783 by Archibald Cunningham, and in that year the Grand Treasurer was Samuel Kerr, a representative Scotch merchant.

Chancellor Livingston was Grand Master from 1784 till 1800, and most of the members of his family belonged to the order. Throughout its history Scotsmen have all along been active in New York's Grand Lodge, and that activity still continues. Mr. William A. Brodie, a native of Kilbarchan, was Grand Master in 1884, and that high and honorable office is now held by Mr. John Stewart—who never fails to boast that he has Scotch blood in his veins.

With this chapter we close our study of the Scot in America. The theme has been an interesting one and has led us into innumerable walks of life, and its subject-matter might easily have been extended over a series of volumes. But enough, more than enough, has been adduced to prove that the record is an honorable one, and that whatever welcome has been given to the expatriated Scot on landing in America, or whatever honors may have been heaped upon him, are amply repaid by his devotion to the country by the care with which he fosters its best interests, and the patriotic efforts he makes to add to its wealth and to its dignity among the nations. The Stars and Stripes raise no loftier feelings or inspire more loyalty in the heart of a descendant of one of the Mayflower party than in the heart of the wanderer from Scotland who has made his home in the United States. The flag becomes his flag, the country becomes his country, and to the defense of the one his blood will be shed if needed, while to develop the interest and maintain the integrity of the other he will devote the same enthusiasm and the same common sense that have served his own country so well. A believer in law, he is ever on the side of authority; a believer in religion, he is a staunch upholder of public and private morals and of honesty in politics; he does not aspire to political influence, to control a caucus, or lead a district; but he treasures his ballot as the outcome of his civil liberty, the charter of his freedom and equality in the Commonwealth. Whatever adds to the material wealth of the country finds him an effective supporter; in the cause of education he is ever in the ranks of the foremost workers, and in charity his liberality and practical interest are everywhere apparent. Take him all in all, he is a useful citizen, and in that regard is second to none. His patriotism is not that of the orator who believed in " the old flag and an appropriation;" but it is true, reverent, and from the depth of his heart. So, too, in the great Dominion north of the St. Lawrence, no native has a deeper affection in his heart of hearts for "This Canada of Ours" than the Scot who has thrown in his lot in that part of the continent, and he is as proud of the maple leaf as he is of the thistle.

But, while giving himself thus up to the land of his adoption, the Scot in America does not forget the land of his birth. It may be to him but a sentiment, yet the sentiment burns deeper into his heart as the years roll on. It may be forever to him a reminiscence, a dream of the past, and the mournful notes of " Lochaber no more " may sound in his ears as he conjures back to memory the once-familiar scenes and recalls once weel-kenned faces. But, as time creeps on its very name becomes sacred, and his highest hopes are that all that is grand in Scotland, all that has lifted her up among the nations, that has made her be regarded as an unfaltering champion of civil and religious liberty, may be transplanted, preserved and perpetuated in the land which has become his own. He never thinks of Scotland without a flutter, without a benediction; and he is ever ready to re-utter in his own words the sentiments of good old Isabella Graham, when, nearing the end of her earthly pilgrimage, she wrote:

"Dear native land! May every blessing from above and beneath be thine—serenity of sky, salubrity of air, fertility of soil; and pure and undefiled religion inspire thy sons and daughters with grateful hearts to love God and one another."

INDEX.

ABERCROMBIE, Hon. Jas., 414.
Adam, Meldrum & Anderson, 266.
Affleck, Robert, 231.
Ainslie, Hew, 190, 388.
Aitken, Robert, 244.
Alexander, Sir William, 45.
Alexander, Gen. William, 117, 308, 420.
Allan, John, 128.
Allan, John, (antiquary,) 13.
Allan, Robert, 386.
Anderson, William, 408.
Auchmuty, Family, 307.

BARCLAY, Robert, of Ury, 85.
Bell, A. Graham, 214.
Bell, A. Melville, 214.
Bennett, James Gordon, 372.
Bethune, Divie, 326, 327.
Bethune, Joanna, 325, 326.
Black Watch, the, 27, 41, 32.
"Boston News Letter," 246.
Boston Scots' Charitable Society, 49, 265, 412.
Craik, James, 205.
British Charitable Society, 265.
Brown, Hon. George, 373.
Bruce, George, 343.
Bruce, Robert, 242.
Bruce, Wallace, 408.
Buchanan, Rev. Dr., 175.
Burden, Henry, 210.
Burns Clubs, 432.
Burns, Robt., first Am. ed., 244.
Burns, Robt., 2d Am. ed., 231.
Burns statue at Albany, 262.
Burtt, Rev. John, 379.

CALDER, A. M., 188.
Caledonian Clubs, 425.

Callender, James Thomas, 353.
Callender, Walter, 267.
Callender, McAuslan & Troup, 266.
Calverley, Charles, 181, 263.
Cameron, Dugald, 56.
Campbell, Alexander, 225.
Campbell, Daniel, 226.
Campbell, Capt. Laughlin, 50.
Campbell, Lord William, 83.
Carnegie, Andrew, 8, 273.
Carter, Robert, 250.
Chalmers, George, 353.
Chisholm, Henry, 212.
Chisholm, William, 212.
Cleland, John, 414.
Cochran, Thomas, 38.
Colden, Cadwallader, 91, 286.
Colden, Mayor Cadwallader D., 93, 231.
Craik, Dr. James, 199.
Craig, Sir James H., 98.
Crawford, D., (St. Louis,) 268.
Crawford, William, 268.
Crerar, D. MacGregor, 404.
Crichton, James D., 405.
Cuming, Sir Alexander, 415.
Curling, 434.

DEMPSTER, W. R., 346.
Denholm & McKay Co., 266.
Dick, Rev. Robert, 211.
Dinwiddie, Robert, 77.
Douglas, David, 204.
Douglas, Sir James, 69.
Drummond, William, 74.
Drummond, Lord, 420.
Dunbar, Sir William, 226.
Dunmore, Earl of, 78, 242, 420.

ECKFORD, Henry, 216.
Erskine, Robert, 202.

Ewing, George E., 188.

FAIRBAIRN, Angus, 394.
Ferguson, James, 217.
Ferguson, Robert, 265.
Fleming, William, 120.
Forbes & Wallace, 266.
Forrest, Edwin, 335.
Fraser, John, ("Cousin Sandy,") 395.
Fraser, Col. Simon, 419.
Freemasonry, 434.
Fulton, Robert, 301.

GALT, John, 242, 362.
Garden, Alexander, 149.
Gardner, Hugh, of New York, 9.
Geddes, Gen. J. L., 35.
Gellatly, Rev. Alexander, 152.
Gilchrist & Co., (Boston,) 264.
Gilfillan, Judge James, 315.
Gordon, Andrew R., 71.
Gordon, Thomas, 302.
Gowans, William, 248.
Graeme, Dr. Thomas, 198.
Graham, Andrew, 10.
Graham, Isabella, 323.
Graham, John, of Edinburgh, 10.
Grant, President U. S., 301.
Grant, Mrs., of Laggan, 319, 377.
Gray, David, 392.
Greenshields, David, 290.
Greig, John, Canandaigua, 310.

HALL, David, 245.
Hall, Rev. Dr. Robert, 154.
Hamilton, Alexander, 57, 123.
Hamilton, Andrew, 86, 302.
Hamilton, Gen. W. B., 271.
Hamilton, John, 271.
Hamilton, John C., 271.
Hardie, James, 285.
Hart, James M., 182.
Hart, William, 181.
Harper, Dr. J. M., 405.
Henderson, D. B., 318.
Henderson, D. M., 404.
Henderson, Peter, 205.
Henry, Joseph, 302.

Hewat, Rev. Alexander, 159.
Hogg, Brown & Taylor, 264, 267, 268.
Hunter, Gov. Peter, 97.
Hunter, Gen. Robert, 87.

IMRIE, John, 407.
Irving, Washington, quoted 18, 59. (Astoria:) 357, (sketch.)
Ivison, Henry, 249.

JAFFREY, Jeannie (Mrs. Renwick,) 14.
Johnston, Gabriel, 81.
Johnstone, George, 80.
Johnston, John, 82.
Johnston, John, (Milwaukee,) 259.
Johnston, John Taylor, 275.
Johnston, Gov., of North Carolina, 159.
Johnston, Gov. Robert, 413.
Jones, Paul, 134.

KEITH, Rev. George, 130.
Keith, Prof. John, 286.
Keith, Sir William, 87, 198.
Kemp, Rev. Dr. William (Bishop), 168.
Kennedy, David (vocalist), 335, 337, 395.
Kennedy, James, 407.
Kennedy, John S., 7, 237, 277, 421.
Kennedy, R. L., 237.
Kennedy, William, 391.
Kidd, Capt., 52.
King, Judge Mitchell, 310, 413.
Kinnear, Peter, 262.
Kirkwood, James P., 217.
Knox, John, 106, 107, 282.

LAIDLIE, Rev. Archibald, 152.
Laidlaw, W. G., 318.
Laing, Joseph, 36, 39.
Latto, Thomas C., 397.
Law, James D., 408.
Lawson, John, 352.
Lawson, James, 372.

INDEX. 445

Lee, James, 273.
Lenox, James, 236, 275.
Lenox, Robert, 235, 274.
Livingston, Family of, 130.
Louden, Samuel, 231.

MAITLAND, David, 233.
Macadam, J. L., 16.
Macdonald, Sir John A., 222.
Maitland, R. L., 274.
Mason, John, 343.
Mason, Rev. Dr. John, 153.
Mason, Rev. Dr. J. M., 154, 164, 326.
Maxwell, Hugh, 311.
Maxwell, William, 230.
Mercer, Gen. Hugh, 111.
Middleton, Dr. Peter, 200.
Milne, Alexander, 223.
Mitchell, Hon. Alex., 256, 257.
Moffat, Rev. Dr. J. C., 368.
Monro, Rev. Henry, 156.
Montgomerie, Major Archibald, 27.
Montgomerie, John, 90.
Morrison, Charles, 195.
Morrison, Gen. David, 36.
Moultrie, Dr. John, 414.
Muir, Rev. James, 160.
Muir, Dr. Samuel, 160.
Murray, Gen. James, 96.
Murray, William, 407.
MacArthur, Judge, Arthur, 316.
Macomb, Gen. Alexander, 123.
Macdonald, Flora, 320.
Macdonald, Hon. John, 278.
Macdonnell, Miles, 101.
Macfarlane, Robert, 367.
Mackenzie, Sir Alexander, 66.
Mackenzie, Donald, 59, 60.
Maclay, Rev. Dr. Archibald, 163.
Maclean, Prof. John, 287.
Maclure, William, 203.
Macmillan, Wm., 205.
Macpherson, Jas., "Ossian," 81.
McArthur, Gen. John, 34.
McArthur, John, 192.
McAuslan, John, 267.
McCallum, Donald C., 218.

McColl, Evan, 402.
McCosh, President, 239, 287, 347.
McCulloch, Hon. Hugh, 314.
McDougall, Gen. Alex., 115.
McGill, James, 288.
McGillivray, Gen. Alex., 20.
McIntosh, Gen. Lachlan, 116.
McIntosh, Wm., Indian chief, 22.
McLachlan, Alexander, 399.
McLean, Andrew, 406.
McLeod, Rev. Dr. Alex., 162.
McLeod, Rev. Dr. J. N., 163.
McNaughton, Dr. James, 202.

NAIRNE, Prof. C. M., 296.
Nelson, Thomas, "Scotch Tom," 223.
North British Society of Halifax, 422.
Norrie, Adam, 232.

OLIVER, John, (Chicago,) 257.
Orr, Robert, 209.

PATON, Susannah, 345.
Pattison, Granville Sharp, 295.
Phyfe, Duncan, 253.
Picken, Andrew B., 382.
Picken, Joanna B., 382.
Pinkerton, Allan, 15.
Pirie, George, 374.

RAFFEN, Capt. J. T., 34.
Ramsay, Donald, 399.
Reid, David Boswall, 206.
Reid, Duncan, 51.
Reid, Robert, ("Rob Wanlock,") 406.
Reid, Hon. Whitelaw, 375.
Reid, William, 263.
Rhind, J. M., 187.
Ritchie, A. H., 184.
Ross, Dr. J. D., 370, 390, 398.
Ross, John, of Philadelphia, 126, 227.
Roy, Andrew, 269.
Russell, Archibald, 273.
Russell, William, 295.

ST. ANDREW'S SOCIETY of Charleston, 149, 157, 246, 311, 413.
St. Andrew's Society of Philadelphia, 416.
St. Andrew's Society of the State of New York, 154, 173, 312, 419.
St. Andrew's Society of Montreal, 423.
St. Clair, Gen. Arthur, 113.
Sandeman, Robert, 142.
Scott, Prof. D. Burnet, 297.
Scott, Rev. Dr. George, 387.
Scott, Walter, 143.
Scott, Mrs., (mother of Sir Walter,) 325.
Scottish Clans, Order of, 429.
Seton, Mgr., 173.
Seventy-ninth Highlanders, (New York,) 36.
Shaw, John, (St. Louis,) 254.
Shepherd, Norwell & Co., 264, 265.
Shirlaw, Walter, 190.
Simpson, Sir George, 67.
Simpson, Crawford & Simpson, 268.
Sinclair, Dr. A. D., 202.
Sinclair, John, (vocalist,) 335.
Sinclair, Malcolm, 40.
Skene, Alexander, 86.
Skene, Prof. A. J. C., 202.
Smibert, John, 178.
Smith, Sir Donald A., 279.
Smith, George, (Chicago,) 281, 256.
Smith, James M., 264.
Smith, W. E., 94.
Smith, W. R., 205.
Smillie, Family, the, 180.
Somerville, Alexander, 363.
Sons of Scotland, Order of, 432.
Spence, Dr. John, 201.
Spence, John F., 261.
Spence, W. W., 261.
Steel, Wm., (Abolitionist,) 11.
Stewart, Dr. A. M., 375.
Stewart, John A., 276.
Stobo, Rev. Archibald, 414.
Stuart, Alexander, 281, 238.
Stuart, Gilbert C., 179.
Stuart, Kinloch, 238.
Stuart, Robert, 59, 62.
Stuart, R. L., 238, 281.
Stuart, Mrs. R. L., 239, 281.
Sturoc, W. C., 407.
Swan, James, 120.

TAYLOR, Rev. Dr. W. M., 165.
Thom, James, 186.
Thomson, Rev. Dr. J., 166, 248.
Thomson, Robert, 187.
Thorburn, Grant, 205, 240.
Troup, John E., 267.
Turnbull, Rev. Robert, 365.
Tytler, James, 383.

WADDELL, Thomas, 271.
Walker, Wm., (Quebec,) 280.
Wait, George M., 220.
Wanless, Andrew, 406.
Washington, George, 21, 29, 107, 179, 202, 302.
Watts, Family of, 125.
Webster, William, 40.
Wells, Robert, 246.
Wellstood, Family of, 190.
Whittet, Robert, 404.
Wilkie, Daniel, (Quebec,) 292.
Williamson, Chas., 53, 54, 230.
Williamson, John, 185.
Williamson, Peter, 57.
Wilson, Sir Daniel, 350.
Wilson, John, (vocalist,) 336.
Wilson, John, (printer,) 247.
Wilson, James, (Signer,) 419.
Wilson, Wm., (Poughkeepsie,) 390.
Wingfield, Alexander, 403.
Witherspoon, Rev. Dr. John, 104, 107, 244, 324, 325, 419.
Wood, William, 298.
Wright, Fanny, 331.
Wright, Chief Justice Robert, 413.

YOUNG, Hugh, 39.

www.ingramcontent.com/pod-product-compliance
Lightning Source LLC
Chambersburg PA
CBHW032005300426
44117CB00008B/903